Remittances as Social Practices and Agents of Change

Silke Meyer • Claudius Ströhle
Editors

Remittances as Social Practices and Agents of Change

The Future of Transnational Society

palgrave
macmillan

Editors
Silke Meyer
Department of History and European Ethnology
University of Innsbruck
Innsbruck, Austria

Claudius Ströhle
Department of History and European Ethnology
University of Innsbruck
Innsbruck, Austria

FWF Austrian Science Fund

This publication was funded by the Austrian Science Fund (FWF) (PUB-883-G) and, additionally, by the Research Area Cultural Encounters – Cultural Conflicts at the University of Innsbruck.

ISBN 978-3-030-81503-5 ISBN 978-3-030-81504-2 (eBook)
https://doi.org/10.1007/978-3-030-81504-2

This Palgrave Macmillan imprint is published by the registered company Springer Nature Switzerland AG.
The registered company address is: Gewerbestrasse 11, 6330 Cham, Switzerland

Acknowledgements

The fact that this book has come together so well is due to the enthusiasm and effort of many people, whom we would like to thank here. The book is based on the research undertaken in the project "Follow the Money: Remittances as Social Practices", which was generously funded by the Austrian Science Fund (2016–2020, P 28929). The project was led by Silke Meyer who, together with Fatma Haron and Claudius Ströhle, examined remittance relations between Austria and Turkey in the context of labor migration. In September 2018, the research team organized the international and interdisciplinary conference "More than Money: Remittances as Social Practices" at the University of Innsbruck. This event can be considered the foundation of this book. We sincerely thank all the participants for their excellent papers, the lively discussions, enthusiastic hikes in the Alps, and inspiring evenings. On our journey to publication, we invited more scholars from various geographical and institutional contexts to contribute their work to this volume, and we are grateful for their trust in our editorship. We also express our gratitude to the research area "Cultural Encounters – Cultural Conflicts" at the University of Innsbruck for further subsidizing the publication.

The fact that the book is now published is above all due to the reliable and dedicated work of all the authors and the editing process—we learnt a lot from this scholarly exchange. Moreover, we would like to express our sincere thanks to the fantastic Tim Corbett for his meticulous proofreading with regard to both content and language. Our final chapter benefited enormously from the constructive criticism of Marta Bivand Erdal, Konrad Kuhn, and Teresa Millesi.

Publishing open access has become possible through the funds of the Austrian Science Fund (FWF). Here, we would like to thank Doris Haslinger and Sabina Abdel-Kader for their support.

Furthermore, we would like to thank our senior editor Elizabeth Graber and our project manager from books production, Shenbagavalli Saravanan, from Palgrave Macmillan/Springer Nature for guiding us through the publishing process. Global open access publishing is not free of complications. It took a long time to publish this book and we would like to thank the authors that they patiently stayed with us. However, the delay in time resulted in considerable lacunae which we are aware of. The effects of the Covid-19 pandemic on remittances and the global changes in money flows due to the Russian war against Ukraine would have to be part of the next chapters in remittances studies.

Finally, and most importantly, we would like to thank all the people who have given us insights into the practices and meanings of saving, sending, and receiving remittances. Their perspectives and reflections are not always represented in international migration and remittance research, yet they are indispensable for understanding the challenges and potentials of future transnational societies.

Silke Meyer and Claudius Ströhle
April 2023, Innsbruck and Berkeley, CA

Contents

Notes on Contributors

Rina Malagayo Alluri is Assistant Professor at the Unit for Peace and Conflict Studies, University of Innsbruck. She is co-editor of *Business, Peacebuilding and Sustainable Development: Beyond the UN SDGs* (2019). Her research interests include diaspora and migration, the politics of belonging, Sri Lanka, business and peace, de-colonization of peace, and transnational peacebuilding.

Samuel Weniga Anuga is a PhD Environmental Science student at the Institute for Environment and Sanitation Studies (IESS), University of Ghana. He has worked as a Research Fellow at the CGIAR Research Center, International Centre for Tropical Agriculture (CIAT) in Colombia. He is an Alexander von Humboldt Research Fellow at the Institute for Environmental Economics and World Trade at the Leibniz University in Hannover, Germany. His research interests include sustainable agriculture, rural livelihoods transformation, and climate policy.

Rochelle Bailey is a Research Fellow in the Department of Pacific Affairs at the Australian National University. She has conducted long-term ethnographical fieldwork in Vanuatu investigating the economic, cultural, political, and social outcomes of Pacific labor mobility in Australia's Seasonal Worker Programme and New Zealand's Recognised Seasonal Employer Scheme (RSE).

Ivana Bajić-Hajduković is Adjunct Professor at Syracuse University in London. Her book *"Can You Run Away From Sorrow?": Mothers Left Behind in 1990s Belgrade* was published in 2020 in the New Anthropologies of Europe series. Bajić-Hajduković has published on the material culture of migration, remittances, and family relationships. She is writing a book about early twentieth century migration from Bosnia-Herzegovina to Serbia and Macedonia based on family history.

Eric Bayala leads the project "Collective Diaspora Supports in Burkina Faso" at the Institute of Sociology at the University of Innsbruck. He also works at the Health University of Applied Science Tyrol. His research interests include migration, African diaspora, health, and international development.

Sara Bernard is Lecturer of Societal Transformations at the University of Glasgow. She is the author of *Deutsch Marks in the Head, Shovel in the Hands and Yugoslavia in the Heart: The Gastarbeiter Return to Yugoslavia (1965–1991)* published in 2019. Her main research interest is international labor migration in the twentieth century with a focus on the Balkans and the Mediterranean. She is also interested in the role of migrants and diaspora communities in the creation of nation states and national identities in Southern Europe.

Brigitte Bönisch-Brednich is Professor of Cultural Anthropology at Victoria University of Wellington, New Zealand. She has published widely on migration, storytelling and narrative framing, ethnographic writing, and ethnographic theory. She is currently working on migrant academics and their experiences of mobility in the knowledge economy.

Stefanie Bürkle is an Artist and Professor of Visual Arts at the Technical University in Berlin. Among her recent projects and exhibitions are Migrating Spaces (2013–2016) and MigraTouriSpace (2018–2021). Her research interests include urban studies, migration, and visual anthropology.

Marta Bivand Erdal is Research Professor at the Peace Research Institute Oslo (PRIO) and Co-director of the PRIO Migration Centre. She has written extensively on migration studies, among other topics of remittances, migrant transnationalism, and migration-related diversity.

Marie Johanna Karner is an Early Career Researcher at the Institute of Geography at the Johannes Gutenberg University Mainz. Apart from topics related to migration, diaspora, and urban geography (e.g. historic urban quarters and nightscapes), her research interest includes tourism geography (e.g. cruise tourism and film-induced tourism).

Hasan Mahmud is Assistant Professor of Sociology at Northwestern University in Qatar. He explored why migrants send remittances to home in his PhD dissertation research among Bangladeshis in Tokyo and Los Angeles. His research interests include globalization, migration, development, immigrants' incorporation, sociological theories, qualitative research, and identity politics.

Silke Meyer is Professor of European Ethnology at the University of Innsbruck. She also serves as Head of the Innsbruck Research Area "Cultural Encounters—Cultural Conflicts." Her research interests are migration, remittances, transnationalism, and inequality as well as narrative.

Aleksandar R. Miletić is Fellow at the Institute for Recent History of Serbia in Belgrade and Director of the Center for History Studies and Dialogue in Novi Sad. He is the author of the book *Journey under Surveillance: The Overseas Emigration Policy of the Kingdom of Serbs, Croats and Slovenes in Global Context, 1918–1928* (2012). His research interests are social and economic history of East-Central and Southeast Europe.

Gökhan Mura is an Assistant Professor in the Department of Visual Communication Design at Izmir University of Economics, Turkey. He studied industrial design and visual communication design. His research interests encompass various design disciplines with a keen interest in the relationship between design and technology, storytelling through design, visual culture, and material culture.

Justice Issah Musah-Surugu holds a PhD in Public Administration and Policy Management and recently completed a joint postdoctoral fellowship with the United Nations University and the UN Framework Convention on Climate Change Secretariat, Germany. Musah-Surugu has a growing publication and research interest in the field of climate change governance, climate finance, adaptation across sub-national government, and the role of the third sector in adaptation.

Eveline Odermatt is a Researcher and Lecturer in the Department of Sociology, Social Policy, and Global Development at the University of Fribourg. Her areas of research include intra-European migration, migration and development, return and post-return reintegration, and transnational configurations. She previously worked on migration issues as a Research Fellow in the School of Global Studies at the University of Sussex and as a consultant to development agencies (e.g. for the SDC and GIZ).

Dirk Rupnow is Professor at the Institute for Contemporary History at the University of Innsbruck, where he currently also serves as Dean of the Faculty of Philosophy and History. His research focuses on Holocaust and Jewish studies, the history of knowledge and migration, memory cultures and the politics of memory, and museology.

Annemarie Steidl is an Associate Professor at the Department of Economic and Social History at the University of Vienna. Her research interests include migration studies from the eighteenth to the twentieth centuries, industrialization and urbanization, and the history of artisans, gender studies, and quantitative methods. Her most recent book was published in 2021 (*On Many Routes: Internal, European, and Transatlantic Migration in the Late Habsburg Empire*).

Claudius Ströhle is a PhD candidate in the Department of History and European Ethnology at the University of Innsbruck. His research focuses on material culture, migrant transnationalism, ethnographic methodology, economic anthropology, and inequality. As part of his fellowship at the International Research Center for Cultural Studies (IFK) in Vienna, Austria, Ströhle is currently a Visiting Scholar at the Institute of European Studies (IES) at UC Berkeley, USA.

Lore Van Praag holds a PhD in Sociology, Ghent University and is Head of the Centre for Migration and Intercultural Studies at the University of Antwerp. Her research interests include ethnicity, gender, climate/environmental change, migration, and education.

List of Figures

List of Tables

CHAPTER 1

Introduction: Theorizing Remittances — Social Positioning and the Making of Migrant Subjectivity

Silke Meyer

Migration means change. In fact, the motivation to migrate in many cases is to achieve change on an individual and collective level. Migrants aim for a better life in their place of destination, they want to improve their financial situation, they seek more security, stability, and personal freedom, they hope for better education and healthcare, all for themselves, their families, and their communities. Collective remittances facilitate the extension of infrastructure like health centers and churches, support hometown associations, and strengthen the social ties between diaspora communities with their places of origin. For the desired improvements do not only affect migrants in their new places of residence, but also transform their homelands.

We claim in this volume that many aspects of these transformations are incited, encouraged, and implemented by remittances. With migrants'

S. Meyer (✉)
Department of History and European Ethnology, University of Innsbruck, Innsbruck, Austria
e-mail: silke.meyer@uibk.ac.at

S. Meyer, C. Ströhle (eds.), *Remittances as Social Practices and Agents of Change*,
https://doi.org/10.1007/978-3-030-81504-2_1

remittances, state programs, organizations, and individuals can transform infrastructure and the lives of non-migrants by channeling funds into education, healthcare, housing, agriculture, and technologies. Remittances are more than money: they encompass social capital, objects, ideas, values, and norms. They bring new attitudes toward learning, well-being and health-seeking behavior, gender roles, and political participation. Their transformative effects are mostly welcome and seen as improving the quality of life, but remittances can also bring irritation, discord, and controversy (Grabowska et al. 2017). As they stand for preferences of spending versus sending, of building a life or founding a business in the place of residence versus supporting family, villages, and the economy in the place of origin, the priorities are not without inner or outer conflict and reflect difficult decisions and painful choices. Remittances thus constitute a source of social conflict as well as of social cohesion. Both result from the fact that remittances are structured by asymmetrical relations arising from global inequalities and neocolonial power constellations (Weiss 2005). Remittances bridge these "divides of global inequality" (Carling 2014, p. 218) and, at the same time, they project this divide into intimate personal relationships.

The aim of this volume is to study the transformative effects of remittances with regard to relational asymmetries in different geographical and historical settings. To this end, we examine both the value and materiality of remittances (what is sent) as well as the changes the transfers elicit (the effects). Our hypothesis is that migration and social change go hand in hand and in many cases, they are hinged by remittances as the ignition and agents for social transformation. However, it is important to note that transformative effects do not equal development. In fact, it is one of our objectives to challenge the narrative of remittances as the key to development and modernization (de Haas 2020). In order to go beyond the migration-development nexus with the "remittance mantra" (Kapur 2005), that is the idea that remittances change poor countries for the better, we take a critical approach, analyzing remittances in their complexity, ambiguity, and ambivalence: How do remittances contribute to transnational social inequalities, foster structures of dependency, reproduce colonial power structures, and thus contribute to a neocolonial world order? In what way are they part of the "transnational social question" (Faist 2014; see also Ströhle & Meyer in this volume)? To answer these questions, we address four different approaches in this volume: first, and in order to pave the way for studying transformative effects, we look at historical remittance transactions and examine their development over time. How have remittance practices changed over time and what were the effects on social relations and family dynamics (Bajić-Hajduković & Bernard in this volume)? What were the contributions of sending and receiving states, for example channeling programs (Miletic in this volume)? Second, we investigate the collectivity of remittance in their transformative effect: What new communities are brought to life by remitting and how do sending and receiving groups change? How does the nation state influence remittance practices? Third, we follow the perspective of material remittances and study the production of symbolic capital in relation to industrial objects and gifts. The fourth approach addresses the future of transnational society by examining the role of remittances in climate change, conflict, and academic economies. Neocolonial structures are made visible in these contributions.

In this introduction, I will offer a theoretical framework of remitting by combining it with theories of social positioning and subjectivity. To this end, I will first review the characteristics of transnationalism in order to provide the necessary context for remittance research. Second, I will pursue the concept of remittance scripts (Carling 2014) for a theory of remittances as a way of social positioning. I conceptualize remitting as ways of being and belonging (Levitt and Glick Schiller 2004) and add the perspective of becoming. According to Levitt and Glick Schiller, ways of being refer to "actual social relations and practices individuals engage in" like caring for family members or supporting communities. Ways of belonging constitute "a conscious connection to a particular group" (Levitt and Glick Schiller 2004, p. 1010), an act of demonstrating membership like wearing a college tie or cooking a particular national or ethnic dish. The ways of belonging include both the practice and the awareness of its symbolic meaning. The notion of subjectivity adds ways of becoming to the expression of belonging and membership. Through ways of becoming, migrants internalize mechanisms of identity formation, adopt specific subject positions like the caretaker, the investor, or the modernizer, and constitute a transnational self. I argue that if we want to conceptualize a transnational (social field) perspective on society, we need to examine the ways in which historical constellations of colonialism, contemporary power structures like border regimes, immigration laws, and work permits as well as cultural hegemonies in places of residence contribute to negotiations of belonging and identity politics. My proposition is that remittance practices represent ways of being, belonging, *and* becoming and that by examining ways of becoming as a process of subjectification, we can better understand the asymmetries and thereby the kernel of the remittance transaction.

Transnationalism: A Society in the Making

Contemporary society is transnational and global at the same time: nation states, businesses, organizations, and people have multiple networks with nodes in a number of places and nation states. Whereas the perspective of globalization is directed onto the macro-level of interaction of businesses and trade, transnationalization describes "the processes by which immigrants forge and sustain multi-stranded social relations that link together their societies of origin and settlement" (Basch et al. 1994, p. 6). Contrary to globalization, transnationalism works "from below" (Smith and Guarnizo 1998). Transnationalism thus describes the economic, political, cultural, and social ties between migrants and their homelands and refers to practices and commitments that constitute and reproduce those bonds.

In migration studies, the emergent transnational perspective has helped scholars over the past 30 years to overcome the early focus on migrants' otherness, their alleged deficits, and the corresponding need to adapt and integrate. The transnational turn has challenged migration studies in questioning linear movements, push-and-pull models, and assimilation theories. This epistemological shift marks the turn away from two separate ways of life in the countries of origin and destination toward an understanding of migration as a network of people, their social relations, international organizations, and the authority of national states (Faist 2010). Remittances play a key role in establishing, maintaining, and fostering these networks. From the early works by Basch et al. (1994), Portes et al. (1999), Levitt (2001), Vertovec (1999), and others, we have learned that transnationalization is a social process that is driven by migrants and their cross-border activities and commitments, but that its effects are not limited to migrants but involve the entire society of both countries of origin and destination. The transnational perspective is therefore directed onto a given society as a whole and not onto ethnic or national groups within that society. It encompasses migrants and non-migrants and how they are affected by institutions, organizations, laws, and economies in more than one nation state. It also takes into account how locality interacts with transnational bonds (Nowicka 2020, pp. 3–4). Migration studies with a transnational perspective does not mean studying migration (anymore): it means examining how society deals with migration; how mechanisms of inclusion and exclusion are produced with regard to ethnicity and nationality; and how ways of being, belonging, and becoming are negotiated within power relations and cultural hegemony.

Furthermore, the transnational perspective has taught us to overcome "the receiving country bias" (Castles et al. 2014) and "methodological nationalism" which runs the risk of conflating society and the nation state (Wimmer and Glick Schiller 2002). A transnational research design does not focus on a group of migrants in (mainly northern) destination states but "follows the people" (Marcus 1995), taking into account the regional differences and local specifics of geography, politics, economy, and culture in the countries of origin. By doing so, we can also fulfill an important prerequisite of transnational research, which is to examine the changes in the lives and social positions of people resulting from migration (Nowicka and Šerbedžija 2016b, pp. 10–13). In other words: What changes when people become migrants? Only with answers to this question can we achieve the goal of studying migration as a perspective on society and an agent of social change.

Living transnationally has become normal for most migrants and also for non-migrants as migration permeates all of society. On a larger scale, everybody could claim to lead a more or less transnational life in consumption, communication, work, and leisure. However, there are differences between migration, mobility, and tourism, and participating in a global popular culture is not the same as living a transnational life. Research on transnationalism has been criticized for using the concept so broadly that it loses its analytical value. Besides, not everything a migrant does or does not do is a transnational practice. In the next section, I will focus on four characteristics of transnationalism that manifest the concept's analytical value, namely spatiality, temporality, capital, and connectivity/disruption.

First, regarding the spatial dimension of border regimes and attention to the nation state: what makes individual and collective transactions transnational is the fact that they cross state borders and thus map out a new transnational space. This space has a dynamic and liminal character which is constantly updated by economic and social exchanges between migrants and non-migrants, by work, communication, and travel. Although borders are overcome regularly from this perspective, they are still a constitutive element of transnationalism. Nation states have the power to regulate territorial border politics and decide who is granted access to immigration and who is not (Nieswand 2018). Beyond immigration laws, national border regimes furthermore create constant challenges and problems for people on the move, for example through import and export laws on goods, citizenship regulations, and passport politics. Moreover, once migrants have encountered the nation state in crossing the border, they are further "confronted with and engaged in the nation building processes of two or more nation-states" (Basch et al. 1994, p. 22). Beyond the legislative, nation states act on the level of the symbolic and negotiate the rights and means not only to immigrate, but also to belong. Being granted permission to apply for and acquire citizenship, residence, and work, to buy property and obtain access to healthcare and education, are constant tasks of living transnationally. Locality is thus a place and a claim at the same time. Transnationalism is not a counter-narrative of nationalism. On the contrary, we need to keep in mind the narratives of nationalism in order to understand transnational identity. The transnational can serve as a stepping stone for national loyalty, as can be seen in the long arm of Recep Tayyip Erdoğan, the ultraconservative president of the Turkish Republic who has a strong influence on German and Austrian Turks and their politics of identity (Faist and Ulbricht 2013).

Nationalism is more than a political and organizational structure, it is a structure of feeling, of experiencing everyday life, and of shaping belonging. Transnationalism can also be used as a stepping stone to a new everyday "banal nationalism" (Billig 1995), as we can see when second- and third-generation Turkish migrants in Vienna cultivate a diasporic "Turkish taste" in popular culture and aesthetics (Savaş 2014) or in the national conflicts over the national identities of Turks and Kurds, fought out in diaspora media (Keles 2015). Media platforms can also offer a way of forming diaspora groups independent from national space (Karner in this volume).

The second dimension of transnationalism is temporal. Transnational lives are characterized by the scaling and simultaneity of acting in two different spheres: speaking two or more languages, buying property and building houses, starting businesses, participating in social life, and following political, cultural, and popular trends in more than one place (Erdal 2020). Social media and new communication technologies help with being in two places at the same time. People follow family events over Instagram and share important moments like birthdays, weddings, and religious ceremonies via video calls. Temporality in transnational lives can also mean a social rhythm of movement, like spending the holidays in one's place of origin or temporary return migration after retirement.

Third, dealing with multi-locality and simultaneity is a skill. Nowicka has shown how migrants make use of their economic, social, and cultural capital in order to find their place in more than one society (Nowicka 2013, 2015). If we consider mobility a resource, that is, an experience from which people derive abilities and skills, then we can conceptualize these skills as transnational capital that allows social differentiation in multiple belongings (Erel 2010; Moret 2018). Remittance can be considered a valorization of transnational capital, a currency that senders and receivers use in the process of cross-border social positioning (Meyer 2019). As with other forms of capital, transnational capital can be converted into economic capital, that is financial remittances, and into social capital, that is the social status that comes with sending and receiving remittances. Patterns of capital conversion follow transnational social conventions and scripts. Thus, remitting "is not just about the economy" (Levitt and Lamba-Nieves 2011), but it is about the forms, conversions, and currency of capital.

Trying to balance capital and debit, the fourth aspect is the reminder that the transnational perspective is directed at connectivity as well as at friction and tension (Waldinger 2015). Transnational space is characterized by connections but also by asymmetries and differences (Nowicka 2020). Waldinger and Nowicka reminded us further that connectivity should not be confused with collectivity: being in contact with relatives and friends abroad does not necessarily lead to a sense of solidarity. In order to avoid romanticizing the idea of community (Joseph 2002), we need to soberly examine the various forms, practices, and temporal durations of transnational social ties and their transformation. The focus must be on the moment, place, relation, or object in which two spheres come together and social norms, practices, and dispositions coincide, conflate, or collide. Tsing (2005) described these encounters as frictions, a metaphor that helps us examine the transformative effects of transnationality: in transnational space, both sides of the encounter change through contact, they rub off on each other and level out. A new condition emerges and produces a distinct liminal social position and quality of belonging, a "betwixt and between" (Turner 1964), engaging with the "there" and "here." By directing our research perspective toward this transnational position, we can go beyond traditional migration research with its focus on adapting and assimilating. Instead, we look at the transformative effects that the transnational condition and disposition have on society: how it changes individual practices, values, and ideas, and how it transforms collectives both in the place of origin and in the place of residence.

Remittances play a key role in these transformative processes. Our interest in this volume is how social ties are reflected and altered in remittance practices: how some of them become reinforced over time, how some of them fade, and how some change their form, meaning, and rhythm of exchange. For example, when remittances are sent no longer as financial aid, but as a part of Islamic charity, this changes not only the amount and frequency in the financial transfers, but also the relationship between sender and receiver, their self-image, and their position in society (Erdal in this volume, Erdal and Borchgrevink 2017). We propose studying transnational lives and the production of multiple belongings, practices, and dispositions by examining remittances. When we study the transformative effects of remittances, we study social change in transnational society.

What Are Remittances?

Remittances are financial, material, social, knowledge-based, and symbolic means of support given by migrants to family, kin, friends, neighbors, and associations in their countries of origin. As such, they recognize, maintain, and affirm social relationships and connect people despite their physical distance. Changing remittance flows can strengthen or weaken social effects (Carling 2020). Moreover, remittances represent the purpose and goal of migration for senders and receivers, for the prospect of remitting can be the incentive for migration aspirations in the first place. To be able to care financially for family, to support the community, to invest in a house or a business in the community of origin are often the reasons for migrating (Carling 2008). The decision to become mobile is thus in most cases connected to the hope of financial advancement, access to work, prosperity, and security; a decision not made individually, but by families, neighborhoods, and villages. It is not only the mobile who profit from this advancement, but also those who stay behind, for the gains of mobility are shared between the place of destination and origin.

The transformative effects of these transfers for the countries of origin are undisputed: successfully established remittance transfers improve living conditions, provide food, clothing, housing, and transport, and facilitate access to education and health services. They enhance agriculture and further technologies for improving crops and water supplies. Technological advancements contribute to the fight against climate change where it is needed the most (Musah-Surugu & Anuga and Van Praag in this volume). The financial flows can free unbanked households from credit constraints and enable the accumulation of capital. Social remittances broaden the horizon of non-migrant communities by promoting peacebuilding processes, political participation, democratic rights, and gender equality. Collective remittances allow the building of infrastructure like community centers and churches, support hometown associations, and connect communities between the diaspora and the homeland (Odermatt and Bayala in this volume). On a macro-level, remittances boost a country's economy, attract investments, and promote economic growth. Access to foreign currencies also stabilizes the national economy.

The other side of the remittance coin encompasses financial and social dependencies between migrants and their communities of origin. When the money stream runs dry, the possibilities for social change toward a better life become sparse. Remittances also have the bad reputation of lowering labor force participation because recipients may be discouraged from seeking employment and work (the "moral hazard effect"). Beyond the household level, remittance flows substitute state financing and lead to privatizing processes, for example in the health and education sector, and thus have a neoliberalizing effect on social infrastructure. This is because, as the sum of private transfers from abroad rises, state investors see less incentive to promote public hospitals, schools, and other educational institutions (Orozco 2013, Ströhle & Meyer in this volume). Furthermore, remittances sometimes come under scrutiny, for example, being suspected of financing crime and terrorism (Horst et al. 2014).

Remittance money is thus special money and is valued differently from other monies (Singh et al. 2012; Thai 2014). At their core, remittance transactions are manifestations of social relations: they are expressions of solidarity, loyalty, and guilt, they represent measures of support and control, and they are accompanied by conflict and cognitive dissonance over the question of where and how to spend money. For the senders, remittance practices represent nostalgic bonds, generosity, and a willingness to help, as well as a means of influence and control. Simultaneously, expectations that migrants will share their ostensibly better life with those they left behind are high and result in social pressure (Lindley 2010). From the point of view of the beneficiaries, the money is earmarked with attributions of subsistence aid, gratitude, but also interference from outside, even blackmail in cases where the transfers arrive with explicit instructions on how the money is to be spent.

Moreover, opinions on remittances frequently surpass the communities involved: where money is sent abroad and not invested locally, migrants are accused of freeloading in their place of residence. In the place of origin, consumption enabled by money sent from abroad represents, on the one hand, freedom of choice and the possibility of expressing individuality, while on the other hand, enhanced consumption leads to criticisms of materialism and superficiality. Eckstein showed how in Cuba remittance money used to carry attributions of conspicuous consumption and of political ideologies and would thus be rejected: "we did not fight a revolution for Colgate toothpaste," she quoted an interview partner who remembered how he loathed the packages sent from the USA (Eckstein 2006, p. 147). Rejecting remittances can be an expression of agency and resistance and can hinder or redirect social change (Grabowska et al. 2017, pp. 125–168). Sometimes, remittances are rejected for practical, emotional, or aesthetic reasons. Occasionally, migrants as well as non-migrants fight change in the community of origin in order to preserve traditions and forms of cultural autonomy, what Peggy Levitt called an ossification effect (Levitt 2009, p. 1237), and they do so by refusing remittances.

It is evident that remittances are far more than a sum of money. In her seminal work on remitting, Levitt coined the phrase "social remittances" in order to capture these multi-dimensional workings. Social remittances are "the ideas, behaviours, identities and social capital that flow from receiving- to sending-county communities" (Levitt 1998, p. 926). Beyond money, remittances encompass objects, foodstuffs, clothing, home furnishings, furniture, carpets, and tools, but also notions of gender roles, of family and childhood, of climate protection and recycling, health and care, democracy and freedom, but also nationalism and fundamentalism, imitation of materialism and consumption in Western regions, and many other issues. Remitting thus goes hand in hand with the transfer of values, norms, narratives, practices, identities, and social relationships (Boccagni and Decimo 2013; Levitt and Lamba-Nieves 2011; Nowicka and Šerbedžija 2016a; Vari-Lavoisier 2020).

This broadening of the concept of remittances from financial transfers to social exchange has opened up a multitude of aspects in the transnational fields. The focus on symbolic representations and social relations between migrants and non-migrants has contributed to the study of remittances as social practice and opened up the dimension of transformation in the sending and receiving societies. Foregrounding the social in remitting allows for embedding exchange in local contexts as well as in historical and geopolitical dynamics. Lacroix suggested juxtaposing the circulation of people and money with the circulation of objects and practices in order to better understand "how objects and subjects, structures and agents, although ontologically distinct, maintain a reciprocal relation of co-production" (Lacroix 2014, p. 658), or more precisely: the coproduction of a transnational field.

Remittances have a material dimension and, as such, they work as bridges in transnational aesthetics: they frame objects as souvenirs, as place-holders for relationships, and as symbols of otherness, as Gökhan Mura and Claudius Ströhle show in their analyses of mutable mobiles (Nowicka and Šerbedžija 2016b, pp. 13–16) and the industrial other. These concepts describe objects that transform while being transferred. Mura reveals how an everyday object like soap changes into an industrial exotic, holding and reproducing the promises of migration as an improvement of life, when remitted from Germany to Turkey in the 1960s. Taking their materiality as a starting point of his analysis, Ströhle looks into the potential of affordance theory in remittance research. Remitted objects have a history which is inscribed in the material but also in the ways they are handled and are therefore embodied in migrant and non-migrant users. The transformative effect of remittances is particularly obvious in their materiality: housing landscapes expand in size and style (Boccagni and Erdal 2020; Erdal 2012; Lopez 2015; see also the visual examples offered by Bürkle in this volume), households modernize, transport becomes possible, technologies like solar energy allow for new leisure pastimes and electronic entertainment, but also for new ways of access to education (Bailey in this volume).

However, we need to be careful that the focus on the social and the material in remittances does not overlay the fundamental economic inequality in which they are embedded and from which they gain their symbolic significance (otherwise we will slip into the developmental approach to remitting). What makes remittances "more than money" is the "embodied symbolism and its meaning for the community of users" (Isaakyan and Triandafyllidou 2017, p. 4), embedded in global asymmetries. These asymmetries constitute the essence of remittances and distinguish gift-giving or financial transactions from remittance transactions. Moreover, the social and the economic in remitting practices cannot be regarded separately because it is the simultaneity of economic, social, symbolic, and relational effects that lies at the core of remittance transfers. The starting point, however, is the situation of global economic inequalities, their history, and their consequences in reproducing neocolonial power relations (Rupnow and Ströhle & Meyer in this volume). Remittances bridge the "divides of global inequality" (Carling 2014, p. 218) and project this divide onto intimate personal relationships. Looking at remittance flows today, it soon becomes obvious that they usually follow the historic formation of a powerful European center with a periphery of poverty. In other words: remittances affirm and perpetuate colonial structures between the "West and the Rest" (Hall 1992). Focusing on development contexts and the idea of empowering developing regions through remittances contributes to and reinforces neocolonial structures and dependencies. However, remittance directions are not given and here, the historical perspective is illuminating. Steidl (in this volume) demonstrates the impact of remittances from America on the economy of the Habsburg Empire. It is therefore a seminal task in remittance research to uncover how remittances are interwoven into historic power constellations and contribute to reaffirming and reproducing neocolonial relations and global inequality. Bönisch-Brednich (in this volume) shows how academic economies, with their Eurocentrism in knowledge production, with English as their *lingua franca*, and with publishing houses located mainly in Europe and North America, echo remittance trajectories.

The relationship between the economic, the social, and the political in the transnational field can be grasped by taking into account the forms of capital remittances generate. Economic capital interacts with cultural and symbolic capital in the social field and generates transnational capital. Financial transactions convey material outcomes as well as symbolic and emotional significance. Ilka Vari-Lavoisier (2016) shows how economic power increases the influence of Senegalese diaspora communities in France and the USA. The presidential election in Senegal in 2012 was decided in Paris and New York rather than in Dakar. Political scientists have explored the same line of research and shown how financial transfers influence political agendas. With economic support from abroad, for example, clientelism becomes costly because, through remittances, voters are more independent from corruption and clientelistic arrangements (Pfutze 2014, p. 306; Pfutze 2012). This can also influence their voting behavior and decrease interest in political participation (Tertytchnaya et al. 2018).

Remitting is aligned with global economics, national politics, and social discourse. As such, it is "a social practice, not just an individual's choice" (Page and Mercer 2012, p. 4; Mahmud 2021). Carling described the complexities of remittance transfers as diverse and compound transactions with material, emotional, and relational elements (Carling 2014, p. 219). A social theory of remittances is needed in order to achieve a relational interpretation that combines individual priorities with social norms and collective expectations in the fundamentally asymmetrical transnational field: it is not just geographical distance, but the distance between an assumed center and periphery that needs to be compensated in transnational mother-, father-, and childhood, when physical absence is balanced with financial and material presence. The temporal dimension is not just the time spent away from family, but also the time and efforts spent on adapting to another environment and culture. The remittance decay hypothesis assumes that migrants remit less the longer they stay abroad, but it is not only the time but also the quality of social inclusion that influences the amount of money sent to the place that migrants used to call home. Remittance decline and growth are multilayered (Meyer 2020). The nation state and its immigration policy influence this quality of social inclusion, as Hasan Mahmud (in this volume) shows in his comparison of Bangladeshis' remittance practices in Japan and the USA. The possibility to settle permanently and reunify with one's family lowers remittances considerably.

Examining the characteristics of remittance exchange, we need to ask: What makes a social and economic transaction a remittance transaction? For an answer, we must not reduce remittance relations to their context of migration but rather examine the structural impact in the context of migration. The difference between a gift from abroad and material remittances, between financial support between families and remittance money, and between caregiving in the family and as a remittance practice (Krzyżowski and Mucha 2014) lies in global inequalities and how they effect and entangle personal, discursive, and structural relations. In short: how they determine the social scripts and positions of remitting.

From Ways of Being and Belonging to Becoming: Remittance Scripts and Migrant Subjectivity

Remittances negotiate, adjust, and compensate for inequality and difference. At the same time, they cannot equalize disparities, and they negotiate different values: economic stability, health, education, consumption, absence, loneliness, pressure, and care are all parts of the composite transaction that is asymmetrical in its very nature. What does it take to negotiate these asymmetries in social relations?

Ways of Being and Belonging: Remittance Scripts and Social Positioning

Remittances represent "unceasing relational work" revealing efforts of "establishing, transforming, and sometimes terminating interpersonal relations" (Zelizer 2014, p. 4). In order to accomplish this task, they need to take a form that holds a winning prospect in the struggle for recognition (Honneth 1995) for senders and receivers as well as the respective communities. Jørgen Carling introduced the concept of remittance scripts to describe the types of negotiation that take place in remittance contexts. Scripts are "structures of expectations for specific types of situations, which facilitate social interaction" and thus provide patterns of motivation, expectation, and communication (Carling 2014, pp. 220–221).

As such, they produce social positions, that is, the role we play in society and the social status derived from this role. Social positioning is shaped through economic, social, and transnational capital (Bourdieu 2006) and practiced in remittance transactions (Carling 2014, pp. 246–247; Isaakyan and Triandafyllidou 2017, p. 5). Especially asymmetrical relations benefit from scripted practices and communication because they can reconcile reverse social positions and promise recognition and acceptance in a potentially strained and intricate situation. Looking at the motivations and meanings of remittances, their asymmetrical natures again show that motives like help, support, allowance, donation, control, and compensation all imply an unequal status between the actors of the remittance transaction. While it is undisputed that remittances indicate multiple belongings, it is also clear that these practices of transnational participation come with very different portents and variant meanings. Supporting a religious community is an expression of membership and a way of belonging, whereas sending money home to buy food and medicine for parents and siblings is a way of being.

Carling described remittance scripts which help to facilitate and communicate economic transactions as social transactions and to produce a social position distinct from the transnational social field. Financial payments can be sent and received for providing care for migrants' children or elderly relatives, looking after property and businesses, or overseeing building projects. In theory, as Carling spelled out, this could be a balanced exchange: work for money. In the transnational relationship, however, this money is not just a salary payment, it is compensation for physical absence, and it produces the position of the migrant employer and the non-migrant employee. The authorization script generates the role of a middleman when remittances are sent to a person who does not keep the money but is responsible for distributing it and overseeing its purpose. His function as a broker is a key position in the migration context. The allowance script is based on the role of the usually male breadwinner in transnational families. Obligation and entitlement produce the positions of the deserving ones (those being taken care of) whereas when remittances fail to materialize, disappointed non-migrants feel like they do not or no longer deserve this kind of transnational care. Carling gave an example in which a disappointed man lists all his relatives abroad but then complains: "But none of them help, man! They never sent anything" (Carling 2008, p. 1462). The script of sacrifice also holds a distinctly transnational moral subtext by implying that migrants have to endure all kinds of forgoing and sacrifice in order to take the position of the giver and caretaker. The pressure involved in such transnational relations is described in the script of help. The logic of help remittances assigns a moral virtue to the sender as benefactor while the recipient is subjected to a passive role, although empowered with money. The script of investment provides the social position of a generous benefactor or greedy businessman.

The special value of remittances is derived from the context of migration. At first glance, remittances scripted with investment seem to reverse the one-sided direction of global economics: migrants can make it abroad. Examined more closely, transnational transfers only reaffirm the divide between immigrant and emigrant countries. Remittance scripts are fundamentally structured by asymmetries (e.g., compensation, authorization, donation, allowance, investment, obligation, and entitlement). This is what makes the money special: it carries the notion of sacrifice, risk, bravery, endurance, success, hope, solidarity, gratitude, and humility. On top of financial support, as an expression of being connected to the transnational community, it produces the social position of the loyal provider, the ostentatious spender, the revolutionary, the dreamer, and the loser (Thai 2014), the caretaker and those being taken care of, the modernizer and the traditionalist, the globalist and the local expert, the broker and middleman, the healer and the patient, the absent parent/child and the responsible, caring parent/child, the altruist and the hedonist, the landlord and the tenant, the boss and the worker, the compatriots and those who left without looking back. Remittances are mostly success stories generating the role of heroes and victims, but also fools and villains. And there are other stories worth listening to when remittance practices break with conventional social systems and challenge hierarchies, for example in gender roles, when women become the head of the household and keepers of monies sent (e.g., Taylor et al. 2006), or when young people support parents and grandparents from abroad and decree their elders' actions (Richman 2005). Remittance hierarchies can instigate change by challenging the social order, but they can also bring conflict when the remittance-induced social positions clash with intrinsic ones.

Becoming: Remittances and the Production of Migrant Subjectivity

Remittance scripts help us understand the ways of being and belonging in the communicative acts of giving and receiving. They show patterns of meaning in actual practices as well as in claims of memberships and social positioning. In order to understand the inner needs and constraints characterizing migrant identity in the context of remittances, we can examine remittance scripts and social positioning through an analysis of identity formation as migrant subjectivity. To begin with, a remittance script often involves the discursive subject of the "ideal migrant" as an industrious, diligent, and loyal individual living and working in the Global North but keeping up meaningful relations to his or her community of origin in the Global South. He or she is part of a diaspora which differs from the migrant population in the financial and emotional commitment to the homeland embedded in a context of development (Page and Mercer 2012, p. 2). At the receiving end, family and household members are expected to be grateful and, with the money, accept the earmarking of development and aid, meaning they are supposed to spend the money on modest daily provisions, education, and health, and not to consume conspicuously. They are also expected to join efforts of development, build "better" houses, pursue an education, and accommodate the transnational vision of home expressed by the migrants.

Although the empirical reality of migrants often differs, subjectivity in the context of migration is governed by the positionality of free and successful agents making the best of their human capital, by exploited workers and passive victims (Deshingkar 2019), and by their either grateful or worried family and kin. These roles are distributed by regimes of mobility that recognize that mobility is stratified by status and rights, by the intersection of gender, class, and race, and by an imaginary of the destination parading migration as a promise for a better life (Glick Schiller and Salazar 2013; Van Hear 2014).

Remittances offer a way of negotiating the migration regime by producing a specific subject position. For example, many migrants have to take work in fields other than what they were qualified or trained for, like domestic, factory, or construction work, and they balance their experience of selling short their training by economic and social remittances. Supporting schools and education facilities at home often compensates the downward mobility of migrants, who can reestablish their position as educated and intellectual individuals by remitting toward educational causes (Isaakyan and Triandafyllidou 2017, p. 14; Parreñas 2015). The pressure of success is immense in migrant biographies: migrants feel an inner need to make up for the loss of social status and experiences of exclusion and discrimination in their host society; they feel the pressure of supporting their home and diaspora communities as well as perhaps a newly discovered solidarity and sense of patriotism triggered by conflict, war, or economic crises in their place of origin (see Alluri in this volume). By remitting, they can regain their lost status as skilled professionals, restore their social status in their communities, and make up for their absence in times of need.

Against this background, we can read remitting as a social practice in which migrant subjectivity is negotiated between normative expectations and individual needs. The making of the migrant follows a path of individual will, agency, and skills, collective expectations and moral obligations, legislative constraints in the host society, organizational structures, and discursive patterns, in short: "the interplay of migrant regimes and migrant subjectivities" (Collins 2021, p. 3). Awumbila et al. (2019) demonstrated how Ghanaian future migrants are molded into subservient domestic workers even before they leave their village: they are taught to dress appropriately, to say "please" and "thank you," and to use terms of respect like calling their employers Mummy and Daddy. Females from Indonesia receive a "resilience training" before their departure that is supposed to foster a strong mind, professional attitudes, and self-esteem, and to shape the future migrant workers into "supermaids" (Chee 2020). Cabalquinto and Wood-Bradley (2020) further referred to the role of media technologies and their affective impact on users. Migrant subjectivity is also constructed by devices, strategies, and digital practices of connectivity services, enabling migrants to remit and keep in touch with their families and places of origin.

The production of migrant subjectivity is thus multifaceted: it is shaped by recruiters and employers, NGOs and state agencies, media platforms, and marketplaces. Migration regimes in the destination countries, that is, the national immigration programs, remittance conditions, the legal status of immigrants, and political and societal discourses on migration, all contribute to turning people into migrants. Their appeals (*Anrufung*) and requirements blend with migrants' senses of duty and inner needs of solidarity and loyalty and thus produce the obliging, disciplinary, and regulatory techniques of migrant governance. Because transnational governance is not connected to one nation state, its history, laws, and constitution (Nowicka 2019, pp. 28–31), it operates by internalizing demands of flexibility, self-responsibility, and self-initiative. This process of neoliberalization can be scaled from the level of migrant subjectivity to development organizations and state governance.

Migrant subjectivity is moreover gendered, classed, age-specific, and ethnicized and/or racialized, and therefore requires an intersectional approach. Nowicka showed how the ethos of hard work and diligence became a Polish quality in the context of Polish migration to the UK (2020, p. 9), whereas the aptitude of female caregivers became linked to their ethnic (often Asian) background as well as their gender (e.g., Miyawaki 2015). Remittances produce a gendered neoliberal governmentality in the hierarchy of the productive and highly valorized male migrant and the less valued non-migrant woman (Kunz 2011). Among the most desired qualities in the discursive position of "the good migrant" are productivity, a willingness to work, diligence, and loyalty. All these qualities can be produced and demonstrated through remittances, and vice versa: remittance practices produce and demonstrate a work ethos, the subject position of the migrant hero with a successful life abroad, and loyalty toward the community at home.

Conclusion

Remittance practices are a key element of migrant subjectivity because they are a manifestation of "having made it abroad": from the decision whether to send money, how much, how often, and to whom, to communicating a purpose—all these acts contribute to a social positioning and subjectivity of migrants (regardless of their actual success or failure in the place of residence). On the other end of the transaction, remittances also produce the position of virtuous and deserving non-migrants, who accept checks, reciprocate with gratitude, and thus maintain the connectivity of transnational networks. Interpreted in this light, remittances become a governmental technique that creates subjectivity by finding and attuning the migrant within the transnational social field.

All of this is not to say that actual people only "do stuff" in order to become somebody, just as scripts are not a social contract and do not entail instructions regulating behaviors and outcomes (Carling 2014, p. 222). Recipients may refuse to express gratitude in order to level out the asymmetry of the social relationship and prefer social distance in order to avoid shame (Carling 2014, p. 247). They may prove to be moral *hazardeurs*, accepting the money and support but not fulfilling their end of the bargain, instead ignoring the obligation to reciprocate through appreciation and humbleness. They may dodge developmental projects and stick to traditional ways of dwelling. The effects of remittance practices on migrant subjects are manifold, diverse, and sometimes unexpectedly irritating. For a concise analysis of the subjectivity of remittance sender and receiver, we return to the key question of what changes when people become migrants. Obviously, one finds care relations, gift-giving, and financial support in non-transnational families: What are the social hierarchies there? People give money to relatives, pay for healthcare for parents and children, finance education, and support livelihoods outside the migration context. This is why the transnational perspective is so important: it helps us not to reduce people to their migrant positionalities, but explain what is particular about being a migrant in specific local and transnational conditions. What turns gifts, help, allowances, and donations into remittances? Again, we are pointed toward the asymmetries in remittance relationships. Remittances are a way of attuning oneself to the structural inequality of the global world, of overcoming injustice, and, at the same time, of reproducing the very same dependency between center and periphery, Global North and Global South, migrant and non-migrant. Still, by becoming a caregiver, an investor, or something similar, remitting is a way of dealing with inequality, with absence, with nostalgia, and with homesickness. It is a position of agency in an environment where many migrants have few means of changing anything.

In their analysis of ways of being and belonging, Levitt and Glick Schiller conceptualized the appeals and expectations of the transnational social field as a kind of citizenship (2004, pp. 1024–1026). We can understand the process of becoming in its legal, cultural, social, and moral dimensions as an acquisition of transnational citizenship with rights and duties specific to migrants. Remittances are an expression of participating and engaging with rights (to work, to buy property, etc.) and duties (to take responsibility, to care for family in places of origin and residence). They allow individuals to turn their ways of being and belonging into transnationally meaningful ways of becoming. In transnational society, they can be seen as allocating social positions, and governing the migrant self through economics, laws, and politics of belonging. When we study migration as part of society, we need to identify the specific practices of identity formation in the context of migration. Remittances as social practices are certainly one of these.

References

Awumbila, M. et al. (2019). Please, Thank You and Sorry: Brokering Migration and Constructing Identities for Domestic Work in Ghana. *Journal of Ethnic and Migration Studies*, 45(14), 2655–2671.

Basch, L. G., Glick Schiller, N., & Szanton Blanc, C. (1994). *Nations Unbound: Transnational Projects, Postcolonial Predicaments, and Deterritorialized Nation-States*. Routledge.

Billig, M. (1995). *Banal Nationalism*. SAGE.

Boccagni, P. & Decimo, F. (2013): Mapping Social Remittances. *Migration Letters*, 10(1), 1–10.

Boccagni, P. & Erdal, M. B. (2020). On the Theoretical Potential of 'Remittance Houses': Toward a Research Agenda across Emigration Contexts. *Journal of Ethnic and Migration Studies*, 1–18.

Bourdieu, P. (2006). The Forms of Capital. In H. Lauder et al. (Eds.), *Education, Globalization and Social Change* (pp. 105–118). Oxford University Press.

Cabalquinto, E. C. & Wood-Bradley, G. (2020). Migrant Platformed Subjectivity: Rethinking the Mediation of Transnational Affective Economies via Digital Connectivity Services. *International Journal of Cultural Studies*, 23(5), 787–802.

Carling, J. (2008). The Determinants of Migrant Remittances. *Oxford Review of Economic Policy*, 24(3), 581–598.

Carling, J. (2014). Scripting Remittances: Making Sense of Money Transfers in Transnational Relationships. *International Migration Review*, 48(1), 218–262.

Carling, J. (2020). Remittances: Eight Analytical Perspectives. In T. Bastia & R. Skeldon (Eds.), *Routledge handbook of migration and development* (pp. 114–124). Routledge.

Castles, S., de Haas, H. & Miller, M.J. (2014). *The Age of Migration: International Population Movements in the Modern World*. Palgrave Macmillan.

Chee, L. (2020). "Supermaids": Hyper-resilient Subjects in Neoliberal Migration Governance. *International Political Sociology*, 14, 366–381. https://doi.org/10.1093/ips/olaa009.

Collins, F. L. (2021). "Give me my Pathway!": Multinational Migration, Transnational Skills Regimes and Migrant Subjectification. *Global Networks*, 21(8), 18–39.

Deshingkar, P. (2019). The Making and Unmaking of Precarious, Ideal Subjects: Migration Brokerage in the Global South, *Journal of Ethnic and Migration Studies*, 45(14), 2638–2654.

Eckstein, S. (2006). Transnational Family Based Social Capital: Remittances and the Transformation of Cuba. *International Journal of Sociology of the Family*, 32(2), 141–171.

Erdal, M. B. (2012). "A Place to Stay in Pakistan": Why Migrants Build Houses in their Country of Origin. *Population, Space and Place*, 18(5), 629–641.

Erdal, M. B. & Borchgrevink, K. (2017). Transnational Islamic Charity as Everyday Rituals. *Global Networks*, 17(1), 130–146.

Erdal, M. B. (2020). Theorizing Interactions of Migrant Transnationalism and Integration through a Multiscalar Approach. *Comparative Migration Studies*, 8(31), 1–16.

Erel, U. (2010). Migrating Cultural Capital: Bourdieu in Migration Studies. *Sociology*, 44(4), 642–660.

Faist, T. & Ulbricht, C. (2013). *Doing National Identity through Transnationality: Categorizations of Inequality in German Integration Debates*. COMCAD Arbeitspapiere – Working Papers, 120. COMCAD – Center on Migration, Citizenship and Development.

Faist, T. (2014). On the Transnational Social Question: How Social Inequalities are Reproduced in Europe. *Journal of European Social Policy*, 24(3), 207–222.

Faist, T. (2010). Towards Transnational Studies: World Theories, Transnationalisation and Changing Institutions. *Journal of Ethnic and Migration Studies*, 36(10), 1665–1687.

Glick Schiller, N. & Salazar, N. B. (2013). Regimes of Mobility Across the Globe. *Journal of Ethnic and Migration Studies*, 39(2), 183–200.

Grabowska, I. et al. (2017). *Migrants as Agents of Change: Social Remittances in an Enlarged European Union*. Palgrave Macmillan.

Haas, H. de (2020). Paradoxes of Migration and Development. In T. Bastia & R. Skeldon (Eds.), *Routledge Handbook of Migration and Development* (pp. 17–31). Routledge.

Hall, S. (1992). The West and the Rest: Discourse and Power. In S. Hall & B. Gieben (Eds.), *Formations of Modernity* (pp. 275–331). Polity Press.
Honneth, A. (1995). *The Struggle for Recognition: The Moral Grammar of Social Conflicts.* Polity Press.
Horst, C., Erdal, M. B., Carling, J., & Afeef K. F. (2014). Private Money, Public Scrutiny? Contrasting Perspectives on Remittances. *Global Networks*, 14(4), 514–532.
Isaakyan, I. & Triandafyllidou, A. (2017). "Sending so Much More than Money": Exploring Social Remittances and Transnational Mobility. *Ethnic and Racial Studies*, 40(15), 2787–2805.
Joseph, M. (2002). *Against the Romance of Community.* University of Minnesota Press.
Kapur, D. (2005): Remittances: The New Development Mantra. In: S. M. Maimbo & D. Ratha (Eds.): *Remittances: Development Impact and Future Prospects.* World Bank, 331–360.
Keles, J. Y. (2015). *Media, Diaspora and Conflict. Nationalism and Identity amongst Kurdish and Turkish Migrants in Europe.* Tauris.
Krzyżowski Ł. & Mucha J. (2014). Transnational Caregiving in Turbulent Times: Polish Migrants in Iceland and their Elderly Parents in Poland. *International Sociology.* 29(1), 22-37.
Kunz, R. (2011). *The Political Economy of Global Remittances: Gender, Governmentality, and Neoliberalism.* Routledge.
Lacroix, T. (2014). Conceptualizing Transnational Engagements: A Structure and Agency Perspective on (Hometown) Transnationalism. *International Migration Review*, 48(3), 643–79.
Levitt, P. (1998). Social Remittances: Migration Driven Local-Level Forms of Cultural Diffusion. *International Migration Review*, 32(4), 926–948.
Levitt, P. (2001). *The Transnational Villagers.* University of California Press.
Levitt, P. (2009). Roots and routes: Understanding the lives of the Second Generation Transnationally. *Journal of Ethnic and Migration Studies*, 35(7), 1225–1242. https://doi.org/10.1080/13691830903006309.
Levitt, P. & Glick Schiller, N. (2004). Conceptualizing Simultaneity: A Transnational Social Field Perspective on Society. *International Migration Review* 38(3), 1002–1039.
Levitt, P. & Lamba-Nieves, D. (2011): Social Remittances Revisited. *Journal of Ethnic and Migration Studies*, 37(1), 1–22.
Lindley, A. (2010): *The Early Morning Phonecall: Somali Refugees' Remittances.* Berghahn.
Lopez, S. L. (2015): *The Remittance Landscape: Spaces of Migration in Rural Mexico and Urban USA.* Chicago University Press.
Mahmud, H. (2021). Beyond Economics: The Family, Belonging and Remittances among the Bangladeshi Migrants in Los Angeles. *International Migration*, 1–15.

Marcus, G. E. (1995). Ethnography in/of the World System: The Emergence of Multi-Sited Ethnography. *Annual Review of Anthropology*, 24, 95–117.
Meyer, S. (2019). Remittances und transnationales Kapital. In K. Braun et al. (Eds.), Wirtschaften: Kulturwissenschaftliche Perspektiven (pp. 64–80). MakuFEE.
Meyer, S. (2020). “Home Is Where I Spend My Money”: Testing the Remittance Decay Hypothesis with Ethnographic Data from an Austrian-Turkish Community. *Social Inclusion*, *8*(1), 275–284.
Miyawaki, C. E. (2015). A Review of Ethnicity, Culture, and Acculturation among Asian Caregivers of Older Adults (2001–2012). *SAGE Open*, 18, 1–18.
Moret, J. (2018). *European Somalis' Post-Migration Movements: Mobility Capital and the Transnationalisation of Resources.* Springer.
Nieswand, B. (2018): Border Dispositifs and Border Effects: Exploring the Nexus between Transnationalism and Border Studies. *Identities* 25(5), 592–609.
Nowicka, M. (2013). Positioning Strategies of Polish Entrepreneurs in Germany: Transnationalizing Bourdieu's Notion of Capital. *International Sociology* 28(1), 29–47.
Nowicka, M. (2015). *Bourdieu's Theory of Practice in the Study of Cultural Encounters and Transnational Transfers in Migration*, MMG Working Paper Series, www.mmg/mpg.de/workingpapers.
Nowicka, M. & Šerbedžija, V. (Eds.). (2016a). *Migration and Social Remittances in a Global Europe.* Palgrave Macmillan.
Nowicka, M., & Šerbedžija, V. (2016b). Migration and Remittances in a Global Europe. In M. Nowicka & V. Šerbedžija (Eds.), *Europe in a Global Context: Migration and Social Remittances in a Global Europe* (pp. 1–20). Palgrave Macmillan UK.
Nowicka, M. (2019). Transnationalismus. Studienkurs Soziologie. Baden-Baden: Nomos. https://doi.org/10.5771/9783845292311.
Nowicka, M. (2020). (Dis)connecting Migration: Transnationalism and Nationalism beyond Connectivity. *Comparative Migration Studies*, 8(20), 1–13.
Orozco, M. (2013). *Migrant Remittances and Development in the Global Economy.* Lynne Rienner Publishing.
Page, B. & Mercer, C. (2012). Why Do People Do Stuff? Reconceptualizing Remittance Behaviour in Diaspora-Development Research and Policy. *Progress in Development Studies* 12(1), 1–18.
Parreñas, R. S. (2015). *Servants of Globalization.* University of Stanford Press.
Pfutze, T. (2012). Does Migration Promote Democratization? Evidence from the Mexican Transition. *Journal of Comparative Economics*, 40(2), 159–175.
Pfutze, T. (2014). Clientelism Versus Social Learning: The Electoral Effects of International Migration. *International Studies Quarterly*, 58(2), 295–307.
Portes, A., Guarnizo, L. E., & Landolt, P. (1999). The Study of Transnationalism: Pitfalls and Promise of an Emergent Research Field. *Ethnic and Racial Studies*, 22(2), 217–237.

Richman, K. E. (2005). *Migration and Vodou.* University Press of Florida.
Savaş, Ö. (2014). Taste Diaspora: The Aesthetic and Material Practice of Belonging. *Journal of Material Culture*, 19(2), 185–208.
Singh, S., Robertson, S. & Cabraal, A. (2012). Transnational Family Money: Remittances, Gifts and Inheritance. *Journal of Intercultural Studies*, 33(5), 475–492.
Smith, M. P., & Guarnizo, L. (Eds.) (1998). *Transnationalism from Below.* Transaction Publishers.
Taylor, M. J., Moran-Taylor, M., & Rodman Ruiz, D. (2006). Land, Ethnic, and Gender Change: Transnational Migration and its Effects on Guatemalan Lives and Landscapes. *GeoForum*, 37, 41–61.
Tertytchnaya, K. et al. (2018). When the Money Stops: Fluctuations in Financial Remittances and Incumbent Approval in Central Eastern Europe, the Caucasus and Central Asia. *American Political Science Review*, 112(4), 758–774.
Thai, H. C. (2014). *Insufficient Funds: The Culture of Money in Low-Wage Transnational Families.* Stanford University Press.
Tsing, A. (2005). *Friction: An Ethnography of Global Connections.* Princeton University Press.
Turner, V. (1964). Betwixt and Between: The Liminal Period in Rites de Passage. *Proceedings of the American Ethnological Society. Symposium on New Approaches to the Study of Religion.* University of Washington Press, 4–20.
Van Hear, N. (2014). Reconsidering Migration and Class. *International Migration Review*, 48, 100–121.
Vari-Lavoisier, I. (2016). The Economic Side of Social Remittances: How Money and Ideas Circulate between Paris, Dakar, and New York. *Comparative Migration Studies*, 4(1).
Vari-Lavoisier, I. (2020). Social Remittances. T. Bastia & R. Skeldon (Eds.), *Routledge Handbook of Migration and Development* (pp. 125–135). Routledge.
Vertovec, S. (1999). Conceiving and Researching Transnationalism, *Ethnic and Racial Studies*, 22(2), 447–462.
Waldinger, R. (2015). *The Cross-Border Connection: Immigrants, Emigrants, and their Homelands.* Harvard University Press.
Weiss, A. (2005). The Transnationalization of Social Inequality: Conceptualizing Social Positions on a World Scale. *Current Sociology*, 53(4), 707–728.
Wimmer, A. & Glick Schiller, N. (2002). Methodological Nationalism and Beyond: Nation-State Building, Migration and the Social Sciences. *Global Networks*, 2(4), 301–334.
Zelizer, V. A. (2014, 19 September). Remittance Circuits. Working Paper Presented at the Workshop "Following the Intangible Flows: Transnational Approaches to Immaterial Remittances", Princeton University, 1–5. https://projects.iq.harvard.edu/files/tsi/files/8-zelizer2015_tsiworkingpaper.pdf.

PART I

Historical Perspectives in Remittance Research

Historical perspectives in remittance research are rare but indispensable if one wants to examine transformative effects in transnational society. It seems almost banal to say: Social change can only be studied with historic depth in the analysis. The role of remittances is wide-ranging in the context of social transformation. Lopez described with regard to Mexico in the 1920s how a remitted watch changed not only the social status of the recipient but also the perception of timeliness in a rural area which had previously run according to natural time like the rise of the sun. Daily routines, work-life, self-image, and the landscape were affected: Sewing machines and technological tools changed the pace in production, and remitted overalls transformed the perception of workers and work. Finally, the automobile bought with money sent from the USA completely changed the Mexican remittance landscape: Streets and highways were built and remote areas could now be reached by car (Lopez 2015, pp. 14–17).

Hence, if we wish to describe "present" transnationalism, we need to investigate "past" transnationalism, perhaps even transnationalism before nations. Historically, space has been constituted not only through national borders but also through religion, language, values, and tradition as well as the density of communication. Transnational networks in the early modern period were elite trading communities, like the ones in Venice and Genoa and the Hanseatic League, religious networks like the Jesuit Order, or academic circles like the one surrounding John Amos Comenius (1592–1670) (Krieger 2004). Likewise, transnational networks broadened with political changes: The revolutions of 1789 (Pestel 2017) and 1848 (Weyland 2009) were accompanied by displacement and migration movements. Out of these expatriate communities emerged a transnational network of political exile.

By comparison, we quickly see that transnationalism today is distinct with regard to the large number of people on the move, the regularity and instantaneity of their communication, and the resulting simultaneity of being "here" and "there" (Portes et al. 1999, p. 224). Glick Schiller noted a structural difference between migration in the nineteenth to early twentieth centuries and today: As it was more difficult and expensive to keep in touch with their places of origin, earlier migrants tended to locate themselves economically, socially, and culturally more intensely in their place of destination. By contrast, today's migrants lead their lives transnationally and connect their places of residence and origin through a tight and lively network of communication and exchange (Glick Schiller 2014, pp. 162–163). Whereas in historic migration, economic success and social recognition depended on a rapid process of integration into the mainstream host society, today's migrant actors rely on cross-border networks and draw social capital from transnational ties (Portes et al. 1999, p. 226).

However, despite the underdeveloped technologies and means of communication, historic transnational communities remained in contact with their homelands: They visited periodically, many migrants returned, and of course, they sent remittances via letters, banks, and so-called pocket remittances, meaning cash or bank drafts which were carried by travelers and visitors. Thereby, long distances fostered cross-border projections, sentiments, and dual strategies, as Madeline Hsu highlighted in her historical analysis of Chinese migration to the USA: Even after the gold mines in California dried up, the migrant workers stayed, found new jobs, and sent remittances, mirroring their dreams of gold as well as of home (Hsu 2002). In her chapter in this volume, Annemarie Steidl shows how remittances from the USA to the Habsburg Empire between 1890 and the 1930s were considerable in number and far-reaching in their effects. Not only the amount of remittances sketched in her chapter are enlightening, but also the direction of the money flows. Likewise, Magee and Thompson (2006) demonstrated how Europe was the recipient rather than the sender of remittances in their analysis of the funds sent from the USA to the UK between 1875 and 1913.

In this section, European states are portrayed as both sending and receiving countries, a perspective that reminds us of the fact that remittance networks are dynamic, and the contemporary configuration as a one-way street from the Global North to the Global South is not a given. Dirk Rupnow shows in his analysis of Austrian social science research on migration and remittances from the 1970s that the Eurocentric and neocolonial paradigm shaped not only research perspectives but also public discourse. He brings to mind that remittance research needs a sound post-colonial basis if we wish to transcend the migration-development nexus.

Furthermore, a comparative perspective is worthwhile with regard to historic and contemporary remittance politics. In his chapter, Aleksandar Miletić investigates monarchist and socialist Yugoslav state programs and their attempts to channel remittances into public projects. However, the great transformation the state officials had hoped for never materialized. The policymakers' conception of remittances as a disposable public resource represents a fundamental misunderstanding of remittance capital. Remittance management today can learn from such historic blunders in utilizing and administering remittances.

Finally, this opening section paves the way for studying the transformative effects of remittances by focusing on changing remittance practices, scripts, and the development of diasporic networks. Ivana Bajić-Hajduković and Sara Bernard apply this comparative perspective to socialist and contemporary Serbia and relate changing remittance practices to remittance scripts: Post-1990 migrants who originated from urban parts of Serbia remit much less than the generations before them and, indeed, their families do not even expect them to do so. Moreover, if remittances are sent on an irregular basis, they are perceived as gifts rather than as financial aid and are not spent on everyday expenses. Receiving money from one's children is inacceptable for today's middle-class urban parents, whereas it was common practice to use money sent by "guest workers" on temporary work in Germany in the 1970s and 1980s. Thus, the changing remittance script is here related to social class and identity politics. Marie Karner analyzes how diasporic remittances shape landscapes by focusing on a village in Lebanon. She shows that diaspora communities have become more accessible and important due to new media, increased mobility, and continuous remittance flows. They have also become more complex and wider-ranging than the two-dimensional structures of origin and destination that were characteristic of historic migration. The historical perspective laid out in this section helps us to identify and understand these processes of social transformation in remitting and in constituting diasporic communities.

References

Glick Schiller, N. (2014). Das transnationale Migrationsparadigma: Globale Perspektiven auf die Migrationsforschung. In B. Nieswand & H. Drotbohm (Eds.), *Kultur, Gesellschaft, Migration: Die reflexive Wende in der Migrationsforschung* (pp. 153–178). Springer VS. https://doi.org/10.1007/978-3-658-03626-3_6

Hsu, M. Y. (2002). Dreaming of Gold, Dreaming of Home: Transnationalism and Migration between the United States and South China, 1882–1943. Stanford University Press.

Krieger, M. (2004). "Transnationalität" in vornationaler Zeit? Ein Plädoyer für eine erweiterte Gesellschaftsgeschichte der Frühen Neuzeit. *Geschichte und Gesellschaft, 30*(1), 125–136.

Lopez, S. L. (2015). The Remittance Landscape: Spaces of Migration in Rural Mexico and Urban USA. University of Chicago Press.

Magee, Gary & Thompson, Andrew S. (2006). Lines of Credit, Debts of Obligation: Migrant Remittances to Britain, C. 1875–1913. *Economic History Review, 59*(3), 539–577. https://doi.org/10.1111/j.1468-0289.2006.00349.x

Pestel, F. (2017). French Revolution and Migration after 1789. *European History Online*. http://ieg-ego.eu/en/threads/europe-on-the-road/political-migration-exile/friedemann-pestel-french-revolution-and-migration-after-1789

Portes, A., Guarnizo, L. E., & Landolt, P. (1999). The study of transnationalism: pitfalls and promise of an emergent research field. *Ethnic and Racial Studies, 22*(2), 217–237. https://doi.org/10.1080/014198799329468

Weyland, K. (2009). The Diffusion of Revolution: '1848' in Europe and Latin America. *International Organization, 63*(3), 391–423. https://doi.org/10.1017/S0020818309090146

CHAPTER 2

Postcolonialism, Transnationalism, and Remittances: New Perspectives on "Guest Worker" Research in Austria

Dirk Rupnow

Introduction

This chapter explores the so-called discovery of immigration (Berlinghoff 2013) during the 1970s—"after the boom"—and the emergence of socio-scientific research on so-called guest workers, focusing especially on the role of remittances in this context. The aim is to apply the perspectives of transnationalism and postcolonialism to early migration and remittance research in Austria.

The early 1970s were a phase of profound changes in several social spheres in Austria, including migration and diversity. After recruitment agreements were signed with Turkey (1964) and Yugoslavia (1966), between 10,000 and 20,000 people came to Austria per year; at the beginning of the 1970s, the number rose to between 25,000 and 40,000. At its peak in 1973, about a quarter of a million people from abroad worked in

D. Rupnow (✉)
Institute for Contemporary History, University of Innsbruck, Innsbruck, Austria
e-mail: dirk.rupnow@uibk.ac.at

S. Meyer, C. Ströhle (eds.), *Remittances as Social Practices and Agents of Change*,
https://doi.org/10.1007/978-3-030-81504-2_2

the country, constituting 10 percent of employees nationwide (Biffl 1986, p. 40). Approximately 80 percent of these were from Yugoslavia and about 12 percent from Turkey. The demand was caused by a rapidly growing economy, which was no longer able to cover its demand for labor domestically. The unions, which tended to reject the opening of the Austrian job market, though unable to completely ignore the demands of the economy, arranged that in the admission of contingents of foreign workers a very restrictive regime for "guest work," including preferential treatment of nationals and a principle of rotation, was introduced (Matuschek 1985, pp. 159–198; Wollner 2007, pp. 213–225). Domestic workers were thus given preference over foreign workers in the labor market, while the "guest workers" regularly had to return home and be replaced.

When Austria Discovered Immigration

Corresponding to the changing labor market and its policies in the late 1960s and early 1970s, public debates about the employment of foreigners and its social consequences increased and took on a negative tone. In March 1974, the oil crisis and the deceleration of economic growth were used as an argument to reduce tourist employment and block guest worker employment to the level of October 1973. This paralleled the recruitment stop in the Federal Republic of Germany, which had already been enacted in November 1973. While in Austria, a quarter of the foreign work force had their residence and work permits withdrawn, residence and chain migration nevertheless frequently continued, with family reunification increasing as an unintended side effect. During this peak and the subsequent reduction of immigration, an intense social-scientific research activity emerged that focused on the societal consequences of foreign workers' employment. The vast majority of the published articles focused on the costs and benefits of labor migration as well as on integration processes. With regard to the Federal Republic, Czarina Wilpert at an early stage labeled the second half of the 1970s—after a first phase of recruitment until 1973—as a phase of debates on infrastructure and research oriented toward social problems (Wilpert 1984, p. 306). This era can also be viewed as the "discovery of immigration" (Berlinghoff 2013).

The social partners (the Economic Chamber, the Workers' Chamber, the Federation of Austrian Industries, and the Trade Union Federation), the essential agents in the field of foreign workers' employment in Austria, founded the "Task Force for Economic and Sociological Studies" in

1971 in order to "cultivate timely and substantiated knowledge on the essential difficulties emerging in foreign workers' employment and to propose appropriate actions" (Arbeitskreis 1973, p. 8).[1] Initially, four studies were conducted, focusing on the attitude of Austrians toward the guest workers, on the experiences and opinions of Austrians in residential areas with a large proportion of guest workers, on the problems and experiences of Austrian industrial enterprises with guest workers, and on the process of integration of guest workers in Austria. The main results were published in one volume in 1973.

It is striking that the publication stated right at the beginning that not only the short- and long-term aims of the recruitment countries, but also of the foreign work force themselves and the sending countries would be considered. There were also frequent references to the fundamental meaning of human rights in this context. The set of aims included the following: along with economic questions ("balance of supply and demand on the job market" and "increase of business efficiency"), we find not only the social interests of the Austrian population ("securing advantages for Austrians, for example, through relative social advancement, new supervisory roles, as well as the prevention of disadvantages, for example through competition") and the "prevention of social tensions as one of the biggest threats and a potential matter of expense of the use of guest workers," but also the "integration of guest workers into the Austrian population" as well as ultimately the "betterment of guest workers as an immediate humanitarian aim"—not to mention their economic integration as consumers and the improvement of international relations with the countries of origin (Arbeitskreis 1973, pp. 8–9).

Integration was here seen as the "effect of a long-lasting process of assimilation," which was seen to "develop to varying degrees": "The largest degree of integration is complete absorption into the nationality of the host country." At this point, it was also acknowledged that integration occurs not only in one direction: "Through contact with the incomers, the people of the host country also experience an assimilation towards them, albeit to a lesser degree." Only for a very small part of the "guest workers," however, was a full-scale integration deemed desirable. The task force's inquiry showed that merely 5 percent of Austrians favored a "permanent inclusion of guest workers into the domestic population," whereas 90 percent strongly rejected this. Even the City of Vienna only saw an

[1] All translations from the material published in German are my own.

approval rate of 10 percent, although "a large-scale historic process of integration still remains present in local memory" (Arbeitskreis 1973, p. 93).

Though in a vague and covert way, the latter is most likely a reference to the large migration movements that occurred in the late phase of the Habsburg Monarchy. At the time, hundreds of thousands of people from the Bohemian lands, the Hungarian part of the monarchy, the Austrian hereditary lands, Galicia, the Bukovina, and Dalmatia came to the capital and residential city of Vienna. This indeed became a central historical point of reference for labor migration in the Second Republic, including the proverbial reference to Slavic names in the Viennese telephone book—which also stood for successful integration and normalization after a few generations (see also Hofstetter 1973, p. 59). This is represented in the iconic Kolaric poster campaign in the Viennese dialect: "I haaß Kolaric, du haaßt Kolaric, warum sogns' zu dir Tschusch?" (My name is Kolaric, your name is Kolaric, why do they call you Tschusch? "Tschusch" is a pejorative term for foreigners, especially people of Southeastern European origin.) The poster was designed in 1973 by the Lintas agency on behalf of the Aktion Mitmensch of the Austrian advertising industry (see also Fischer 2008, pp. 327–353; Hemetek 2000) (see Fig. 2.1).

With its—from today's perspective—rather problematic imagery, this campaign can be read as a plea for humanity and equality at the height of the employment of "guest workers" and the increasingly controversial discourse that accompanied it. In fact, it emerged as a trivial effort of improving the image of advertisement generally; the content was thus actually interchangeable, but the choice of subject here was simultaneously quite significant. Meanwhile, in Germany there was a dominance of references to the history of colonialism and slavery—partly by circumvention, partly by explicit inclusion of the recent Nazi past (see also Geiselberger 1972, pp. 9–13; Klee 1971; Meinhof 1995, pp. 97–107).

The study assessed prejudices toward foreign workers from Turkey and Yugoslavia as harmless. It is significant, however, that these workers were regarded as "primitive, dirty, clumsy and unreliable as well as overall culturally strange" (Arbeitskreis 1973, p. 81). There was here already some sense of the threat that with the increasing integration of "guest workers" and especially their social advancement, prejudices would also increase (Hahn and Stöger 2014, pp. 32–33). For that reason, a "general atmosphere of tolerance, humanity and a continuing emphasis on the advantages of the use of guest workers" was called for in order to avoid an

Fig. 2.1 The Kolaric poster campaign, 1973. Reproduced with kind permission of the Initiative Minderheiten Austria

escalation of social tensions. In this context, a crucial role was attributed particularly to the mass media, cultural institutions, the education system, and "the big organizations." Following the right-wing populist "Schwarzenbach-Initiative" against "Überfremdung" (hyperxenesis) in Switzerland in 1970, a "systematic agitation against foreigners" was (at that time) seen as unlikely in Austria (Arbeitskreis 1973, p. 88). At the same time, the study held that there was a "threshhold of hyperxenesis," which in small towns lay at 20 percent and in larger towns at 30 percent, respectively (Arbeitskreis 1973, pp. 89–92). However, it was also stated that there were no absolute critical limits: "Tensions do not simply arise from the existence of guest workers, they must have causes—either actual conflicts of interest or factitious prejudices. Such causes may already take effect in residential areas with a relatively low density, presumably in areas with a number of guest workers of about ten per cent" (Arbeitskreis 1973, p. 92).

A proportion of 10 percent of foreign employees was seen as the crucial threshold "at which social problems apparently arise": "In the long run, the economic benefits of foreign workers' employment for the host country decline, while simultaneously political and social considerations gain in importance" (Butschek and Walterskirchen 1974, pp. 214, 224). The "Schwarzenbach-Initiative" in Switzerland also aimed at curtailing the proportion of foreign workers at 10 percent. In general, however, the necessity and benefit of foreign workers were not called into question (see also Hofstetter 1973).

Costs and benefits were henceforth repeatedly weighed up against each other, which resulted in the issue of foreign workers moving from the economic sphere to domestic and social politics. In this context, the question was raised whether it even still made sense to maintain businesses with a proportion of foreign workers exceeding 80 percent: "Would it not be more reasonable to move such enterprises to foreign countries?" (Hofstetter 1973, p. 59). In light of the neoliberally motivated relocation of production to newly industrialized countries that has genuinely occurred in recent decades, this was a remarkable proposal by an Austrian union official. This was, after all, the time when the demand for "integration before new immigration" came up, which was upheld throughout the 1990s and into the present day: "Still, the number of foreign workers cannot and must not go sky high. Obviously, the development of our infrastructure has not kept pace with the expansion of the population through foreigners. Thus, our next aim must be to provide the appropriate conditions for the number of foreigners that we already employ" (Hofstetter 1973, p. 59).

The studies went on to outline three problem scenarios that were to be prevented in the future: the "ghetto problem" (the formation of a segregated subgroup), the "pogrom problem" (the development of aggressive tendencies toward foreigners and the radicalization of the majority population), and the "proletarianization problem" (the modification of culture and society due to the successful assimilation of the foreign workers, but also their "confinement to lower social classes") (Gehmacher 1972, p. 14). These problems were also identified and formulated in the study "Möglichkeiten und Grenzen des Einsatzes ausländischer Arbeitskräfte" (Opportunities and Limitations in the Use of Foreign Workers) of the Beirat für Wirtschafts- und Sozialfragen (Advisory Board for Economic and Social Questions), a kind of early think tank of the Austrian social partners. To avoid crisis scenarios, two preemptive strategies were proposed to reduce social tensions, namely either the integration of the foreign workforce on several social levels or their rotation through flexible governance (Beirat 1976, p. 38).

Remittances in Social Science Research of the 1970s

It was clear to the recruiting countries from the very beginning that hiring "guest workers" would stabilize prices domestically and exert a counter-inflationary effect because of low consumption on behalf of the labor migrants and their payment of remittances, while the production and amount of goods would increase. Remittances were not seen by economic researchers as a serious threat to the balance of payments, while one of the greatest prejudices relating to guest workers was that the export of currency was dangerous (Österreichisches Komitee für Sozialarbeit 1972, p. 83; Zur Beschäftigung 1962). Remittances were also widely seen as a benefit for the sending countries. In the lists of advantages and disadvantages for the receiving and sending countries, the advantages included a reduction in unemployment and thus of the burden of state benefits as well as of domestic political tensions alongside the conveyance of a modern approach to continuous and well-organized labor. The disadvantages cited on the other hand included the depopulation of regions and villages, the temporary loss of good labor forces, the permanent loss of labor forces generally, and "thus a long-term deterioration of genetic potential," as well as a danger of mass remigration, since remigrants exacerbated the oversupply of small-scale businesses (Arbeitskreis 1973, p. 128).

At the same time, remittances were seen as advantageous to the receiving countries in the long run, because they would eventually increase the external demand for consumer goods and thereby increase exports of goods and services (Beirat 1976, p. 32). This fact in particular was seen as a kind of neocolonial aspect of the labor migration arrangement of the 1950s to the 1970s: the sending countries would only experience an ostensible improvement in their trade balance through the remittances of the emigrants, while at the same time these payments would have an inflationary impact, as they would lead to more consumption than production. While the receiving countries tried to present remittances as a form of development aid, they would in fact primarily benefit the demand for capital goods—once the "guest workers" had become accustomed to cars and electronic appliances—thus also once more benefitting the receiving countries, while the trade deficit of the sending countries increased (Geiselberger 1972, pp. 18–20, pp. 167–171; see also Klee 1971, p. 25).

Above all, remittances were understood as an important indicator of emigrants' ties to their countries of origin (Mehrländer 1974, pp. 231–239) and their willingness to return (Lichtenberger 1984, p. 173). As the Advisory Board for Economic and Social Questions noted: "The primary motive for accepting work abroad is the higher wage, which is mostly connected to very specific saving targets." A distinction was here made between "saving targets for the homeland" (which included the means to build homes, buy property, establish businesses, repay debts, and provide for relatives), "saving targets that can be realized both in Austria and in the homeland" (which included cars and other long-term consumer goods, clothes, and education for one's children), and "saving targets for Austria" (which included accommodation and furniture). These "saving targets for Austria" offered to contemporary researchers "a good indication of the willingness to integrate and the level of integration already achieved" (Beirat 1976, p. 50). These distinctions were viewed as a direct reflection of the level of integration: "Of the Turkish workers in Vienna, for example, forty per cent accepted work abroad to pay off their debts while 31 per cent aimed to make themselves independent with the income they could save thereby, with a further 15 per cent having at least considered the latter option. A survey of the saving targets of foreign workers in the Federal Republic of Germany revealed that 60 per cent of saving targets were clearly geared toward the homeland, while the remaining indications could not be clearly attributed as pointing toward either the homeland or the host country" (Beirat 1976, p. 50).

The saving practices of the "guest workers" were thus used to legitimize the rotation principle, while an understanding was also explicitly expressed for the fact that changes in the workers' individual goals were dependent on the conditions reigning in the recruiting country: "In sum, the available research findings lead to the conclusion that the primary goals of the bulk of the foreign workers predominantly favor rotation. The longer they remain, the more positive the attitude to integration emerging among a portion of the foreign workers, provided that—particularly if the conditions for integration are good—a successive change in subjective targets takes place" (Beirat 1976, p. 54).

Interestingly, social science research on domestic and foreign migration also emerged in Turkey, as one of the major sending countries, during the era of guest worker migration, especially following the establishment of a state planning office in 1960 and the introduction of university autonomy in 1961—thus even somewhat earlier than in most host countries. At this point in time, migration also became a focus of state planning and government policy in Turkey, relating alongside questions of population growth and unemployment especially to the migrants' potential savings as an important source of income and as a motor of national economic development. Thus, it is not surprising that wages, salaries, savings, and remittances constituted by far the most studied topics in Turkish social science research between 1960 and 1984 (Abadan-Unat 1986, pp. 45–57, esp. 47–48, 50–51; Abadan-Unat 1976; Akgündüz 2016, pp. 53, 55–56, 67–68). In an inversion of the notion that guest worker recruitment constituted development aid to the sending countries, Turkish researchers assumed that it was above all unemployed workers who emigrated and that this emigration would thus not constitute a domestic workforce drain. The emigrants were mostly considered to be unskilled workers who would return with useful know-how for Turkish industry. This was already refuted empirically at an early stage. In any case, it demonstrates that the sending countries also subjected guest worker migration to cost/benefit considerations (İçduygu 2014, pp. 117–123).

Reclaiming Postcolonial and Transnational Perspectives

This contemporary interpretation of remittances as an indicator of migrants' willingness to return or to stay and "integrate" demonstrates the need to place the financial and social transfers in a wider context. The continuing connection to their countries of origin (including the purchase of property and the construction of homes) could not yet be seen as part of a "transnational lifestyle" as it is regarded today. Moreover, the migrant actors themselves were not regarded as active agents, but as labor subjects, who had to be controlled and optimized. Their voices and perspectives remained silent in early "guest worker" research.

In the interpretative paradigm of postcolonialism, the denial of representation and an independent voice is a practice that seamlessly perpetuates colonial forms of rule and discourse—which is, of course, what the concept of postcoloniality focuses on: not simply the chronological "thereafter," but the continuities and traditions of othering as phenomena that were not concluded with but rather continued to exert an influence beyond the rupture of decolonization. If, following Gayatri Chakravorty Spivak (1988, pp. 271–313), one of the preeminent scholars of postcolonial theory, we ask the question "Can the Subaltern Speak?," we can only answer with "yes." The postcolonial twist in this communication is: of course, the subaltern can speak. But who listens to a voice that does not represent the cultural hegemony?

Colonialism Without Colonies

Recent research on labor migration in the second half of the twentieth century has repeatedly described and interpreted this as a post- or neocolonial phenomenon and/or as a specific form of internal colonization, equating labor migrants with the subaltern of postcolonial discourse.[2] In many European countries, this "colonialism without colonies" is in fact related directly to these countries' colonial pasts—a claim that can even be applied to Austria when considering the internal colonization status of Bosnia and Herzegovina within the Habsburg Empire (Müller-Funk and Wagner 2005; Todorova 2009). Indeed, if we follow Jürgen Osterhammel's (2006, pp. 19–26) definition of colonialism, we find that the following traits apply to the labor migration of the 1950s and 1960s: (a) hegemony over cultural foreignness and the construction of inferior otherness; (b) the belief in a mission and a duty of guardianship, albeit today in weaker form; (c) differentials and dependencies between centers and peripheries (particularly present in remittance transfers to places of origin); and presumably also (d) the utopia of the non-political that reduces everything to

[2] The debate in German-speaking migration studies can be followed in Steyerl and Rodriguez (2003, pp. 56–107). See also Dhawan (2007). Spivak insisted that labor migrants in Northern countries have always been more privileged than the subaltern in the South, who do not have any access to mobility.

administrative acts while at the same time the locals (ironically) feel colonized by the immigrants. Seen like this, we are looking at a system of exploitation, with the colonized invariably existing only to serve the dominant culture in which they themselves remain marginalized. This is still reflected today in those popular political and economic arguments that praise migration as compensation for the demographic decline of the indigenous population and thereby try to make it more palatable to the fearful autochthonous population, which tends toward racist exclusion. Even if one is not entirely prepared to accept this comparison between colonial exploitation and labor migration, it is obvious that the denial of representation is a central problem in both and, due to the changes taking place in our society through migration, that a new take on national history is required.

Austria as a Migration Society

Migration processes have led to changes in Austrian society that necessitate a transnational history of Austria as a migration society. This signifies an important paradigm shift: society as a whole is currently being transformed to a significant degree by migration processes. This affects natives and immigrants alike, just as colonialism did not just affect and transform the colonies, but also the metropoles. This also complicates the notion of "integration," which presupposes a linear process of assimilation as was proffered by the Chicago School as far back as the 1920s through the 1940s. Immigrants do not assimilate up to the point that they disappear completely within their host society, which itself remains unchanged. Rather, our society, culture, and everyday lives are transformed under the influence of migration. The conventional notion of immigrant societies therefore seems inappropriate these days, as it continues to delegate the issue to an ostensibly clearly defined group ("the immigrants") who are not viewed as an integral part of society, but at best as an appendage (Broden and Mecheril 2007). Social science research should not contribute to this view and further ghettoize migrants by singling them out as research topics. Glick Schiller has addressed this approach as methodological nationalism and pointed toward its inherent dangers (Wimmer and Glick Schiller 2002). What we should do instead is take into account the entire society in our research. Social "problems" or "issues" should not be passed down to the "immigrants," as has long been the case in public discourse and continues to predominantly be the case today.

The Perpetuation of Racism in Migration Discourse

With specific regard to Austria, further special conditions prevailing in this migration society need to be taken into account: This is a post-Nazi, post-genocidal society. The concept of post-Nazism—like postcolonialism—points toward the continuities and traditions that exist beyond the ruptures, toward remains and traces, residues, and effects that by no means simply disappeared after the end of Nazi rule. It is not possible to talk about foreignness and constructions of the "other" in Austria or Germany without taking into account these countries' catastrophic histories of racism, persecution, expulsion, and genocide. These histories also include colonial experiences of racism and violence, regardless of whether there was a direct path leading "from Windhoek to Auschwitz" (Jürgen Zimmerer) or not. This is evident in the introduction of terms such as "xenophobia" in the 1970s, since (structural) racism was after the Holocaust not perceived of as such or was systematically denied (Goldberg 1993; Terkessidis 1998). Conventional references to "prejudices" also reduce racism and antisemitism to individual faults while at the same time masking the fact that these are not exceptional phenomena, but rather dominant ideas of some members of society about their society, constituting a complex form of "racist knowledge" (Terkessidis 1997).

One can also not discuss "guest workers" and their remittance practices without taking into account the history of forced and foreign labor during World War Two. Beyond this history, which Austria and Germany have in common, Austria's specific prehistory of interior migration within the Habsburg Empire naturally also needs to be considered, especially migration from Bohemia, Moravia, Silesia, and Galicia into the metropolis Vienna. By 1840, 40 percent of the population living and working in the imperial residence were "foreign." In this context, "colonial attitudes" toward the immigrants from the provinces became ubiquitous (Csáky 2010, pp. 222–230, pp. 345–356).

National Histories and Transnational Society

From today's perspective, migration is a distinctly transnational phenomenon. The traditional framework of the nation state remains intact therein, not least of all because of the significance of the different national legal systems between states, yet this framework is repeatedly disrupted and circumvented (Waldinger 2015). Other levels—such as the local and the regional—become more prominent in this context: migration systems and migrant biographies and networks moreover connect spaces to Austrian history that were not classically a part of this history, especially the migrants' places, regions, and countries of origin along with their respective histories, which enticed the migrants to emigrate in the first place, as well as the places to which, having been transformed themselves, they migrate onward or back (Römhild 2004). Migration not only opens up (more) complex spaces but, through manifold connections in memory, also (more) complex chronological interrelations. Transnationality therefore has to be regarded as a research perspective in which the nation remains significant as a frame of reference, but where the established logic of the national is repeatedly and fundamentally challenged and called into question. Transnational and national developments exist in a complex interrelationship, just as various transnational processes that are described for example as Europeanization or globalization exert an influence on each other, overlay each other, and compete with each other. The national framework is not simply dissolved, but it is very much influenced, overlaid, and intersected by transnational currants. The global and the local/regional get mixed up in the process—a process of hybridization or "glocalization" (Robertson 1998, pp. 192–220).

Migration, cross-border lifestyles, and multiple belongings expressed in remittance practices disrupt ideas of distinct belongings and homogenous identity constructions based on clear boundaries, of solid, untraversable borders, and of equally immutable, clearly delineated cultures. Remitting as a genuinely transnational phenomenon places the focus on the spaces both below and above the national, meaning the local/regional and international, respectively, while also complicating this classic gradation. At the same time, remittances reproduce a neocolonial gaze by projecting global inequalities onto social relations (see Meyer in this volume). They demonstrate that today's society is no longer a national society (if it ever was that), but at the same time, they point toward the hierarchy between places and societies, for example by reinforcing the relation of center and periphery from the characteristics of postcolonialism outlined by Osterhammel.

If we want to begin analyzing remittances as transnational practices, we must start by deconstructing national history (Bojadžijev 2009, pp. 102–105). After all, it was national history that produced and legitimized exclusions to begin with. The establishment of historiography and the nation state were closely related to one another. It was not least of all through a history constructed as specific, separate, and primordial that nation states drew their ostensibly inviolable legitimacy throughout the entire nineteenth century and well into the twentieth century. The establishment and development of museums also played a central role in this respect. These served, like historiography, to generate a national past and a shared culture in the first place. This entailed not only the drawing of clear boundaries toward the outside, but also the production of a homogenous interior: populace, culture, and territory were constructed as a natural entity and no distinction was here made between nation and peoplehood. On the contrary, the idea of nation was always ethnically contaminated (Anderson 1983). This is why it remains difficult to this day to conceive of ethnic and cultural diversity as well as of various historical interrelationships within national contexts.

The process of inscribing migration into (national) history always entails the danger of essentializing and homogenizing the very phenomena that are supposed to be integrated. Problematic ascriptions and inappropriate definitudes are unfortunately necessary for linguistic understanding alone. In reality, however, neither migrants nor the autochthonous Austrian population are homogenous entities. Moreover, neither is defined exclusively by their origins. Instead, they can all be equally divided into various groups, networks, and individuals. However, identities are always ascribed in abridging territorial forms. It is especially important that the integration of migration and migrants into national history does not simply serve as a form of appropriation and to once again reinforce the myth of the nation, in the manner that dominant cultures are currently trying to exploit hybridity and heterogeneity as economic resources. The historical normalization of migration is similarly ambivalent, as it is currently serving the needs of globalization: of course, it is true that migration processes of various scopes constitute the rule rather than the exception in history. However, this realization should not lead to centuries of perpetual and effective practices of inequality, exploitation, and difference being concealed or even justified.

Who Tells the National History? Whose Voice Is Heard?

Postcolonial theory is especially suited in this context to hone our focus on ubiquitous forms of essentialization and exoticization, on exclusions and suppressions. Postcolonial theory also reminds us of the import of positionality, criticism, and self-reflection—and not least of all of one's own position as a narrator (Ha 2009, pp. 43–60). Especially with topics relating to historical and contemporary exclusions and marginalizations as well as racist ascriptions, it is never irrelevant who is speaking. Integrating migration and migrants into national history cannot be a comfortable exoticism, but should instead engender a critical view toward the present and the future.

A scholarly engagement with migration societies therefore demands a break with the inherited and established methodological nationalism (Wimmer and Glick Schiller 2002). The transnational gaze expands the national sphere without dissolving it. Spaces need to be set in relation to one another and to be connected with one another beyond the logic of the nation. As this volume shows, such a perspective is needed because a history of migration and social change—precisely following postcoloniality—can never just be a history of elites, but must always give migrants a voice and a subject position of their own, while fathoming their agency within the prevailing societal power structures. This ultimately prevents the reduction of migrants to their economic significance, as happens so often in public discourse.

Provincializing Europe

A transnational history of Austria as a migration society necessarily entails a European perspective. The transnational labor migrations that began in the 1950s were initially an interior European migration, moving above all from the European countries around the Mediterranean to the industrialized states of Central, Western, and Northern Europe. The transfer of labor forces within the European Economic Community (EEC) was from the outset connected to questions of European integration, above all with free movement on the labor market, which would later render the recruitment halts largely ineffective with regard to other member states (this applied to Italy, as a founding member, from the very beginning, and furthermore from 1981 to Greece and from 1986 to Spain and Portugal). Immigration policies were already being coordinated within the EEC by the 1970s. Thus, national policies can no longer be understood outside of the supranational framework of the European Union. The former countries of origin have by today mostly turned into destination countries. In Austria, too, immigration from Africa and Asia is increasing, albeit slowly. Migration has become one of the key issues for Europe, as becomes obvious with regard to developments following Lampedusa and Ceuta.

European discourses and policies regarding migration and its international entanglements shine a light not only on the process of European integration, but also on the attempt to construct a European identity. Unfortunately, this identity construction has also gone hand in hand with the exclusion of the "Other," which is defined culturally as well as very practically and politically, and which the border regime FRONTEX is attempting to keep out of "Fortress Europe." Here, the European dimension opens up into the global context, particularly as it relates to the past and present in Africa and Asia.

The topic of migration, which has hitherto remained marginalized in institutionalized contemporary history, allows for Austrian as well as European contemporary history more broadly to be reconceived and reconfigured, above all spatially and chronologically: spatially with regard to the global context, combining international relations and transnational entanglements, and chronologically with regard to incorporating the history and above all the aftermath of colonialism on equal footing alongside the history and aftermath of the Holocaust and World War Two. Such a reconceived history would not only open up new horizons and overcome historical rivalries, it would moreover offer manifold opportunities for collaboration within the field of history while simultaneously fostering an intense transdisciplinary network—not least of all with those disciplines that have to date dealt with the issue of migration, but also with other fields in the humanities, the social sciences, and cultural studies.

Migration is surely one of the most incisive elements in our understanding of European postwar history and the European present. It is also perhaps the greatest current challenge in European society. Few other events and processes have had a comparable effect on our societies. The Cold War was followed by an era that Samuel Huntington already before 9/11 described as the "Clash of Civilizations" (Huntington 1998). Turning away from his own position conveyed in his classic work "Orientalism," Edward Said countered Huntington's argument with the observation that cultures are constantly changing, exchanging with one another, and enriching each other—despite their simultaneous histories of conflict and violence (Said 2001; see also Said 1979). How great the subsequent shifts have been is evident for example in the fact that during the Cold War, with the Association Agreement concluded with the EEC in 1963/64 and the determination of its essential eligibility to join as a member state, Turkey could naturally be regarded as a part of Europe, whereas today this belonging is constantly being challenged through culturalistic arguments

(Clemens 2007). Following Dipesh Chakrabarty's (2008) classic work, we need to provincialize Europe and correct Eurocentrism on the global stage while not declaring Europe and its perspectives obsolete or losing them from sight.

Conclusion

In the early 1970s, the social sciences were deeply involved in the development of controversial discourses on foreigners and thereby also their remittance practices: they created and reaffirmed patterns of perception; they established connections and tried to offer solution strategies (see also Lanz 2007, pp. 86–96; Treibel 1988). Interestingly, the numerous Austrian studies from this time were hardly considered or investigated, neither as records for a history of science or a history of knowledge in the narrower sense nor as crucial testimonies of the development of the social and political engagements with migration and migrants. (That being said, they were taken into account in: Bergkirchner 2013, pp. 93–102; Gächter 2016, pp. 50–54; Matuschek 1985, pp. 182–184; Mayer 2009, pp. 136–138.) They did not even feature in a recent anthology focusing on the connection between research and politics in the field of migration, asylum, and integration (Karasz 2017).

The contribution of early social science to the controversial discourse on foreigners can also be tracked in their contributions regarding "guest workers'" remittances. Rather than investigating motives of supporting family and kin at home, the money transfers were viewed in their purely economic impacts. Research was thus limited to financial transfers, whereby remittances were not seen as a serious threat to the Austrian balance of payments, while the studies also highlighted the benefits for the economies of the receiving countries, namely Turkey and Yugoslavia. Above all, remittances were understood as an important indicator of emigrants' ties to their country of origin and their willingness to return, thus legitimizing the rotation principle of the guest worker regime.

In actuality, remittances allow for cross-connections and interactions between politics, the economy, education, science, and religion can be taken into account as well as a transnational (and not only Western European) history can be told. The fact that numerous phenomena were already documented and interpreted by the social sciences at the time raises, of course, specific methodical challenges as to how this "social data" and the theories and explanatory models of the time can be historically investigated and classified (Doering-Manteuffel and Raphael 2012, pp. 30–31, 115–117). A historicization of early research on the so-called guest worker migration and its economic, social, and cultural consequences is necessary to deconstruct current discourses on migration and integration. It shows how deep colonial structures protrude into systems of knowledge production and academic economies (see also Bönisch-Brednich in this volume).

This is in line with an understanding of contemporary history as a history of problems and challenges in the present (Hockerts 1993, pp. 98–127). Thereby, questions are raised not only internal to scholarship, regarding for example traditions and models, methods and theories, and the transfer of concepts and ideas, but also regarding external scientific issues, such as the complex interaction between science, politics, and society, agents and institutions, European and international networks, as well as the role of expert knowledge in political decision-making and the public (see also Boswell 2011). The studies from the early 1970s not least of all offer insights into a future in the past: the then-assumed future of a migration society, even before this concept existed at a time when an understanding of migration-driven change of society gradually started to emerge. The same is important when studying remittances: money, object, ideas, and norms are not simply sent to the places of origin, but have transformative effects on actors and societies that transcend national borders. These effects determine the present, which is simultaneously a continuation of this history.

References

Abadan-Unat, N. (1976). Turkish Workers in Europe 1960–1975: A Socio-Economic Reappraisal. Brill.

Abadan-Unat, N. (1986). Die ersten 25 Jahre der türkischen Migration: Versuch einer wissenschaftlichen Bilanz. In H. Bausinger (Ed.), *Ausländer – Inländer: Arbeitsmigration und kulturelle Identität* (pp. 45–57). Tübinger Vereinigung für Volkskunde e.V.

Akgündüz, A. (2016). *Labour Migration from Turkey to Western Europe, 1960–1974: A Multidisciplinary Analysis*. Routledge.

Anderson, B. (1983). *Imagined Communities: Reflections on the Origin and Spread of Nationalism*. Verso.

Arbeitskreis für ökonomische und soziologische Studien Vienna (Ed.). (1973). *Gastarbeiter. Wirtschaftliche und soziale Herausforderung*. Europaverlag.

Beirat für Wirtschafts- und Sozialfragen (Ed.). (1976). *Möglichkeiten und Grenzen des Einsatzes ausländischer Arbeitskräfte*. Überreuter.

Bergkirchner, C. (2013). *Zur Genese des Ausländerbeschäftigungsgesetzes 1975* [unpublished thesis]. University of Vienna.

Berlinghoff, M. (2013). *Das Ende der "Gastarbeit": Europäische Anwerbestopps 1970–1974*. Verlag Ferdinand Schöningh.

Biffl, G. (1986). Der Strukturwandel der Ausländerbeschäftigung in Österreich. In H. Wimmer (Ed.), *Ausländische Arbeitskräfte in Österreich* (pp. 33–87). Campus-Verlag.

Bojadžijev, M. (2009). Geschichte der Migration neu schreiben: Erkundungen und Entdeckungen jenseits der Grenzen nationaler Geschichtsschreibung. In N. Bayer, A. Engl, S. Hess & J. Moser (Eds.), *Crossing Munich: Beiträge zur Migration aus Kunst, Wissenschaft und Aktivismus* (pp. 102–105). Edition Metzel.

Boswell, C. (2011). *The Political Uses of Expert Knowledge: Immigration Policy and Social Research*. Cambridge University Press.

Broden, A. & Mecheril, P. (2007). Migrationsgesellschaftliche Re-Präsentationen: Eine Einführung. In. A. Broden & P. Mecheril (Eds.), *Re-Präsentationen: Dynamiken in der Migrationsgesellschaft* (pp. 7–28). IDA-NRW Eigenverlag.

Butschek, F. & Walterskirchen, E. (1974). Aspekte der Ausländerbeschäftigung. *WIFO-Monatsberichte* 4, 214–224.

Chakrabarty, D. (2008). *Provincializing Europe: Postcolonial Thought and Historical Difference*. Princeton University Press. (Original published 2000).

Clemens, G. (Ed.). (2007). *Die Türkei und Europa*. LIT Verlag.

Csáky, M. (2010). *Das Gedächtnis der Städte: Kulturelle Verflechtungen – Wien und die urbanen Milieus in Zentraleuropa*. Böhlau.

Dhawan, N. (2007). Can the Subaltern Speak German? And other Risky Questions: Migrant Hybridism vs. Subalternity. *Translate, Webjournal of Eipcp – European Institute for Progressive Cultural Policies*. http://translate.eipcp.net/strands/03/dhawan-strands01en. http://translate.eipcp.net/strands/03/dhawan-strands01en.html.

Doering-Manteuffel, A. & Raphael, L. (2012). *Nach dem Boom: Perspektiven auf die Zeitgeschichte seit 1970* (3rd ed.). Vandenhoeck & Ruprecht.

Fischer, W. (2008). "I haaß Vocelka – du haaßt Vocelka": Der Diskurs über die 'Gastarbeiter' in den 1960er bis 1980er Jahren und der unhistorische Vergleich mit der Wiener Arbeitsmigration um 1900. In M. Scheutz & V. Vales (Eds.), *Wien und seine WienerInnen: Ein historischer Streifzug durch Wien über die Jahrhunderte* (pp. 327–353). Böhlau.

Gächter, A. (2016). 50 Jahre jugoslawische Gastarbeit in Österreich. In A. Özbaş, J. Heinzl & H. Özbaş (Eds.), *50 Jahre jugoslawische Gastarbeit in Österreich* (pp. 40–55). CLIO Verein f. Geschichts- & Bildungsarbeit.

Gehmacher, E. (1972). Die soziale Problematik der Gastarbeiter. In Österreichisches Komitee für Sozialarbeit (Ed.), *Gastarbeiter in Österreich. 3. Österreichische Konferenz für Sozialarbeit* (16. bis 18. November 1971, Vienna) (pp. 14–20). Verlag Jugend & Volk.

Geiselberger, S. (commissioned by Bundesvorstand der Jungsozialisten). (1972). *Schwarzbuch: Ausländische Arbeiter*. Fischer Taschenbuch Verlag.

Goldberg, D. T. (1993). *Racist Culture: Philosophy and the Politics of Meaning*. Blackwell Publishers.

Ha, K. N. (2009). *Unrein und vermischt: Postkoloniale Grenzgänge durch die Kulturgeschichte der Hybridität und der kolonialen "Rassenbastarde"*. Transcript.

Hahn, S., & Stöger, G. (2014). *50 Jahre österreichisch-türkisches Anwerbeabkommen*. Studie im Auftrag des Bundesministeriums für Europa, Integration und Äußeres. Salzburg. Universität Salzburg. https://www.uni-salzburg.at/fileadmin/multimedia/Geschichte/docsuments/Studie_Anwerbeabkommen_-_Uni_Salzburg.pdf.

Hemetek, U. (Ed.). (2000). *Am Anfang war der Kolaric: Plakate gegen Rassismus und Fremdenfeindlichkeit*. Mandelbaum.

Hockerts, H. G. (1993). Zeitgeschichte in Deutschland: Begriff, Methoden, Themenfelder. *Historisches Jahrbuch* 113, 98–127.

Hofstetter, E. (1973). Ausländische Arbeitskräfte: Ist die Grenze erreicht? *Arbeit & Wirtschaft* 11, 53–59.

Huntington, S. (1998). *The Clash of Civilizations and the Remaking of World Order*. Simon & Schuster.

İçduygu, A. (2014). Turkish Emigration and its Implications for the Sending and Receiving Countries. In M. Bommes, H. Fassmann & W. Sievers (Eds.), *Migration from the Middle East and North Africa to Europe: Past Developments, Current Status and Future Potentials* (pp. 99–136). Amsterdam University Press.

Karasz, L. (Ed.). (2017). *Migration und die Macht der Forschung: Kritische Wissenschaft in der Migrationsgesellschaft*. ÖGB Verlag.

Klee, E. (1971). *Die Nigger Europas: Zur Lage der Gastarbeiter. Eine Dokumentation*. Patmos-Verlag.

Lanz, S. (2007). *Berlin aufgemischt: Abendländisch – multikulturell – kosmopolitisch? Die politische Konstruktion einer Einwanderungsstadt*. Transcript.

Lichtenberger, E. (1984). *Gastarbeiter: Leben in zwei Gesellschaften*. Böhlau.

Matuschek, H. (1985). Ausländerpolitik in Österreich 1962–1985: Der Kampf um und gegen die ausländische Arbeitskraft. *Journal für Sozialforschung 25*(2), 159–198.

Mayer, S. (2009). Rotation, Integration, and Social Exclusion: Discourse and Change in/of Migration Policies in Austria. *Ethnologia Balkanica 13*, 129–146.

Mehrländer, U. (1974). *Soziale Aspekte der Ausländerbeschäftigung*. Neue Gesellschaft GmbH.

Meinhof, U. M. (1995). Kuli oder Kollege: Gastarbeiter in Deutschland. In U. M. Meinhof (Ed.), *Deutschland, Deutschland unter anderem: Aufsätze und Polemiken* (pp. 97–107). Wagenbach.

Müller-Funk, W. & Wagner, B. (Eds.). (2005). *Eigene und andere Fremde: "Postkoloniale" Konflikte im europäischen Kontext*. Turia + Kant.

Osterhammel, J. (2006). *Kolonialismus: Geschichte, Formen, Folgen* (5th ed.). C.H. Beck.

Österreichisches Komitee für Sozialarbeit (Ed.). (1972). *Gastarbeiter in Österreich. 3. Österreichische Konferenz für Sozialarbeit* (16. bis 18. November 1971, Vienna). Verlag Jugend & Volk.

Robertson, R. (1998). Glokalisierung: Homogenität und Heterogenität in Raum und Zeit. In U. Beck (Ed.), *Perspektiven der Weltgesellschaft* (pp. 192–220). Suhrkamp.

Römhild, R. (2004). Global Heimat Germany: Migration and the Transnationalization of the Nation-State. *Transit* 1(1). http://escholarship.org/uc/item/57z2470p.

Said, E. (1979). *Orientalism*. Vintage Books.

Said, E. (2001, October 4). The Clash of Ignorance, *The Nation*. https://www.thenation.com/article/archive/clash-ignorance/.

Steyerl, H. & Rodriguez, E. G. (Eds.). (2003). *Spricht die Subalterne deutsch? Migration und postkoloniale Kritik*. UNRAST Verlag.

Spivak, G. C. (1988). Can the Subaltern Speak? In C. Nelson & L. Grossberg (Eds.), *Marxism and the Interpretation of Culture* (pp. 271–313). University of Illinois Press.

Terkessidis, M. (1997). Woven into the Texture of Things: Rassismus als praktische Einheit von Wissen und Institution. In A. Disselnkötter, S. Jäger, H. Kellershohn & S. Slobodzian (Eds.), *Evidenzen im Fluß: Demokratieverlust in Deutschland – Modell D – Geschlechter – Rassismus – PC* (pp. 172–187). DISS.

Terkessidis, M. (1998). *Psychologie des Rassismus*. Westdeutscher Verlag.

Todorova, M. (2009). *Imagining the Balkans*. Oxford University Press.

Treibel, A. (1988). *Engagement und Distanzierung in der westdeutschen Ausländerforschung: Eine Untersuchung ihrer soziologischen Beiträge*. F. Enke Verlag.

Waldinger, R. D. (2015). *The Cross-Border Connection: Immigrants, Emigrants, and their Homelands*. Harvard UP.

Wilpert, C. (1984). International Migration and Ethnic Minorities: New Fields for Post-War Sociology in the Federal Republic of Germany. *Current Sociology* *32*(3), 305–352.

Wimmer, A. & Glick Schiller, N. (2002). Methodological Nationalism and Beyond: Nation-State Building, Migration and the Social Sciences. *Global Networks* 2(4), 301–334.
Wollner, E. (2007). Die Reform der Beschäftigung ausländischer Arbeitskräfte Anfang der 1960er Jahre in Österreich. *Zeitgeschichte 34*(4), 213–225.
Zur Beschäftigung ausländischer Arbeitskräfte (1962). *Monatsberichte des Österreichischen Instituts für Wirtschaftsforschung 35*(5), 232–236.

CHAPTER 3

"You Can't Have Your Pudding and Eat It"? Remittances and Development in Yugoslavia, 1918–1989

Aleksandar R. Miletić

Introduction

The role of remittances in the global economy has once again become important as a vital ingredient of the migration-development nexus introduced by the ruling neoliberal agenda. Optimistic accounts of mutually beneficial migration outcomes and exchange between the global North and South have been dominant in official UN papers and its policy guidelines since the 1990s, especially in the 2000s (Gamlen 2010; De Haas 2010; United Nations Development Programme 2009). The migration-driven enthusiasm reached such a level in that period that some analysts wrote about a global craze or frenzy about mobility and the freedom of movement. However, as pointed out by Gamlen, the global recession during the late 2000s triggered a new wave of critical if not entirely pessimistic attitudes about migration-development outcomes. This change of heart in scholarly production was again beneficial for the business and

A. R. Miletić (✉)
Institute for Recent History of Serbia, Belgrade, Serbia

S. Meyer, C. Ströhle (eds.), *Remittances as Social Practices and Agents of Change*,
https://doi.org/10.1007/978-3-030-81504-2_3

power structures as it coincided with the tightening of immigration controls in receiving countries (Gamlen 2014).

Looking back to the past, a similar scheme can be attributed to the neo-Marxian and structuralist critique of the migration-development concept in the recessionary 1970s and 1980s. A comprehensive critique of power structures contributed to its short-term consolidation in those recessionary periods. This brings us closer to our case, since most of the credible scholarly interpretations of the impact of remittances on the social and economic development of socialist Yugoslavia derive from that period. On the one hand, the literature echoed the very same negative appraisal of the developmental outcomes of the migration process (Baučić 1979; Bohning 1975; Vedriš 1978). On the other hand, and in line with the presupposed neoliberal craze about remittances, the prevailing public attitude and standard state agendas in post-Yugoslav (post)transitional countries appeared to be optimistic, praising the favorable outcomes of the stable inflow of hard currency. However, at least in academia, this optimism has been counterbalanced by reservations regarding the sustainability of remittance-related development (Jakobsen and Štrabac 2015; Nikolić 2009).

This chapter does not attempt to embark on a futile arbitration between optimistic and pessimistic approaches to the predetermined causality between migration and development. Instead of challenging prevalent pessimistic narratives on remittance management in Yugoslav studies, it aims to broaden the interpretative framework by shifting between scales of analysis and by introducing new concepts and comprehensive comparative perspectives. The analysis brings together insights from existing literature (Brunnbauer 2016a, b; Đikanović 2016; Miletić 2012; Miletić 2009) and new empirical data provided by archival sources, contemporary newspapers, and other publications of the period under review.

The focus of this chapter is on state remittances and repatriation programs in the period from 1918 to 1989. I will show that state policy was paradoxically inclined to both developmental strategies, hence facing the problem indicated in the title: "You can't have your pudding and eat it," as the Zagreb-based Emigration Commissariat (EC), Artur Benko Grado, pointed out in 1920. Of special interest is the difference in interpreting remittances as a private and/or public resource in Yugoslavia. The tension between these two notions is evident in the discrepancy between emigrants' investment and consumption patterns and the governmental mindset that was operating toward actual or at least symbolic appropriation of remittances.

This chapter is divided into five sections. The first section is dedicated to a survey of the main developments in the Yugoslav emigration process and its emigration policy in the interwar (1918–1928) and socialist periods (1945–1989). The second and third sections emphasize the aforementioned decision makers' oscillation between repatriation and remittance developmental agendas. The fourth and fifth sections analyze the macro- and meso-levels of remittance-related developmental dynamics.

Main Trends in Yugoslav Emigration

The first Yugoslav state was born out of the violence of World War I, which also had a considerable impact on migration following a breakdown of the global labor market. The Yugoslav emigration authorities began operating at a moment when mass migration had already been halted. The process of migration control through issuing passports and visa requirements enabled national governments to control population movement in accordance with a wide range of newly introduced criteria, according to the perceived economic, political, and military needs of the country, and to support national, demographic, eugenic, or even racial policies (Miletić 2012, pp. 17–52; Idem 2009, pp. 96–104; Brunnbauer 2016a, pp. 126–130).

In line with these unfavorable trends, the emigration rates from Yugoslavia were almost negligible, especially when compared with the prewar data. The above-cited Artur Benko Grado, one of the leading Yugoslav experts on migration in the interwar period, claimed that the country had a positive migration balance, meaning a negative net emigration, for the period between 1918 and 1923: "Before the war, it was quite a different situation. [...] In only one year, we had more emigrants from Croatia and Slavonia who left for the US than left in five years from the whole kingdom across the world" (Grado 1924, p. 16). Approximately, this ratio (one to five) applies to the overall Yugoslav statistics for the interwar period when compared with the Croatian-Slavonian prewar data. While the average annual net emigration from this Austro-Hungarian province to the US in the period 1901–1913 constituted 42 emigrants per 10,000 inhabitants, in interwar Yugoslavia, the ratio for overall emigration was around eight (Iseljenički odsjek 1920; Statistički godišnjak, 1940 (1941), pp. 137–138, 143, 147). This calculation is related to the 1910 and 1931 census data for Croatia and Yugoslavia, respectively (Signjar 1915, p. 2; Opšta statistika 1938, p. 4).

Relieved by this decrease in the net volume of emigration, the Yugoslav emigration service could focus on its hidden agenda, namely facilitating the departure of ethnic minorities and, conversely, preventing emigration of ethnic nationals. This policy accounts for the low levels of emigration of ethnic Yugoslavs and the large share of officially designated non-Slavic minorities in the annual contingents of emigrants from the country in the 1920s (Miletić 2012). The ethnic criterion also facilitated an administrative distinction between emigration to Anglo-Saxon countries, effectively reserved for the passport applicants belonging to the constitutive ethnic groups, and Central and South American countries, which became a destination for unwanted minorities. The importance of this distinction was highlighted on several occasions in 1924 and 1925 by high officials of the Yugoslav EC (Miletić 2012, pp. 97–99; Aranicki 1925a; Idem., b). The ethnic agenda and concerns for the co-ethnic emigrants' well-being in their destination countries interfered one with another in a way that eventually did not correspond with the presupposed state interest. The countries' balance of payment might have indeed benefited from the remittances sent by the co-ethnic diaspora. However, the minority migration balance at the same time became compromised since a huge number of minority migrants returned to Yugoslavia from the unsettled countries of South America. The Yugoslav authorities could have accomplished their ethnic agenda by allowing them to emigrate to the more prosperous Anglo-Saxon countries, yet in that case they would have deprived the national economy of the hard currency influx.

While minorities were expected to permanently leave the country, co-ethnic migrants were preferred as temporary labor emigrants in the inter-war period. Whenever possible, the authorities tried to prevent co-ethnic migrants from emigrating with their family members in order to secure their eventual return to Yugoslavia. On at least two occasions, Fedor Aranicki, the chief of the EC, advocated this strategy in plain words. In 1923, he argued against the departure of emigrants' spouses to America, "since we are thereby permanently losing entire families. In any case, it would be better to reserve the quota [i.e., the US immigration quota] for men who will work there and send money here, thus remaining in a more intensive material and moral contact with the homeland" (Iseljenički komesarijat, 1923, p. 1). Regarding emigration to Canada in the 1920s, he commented: "one can be even more at ease about this emigration as women do not emigrate there, which means that both the emigrants and their savings are preserved for our state" (Aranicki 1924, p. 2). Grado even proposed that his superiors initiate procedures for the codification and recognition of the legal status of temporary migrants at the level of international law (Grado 1924, p. 19). The ideal outcome of the migration process for the Yugoslav officials was to receive the benefits of remittances while maintaining the demographic substance of ethnic Yugoslavs.

While the emigration policy of interwar Yugoslavia was dominated by ethnic and remittance-related issues, the new socialist Yugoslavia in its formative period assumed a strict ideological attitude to migration. Labor migration to capitalist countries was perceived as a sign of weakness and as an embarrassment for their utopian society under construction. For most of the socialist era, state officials did not even use the term "emigration," which only referred to the labor movements before socialism. This corresponded ideologically to Soviet practices (Miletić 2012, p. 37). In the Yugoslav official statistical yearbook, the term "emigration" was only mentioned in the annual issues between 1958 and 1969, in which the presented data referred to the period between 1953 and 1968 (Statistički godišnjak, 1945–1987). From 1973 on, it reappeared in the official statistics under the euphemistic and rather cumbersome legal phrase designating "workers temporarily employed abroad." However, the statistics did not include annual migration developments, but only census data from 1971 and 1981 on the actual number of workers abroad. Annual net emigration for the period from 1953 to 1968 was around 12 emigrants per 10,000 inhabitants (census 1961), which is still considerably below the pre-1914 rates in Croatia, but higher than the interwar Yugoslav standards. From the mid-1960s on, socialist Yugoslavia began facilitating the emigration process to such an extent that in the following period it became more liberal in terms of freedom of movement than it had been in monarchist Yugoslavia.

In 1971, the number of Yugoslav workers abroad totaled almost 770,000, including family members; in 1981 it was more than 870,000. In this period, a striking shift in the regional distribution of emigration contingents was taking place. While in the interwar period, most emigrants originated from Dalmatia and the northern provinces (Slovenia, Croatia-Slavonia, and Vojvodina), in the socialist period the other Yugoslav provinces also began to participate in the mass migrations. These provinces, which had only provided around 10 percent of the Yugoslav emigration contingents in the 1920s, had risen to around 50 percent of the corresponding ratio in 1971, and around 62 percent in 1981 (Miletić 2012, p. 58; Statistički godišnjak, 1983 (1983), p. 441). This rather sudden shift in the patterns of labor mobility in these provinces proved to be of the greatest importance in terms of their participation in the European and global labor markets.

Repatriation Agenda

Throughout the monarchist and socialist periods in Yugoslavia, the emigration authorities strived to maintain a cross-border political community that was not only inclusive toward non-resident citizens, but usually appealed to their patriotic sentiments and asked them to actively support their homeland. From time to time, state officials thought they could exercise more influence on their citizens or co-ethnics living abroad. Among the state agendas, repatriation proved to be one of the most ambitious and it had been almost constantly pointed out by authorities, yet the degree of insistence on it varied depending on the current political and international constellations.

The repatriation program was advocated by the officials of the Zagreb emigration department of the provincial Croatia-Slavonia government from 1919 to 1921, at the very beginning of the Yugoslav state's existence. Their administrative practice did not distinguish between emigration and repatriation responsibilities, and when the first Yugoslav migration decree was drafted, Zagreb experts proposed that it should also include six articles dedicated to repatriation and even refer to repatriation in the title (Iseljenički odsjek 1921). Although these proposals were not included in the Yugoslav decree nor the later law on emigration of 1921, the state officials maintained some expectations regarding the outcomes of repatriation. Given the considerable annual rates of returnees, they specifically hoped that the country would benefit from the knowledge and industrial and technical skills they brought back to Yugoslavia. The odds seemed in their favor, as throughout the period between 1921 and 1928, less than 5 percent of female and 9 percent of male emigrants from Yugoslavia were skilled workers.

In a report written in 1922, one official from the Yugoslav General Consulate in Chicago explained why their expectations did not materialize. The returnees were usually those who could not adapt to the American way of life and work; they did not acquire knowledge of modern technology since most of them were hired as unskilled labor: "Usually, in this ocean of people and work, they become lonelier than they had been in their village. Very often they come back [to Yugoslavia] less cultured than they were before" (Miletić 2012, pp. 141–142). Immigrants who acquired some skills and knowledge were usually among those who decided to stay in America. Yet another negative outcome of the emigration process became evident in 1927 when Grado warned superiors about the rising share of skilled and qualified labor in emigration contingents, at the expense of unskilled workers (1927, p. 1). This was in anticipation of a problem that would mark the subsequent decades and almost a century of the emigration process into the present day.

It was only in the formative socialist period after World War II and well into the 1950s that the repatriation agenda was considered such a priority that it became effectively the only state program regarding migration. As if nothing else mattered, all the state resources meant for emigration affairs were channeled into the master project of repatriation. An impressive yet impossible goal was set to repatriate all the so-called economic migrants who had left the country during the allegedly reactionary and repressive monarchist regime of old Yugoslavia. Like other socialist utopian causes, the lion's share of the input in this project relied on propaganda enthusiasm, since material resources were scarce. Returnees arriving on state-operated steamships were greeted in Yugoslav ports by reputedly spontaneous crowds, who shouted political slogans and welcomed their compatriots returning from abroad. The returnees were provided with free meals, hotel accommodation, and transportation to their homes. The machinery, tools, and vehicles they brought with them were either exempted from taxation or charged at reduced rates (Brunnbauer 2016a, pp. 262–70). In order to facilitate repatriation from other European countries in one place, a huge barrack settlement with the capacity to accommodate around 500 lodgers was constructed in Kamnik, Slovenia (Moskovljević 1948, pp. 1–4; Bekavac 1948, p. 1).

Despite poor infrastructure, a lack of food and clothing, and limited available housing, the Yugoslav socialist authorities did their best to accommodate, supply, and find adequate employment for the repatriates. They received double rations of food and clothing compared to domestic laborers and were immediately provided with appropriate housing. This privileged position caused the returnees to become the target of resentment and complaints by their colleagues and neighbors. However, no matter how privileged they might have been in Yugoslavia, their standard of living and their personal income was much lower than what they had become used to in their countries of emigration. Most of the able-bodied skilled workers decided to emigrate back to their previous continental or overseas destinations, while the weak, old, and sick remained in Yugoslavia. (Brunnbauer 2016a, p. 266).

By the end of the 1950s, the repatriation agenda as an almost exclusive approach to migration problems was abandoned. In the 1960s, Yugoslav emigration policy became ever more liberalized, and the focus of the country's migration concern shifted toward an emigration agenda. In the 1970s and 1980s, the repatriation narrative reappeared, however. Under the circumstances, it became intrinsically linked with attempts to channel emigrants' hard currency savings for the benefit of the home economy and the state's balance of payments. Since this policy emphasizes the importance of remittances over that of the emigrants themselves, it will be analyzed in the next sections.

Influx of Remittances

When it peaked between 1980 and 1982, the average annual gross remittances to Yugoslavia totaled around US$4.5 billion, while in 1988 it was estimated that around US$10 billion were deposited in private savings abroad. The data is even more striking when compared with other European source countries. According to Bogoev's data (1989, p. 130) referring to the period from 1977 to 1983, the aggregate amount of Yugoslav gross remittances was bigger than that of Greece (by 3.6 times), Turkey (by 2.1 times), Spain (by 2.9 times), and Italy (by 3.3 times). In monarchist Yugoslavia, according to the estimates of the experts from that period, the average annual remittance inflow ranged between US$10 and US$20 million (Đikanović 2016, pp. 106, 112). In the period between 1926 and 1929, the influx was around 2.7 billion dinars, or around US$45 million—an amount that not only compensated for the deficit of the balance of payment in that period, but exceeded it by almost 60 percent (Miletić 2012, p. 136). In spite of the fact that they did little to help emigrants with their endeavors, the authorities in both monarchist and socialist Yugoslavia had, from early on, a fairly good insight into and high expectations of the remittances sent by emigrants and the savings brought back to the country by returnees.

The priority, in either case, was to facilitate the influx of hard currencies through official state channels in order to claim these as a net gain for the state's balance of payments. In the 1920s, Yugoslav emigration and banking experts were pointing out the devastating consequences of semi-legal activities by small exchange bureaus, which kept foreign exchange outside the national banking system. Ljubomir Kosijer, a banking expert, even proposed a system of state-organized transportation and reception of returnees to the authorities with the aim of facilitating a legal conversion of foreign exchange (Grado 1924, p. 17; Kosijer 1924, pp. 93–94). This proved to be a big concern for the state even during its most utopian socialist period immediately following World War II. No matter to what extent they despised the bourgeois order, the socialist comrades were more than willing to lay their hands on the remittances earned there. At the steamship liners, the procedure for the exchange of hard currencies would often begin on the open sea, even before the steamships entered domestic ports. If not on the boat, the currency exchange was arranged in the port immediately upon disembarkation (Savet 1964, pp. 1–2). The state officials in charge of organizing the reception in the ports wrote about a close inspection of returnees' movements in order to prevent the illegal exchange of the currency (Japunčić 1947, p. 3). It bears mentioning that these extortionist practices took place in the midst of festive official welcome receptions. Many of the returnees brought sacks of flour with them, which indicates that they knew very well about the economic situation in Yugoslavia. In this period, the comrades from the reception committees often complained about those non-financial means of support.

In 1947, one repatriation official suggested that his superiors launch a subtle propaganda campaign among emigrants to persuade them to send financial remittances rather than parcels to their relatives (Japunčić 1947, p. 4). The same issue was raised in a discussion over exchange rates payable to the remittance receivers in Yugoslavia in 1954. A more generous rate was proposed in order to prevent the practice of sending parcels instead of money, which had allegedly already been advertised and instructed by anti-Yugoslav propaganda abroad (Savet 1954, p. 1). This sensitive issue was finally resolved in 1959 when high tariff taxation was imposed on the contents of parcels sent from abroad. The decision was explained in the journal *Zavičaj* (Homeland), the official organ of the Matica of emigrants from Serbia ("Novi carinski propisi" 1959, p. 7).

The justification for the introduction of the tariff was a rather suggestive advertising of the benefits of sending remittances instead of foreign-produced goods. Allegedly, these goods were more affordable in Yugoslavia, which had developed a strong industrial basis to produce consumer goods. The tariffs were thus meant to protect the interests of the parcel recipients. According to the article, by sending remittances, emigrants opted for a more convenient and more affordable way of helping their relatives. However, if the emigrants still decided to send parcels, there was a special offer by the Belgrade merchant company Jugoeksport, which came forward with a great variety of domestic products that could be bought for remittances. These were to be exchanged at generous rates and sent on to the postal recipients in Yugoslavia. Both options advertised by this journal included a hard currency gain for the national balance of payments.

The state apparatus of monarchist Yugoslavia was also concerned about the uninterrupted flow of remittances. An interview conducted with Milorad Nedeljković, director of the Yugoslav Poštanska štedionica (Postal Savings Bank) in 1927, reveals that the state mediated and provided help in negotiations between this bank and American and Canadian postal authorities. According to Nedeljković, the contract concluded between the three national postal companies enabled Yugoslav emigrants to send their remittances from any post office in these North American countries. The procedure was quite simple, as the emigrant only had to write down the address of the postal destination in Yugoslavia. The Head Post Office in the US collected these remittances and at least once a week sent them to the Belgrade headquarters of Poštanska štedionica.

Apart from providing state-facilitated banking and postal channels to bring home remittances, Yugoslav state officials often raised the issue of how to employ remittances in a more concentrated and useful way. This question was discussed by Yugoslav emigration representatives and policymakers at their 1924 conference in Zagreb, where it was pointed out that almost all the remittances had been spent on either personal consumption or housing improvements. A few speakers suggested measures that would facilitate a more active role for the National Bank of the Kingdom of Serbs, Croats and Slovens (SCS) in the management of remittances. They argued that the central bank should not have been limited only to the conversion of emigrants' remittances (as any other financial institution could do this). Rather, it should have engaged in a more ambitious project of establishing an American branch to collect all emigrants' savings and remittances in one place. Only in this way could the huge potential of emigrant finances be used for large-scale investment projects in Yugoslavia.

This initiative was not realized during the interwar period, yet it shows that remittances were perceived as a public resource, at the disposal and within the effective reach of the state machinery. This was even more evident in a memo by Grado in 1920, in which he wrote that the authorities had to choose whether to pressure emigrants to return home and bring all their savings with them or to stay in America and continuously send small remittances to their family members. Grado pointed out the dilemma in slightly inaccurate English: "You can't eat the pudding and have it" (Grado 1920).

In socialist Yugoslavia, after the above-mentioned tariff policy change of 1959, the state agenda clearly became more mercantilist and market-oriented with regard to the process of channeling hard currency into the country's banking system. During the 1960s, the main concern was to attract remittances, while in the 1970s and 1980s, the state also facilitated schemes of investing hard currency savings and remittances into the social sector of the economy. A hard currency-driven enthusiasm was particularly evident in the second half of the 1960s in the reports and policy proposals by the Federal Council for Emigration Issues.

The president of the council, Đuro Stanković, was a prewar member of the communist party. During the war, he was a political commissaire of the Sixth Lika Brigade, one of the most celebrated units of the partisan army. He might be considered a party hardliner since he was implicated in the indiscriminate liquidations of political opponents in 1944 and 1945 (Cvetković 2006, p. 174). However, his reports in 1964 and 1967 only evince economic and market-oriented reasoning disassociated from any ideological narrative or connotation. He took pride in pointing to a huge annual increase in remittances, as though this were an accomplishment of his emigration council. At one point, Stanković stressed that just one donation from abroad in 1966—a US$65,000 donation for the construction of a local infirmary—was worth more than the total federal expenditure for all the emigration services in the country. The comparison was closely related to Stanković's own agenda, namely to convince the federal authorities to increase the funding available to emigration offices in line with the increase of the hard currency influx into the country (Stanković 1967, p. 3). The former communist hardliner identified himself with the role of a market-oriented manager to such a degree that it included an expectation of sharing the profit with federal authorities.

One of the political agendas of the Yugoslav regime throughout the 1960s was to pacify political emigration and to gradually transform it into economic migration. The process was announced by the amnesty law of 1961, while in Stanković's report the pacification of political emigration could reattach the emigrants and their immense resources to Yugoslavia. He thought these emigrants, together with the prewar diaspora, should be attracted by commercials and propaganda to visit Yugoslavia. Stanković estimated that each of them would spend at least US$1000 per visit, which he calculated with simple arithmetic, and again included an enthusiastic account of how the state would benefit from this tourism. Compared with the previous postwar repatriation agenda, this 1967 attitude was almost on the opposite pole of the ideological spectrum. Instead of viewing labor emigrants as would-be returnees and political emigrants as enemies, both groups were now invited to come to Yugoslavia as tourists. In the 1970s and 1980s, innovative and rather complicated institutional frameworks were designed to attract migrants' remittances into the companies belonging to the social sector of the economy.

Remittances on the Macro-Scale

Practices surrounding remittances belong, first and foremost, in the private domain of personal and family concerns (Horst et al. 2014). The public utilization of these resources is usually only circumstantial and unintended, especially as regards anticipated macro-economic outcomes. However, at the birth of the Yugoslav state in 1920, the huge asset of hard currency influx could hardly escape being envisaged for appropriation in either symbolic or real terms. Symbolic appropriation refers to both the governmental mindset and the narrative representation of private remittances as a government's active and disposable national resource.

One finds this very attitude and almost the same notion in the late 1980s, in the last years of socialist Yugoslavia. In 1988, officials of the federal fund for facilitation of credit support for the industrial development of the Yugoslav republics and Kosovo lamented in a memo their inability to obtain a loan of DM2 million for the purpose of creating employment for the returnees from West Germany. The memo highlighted that the painstaking negotiations with the West German government had gone on for more than two years, "notwithstanding the fact that the estimated savings of our workers temporarily employed in West Germany [was] around DM10 billion!" (Kaćanski 1988, p. 100). The undertone implies that the state could somehow have had access to those billions of hard currency, which was certainly not the case.

Apart from symbolic appropriations, there were also some actual appropriations of remittances by the state. These included unfavorable and sometimes even extortionist official exchange rates and a variety of restrictions regarding the disposal of private hard currency deposits in Yugoslav banks. When more rigorous limitations were introduced in that domain of banking operations by the federal government of Milka Planinc in October 1982, it deeply affected rates of remittances arriving in Yugoslavia via official channels. While the gross influx of remittances in 1982 was around US$4.4 billion, the corresponding amount for the subsequent year was no more than US$2.9 billion, and it remained considerably below the 1982 level in the following period (Bogoev 1989, pp. 128, 137). There was no better proof of the actual limits of the government interference in remittances, as well as of the undeniably private character of remittance transactions.

A specific pattern of the symbolic appropriation of remittances is evident in the semantics of the Yugoslav emigration authorities, who often quoted official statistics on remittances as though they were the outcome of their own activities. The steady inflow of remittances and ever-rising rates of the hard currency influx in the 1920s and during the period from 1965 to 1982 had set the stage for grand-scale, nationwide, investment projects and the rapid development of underdeveloped regions in Yugoslavia. The frustration of the state bureaucrats and experts in the field arose from the fact that most of the money sent from abroad usually ended up in the extended consumption of the individuals who received it. A beneficial impact of remittances on the country's balance of payments was usually taken for granted or otherwise neglected in such grandiose and unrealistic schemes (Grado 1924). However, according to Anthony Thirlwall's theoretical model, the trade balance performance proved to be a decisive ingredient of economic growth, especially for developing countries (McCombie and Thirlwall 2004).

This model stems from the post-Keynesian demand-driven concept of productivity growth. It suggests that running a long-term deficit will result in a constant foreign exchange shortage that will eventually cause a constraint on demand of the overall national economy. Thirlwall and his followers have tested this formula for GDP growth in many nation states, and they particularly stressed its significance in developing countries. The Yugoslav economy might also have benefited from the steady inflow of hard currency, yet there was a huge discrepancy between gross volume and net income in remittances.

Net income refers to the deposits which were effectively converted into domestic currency through official channels and thus became disposable assets of the National Bank of Yugoslavia. However, due to unfavorable exchange rates and state interference in private deposits, net income decreased in the 1970s, from around 75 percent of the gross inflow in 1971 to around 50 percent in 1979. By the end of the 1980s, it constituted less than 30 percent of the gross inflow (Bogoev 1989, p. 136). The state was running deficits in the period from 1976 to 1980, which would have also been the case in the 1980s if not for the net income of remittances in that period. However, the data on annual GDP growth in Yugoslavia and its balance of payment performance, at first sight, seems unrelated in terms of Thirlwall's theory. This is because, during the deficit period from 1976 to 1980, the average annual GDP growth was between 4 and 5 percent, while in the 1980s, when the balance of payment was positive, growth was negative or close to zero.

The constrained growth in the 1980s had much to do with administrative restrictions on the availability of foreign exchange imposed by the federal government. This was a follow-up of the strict fiscal responsibilities assumed by the state before the consortium of foreign creditors. The balance of payment became positive, however, at the cost of constrained growth (Marsenić 1990, pp. 99, 219, 302). One way or another, the role played by remittances in this macro-economic context was to a great extent positive regarding the developmental agenda. One could only contemplate the multiplying effects of the residual amounts of remittances which never entered the state-facilitated banking system.

Rising unemployment in Yugoslavia was yet another macro-economic feature interrelated with mass migrations. In 1971, when there were around 9 million active laborers in the country, 672,000 of them constituted guest workers abroad, while the number of unemployed in Yugoslavia was around 300,000. In 1981, the corresponding numbers were 10 million, 625,000, and around 800,000. Apart from the unemployed and the guest workers, around 4 million people were employed, or rather trapped, in agriculture, where only a small share of the production was organized in an efficient and profit-oriented manner. The perennial problem of underemployed labor in the countryside was even more acute in interwar Yugoslavia, which was a predominantly agrarian country.

It has already been pointed out by Brunnbauer (2016a, p. 308) that Yugoslav migration outcomes did not correspond with the model predicted by neoclassical theory. Not only was there no convergence of factor prices or other related equalizing effects, but the wage gap between Yugoslavia and the destination countries became ever more pronounced. According to Ivo Baučić, the leading Yugoslav expert in the field, Yugoslav migrant workers in the 1970s could earn around 3.5 times more abroad than in Yugoslavia, while in the late 1980s this ratio almost doubled (Kaćanski 1988, p. 39). This fits almost perfectly with Myrdal's predictions on circular cumulative causation as a result of an unrestricted market exchange of labor and goods between developed and underdeveloped countries (Myrdal 1957, pp. 11–49). Ever since it has been reintroduced in migration studies, Myrdal's theoretical model serves as an ultimate evidence of the pessimistic conclusions on the nature of the migration process. However, Myrdal himself was far from being a defeatist or complainer. His scholarly wisdom also included a variety of proactive measures intended to minimize the negative effects of cumulative causation. In the first place, these entailed a meaningful state intervention by underdeveloped countries in both internal and foreign market operations, as well as meticulous and long-term planning of their development strategies (Myrdal 1957, pp. 81–99).

In our days, when neoliberal values dominate politics and global scholarship, it is no wonder that this optimistic and proactive component of Myrdal's conceptions has been entirely overlooked or forgotten even by authors who make use of his theoretical system. However, socialist Yugoslavia in the 1970s and 1980s was not entirely helpless before the scrutiny of the global market: it did intervene in markets and seriously plan its development strategy. Yet again, it ended up in the worst circular cumulative causation of economic stagnation, rising unemployment, and overall dependency. The Turkish case provides us with a significantly different story, at least when it comes to the 1980s. Throughout the 1970s, the balance of payment in this country was almost entirely dependent on remittances, which totaled up to seventy and as much as 90 percent of the country's exports. In the second half of the 1970s, the percentage ratio of the total gross inflow of remittances and exports was around 60 percent in Turkey and 45 percent in Yugoslavia. In the first half of the 1980s, the corresponding ratio declined to 33 percent in Turkey and 35 percent in Yugoslavia (Aydaş 2003, p. 64; Bogoev 1989, p. 143).

The relative importance of remittances in the Turkish economy declined due to the export-oriented economic reforms introduced after the military coup in 1980. The shifting priorities in economic policy brought about an unprecedented rise in annual rates of exports (Togan and Balasubramanyam 1996; Şenses 1991; Aksel 2019, pp. 61–62, 69). In the first half of the 1980s, the average annual growth rate of exports in Turkey was around 23 percent, while in Yugoslavia in the same period it was no more than 4 percent. If one disregards developments in 1981, it was close to zero (Aydaş 2003, p. 64; Bogoev 1989, p. 143). This enormous rise in Turkish exports had nothing to do with the previous dependence on foreign exchange derived from remittances, nor was this the case with the stagnation of the Yugoslav economy in the 1980s. Migration literature has already pointed to the multi-causality of growth-related factors in developing countries.

Remittances on the Meso-Scale

Underneath the macro-economic surface, there is a meso- and micro-universe of everyday life and societal interaction triggered by remittances. Brunnbauer (2016a, pp. 319–320) has already pointed out the transformative impact of emigration and the widespread transnational character of social networks and practices in the Balkan countries on the local level. With regard to remittance utilization, I will focus here on the developments in the domain of investment in housing and socialist enterprises. According to one survey conducted in Croatia in 1970/1971, investment in the housing sector constituted a predominant share of labor migrants' expenditure. The results indicate that among the contingent of the migrants who actually spent their savings, around 73 percent invested them in housing construction and appliances, around 17 percent decided to buy a car, and a residue of around 10 percent of the interviewees invested their savings in agriculture machinery (Baučić and Maravić 1971, p. 92). Yugoslav emigration authorities in both the monarchist and socialist period often complained about this distribution of emigrants' expenditure, which was devoid of any sustainable business-oriented approach. This critical stance included paternalistic complaints regarding the selfish immaturity and irrationality of emigrants' choices. This also impacted the language used by politicians and experts: a basic necessity like providing oneself with a roof over one's head was often considered "consumption" rather than investment; the remittances were "wasted" rather than put to good use (Grado 1924, p. 17. Miletić 2012, p. 135; Kaćanski 1988, pp. 30, 61; Bogoev 1989, p. 125).

In this regard, some inconsistencies become apparent between the daily politics of the Yugoslav emigration offices and the extent of their dissatisfaction with its outcomes. This particularly holds true for the socialist period, when the state tried by all means to encourage and facilitate *Gastarbeiter* investment in housing construction. In line with the state agenda, the banks offered up to 20-percent discounts for the housing units paid for with hard currency. This opportunity was widely advertised by official emigration journals. However, obtaining all the necessary licenses for construction proved to be difficult and housing space was limited (Kaćanski 1988, pp. 40–41). Both constraints were ideologically driven and, in a more general context, they epitomized the inner conflict between market-oriented incentives that developed in the Yugoslav economy after 1965 and the deeply rooted bureaucratic traditions of administrative socialism.

It seems that while arguing against investments in the domain of housing, Yugoslav officials and experts in the field were disregarding the scale of the housing crisis and the poor level of housing infrastructure, particularly those from interwar Yugoslavia that were being rapidly improved in the socialist period. Many of the endemic diseases and health-related disabilities in interwar Yugoslavia were a consequence of inadequate housing conditions (Dimić 1996, pp. 49–69). From this perspective, the improvement of housing standards undoubtedly contributed to the country's long-term development agenda, correlated with the short-term impacts of providing employment and materials in the construction and maintenance sectors. Whenever it served household necessities, such a private initiative supplemented the broader agenda of national housing policy.

The aforementioned tension between pro-market incentives and the ideological approach to the socialist economy brought about unconventional para-market schemes to attract emigrants' hard currency savings into social sector enterprises. The system was inaugurated by decrees issued in 1972 (Vedriš 1977, p. 4) and was later sanctioned in the Law on Associated Labor of 1976. The scheme provided employment for returnees or members of their families as compensation for a certain amount of foreign exchange deposited in a five- to ten-year period years with stable interest rates and for the sake of the companies' current account. The available data indicate sums between DM5,000 and DM10,000 invested by individuals. The most successful campaign was conducted from 1973 onward by the company Pionirka in Imotsko (Aržano plant), which collected around DM500,000 through such a scheme (Brunnbauer 2016b, Ivanković 1977, pp. 45–46; Vedriš 1978). Unfortunately, according to the regulations, only half of these assets were available for the company's purchase of machinery from abroad. Due to a lack of market and business opportunities, the Aržano textile factory did not manage to become a profitable, self-sustaining enterprise during the 1970s (Vedriš 1977, p. 9;

Vedriš 1978, p. 17). Interestingly, a similar scheme of returnee employment conditional on deposited hard currency was proposed by Grado in the 1920s (Grado 1924, p. 18).

By the end of the 1980s, the schemes popularly dubbed "hard currency factories" or "purchasing employment programs" were considered a failure, although it was estimated that around 40,000 people had found employment through them by the end of the 1980s (Kaćanski 1988, p. 33). However, if the average individual deposit was close to the minimal evidenced amount of around DM5000, then the overall sum invested in these factories may have totaled up to DM200 million or more. Nevertheless, the overall program was considered a failure by both the authorities and the experts in the field. One can find similar negative assessments in Turkey regarding analogue investment schemes that operated within the framework of the Turkish Workers Companies. Experts' estimates of money invested in these companies were as high as US$300 million, yet the Turkish authorities generally perceived them as a disappointment (Adler 1981, pp. 62–72). This was a result of the same irrational expectations and high hopes invested in the transformative power of remittances as in Yugoslavia.

Conclusion

A vast Yugoslav diaspora, composed of people of diverse economic, political, ethnic, and citizenship statuses, provided a constant source of discomfort and unrealistic expectations for the control-obsessed authorities of Yugoslavia. This holds true for both interwar and socialist Yugoslavia. However, in territorial terms, the emigration process and diaspora affairs in the monarchist period were predominantly related to the northern Yugoslav provinces and Dalmatia. It was only in socialist Yugoslavia that the rest of the country experienced the phenomenon of mass migration. Moreover, the number of migrants from Macedonia, Kosovo, Serbia, Bosnia-Herzegovina, and Montenegro rose gradually, by the 1980s constituting the majority of Yugoslav *Gastarbeiter*. Over the course of Yugoslav history, all its provinces thus became integrated into the global labor market, while emigrants themselves and their earnings came under the scrutiny of the anxious authorities.

In developmental terms, the Yugoslav authorities almost always hesitated between opting for the final repatriation of emigrants and relying on their remittances. The only period when the state agenda was coherent was during the first post-WWII decade, when all available state resources and immense efforts were invested for the sole purpose of bringing emigrants back home. This huge attempt of facilitating transformative change by repatriating human capital eventually failed, as was the case with a similar scheme that counted on emigrants' financial resources. A comparison with the Turkish Republic and its rapid advance of the export-oriented sector of its economy in the 1980s, despite a huge previous dependence on remittances in the 1970s, points to important conclusions. The overall development seems to have been, to a significant degree, unrelated to remittances in terms of both positive and negative expectations and outcomes. Even when the balance of payment facilitated by remittance inflows provided developmental preconditions as confirmed by the Thirlwall model, the expected outcome was still dependent on the proactive economic policy and overall state agenda. This holds true for both the Yugoslav economic stagnation and the Turkish export boom in the 1980s. As Ulf Brunnbauer already proposed, a typically hysterical tone in migration debates may be calmed down with a historical retrospective focus on the actual developments and outcomes of migration (2016a, p. 322). In our case, this applies to the popular and scholarly debates assuming the essential developmental role of remittances, too.

The Yugoslav model of remittance policy turns out to be indicative of the country's desperate need for developmental resources rather than of a reasonable and comprehensive economic or emigration policy. Similarly, the paternalistic attitudes of state officials, their frustration with the emigrants' supposedly irrational and spendthrift behavior, and their endless designs to appropriate remittances or to facilitate their more productive utilization are much more related to the general fields of the art of governance than to those of the specific domains of migration or development studies. The principal bureaucratic misconception was about the nature of remittances being perceived as a public resource. Ironically, whenever the state tried to interfere with the freedom to dispose of remittances, it would subsequently gain less in terms of both direct and indirect benefits, as was demonstrated by the enforcement of the 1982 banking regulation. Otherwise, the remittances, when recognized and administered as a private resource and a kind of individual self-help scheme, could significantly supplement a broader developmental agenda regardless of actual state policy.

Having observed this, my intention is not to advocate this laissez-faire model as an exclusive model of public policy, nor am I inclined to conform to the neoliberal enthusiasm of the early 2000s regarding the migration-development nexus. Public policy, and especially economic policy in underdeveloped or developing nations, should always include a significant degree of state intervention and overall planning. Only when deprived of such active policy might underdeveloped countries consider emigration of their labor force as a meaningful development strategy. Under such circumstances, the neoliberal enthusiasm for migration seems to derive from the same desperate lack of developmental strategy and is equally unrealistic as were the utopian designs of the Yugoslav emigration authorities.

Acknowledgments This research forms part of the project, funded by the Serbian Ministry of, Science, Technological Development and Innovations and by the Mediterranean Program of the European University Institute in Florence and the Imre Kertész Kolleg in Jena. As regards the writing process and final shaping of ideas and conceptions I would like to express my sincere gratitude to Silke Meyer and Claudius Ströhle for their advice, contributions, and guidance.

References

Adler, S. (1981). *A Turkish Conundrum: Emigration, Politics and Development, 1961–1980.* International Labor Organization.

Aksel, D. B. (2019). *Home States and Homeland Politics: Interactions between the Turkish State and its Emigrants in France and the United States.* Routledge.

Aranicki, F. (1924). Kanada, iseljivanje zemljoradnika, 5837/24, 23. IV 1924. In: Hrvatski državni arhiv. Fond iseljenički komesarijat (1071), b. 560.

Aranicki, F. (1925a). Statistika naše migracije za god. 1925. In: Hrvatski državni arhiv, 1071, kutija 559.

Aranicki, F. (1925b). Cirkular svim velikim županima, 28 februar 1925. In: Hrvatski državni arhiv, 1071. Kutija 558, 1.

Aydaş, O. T. (2003). *Determinants of Workers Remittances: Evidence from Turkey* [MA thesis]. https://core.ac.uk/reader/52939535.

Baučić, I. & Maravić Ž. (1971). *Vraćanje i zapošljavanje vanjskih migranata iz SR Hrvatske. Centar za istraživanje migracija.*

Baučić, I. (1979). *Stanje vanjskih migracija iz Jugoslavije krajem sedamdesetih godina.* Centar za istraživanje migracija.

Bekavac, T. (1948). Izveštaj sa puta u Sloveniji, 4. IX 1948. In: AJ, 25, fasc. 68, a. j.

Bogoev, K. (1989). Devizne doznake u jugoslovenskoj privredi. *Finansije,* 43(2–3), 123–145.

Bohning, W. W. (1975). Some Thoughts on Emigration from the Mediterranean Basin. *International Labour Review,* 111(3), 251–278.

Brunnbauer, U. (2016a). *Globalizing Southeastern Europe: Emigrants, America, and the State since the Late Nineteenth Century*. Lexington Books.

Brunnbauer, U. (2016b). Migration and Economic Development in Socialist Yugoslavia. Ostblog: https://ostblog.hypotheses.org/728.

Cvetković, S. (2006). *Između srpa i čekića. Represija u Srbiji 1944–1953*. Institut za savremenu istoriju.

Đikanović, V. Š. (2016) Iseljenici u Severnoj Americi i jugoslovenska država 1918–1945 [Doctoral dissertation], https://nardus.mpn.gov.rs/handle/123456789/7254?locale-attribute=sr.

Dimić, L. (1996). *Kulturna politika u Kraljevini Jugoslaviji I*. Stubovi kulture.

Gamlen, A. (2010). The New Migration and Development Optimism: A Review of the 2009 Human Development Report. *Global Governance*, 16(3), 415–522.

Gamlen, A. (2014). The New Migration-and-Development Pessimism. *Progress in Human Geography*, 38(4), 581–597.

Grado, A. B. (1920). Organizacija iseljenčke službe u Kraljevini SHS, 15 VIII 1920. In: Hrvatski državni arhiv, Fond Artur Benko Grado (790), kutija 3, fascikla 10.

Grado, A. B. (1924). Anketa o iseljavanju, 16–18 IX 1924. In: Hrvatski državni arhiv, 790, kutija 7, fascikla 4.

Grado, A. B. (1927). Opadanje iseljavanja nekvalifikovanih radnika, 14. IV 1927. In: Hrvatski državni arhiv, 790, kutija 10, fascikla 24.

De Haas, H. (2010). Migration and Development: A Theoretical Perspective. *International Migration Review, 44(01)*, 227–264.

Horst, C., Erdal, M. B., Carling, J. & Afeef K. F. (2014). Private Money, Public Scrutiny? Contrasting Perspectives on Remittances. *Global Networks*, 14(4), 514–532.

Iseljenički odsjek (1920). Pregled o iseljavanju...i vraćanju u domovinu, 15. VIII 1920. In: Hrvatski državni arhiv, 790, kutija 3, fascikla 10/178.

Iseljenički odsjek (1921). Nacrt uredbe o iseljavanju i vraćanju, maj 1921. In: Hrvatski državni arhiv, 790, kutija 5, fascikla 12.

Iseljenički komesarijat (1923). Zahtev za ekspertsko mišljenje, 27. X 1923. In: Hrvatski državni arhiv, 790, kutija 10, fascikla 24.

Ivanković, M. (1977). *Vodič za posao u Jugoslaviji*. Udruženje publicista.

Jakobsen, J. & Štrabac, Ž. (2015). Doznake iz inozemstva, institucije i razvoj u Bosni i Hercegovini. In: Kostić, R., Ćosić, E., Babić, B., (Eds.), *Migracije u funkciji razvoja*. Ministarstvo za ljudska prava i izbjeglice.

Japunčić, J. (1947). Izvještaj o službenu putovanju u Zagreb i Split, 24. IV 1947, Arhiv Jugoslavije, Fond Ministarstva rada FNRJ (25), fasc. 68, a. j. 195.

Kaćanski, V. (Ed.). (1988). Korišćenje štednje građana na privremenom radu u inostranstvu za razvoj. Fond za kreditiranje bržeg razvoja.

Kosijer, L. S. (1924). Anketa o iseljavanju, 16–18 IX 1924. In: Hrvatski državni arhiv, 790, kutija 7, fascikla 4.

Marsenić, V. D. (1990). *Ekonomika Jugoslavije*. Ekonomika.
McCombie, J. S. L. & Thirlwall, A. P. (Eds.). (2004). *Essays on Balance of Payments Constrained Growth: Theory and Evidence*. Routledge.
Miletić, A. R. (2009). (Extra-) Institutional Practices, Restrictions and Corruption. Emigration Policy in the Kingdom of Serbs, Croats, and Slovenes (1918–1928). In Brunnbauer, U. (editor), Transnational Societies, Transterritorial Politics. Migrations in the (Post-) Yugoslav Region, 19th-21st Century. Oldenbourg Verlag, 95–120.
Miletić, A. R. (2012). *Journey under Surveillance: The Overseas Emigration Policy of the Kingdom of Serbs, Croats and Slovenes in Global Context, 1918–1928*. Lit Verlag.
Moskovljević, Ž. (1948). Izveštaj Živojina Moskovljevića. AJ, 25, fasc. 68, a. j. 195.
Myrdal, G. (1957). *Rich Lands and Poor*. Harper & Row.
Nikolić, G. (2009). Efekti iseljeničkih doznaka na ekonomski razvoj Srbije. *Hereticus* 7(4), 69–84.
Novi carinski propisi u Jugoslaviji. Otvorena služba poklon-paketa, *Zavičaj*, 13/ VI 1959, 7.
Opšta državna statistika (Ed.). (1938). *Definitivni rezultati popisa stanovništva od 31. marta 1931. godine*. Vol. II. Državna štamparija.
Savet za pitanja iseljenika (1954). Odboru za privredu SIV-a, 23. IX 1954. In: AJ, Fond Savezno izvršno veće (130), fascikla 594, a. j. 984.
Savet za pitanja iseljenika (1964). Informacija o zameni unetih sredstava plaćanja, 18. IV 1964. In: AJ, 130, fascikla 594, a. j. 984.
Şenses, F. (1991). Turkey's Stabilization and Structural Adjustment Programme in Retrospect and Prospect. *The Developing Economies*, 29(3), 210–234.
Signjar, R. (1915). *Statistički atlas Kraljevina Hrvatske i Slavonije, 1875–1915*. Zemaljski statistički ured.
Stanković, Đ. (1967). Savet za pitanja iseljenika, Saveznom izvršnom veću 5. IV 1967. In: AJ, 130, 594, 984.
Statistički godišnjak 1940 (1941). Opšta državna statistika, Državna štamparija.
Statistički godišnjak 1983 (1983). Savezni zavod za statistiku.
Togan, S. & Balasubramanyam, N. (Eds.). (1996). *The Economy of Turkey since Liberalization*. Macmillan Press.
United Nations Development Programme (Ed.) (2009). *Human Development Report. Overcoming Barriers: Human Mobility and Development*. Palgrave Macmillan.
Vedriš, M. (1977). *Ulaganje ušteda vanjskih migranata u društveni sektor privrede*. Centar za istraživanje migracija.
Vedriš, M. (1978). *Od deviznih ušteda do radnih mjesta u domovini*. Centar za istraživanje migracija.

CHAPTER 4

"Money Can't Buy Me Love": Remittances, Return Migration, and Family Relations in Serbia (1960s–2000s)

Ivana Bajić-Hajduković and Sara Bernard

Introduction

Labor migration and the remittances it produces have long been an essential aspect of socioeconomic and political change in the region of former Yugoslavia. During socialism, guest worker migration affected a significant proportion of the population. Along with the inbound tourism to the Yugoslav seaside, the migration of guest workers generated the most significant inflow of hard currency to socialist Yugoslavia. Migrants' remittances, however, went far and beyond foreign currency deposits in Yugoslav bank accounts. Migrant workers often visited their home villages with savings, consumer goods, tools, and ideas acquired abroad; they built houses,

I. Bajić-Hajduković (✉)
London, UK
e-mail: ibajicha@pm.me

S. Bernard
University of Glasgow, Glasgow, UK
e-mail: sara.bernard@glasgow.ac.uk

S. Meyer, C. Ströhle (eds.), *Remittances as Social Practices and Agents of Change*,
https://doi.org/10.1007/978-3-030-81504-2_4

paved streets, bought workplaces, and opened small businesses. The volume and spread of remittance-related practices to the Yugoslav emigrants' regions of origin was a result of the fact that the vast majority of migrants regarded their stay abroad as temporary. They sent money and brought goods back to their home villages, where some members of their family prepared and waited for their return home.

With the collapse of socialism and the ensuing wars in Yugoslavia, a significant shift occurred in migration patterns. While the typical migrant of the socialist period was a peasant worker with low qualifications and skills searching for savings opportunities, the post-1990 period saw an unprecedented migration of not only displaced and impoverished people but also of highly skilled migrants in pursuit of stability, safety, and better opportunities abroad. The remittance-related practices of the post-socialist Yugoslav migrants represented a paradigm shift and a break from socialist practices. In this later phase of migration, remittances were no longer directed at children and their caretakers to ensure their future in Yugoslavia. Instead, migrants were sending remittances to aging parents and other relatives who could not leave the country. Return migration, if still considered possible or desirable, assumed very different meanings and forms after the socialist period. More broadly, while migrant remittances continued to be a significant financial resource for governments in many former Yugoslav countries, the social function of "informal" remittances and their beneficiaries changed remarkably.

This chapter outlines some of the most relevant changes in remittances and migration practices from the socialist to the post-socialist period in Serbia. It relates these changes to transformations in relationships within migrant families in both urban and rural Serbia. It brings together long-term research on Serbian remittances from a social history and social anthropology perspective. Combining anthropological micro-level research on remittances and motherhood in post-socialist Belgrade and long-term historical analyses on peasant migrants' investments during socialism, this contribution represents a first attempt at providing a long-term and multidisciplinary examination of some of the social transformation in family relationships brought on by the collapse of socialism in former Yugoslavia as evidenced in the phenomenon of migration and the remittances inflow it generated. Exploring family roles across the prisms of gender, generation, and class reveals the complexities of remittance practices that statistical data does not show. This contribution argues that migration and remittance practices had a profound and sometimes traumatic impact on family relations.

The Inflow of Migrant Remittances in (Post-) Socialist Serbia: An Overview

Migration and the remittances have long been important factors of social change in Serbia and the broader Yugoslav region. Before the fall of Yugoslavia and the massive migration movement prompted by the conflict and by post-socialism, labor emigration from Yugoslavia consisted mostly of unskilled labor employed in Western Europe as guest workers. The substantial remittances sent home by guest workers captured the interest of the broader public both at home and abroad. In Yugoslav public and political debate, citizens, migration specialists, and the communist leadership dreamed of the gains generated by the revenues migrants sent back home. Yugoslav migration policies attracted considerable attention by foreign analysts and policy makers because Yugoslavia was the only socialist country in Europe to rely on guest worker remittances to achieve development.

In the 1980s, the rise of youth unemployment fostered an increase in the emigration of young and educated people (Dević 2016, p. 27). The war and the further deterioration of the economy in the 1990s exacerbated this trend. This brain drain diaspora differed from the previous generations of both guest workers and political émigrés who had fled communism. With the fall of Yugoslavia, a new wave of migrants left the country, some as refugees and others as economic and political migrants, but all with the same goal of escaping war, economic collapse, and political turmoil (Vuksanović 2001). The 1990s in Serbia were marked by the United Nations embargo and hyperinflation. Access to foreign currency became a lifeline as prices changed hourly. The suspension of air traffic following the UN embargo and the significance of informal networks suggest that pre-1990s' migrants were sending financial support through informal channels during this period, as well as some of the post-1990s' migrants (Petree and Baruah 2007). As many of the pre-1990s' migrants settled in Germany, Austria, Switzerland, and other Western European countries, their geographical proximity to Serbia enabled them to send remittances via friends or bus drivers, or to deliver them directly to their families, thus helping alleviate the precarious situation of the 1990s.

Pension provisions were a significant source of revenues sent to Serbia by the pre-1990s' generation. While still residing abroad, many retired guest workers spent several months per year in the houses they had built in their home villages (Widmer 2010).

The post-1990s' economic migration in many cases painted a different picture. First of all, the proportion of more highly qualified migrants had significantly increased. The destination countries of the post-1990s' brain drain migrants included overseas countries with settlement programs. Post-1990s' migrants were also younger than the previous guest workers. Thousands of young people left Serbia in the 1990s and early 2000s as highly skilled migrants on settlement visas to Canada, Australia, and New Zealand, in addition to those pursuing better opportunities in Western and Central Europe, as well as further afield in Africa, South America, and elsewhere (Grečić 1994, 2010).

The influx of remittances was also affected by changes in migration patterns. Overall, there is a lot of evidence to suggest that post-1990 migrants from Serbia were sending much less money in foreign currency in comparison to the pre-1990 migrants. Nevertheless, throughout the first two decades of the twenty-first century, the media in Serbia reported an exceptionally high influx of remittances. These reports originated from the World Bank, who in turn collected the data from the National Bank of Serbia (NBS). Despite significant discrepancies in the volume of remittances between these two sources, with the NBS reporting significantly fewer remittances in comparison to the World Bank, Serbia was ranked as one of the top ten remittance recipient countries in the world in the early twenty-first century. With more than 3 billion euros annually, Serbian remittances constitute 15 percent of the country's GDP (Gajić 2020). Divided per capita, Serbian residents are among the top five recipients of remittances in the world.

Bombastic newspaper headlines about the alleged billions of dollars pouring into the country from the diaspora fueled people's imaginations of fortunate parents whose children were sending them money from abroad (Mikavica 2006; Krivokapić 2007). This narrative was part of a broader political discourse about the role of migrants in the newly established, independent Serbia. In the early post-Milošević years, subsequent governments reached out to Serbs abroad for support in restoring national pride and economic wealth. Two critical steps toward building a stronger relationship with the diaspora in the post-socialist period were the creation of the Ministry for the Diaspora and the passage of the Amnesty Law, which allowed army deserters from the wars of the 1990s to return to the country. In more recent years, however, there was another turn in the relationship toward the diaspora. The former Ministry for the Diaspora was replaced by an Office for Cooperation with the Diaspora and Serbs in the Region, governed by the Ministry of Foreign Affairs (Bobić 2009). Over the past few years, the interest in the financial input of the diaspora remained; however, the willingness to create a more dynamic relationship with the diaspora returned to that of the Milošević era. Like in the 1990s, remittances in post-socialist Serbia continue to flow to individuals, with no government-supported programs for diaspora investments.

The high volume of remittances in post-socialism was a continuation from the socialist period, when Yugoslavia was among the top European countries in this respect. Yugoslav guest workers remitted more than their Greek, Turkish, Italian, Portuguese, and Spanish counterparts (SOPEMI 1979, p. 125, 1981, p. 149). According to the annual reports of the Yugoslav National Bank, worker remittances became a vital relief for the external balance of payment deficits from 1967 onward. Despite its socialist ideology, the Yugoslav leadership greeted these remittances with great enthusiasm. The expectation was that workers' savings would finance the development of underdeveloped regions (Bernard 2019).

In both socialism and its aftermath, these expectations about the role of remittances in bringing development to Yugoslavia and later to Serbia were, for the most part, disappointed. Overall, migrants were disaffected with the politics in their homeland. Instead, remittance practices were defined by individual ambitions and family needs. State regulations did indeed affect the ability of migrants to send remittances and their uses. However, rather than support migrants in investing their savings into their home country, government interventions were often perceived by returnees as obstacles to profitable investments (Bernard 2019, pp. 240–242). Migrants and their families primarily used remittances to cope with the failures of socialist and post-socialist development on a political and everyday level, rather than support its achievements.

Social Status and the Rural/Urban Divide

In Serbia and the broader Yugoslav region, the transition from socialism to post-socialism had a profound impact on class identities. While Yugoslavia did not experience a straightforward transition from communism to capitalism, people's experiences of change in their everyday lives in the 1990s embodied the end of socialist values attached to particular social(ist) classes. For these people, as for millions of other Eastern Europeans, the changes brought about by post-communism meant, as Verdery (1999, p. 35) described, "a reordering of people's entire meaningful worlds; [...] a rupture in their worlds of meaning, their sense of cosmic order." Migration was a substantial aspect of this reordering. The changes affected old and new migrants in different ways. While labor mobility and employment opportunities for the former were restricted and became more precarious, new opportunities for employment and professional advancement were offered to the latter.

The open borders and freedom of movement which had characterized socialist Yugoslavia as a unique case in Cold War Europe ended in November 1991 when visa restrictions were introduced. These were gradually relaxed, but only lifted entirely in the 2010s. The sanctions and embargo on Serbia during the wars of the 1990s, as well as more stringent immigration policies introduced in Western Europe after the two oil crises in 1973 and 1979, greatly affected the rural migrants of the socialist period. In the 1980s, their employment had already become increasingly discontinuous and less profitable than in the past (Schierup 1981; idem, 1986). Post-1990 emigration was different. The new urban emigrants possessed qualifications and skills that made their employment in the Western markets profitable. They were young and highly educated, with the skills and knowledge to navigate the intricacy of application procedures. The post-1990s' urban emigrants were leaving their friends and parents behind, often as single individuals who wanted to fulfill their passions, talents, and dreams. They left with the prospect of pursuing successful carriers abroad.

Although they were better positioned in the international labor market than the old generation of unskilled migrants, the post-1990 generation of migrants remitted much less than the guest workers from the socialist period did. Sources suggest that guest workers still contributed most to the staggeringly large pool of remittances to Serbia recorded by the World Bank in the mid-2000s (Petree and Baruah 2007). In the cities, there is no evidence to support the euphoric messages conveyed by the Serbian media and the Serbian government about the wealth that the Serbian diaspora was displaying at home. The ethnographic fieldwork of Bajić-Hajduković in Belgrade in 2005/2006 and from 2007 to 2014 did not uncover the presence of this vast influx of foreign currency into people's everyday lives. Her findings were supported by an International Organization for

Migration (IOM) study that suggested that post-socialist remittances were not channeled to the families of post-1990 migrants from Belgrade (see Bajić-Hajduković 2020; Petree and Baruah 2007). As in the 1970s and 1980s, a large proportion of payments to Serbia were still channeled to the same recipients—the guest workers' families with closer connections to the countryside. The quantitative data from the 2011 census in Serbia also highlighted a discrepancy between urban and rural remittance destinations in the country. The 2011 census recorded that people above the age of sixty from the Belgrade area received the lowest volume of remittances in the country, while most remittance recipients above sixty lived in southern and eastern Serbia (Stanković 2014, p. 98).

In the Belgrade families affected by the post-1990 migration, remittances were never mentioned, nor was there any evidence of additional income within those households. The post-1990s' migrants who originated from urban parts of Serbia remitted much less, either because they did not think they should do so or because their families did not expect them to. For Belgrade mothers, remittances were acceptable only if they remained invisible and unused. In most cases, Belgrade mothers kept their migrant children unaware of the severity of their material circumstances, in line with normative expectations. In the few cases where mothers received remittances, they insisted that the money was not used for everyday consumption. They made a clear distinction between the money that their son or daughter sent occasionally and the remittances that guest workers on temporary work in Germany in the 1970s and 1980s sent to their families. Belgrade-based elderly mothers thought that receiving financial support or a gift with a value that was not purely symbolic was something that only peasants could accept (Bajić-Hajduković 2010, p. 29).

The (In)Visibility of Remittances in Family Relationships

The visibility of peasants' remittances stands in stark contrast with the invisibility of the gifts sent by adult children to their mothers in Belgrade. The guest worker migration of the socialist period was intended to provide financial support to alleviate the poverty of peasant families. Whether used to refurbish houses, buy farming machinery, or secure a job outside of agriculture, remittances were spent for the benefit of the migrant family.

There was no secrecy about the provenance of the acquired wealth. Instead, it was proudly displayed.

Although emigration was prompted primarily by economic necessity, the desire to climb the social ladder was typical for many peasant migrants. The opulent houses that guest workers built in their home villages and the impressive number of tractors dropped off on neglected fields were symbols of the migrants' aspiration for social recognition. Sociological research on rural Serbia has shown that middle-class peasantry in eastern Serbia went abroad primarily to be able to surpass the wealth of rich peasants (Bratić and Malešević 1982; Schierup 1973; Tanić 1974, pp. 83, 305). Within peasant communities, some ethnic minorities were overrepresented among the migrants. They were also more likely to invest remittances to enhance their family's social status rather than to secure employment (Vuksanović 1996; Tanić 1974, pp. 87, 88, 94). For instance, workers' remittances were used to display family wealth in the Vlach community of Ljubičevo (eastern Serbia) where social status was acquired through the marriage of adolescent children with wealthy families (Schierup 1973, p. 46).

The different remittance practices speak not only about the desire to enhance the social status of peasants. More broadly, they account for how migration reshaped class identities and became a social stigma for peasants. This is not, however, a social phenomenon particular to Serbia. The investment of peasant migrants in social status is neither specific to Serbian guest workers nor the wider Balkan region. The building of opulent houses and the import of tractors and expensive consumer goods were widely reported in many rural emigration areas around the world during the twentieth and twenty-first centuries (Körner and Werth 1981; King 1986; Gardner 1995; Dalakoglou 2010; Boccagni and Erdal 2020). As in Serbia, these investments have been described as symbols of the uncultured otherness of peasants. In the case of Serbia, however, the remittance practices of rural migrants acquired a broader significance than in other emigration countries due to the sizeable proportion of the peasant population throughout the entire twentieth century.

Although socialism tried hard to dismantle the peasantry, as it did not fit within the parameters of the classless society Yugoslavia claimed to be, the rural population in Serbia formed the majority until the 1990s. In 2020, the rural population still accounted for 44 percent of the total population (Worldometer 2020). In socialist Serbia, peasants were systematically constructed as the "enemy within" (Bajić-Hajduković 2020, p. 11).

The working class considered peasants backward. Political and intellectual circles often questioned the peasants' loyalty to the communist regime. Left behind by socialist policies of industrialization and proletarianization, peasants found employment abroad to be a way out of economic misery and social exclusion.

Whether migrating within Yugoslavia or further afield, the majority of migrants from Serbia in the socialist era came from the countryside (Burić 1973, p. 251). Before the legalization of temporary employment abroad (1963), large numbers of the agricultural population left the countryside and moved to the urban peripheries in search of a job in the public sector. This immigration led to a notable growth of the urban peripheries (Tanić 1989). Here, self-made houses and informal trade proliferated but were poorly tolerated by the authorities and urban dwellers, who saw the peasants as "others" who were corrupting the urban milieu. Employment abroad did not end this rural exodus, but it transformed the interaction between rural and urban areas. Peasants acquired the status of workers abroad, a status that came with privileges which they wanted to keep once they returned to Yugoslavia. Upon their return, guest workers tried to obtain jobs in industry and to leave the agricultural sector. However, they did not leave their home villages permanently. Peasants populated urban peripheries but kept one foot in the countryside, where they returned daily, weekly, or monthly (Nejašmić 1981; Vedriš 1978).

During socialism, migration and the revenues it generated played an essential role in constructing stereotypes about the otherness of peasants. The investment of guest workers and their flaunting of wealth were widely discussed in political debates and media (Bernard 2019, pp. 95-98, 150-166). When Yugoslav socialism started to tremble, the discrepancy between the wealth displayed by guest workers and the underdevelopment of their regions contributed vastly to the growing antagonism of the urban population toward the peasantry. This dissatisfaction increased in the 1970s, when the employment of workers from the Serbian countryside abroad was booming. From the 1970s, Serbia and the broader Yugoslav region experienced a rise in social inequalities and economic disparities between its republics and within its regions (Pleština 1992). The uneasy incorporation of rural into urban patterns of development was one of the symbols of this unevenness.

This in-between status of the peasantry and the working class which characterized many guest workers was the reason why in cultural productions and media debates the figures of the economic migrant and the peasant often overlapped. However, the meaning of the peasant migrants changed over time. In the 1950s and early 1960s, the peasant was portrayed sympathetically as naïve, warm-hearted, and simple. From the early 1970s, this changed, and the image of the peasant began to become more complex and increasingly negative. (Bernard 2019, pp. 205–212). In these years, employment abroad, a phenomenon until then mostly affecting the impoverished working classes from the northwestern republics, became a widespread practice among peasants in the southeastern Yugoslav regions (Brunnbauer 2009, p. 28).

The Transformation of Value Systems and the Impact of Class on Family Ties

In the 1980s and 1990s, when the economic crisis deepened and stricter limitations on the international mobility of Yugoslav and later Serbian migrant workers were introduced, the pressure of the rural population on the urban peripheries increased. In addition to being viewed as "uncultured," the meaning of the term "peasant" in the 1990s amalgamated the anxieties of nationalism and the eroding socialist system of values—it stretched far beyond a symbol of someone who hailed from the countryside. It became an archetype of post-socialist aesthetics: turbo-folk music, fake Diesel jeans, Nike trainers, and thick gold chains with crosses (Marković 2005; Gordy 1999, pp. 106–110; Bajić-Hajduković 2020, p. 85). This new peasant was someone who lived for the day, who cared how much they earned but not how they earned it, even if this involved illegal activities in the flourishing black market. In other words, this was someone with no morals or regard for the social values of the socialist era. The peasant became an embodiment of the changes that were sweeping away the familiar system of values and social norms. Remittance practices in post-socialism affirmed the class distinction between the "useful" children of peasants and the working class and the "priceless" children of the urban middle class (Zelizer 1994). The concept of "priceless children" emerged with the mass–industrialization of the USA at the turn of the twentieth century, which saw the role of the child changing from a unit of labor to an object of parental sacrifice and unconditional love (Zelizer 1994). A similar phenomenon occurred after World War Two in parts of Yugoslavia. Children born in the postwar period became objects of their mothers' love and sacrifice—"priceless children." Their mothers, even when their dire material conditions in the 1990s and early 2000s suggested otherwise, could not and would not accept financial support in the form of remittances.

In the post-socialist reordering, receiving remittances or other forms of financial support from a migrant child indicated a loss of middle-class status. The socialist middle class had become so impoverished that it had become an empty signifier, clinging on to class values that had become hollow in the new post-socialist class system in Serbia. (Bajić-Hajduković 2020, p. 88).

Nevertheless the socialist middle class still clung to their old habits and beliefs, some of which manifested themselves in their relationships with their children. The social norms relevant to these generations implied that mothers were there to protect their children and to look after them long into adulthood; they did not expect their children to sustain them or materially support them. This was considered something that peasants did, such as those who had guest worker sons or daughters in Germany, Austria, or Switzerland. The old socialist urban middle class was there to support its migrant children in every possible way, and not the other way around (Bajić-Hajduković 2020, p. 88).

Employment abroad, for the peasant, was a family matter which formed a bond between older and younger generations. Rural emigration was conceived of and organized by both the state authorities and the migrants themselves to be temporary. This is pivotal to understanding the relationships in migrant families. The temporary character of guest worker migration meant that the migrants were expected to return and that family unity would eventually be restored. The major investments typical of Yugoslav guest workers symbolized these expectations: the building of a new and bigger house, or the import of machinery to enhance the productivity of the small plot owned and worked by the family. The time and the costs sustained to raise the family's living standards required a commitment by all family members abroad and at home over several decades. Even when guest workers invested in securing jobs outside agriculture, these were principally intended as employment opportunities for family members who were not yet employed abroad. This was the case with the opening of small shops, which were usually run by family members, but also when guest workers took advance of the possibility to "buy a workplace." This practice was introduced in the 1970s by the Yugoslav government to support local development. It consisted in the payment, in hard currency or the equivalent in dinars, of the amount of money required by factories to open a workplace. The vacancy was usually offered to the payers or one of their family members (Ivanović 2010). Well-established informal networks in the local community were essential to ensuring the success of the peasant migration strategy. Family members and their circle of friends and relatives were key actors in guest worker migration strategies. Guest workers from the same villages shared the costs of accommodation abroad and could help driving back remittances and gifts to family members who had remained in their villages to take care of the land.

During socialism, the reliance on the family and the importance of the local community was not a peculiarity of rural migration from Serbia. However, peasant solidarity between home community members and within intergenerational families had a long tradition in Serbia, which was challenged but not eliminated by socialism. Before World War Two, 90 percent of the Serbian population were peasants, with families organized into collective households called *zadruga*. The child in a *zadruga* was considered primarily a unit of labor (Isić 2006). Once social reforms and rapid industrialization began in post-World War Two Yugoslavia, the role of the child began to change.

Nevertheless, this change was slow, and it did not affect all of Yugoslav society equally. Although it became a common feature of the urban classes, this was much less the case in rural areas, where socialist modernity was a contested symbol of identity. Indeed, in rural, underdeveloped areas, reliance on extended family networks remained a response to falling employment opportunities and an overall lack of welfare services. In these settings, children remained economic assets to the family and not vice versa. Children's education and professional careers were determined by decisions taken by the family and for the pursuit of family unity and wellbeing.

The family migration established during socialism survived its collapse, albeit in new forms. The "guest worker" had become a way of life rather than a temporary status. Not even wars or the low economic prospect of return migration could interrupt the investment of an entire working life in one's home village. Moreover, migration had transformed families and community life so radically that both family and societal relations became dependent thereupon. Migrant children today, just like their parents before them, still leave for employment abroad while keeping one foot in their home villages, where aging parents and relatives wait for their return and live on the remittances they send home. This explains why older generations in rural areas have been the principal recipients of remittances in recent decades. The most traumatic changes, however, were wrought on motherhood and the role of women within families more broadly. This was the case in villages and cities—during socialism and thereafter.

Motherhood and Gender Roles

Even though the Belgrade mothers discussed by Bajić-Hajduković were not all in the same financial situation—some were struggling to make ends meet, while others were much better off—what they shared in common was an understanding that, if received, remittances should not be consumed for mundane purposes because they came from their children, whom they considered sacred objects of love and care. This attitude to children is typical of the generation of women born around World War Two who belonged, in their view, to the middle class. Women in socialist Yugoslavia considered motherhood an essential aspect of identity. Milić even argued that Yugoslav women worked and lived for their children (2008, p. 195). While socialism motivated women to pursue education and employment, they were not free from traditional patriarchal norms of having primary responsibility for their families and children. However, employment and (relative) financial independence enabled women to feel respected for their work in the domestic sphere, if not so much by their husbands, then by their social circle and above all their children (Milić 2008, p. 1959).

During socialism, emigration was one of the principal means for women to find employment. Although the communist leadership proclaimed women's emancipation, female unemployment remained very high and even began to rise in the late 1960s (Woodward 1995, pp. 206–209; Davidović 1986). This prompted a significant number of women to find employment abroad. Women from the Serbian countryside usually went abroad with their husbands but had fewer opportunities to gain skills than their spouses. Women were overrepresented among the unskilled and the poorly educated. Unlike the majority of male guest workers, only a small number of female migrants had finished the eight years of compulsory education, which was a precondition for attending vocational training abroad (Archives of Serbia [undated], Socialist Alliances of the Working People of Serbia (dj75), box 1, No. 12). More often than their husbands, women held poorly paid physical jobs. They were rarely members of trade unions (p. 8; Marić 1990, p. 35). Female guest workers were often in a relationship. If they did not have children before leaving, they had them while they resided abroad. Unlike female domestic workers, though, female guest workers did not take maternity leave when they had children. Instead, they continued to work, even working extra hours, because the main reason they had joined their husbands abroad was to save enough money for a decent life in Yugoslavia (Morokvašić 1987, pp. 122–127; Burić 1973, p. 258). As childcare was too expensive and guest worker children underperformed at school, the elderly in the family considered the earlier return of the children to be the best course of action (Vegar 1986; Vuksanović 1995, p. 352; Petrović 1973). In fact, research on Yugoslav women residing abroad during socialism suggests that mothers were more hesitant than their husbands about investments in Yugoslavia. However, their doubts rarely led them to revise their plans to return. Yugoslav mothers abroad lamented in particular the traumatic experience of sending their children back to Yugoslavia to be raised by family members, usually grandparents (Bernard 2019, pp. 246–248; Schierup 1990, p. 105; Morokvašić 1987, pp. 218–222). This wound could never heal properly.

Family migration patterns in the post-socialist context presented different challenges to Belgrade mothers than those faced by rural women under socialism. The fall of Yugoslavia and the massive emigration of grown children that coincided with a change in social norms and values created an incredibly difficult situation for elderly mothers. With the departure of their children, their world collapsed: there was no one left in the inner social circle or family to appreciate these women's sacrifice. Elderly mothers, perhaps more than anyone else, felt the crumbling of socialist values—they lost everything in this process, including themselves.

Mothers of post-1990s' migrants from Belgrade considered it unacceptable to receive material support from their children. Most of the women included in this research lived in small apartments in concrete socialist apartment blocks, furnished with household appliances that were on average thirty years old. The very question of whether they received money from their migrant sons and daughters abroad caused embarrassment among Belgrade mothers. They would blush, look away, and explain that they had not given birth to their child expecting their support (Bajić-Hajduković 2020, p. 77).

The appropriate gift for a mother–child relationship, according to Belgrade mothers, was a gift with little or no material value, a gift that was symbolic and inalienable. Money thereby became a form of inalienable gift that mothers did not use for consumption, but saved so that their children would get it back as their inheritance. The only exception was when it was used for a purpose that transcended consumption, such as treating a severe illness or paying for funeral costs. A gift that came from a "sacred object" of a mother's love and care—a child—could not be consumed in a mundane way. Instead of remittances, what stood out in the research conducted with Belgrade mothers was their loneliness. The elderly mothers talked for hours on end about their loss, their migrant children, and the emptiness, physical and emotional, that remained in the wake of their children's departure. Money could not fill the absence and the profound sense of loss.

The case of the Serbian middle class resonates with Patico's study of consumption in the post-Soviet middle class (2008). The post-Soviet middle class defined itself by having been born and socialized within middle-class families and a middle-class milieu during the Soviet period. The socialist middle class in post-socialist Serbia, like its Russian counterpart, had become impoverished, but people still defined themselves as middle class based on their culturedness. Even though the former occupations of Bajić-Hajduković's interview partners in Belgrade varied substantially in terms of income (including a retired teacher, a seamstress, a company director, a translator, and a housewife), they all shared in common that they lived and had raised their children in Belgrade, socializing them with a socialist middle-class identity and providing the education and skills that subsequently facilitated their children's emigration. The comparison with the Russian self-professed middle class, the diversity of backgrounds, with many an urban dweller in Serbia coming from the countryside, as well as the very different occupations ranging from blue- to white-collar workers to the unemployed, points to the fact that the class discourse in the Belgrade context was highly subjective. In other words, appropriating a middle-class identity was the result of an active process of self-positioning and constructing one's culturedness in opposition to the "Other," embodied as the peasant. The middle class created this new peasant as a way of navigating the murky and tumultuous sea of post-socialist metamorphoses; the peasant was a counter-balance to a crumbling system of socialist middle-class values. As long as one could point out a peasant and their ways, the middle class could still hold on to their values, regardless of how much the realities betrayed their middle-class identity.

The narratives of Belgrade mothers about the different experiences of motherhood between rural and urban families also belong to a broader understanding of modernity and belonging. The Belgrade mothers' narratives about migrant sons and daughters are evocative of the study of the making of the "priceless child" in early twentieth-century America (Zelizer 1994). Zelizer argued that a shift in constructing the "sacred child" emerged as a result of the massive industrialization that took place in America at the start of the twentieth century. Kopytoff argued along similar lines that material affluence in most modern industrial societies has allowed Westerners to "purge relations with kinsmen of much economic content and make them almost entirely 'social'" (Kopytoff 2004, p. 273). According to Kopytoff, parents in Western societies are in a position not to expect any material benefits from their children. This, however, is not the case in poor peasant societies, where arduous material conditions engender rather different relationships between parents and children (Kopytoff 2004, p. 273).

During socialism, economic hardship was indeed a critical factor in shaping parent/child relations in rural areas. However, poverty is not a monolithic factor. There are significant disparities in wealth between different rural areas and within their communities. Moreover, social differences existed within the peasantry to no less extent than between the peasantry and the working class (Ströhle 2016). A closer look at how migration affected gender roles in migrant families during socialism is exemplary of these differences. The employment abroad of women was not welcomed equally in all rural communities.

In some cases, it was even prohibited. Data from the population census held in 1971 allows the geography of these dissimilarities to be discerned. Within the Republic of Serbia, the proportion of female workers among the total number of workers employed abroad varied from 42.7 percent in the autonomous province of Vojvodina, to an average of 35.7 percent in Serbia generally, and down to 4.2 percent in the autonomous province of Kosovo—the total Yugoslav average was 31.4 percent (see Künne 1979, p. 102). Whatever the dominant social convention or underlying economic condition behind female (non-)emigration, remittance practices changed gender roles within the family.

In his extensive work on rural emigration from socialist Serbia, the sociologist Živan Tanić (1974, pp. 32, 33, 99–101) illustrated that emancipation became possible for peasant wives left behind. As the birth rate fell, women were free to take up seasonal jobs outside agriculture and to cultivate their network of solidarity with women in the villages. However, hard physical labor on the land and responsibility for the construction of a new house indicated a masculinization rather than an emancipation of rural women. Remittances could well reproduce patterns of subjugation to the patriarchy rather than challenging them. For example, during his fieldwork in eastern Serbia, Schierup reported that it was typical of women to take on male duties in the field. At the same time, men enjoyed watching the televisions bought with the savings they had earned abroad (1973, p. 10).

The different impact of remittances could also be seen with the children growing up in rural families who were profoundly affected by their parents' employment abroad. Research on the guest worker children growing up in the Serbian countryside has revealed a distinction between poor and relatively rich peasant families. The latter were able to give pocket money and presents to the children left behind, resulting in these children disregarding work. In more impoverished peasant families, remittances were used to make essential improvements in the cultivation of land and in house maintenance. Children had to grow up fast. They assumed adult responsibilities as children while under the care of aging grandparents (Ciglar 1990; Tanić 1974, pp. 99–107). For girls growing up in deprived rural areas which were mostly inhabited by socially excluded minority groups, the status of adulthood would never properly be granted as they were promised, still at adolescent age, to a member of the community employed abroad, where they were sent at the request of the promised husband (Tanić 1974, p. 92).

To be sure, economic hardship could also affect urban migration. Research shows how, under socialism, when urban migration was driven by economic need (because of unemployment of both parents), children were more likely to be sent to an orphanage as urban parents lacked the family network and income from the land on which rural families relied (Burić 1973, pp. 259–261). The extreme poverty of unemployed urban parents is also one reason why family migration was rare during socialism.

Conclusion

Recent data shows that as many as 70 percent of young Serbs would like to emigrate (Rolandi and Elia 2019). This suggests that migration continues to be the principal response of families to the new forms of poverty and deep social inequality that have emerged in post-socialism.

By taking Serbia as a case study, this contribution showed how reports about voluminous remittances can mask deep levels of poverty and social inequality. It did so by looking beyond the data recording a high volume of remittances over a more than fifty-year period. Instead, the study focused on migrant families to examine who received and used remittances, why, and how. It compared remittances practices in rural families during socialism with those adopted by urban families after the collapse of Yugoslavia. It argued that class identity and social(ist) values were more important than economic status to explain why peasant migrants used savings to improve family living standards. By contrast, urban families rejected this practice as immoral. The perceived distance between rural and urban morality, which emerged in the narratives of Belgrade mothers, was contextualized in broader trends of women's emancipation and dichotomous urban/rural modernization from the twentieth into twenty-first centuries.

Albeit in changing forms, the inflow of remittances and their uses will remain a crucial driver of social change and adjustments to the challenges of globalization which socialism and neoliberalism have left unsolved. This prospect makes the study of how remittances (re)shape relations in migrant families in the past, present, and future highly topical.

References

Archives of Serbia (AS). (undated). Socialist Alliances of the Working People of Serbia (dj 75), Koordinacioni odbor za radnike u inostranstvu (Box 1), (Položaj žena i porodice zaposlenih u inostranstvu (No. 12).

Bajić-Hajduković, I. (2010). The Lost Matriarch: The Consequences of Remittances on Mother-Child Relationships in Urban Serbia. *Genero—Časopis za feminističku teoriju i studije kulture*, *14*, 25–48.

Bajić-Hajduković, I. (2020). *"Can You Run Away From Sorrow?" Mothers Left Behind in 1990s Belgrade*. Indiana University Press.

Bernard, S. (2019). *Deutsch Marks in the Head, Shovel in the Hands and Yugoslavia in the Heart: The Gastarbeiter Return to Yugoslavia (1965–1991)*. Harrassowitz.

Bobić, M. (2009). Diaspora kao ekonomski i socijalni kapital Srbije. *Sociološki Pregled*, *43*(3), 361–377.

Boccagni, P., & Erdal, M. B. (2020). On the Theoretical Potential of 'Remittance Houses': Toward a Research Agenda across Emigration Contexts. *Journal of Ethnic and Migration Studies*. https://doi.org/10.1080/1369183X.2020.1804340.

Bratić, D., & Malešević, M. (1982). Kuća kao statusni symbol. *Etnološke Sveske*, *4*, 144–152.

Brunnbauer, U. (2009). Labour Emigration from the Yugoslav Region from the Late 19th Century until the End of Socialism: Continuities and Changes. In U. Brunnbauer (Ed.), *Transnational Societies, Transterritorial Politics: Migrations in the (Post-)Yugoslav Region, 20th–21st Century*, (pp. 17–49). De Gruyter.

Burić, O. (1973). Novi tip nepotpune porodice. Porodice čiji su hranitelji otišli na rad u inostranstvo. *Sociologija*, *15*(2), 245–271.

Ciglar, V. (1990). Jesu li privremeni staratelji primjeren supstitut za roditelje? *Migracijske Teme*, *6*(4), 47–53.

Dalakoglou, D. (2010). Migrating-Remitting-"Building"-Dwelling: House-Making as "Proxy" Presence in Post-Socialist Albania. *Journal of the Royal Anthropological Institute*, *16*, 761–777.

Davidović, M. (1986). Nezaposlenost i društvena nejednakost u Jugoslaviji. *Gledišta*, *27*(7–8), 3–35.

Dević, A. (2016). What nationalism has buried: Yugoslav social scientists on the crisis, grassroots powerlessness and Yugoslavism. In P. Stubbs, R. Archer & I. Duda (Eds.), *Social Inequalities and Discontent in Yugoslav Socialism* (pp. 21–37). Routledge.

Gajić, M. (2020, January 14). Doznake—Koliko novca Srbi iz inostranstva šalju u Srbiju? *Talas*. https://talas.rs/2020/01/14/doznake-koliko-novca-srbi-iz-inostranstva-salju-u-srbiju/.

Gardner, K. (1995). *Global Migrants, Local Lives: Travel and Transformation in Rural Bangladesh*. Oxford University Press.

Gordy, E. (1999). *The Culture of Power in Serbia: Nationalism and the Destruction of Alternatives*. Penn State Press.

Grečić, V. (1994). Oživljavanje priliva doznaka i kapitala naših radnika i iseljenika. In T. Popović (Ed.), *Strategija povratka Jugoslavije na svetsko tržište* (pp. 154–158). Institut ekonomskih nauka.

Grečić, V. (2010). *Srpska naučna dijaspora: 'tamo i ovde'*. Institut za međunarodnu politiku i privredu.

Isić, M. (2006). Dete i žena na selu u Srbiji između dva svetska rata. In L. Perović, (Ed.), *Žene i deca: Srbija u modernizacijskim procesima XIX i XX veka*, (pp. 131–159), Helsinški odbor za ljudska prava u Srbiji.

Ivanović, V. (2010). Durch Ersparnisse zum Arbeitsplatz. Investitionen der Gastarbajteri in die Wirtschaft der Socialistischen Föderativen Republik Jugoslawien. In V. Bakondy, S. Ferfolgia, J. Janković, C. Kogoj, G. Ongan, H. Pichler, R. Sicar & R. Winter (Eds.), *Viel Glück! Migration Today. Vienna, Belgrade, Zagreb, Istanbul*. (pp. 90–103). Mandelbaum Verlag.

King, R. (Ed.). (1986). *Return Migration and Regional Economic Problems*. Routledge.

Kopytoff, I. (2004). Commoditising Kinship in America. In S. J. Taylor, L. L. Layne, & D. F. Wzniak (Eds.), *Consuming motherhood* (pp. 271–278). Rutgers University Press.

Körner, H. & Werth, M. (Eds.). (1981). *Rückwanderung und Reintegration von ausländischen Arbeitnehmern in Europa. Beiträge zu einem internationalen Symposion des Isoplan–Instituts in Saarbrücken am 16. und 17. Oktober 1980*. Breitenbach.

Krivokapić, B. (2007, September 15). Dijaspora pomaže, ali nema investicija. *Blic*. https://www.blic.rs/biznis/dijaspora-pomaze-ali-nema-investicija/336ksqq.

Künne, W. (1979). *Die Aussenwanderung jugoslawischer Arbeitskräfte. Ein Beitrag zur Analyse internationaler Arbeitskräftewanderungen*. Hanstein.

Marić, V. (1990). Organiziranost i druženje u inozemstvu. *Migracijske Teme* 6(4), 33–38. Suplement.

Marković, P. (2005). Srpski Gastarbejteri kao faktor modernizacije u Srbiji. *Istorija XX veka*, *2*, 145–163.

Mikavica, A. (2006, July 10). Dosta šalju—malo ulažu. *Politika*. http://www.politika.rs/scc/clanak/12204.

Milić, A. (2008). Žene u bivšoj Jugoslavili: Drugačiji pogled na učinke socijalizma u promeni društvenog položaja žena. In S. Vujović (Ed.), *Društvo rizika: Promene, nejednakosti i socijalni problemi u današnjoj Srbiji*, (pp. 181–198). Insititut za sociološka istraživanja Filozofskog Fakulteta u Beogradu.

Morokvašić, M. (1987). *Emigration und danach: Jugoslawische Frauen in Westeuropa*. Stroemfeld/Roter Stern Verlag.

Nejašmić, I. (1981). Povratak jugoslavenskih vanjskih migranata i njihovo uključivanje u gospodarski i društveni život zemlje. *Rasprave o Migracijama*, *73* (special issue).

Patico, J. (2008). *Consumption and Social Change in a Post-Soviet Middle Class*. Stanford University Press.

Petree, J. & Baruah, N. (2007). *A Study of Migrant-Sending Households in Serbia-Montenegro Receiving Remittances from Switzerland*. International Organization for Migration.

Petrović, B. (1973). Deca stranih radnika školskog uzrasta u SR Nemačkoj. *Sociologija*, *15*(2), 327–340.

Pleština, D. (1992). *Regional Development in Communist Yugoslavia: Success, Failure, and Consequences*. Westview Press.

Rolandi, F., & Elia, C. (2019, November 25). Escape from the Balkans. *Osservatorio Balcani e Caucaso*. https://www.balcanicaucaso.org/eng/Areas/Balkans/2019-escape-from-the-Balkans-197872.

Schierup, C. (1981). Povratne migracije i nova međunarodna podjela rada. *Revija za Sociologiju*, *11*(3–4), 13–142.

Schierup, C. (1973). *Houses, Tractors, Golden Ducats: Prestige Game and Migration. A Study of Migrants to Denmark from a Yugoslav Village*. Field Report, Århus University.

Schierup, C. (1990). *Migration, Socialism and the International Division of Labour: The Yugoslavian Experience*. Avebury.

SOPEMI. (1979). *Rasprave o Migracijama*, *52* (special issue).

SOPEMI. (1981). *Rasprave o Migracijama*, *72* (special issue).

Stanković, V. (2014). *Popis stanovništva, domaćinstva i stanova 2011. u Republici Srbiji: Srbija u procesu spoljnih migracija*. Republički Zavod za Statistiku.

Ströhle, I. (2016). On Social Inequalities in a Socialist Society: The Creation of a Rural Underclass in Yugoslav Kosovo. In R. Archer, I. Duda & P. Stubbs (Eds.), *Social Inequalities and Discontent in Yugoslav Socialism* (pp. 112–131). Routledge.

Tanić, Ž. (1974). *Seljaci na evropskim raskrnicama. Analiza ekonomska emigracija.* Institut društvenih nauka, Centar za sociološka istraživanja.

Tanić, Ž. (1989). *Beogradska predgrađa i prigradska naselja: sociološka analiza.* Institut društvenih nauka, Centar za sociološka istraživanja.

Vedriš, M. (1978). Od deviznih ušteda do radnog mjesta u domovini. *Rasprave o Migracijama, 46* (special issue).

Vegar, B. (1986). Jugoslavenska djeca u bečkim školama. *Migracijske Teme, 1*(1), 75–80.

Verdery, K. (1999). *The Political Lives of Dead Bodies: Reburial and Post-Socialist Change.* Columbia University Press.

Vuksanović, G. (2001). *Jugoslovenske izbeglice. Izmedju želje i mogućnosti za povratkom.* Filozofski Fakultet, Novi Sad.

Vuksanović, G. (1995). Odnosi autoriteta u porodicama povratnika sa rada u inostranstvu *Sociologija, 37*(3), 343–367.

Vuksanović, G. (1996). Stanovništvo Srbije na radu u inostranstvu tokom XX veka. *Godišnjak Filozofskog Fakulteta u Novom Sadu, 34,* 295–307.

Widmer, H. (2010). Povratnici. Serbische Arbeitsmigrant/innen im Ruhestand. In V. Bakondy, S. Ferfoglia, J. Janković, C. Kogj, G. Ongan, H. Pichler, R. Sicar & R. Winter (Eds.), *Viel Glück! Migration Today. Vienna, Belgrade, Zagreb, Istanbul.* (pp. 398–407). Mandelbaum Verlag.

Woodward, S. (1995). *Socialist Unemployment: The Political Economy of Yugoslavia 1945–1990.* Princeton University Press.

Worldometer (2020). Population of Serbia: Urban vs Rural Population (historical chart), https://www.worldometers.info/world-population/serbia-population/.

Zelizer, V. (1994). *Pricing the Priceless Child: The Changing Social Value of Children.* Princeton University Press.

CHAPTER 5

"Dear Brother, Please, Send Me Some More Dollars...": Transatlantic Migration and Historic Remittance Between the Habsburg Empire and the United States of America (1890–1930s)

Annemarie Steidl

In the summer of 1921, a migrant worker living in Joliet, Illinois, who had been born in the Habsburg Empire, received the following message, translated into English:

> Dear brother, please, send me some more dollars [...]. You know, God gave me many children and I have to support them and I have nothing to support them with [...]. Do not resent me for begging, I am ashamed for begging, but I have to. Please, help us. You know, this country was always poor and will always be poor, and I am lucky to have you send me something. (Anton Nemanich Papers 1921)

A. Steidl (✉)
Department of Economic and Social History, University of Vienna, Vienna, Austria
e-mail: annemarie.steidl@univie.ac.at

S. Meyer, C. Ströhle (eds.), *Remittances as Social Practices and Agents of Change*,
https://doi.org/10.1007/978-3-030-81504-2_5

This letter was sent to Anton Nemanich from Lokvica—by that time situated in the Kingdom of Yugoslavia, today in the Republic of Croatia. Such a message might just as easily have arrived in Joliet in 2020 in the form of an email or WhatsApp text, perhaps sent from a relative in Latin America or the Caribbean. Data from the US census shows that, in 2010, more than a quarter of Joliet's population spoke a language other than English at home, and one-seventh of the city's population today are foreign-born. The 1921 letter, with all its heartbreak and humiliation, indicates that money sent transnationally was an important connector of migrants to their scattered families, then as now (Steidl et al. 2017, p. 250).

Nearly 18 million people left Europe for the United States between 1890 and the 1930s, the vast majority of whom had been born in Eastern and Southern Europe. US immigration records show that at 27.9 percent, individuals from the Habsburg Empire formed the largest group of US-bound migrants between the years 1902 and 1911, followed by people from the Kingdom of Italy and the Russian Empire. Nineteenth-century industrialization, urbanization, and political and economic liberalization encouraged and facilitated these massive transatlantic migrations. From the mid-nineteenth century on, overseas migration was triggered by a growing demand—particularly in the United States—for low-skilled laborers in mines, factories, construction, and urban services. Ever more jobs began attracting Europeans to a more labor-intensive American economy in which even urban service jobs and factories were heavily reliant on temporary employment. This provided the perfect conditions for the growing internationally mobile labor force from Central, Southern, and Eastern Europe. Millions of citizens left the Habsburg Empire before World War One, with between 30 and 40 percent returning to Europe before the war started. Based on data regarding wages and expenses and estimates of remittances, I will follow the money that was sent from migrants in the United States to their dependents back in the Habsburg Empire.

Historic Remittance Practices

Remittances are money transfers earned by migrants abroad and sent back to relatives and dependents in their countries of origin. Today, migrant remittances constitute a significant part of international capital flows, especially for the national income of labor-exporting countries. The World

Bank documented that in most developing countries, remittances are already more than three times the size of official development assistance (World Bank Group 2019, p. 1). Although few scholars would deny the significant contribution of migration and remittances to the income and survival of families in the countries of origin today, flows of remittances by migrants in the past are still a mostly neglected topic of research. However, going abroad to earn higher wages and sending money to relatives and friends back home is hardly new, even though the means of transport and communication were less efficient and reliable then than they are today.

Then as now, remittances were part of a collective strategy that consisted in sending one or more members of one's family abroad so that they could support those left behind. Millions of Europeans had migrated to the United States of America by the 1930s. These people stayed in contact with family members, friends, and neighbors mostly via letters. The letters sent by those who stayed in Europe frequently asked for financial support, while the letters sent by the transatlantic migrants often included remittances, which constituted a source of income that many Europeans in their countries of origin with relatives or friends overseas depended on (Cancian and Wegge 2016, pp. 352–353). As a case in point, in the early twentieth century the mother of Mike Vukasinovich, who had moved to the United States from a village near Bjelovar in Croatia-Slavonia, wrote in a letter to her son: "I do not wish to have it so that I need to find money to win it and what you write that you sent me money but that was too little" (Mike Vukasinovich Papers).

Up to 60 million Europeans left the continent during the long nineteenth century lasting into the 1930s, which resulted in a huge reallocation of the population on an international scale. Many migrants moved to seek out a better existence compared to what they had experienced in their homelands. Individuals moved if they had the financial means or could secure a loan from family members or friends to cover the costs of travel. Therefore, the transatlantic mass migration of the late nineteenth century was accompanied by considerable financial flows between continents, countries, and empires. As many people preferred to use informal channels to transfer their savings, it can reasonably be concluded that a significant share of remitted money sent to Europe in the nineteenth century traveled via "invisible" operations. Banknotes were mailed through ordinary letters, despite the risk of loss or theft, and migrant laborers also used networks of family and friends to whom they entrusted envelopes full of money for the families when they traveled back to Europe. Transatlantic migration was never a one-way street, especially during the decades before World War One. Many migrants to the United States went back and forth or even returned to Europe for good, taking their savings with them. Rui Esteves and David Khoudour-Castéras use the term "pocket remittances" for cash, but also for bank drafts which were carried by those who returned to Europe (2009, p. 954). From this perspective, return migrants can be viewed as important agents of change, as innovators and investors. The general expectation was that so-called pocket remittances, as well as the experience, skills, and knowledge that these people acquired during their time in the United States, would greatly help the economic development of their countries of origin (de Haas 2007, p. 3).

Migration Between the Habsburg Empire and the United States of America

In comparison to other European regions such as the western German lands or the Scandinavian countries, Habsburg citizens were latecomers to transatlantic migration. Although various migration patterns within, from, and to the Habsburg Empire had a long-standing history, transatlantic movements were not a characteristic feature of mass mobility prior to the 1880s (Steidl 2021). By the end of the nineteenth century, transatlantic migration had become easier due to the circulation of knowledge about the wider world. Although some people from the Austrian territories had moved overseas as early as the eighteenth century, a new type of international movement did not emerge before the end of the nineteenth century. According to official surveys, only a few thousand people had left the Habsburg provinces for destinations overseas before the middle of the century, with the numbers of overseas migrants being particularly small for the Kingdom of Hungary and Croatia-Slavonia, totaling only a few hundred persons per year (John 1996, p. 55; Puskás 1982, p. 18). The number of overseas movements was still low in the 1870s but grew apace in the following decades. Booming industrial centers in the United States stimulated transatlantic traffic with a seemingly insatiable demand for cheap laborers (Zahra 2016, pp. 3–6).

By the first decade of the twentieth century, many provinces and regions of the Habsburg Empire had become a major source of labor migrants, who joined Irish, Italian, and German workers in transforming industrial labor in the Americas. Overseas migration had developed into a generally accepted means of improving one's living situation, an instrument for social advancement, and the number of individuals who moved over long distances increased in proportion to the information available regarding particular destinations. While images and visions of "America" as a land of milk and honey corresponded little with reality, they nonetheless influenced migration decisions. US immigration records show that in the 1900s, individuals from the Habsburg Empire comprised the largest group of new arrivals. In 1910, a peak year for transatlantic movement to the United States, 113,218 Austrian subjects crossed the Atlantic (Steidl et al. 2017, p. 114).

In the first decade of the twentieth century, the absolute number of US-bound migrants from the Kingdom of Hungary outstripped those from Imperial Austria. With migration from both parts of the empire falling to 50,000 from more than 350,000 in the previous year, 1908 was a year of retrenchment (Puskás 1990, pp. 43–58). According to the *New York Times*, the economic decline of the US labor market, which was accompanied by a sharp rise of unemployment in these years, resulted in "the most violent reaction in the history of transatlantic travel" (*New York Times*, December 19, 1909). The recovery of the US economy in 1909 prompted a renewed rise in out-migration from the Habsburg Empire, but these numbers failed to approach the 1905 to 1907 levels for the rest of the prewar period, although migration from Imperial Austria reached a new record in 1913. Finally, the onset of war in Europe in the summer of 1914 resulted in a dramatic drop in US-bound movements. The British blockade of the Central Powers made wartime travel for German and Habsburg citizens to and from Europe highly difficult, if not impossible (Feys 2016, pp. 151–162). Even if the necessary preconditions for significant overseas traffic had developed at a relatively late point in time, these routes had become a generally accepted means to improving the living situation of individuals as well as their families, a positively marked instrument for social advancement, and the rise in the number of people who moved over longer distances increased the information available concerning potential destinations. Overall, up to four million people from the Habsburg Empire arrived in the United States during the long nineteenth century (Keeling 2013, p. 62; Deak 1974, p. 34).

Even if the United States had become the preferred destination for a rapidly increasing number of Habsburg citizens, their regions of origin changed dramatically. While in the second half of the nineteenth century, German-, Czech-, and Yiddish-speaking people from the Bohemian Lands and from Vorarlberg accounted for more than 80 percent of all international migrants from the empire, at the end of the century, the new arrivals were primarily Poles, Slovaks, Slovenes, Croats, Serbs, Hungarians, Ukrainians, and Romanians. Therefore, transatlantic migration from the Habsburg territories should not be reduced to only one type of mass movement. Divergent overseas mobility patterns emerged along various regional, ethnic, and cultural lines and during different stages of economic development. Peoples' social status, gender, and religious and ethnic affiliations linked them closely to certain mobility patterns. While in some parts of Imperial Austria, individuals started to move overseas quite early in the first half of the nineteenth century and many had the intention to settle on land for farming, the knowledge that the US labor market was in search of foreign workers did not spread to other areas until the first decade of the twentieth century. Many moved as family groups, such as Czech speakers from the Bohemian Lands in search of free territories in the 1870s and 1880s, while others left their families in Europe with the intention of returning. Most transatlantic travelers were young men and women in employment age, many of them single and hoping for a profitable job or a suitable marriage partner (Steidl and Fischer-Nebmaier 2014). Especially since the end of the nineteenth century, most Habsburg citizens moved within well-developed transatlantic communication and migration networks of family and friends, but there were also adventurous pioneers who made their way to still scarcely populated areas in the West and South of the United States.

Historic Return Migration

Of the Europeans who settled in the Americas, some returned to their countries of origin (Wyman 1993, p. 9). Increasing globalization processes of labor markets modified transcontinental migration patterns from exclusively lifelong commitments to temporary employment. The mainly work-related moves all over the globe had high return rates both because there was little intention of permanent settlement and because new travel possibilities made return much easier. According to official data from the US government and shipping company statistics, nearly half of all European migrants crossed the Atlantic more than once during the first decades of the twentieth century (Steidl 2021, pp. 151–161). Before World War One, the majority did not leave the Habsburg Empire with the intention of settling in the United States for good. Wages were considerably higher in US heavy industry, mining, and construction, and the main goal was therefore to save as much money as possible and to return with these pocket remittances after two to five years (Dustmann and Weiss 2007).

This decision to return was just as likely the result of a positive reason as a negative, and rather than being viewed as failures, return migrants should be recognized as simply a part of a global migration system (Grosjean 2005, pp. 216–232). Some transatlantic migrants returned home with their pockets empty, their health ruined, and their illusions shattered, but not all were actually bankrupt, ailing, or disaffected. Some of those who had originally left home with no thought of returning simply changed their minds. A significant number of migrants went overseas with no intention of settling permanently, but rather with the goal of repatriating the income they hoped to make and thereby improving the economic situation of their families in their home countries. Migrants who intended to return based their decisions not only on their immediate and prospective circumstances in the host economy, but also on the expected future in their countries of origin (Dustmann and Weiss 2007, pp. 236–256). Family networks, networks of neighbors, and clientele were all highly influential when it came to migration; the same was the case for return migration.

About 1.2 million individuals moved from the Habsburg Empire to the United States between 1908 and 1913, of whom about 460,000 returned (Steidl 2021, p. 154). It is estimated that in 1902, for example, the rate of individuals who came back to Hungarian-ruled Liptó/Liptov/Liptau County constituted about 50 percent (Evans Poznan 2011, p. 93). Between 1900 and the outbreak of World War One, most transatlantic migrants from the Habsburg territories planned to stay only temporarily, making use of opportunities to earn money that would relieve financial difficulties back home. "Most of the Bohunks came to America intending to stay two or three years [...] work to the limit of their endurance [...] and then, returning to the Old Country, pay the debt on the old place, buy a few additional fields and heads of cattle, and start anew," recalled Louis Adamic, who left Imperial Austria in 1913 at the age of sixteen (Adamic 1932, p. 104). An oral history survey of Yugoslav migrants in the United States found that two-thirds of the migrants who arrived before 1910 had planned to return (Colakovic 1973, p. 58). Many desired financial independence or at least an improvement in their economic lot, and hoped a few years of work in America would allow them to realize these dreams. It was a common mobility pattern for married men to leave their families behind in Europe and return to join them again after a few years in America. Young couples planned to build houses of their own, others wanted to buy a few acres of land so that they could work for themselves or save up enough to buy a small store or a shop along with the necessary tools. Return migrants also made use of skills acquired in the US labor market. The ability to cope with new technologies and faster production processes in the United States were qualifications in high demand in many industrializing European regions (Gould 1980, p. 51).

Return migration was largely a movement of men (Steidl 2021, pp. 156–157). While men moved on their own for employment reasons, women participated in repeat transatlantic crossings in much lower numbers. In comparison to South and Southeastern Europe, where women had limited opportunities in the labor market, the industrializing process in the United States provided many jobs for women. Besides, at the beginning of the twentieth century, men were in the clear majority of the US population in the age cohort of 18–30 years. These surplus men, when still single, formed a lucrative marriage market. Therefore, young single women were more likely to leave Europe with the intention of permanently settling on a new continent and starting a family of their own (Steidl and Fischer-Nebmaier 2014, p. 85). For women, migration was a way to overcome patriarchal traditions. These routes were therefore often difficult to reverse, because a return to their society of origin might have implied a return to patriarchy (Krauss 2001, p. 13).

For those who left, migration implied a fresh start in a new environment, but for those who stayed behind, the loss of a family member or friend might have had other implications. The social and economic positions that migrants had formerly held became vacant and had to be filled; social configurations needed to be rearranged. The ones left behind, most often women with children, might have had difficulty coping without a male breadwinner present. Not all migrants were able to obtain (or keep) a decent job in the United States, and they might not have been able to support families in Europe. Those left behind did not always welcome those who returned with open arms and might have been distrustful of the returnees' new perspectives or broadened horizons. The administrations in both parts of the Habsburg Empire might likewise have viewed the return of transatlantic migrants with some skepticism, even if they returned with financial means (Puskás 1982). Migrants might have been treated by the sedentary population as "traitors" who had abandoned them on the one hand, or on the other hand might have been seen as shining beacons of a better future for the entire community. It was not uncommon for return migrants to be mocked—the term *chuligani pruscy* was used to refer to Polish migrants who had returned from Germany, and *amerykanie* was used to refer to return migrants from the United States (Esch 2017, pp. 131–188).

The freedom that individuals from the Habsburg territories had enjoyed working and living on two continents ended abruptly with World War One. Although the United States remained neutral during World War One until April 1917, the global conflict had an almost immediate effect on international migration. Congress sought to restrict the admission of new arrivals even before the United States entered the war. In the 1920 fiscal year, return migration grew to more than 288,000, with almost a quarter of a million individuals leaving the United States the following year, too. In 1921 and 1924, however, US Congress passed additional laws restricting immigration that had the effect of discouraging would-be returnees who had not been naturalized and were thus not guaranteed re-admittance to the United States (Steidl et al. 2017, pp. 73–74).

Transatlantic Communications and Sending Money Back Home

People who crossed the Atlantic faced a bigger decision, besides transportation costs, in calculating whether to go west, or back east, and when to make such moves. Drew Keeling (2013) termed this type of migration "risk management," which means that people tried to take advantage of transatlantic demands for their labor and to minimize living costs while maximizing other financial earnings, which included accumulating liquid savings and investing in real estate. Before World War One, the United States benefited enormously from European migrants' ability to adapt to seasonal fluctuations in the American job market. As Susan B. Carter and Richard Sutch wrote, migrants' "involvement in the American economy allowed for longer economic expansions and shorter contractions than would have been the case had employers been forced to rely on domestic labor supplies alone" (Carter and Sutch 1997). An investigation of labor turnover led to a set of questions about how individuals from the Habsburg Empire used their earnings from wage labor (Steidl et al. 2017, pp. 260–282). Which institutions were used to hold the possible savings of the Habsburg migrants and did they invest their money in real estate in the United States or did they transfer their savings to Central Europe?

In 1907, the US Labor Department carried out a survey among Italian, Slavic, and Hungarian-speaking unskilled male labor migrants to compile detailed information on migrants' earnings, savings, and investments. Labor Department administrators estimated that unskilled laborers from Southern and Central Europe earned on average USD1.50 per day in US industry. Having a permanent job and working about 26 full days each month, these laborers could expect a monthly income of USD39, potentially amounting to between USD450 and 500 with full-time employment year-round. The Labor Department further estimated how much these European men spent on housing, food, and clothing, assuming that most of these men were either single or had left their families in Europe. Many spent on average USD12 per month on lodging and food in boarding houses. If they spent another USD1.50 each month on clothing, they could save about USD25 net at the end of each month for further expenses. Without a family to provide for and no further special needs, the Labor Department estimated that these men might have been able to accumulate as much as USD1000 after a bit more than three years of industrious work in the United States (Sheridan 1907, p. 477). Those savings could either be sent via letters or transfered via banks to Europe or brought back by return migrants as pocket remittances. Estimates by the Labor Department did not include expenses for amusements such as beer or cigarettes, nor newspapers or going to the movies. All such expenditures would have eaten into their savings and reduced remittances or delayed a possible return to Europe (Steidl et al. 2017, p. 283).

On the basis of similar documents, Claudia Goldin (1990) prepared a dataset of women wage earners in various US cities. According to her estimates, women who worked as textile laborers, in cigar factories, or other sweatshops could earn about USD25 each month. Based on the 1907 survey, the US Labor Department reported an average weekly wage for women from the Habsburg Empire of USD5.87. Taking Goldin's and the Labor Department's estimates, women who lived on their own or shared accommodation, spent up to USD2.93 per week on lodging and board, with another forty cents needed for public transportation. Goldin estimated that single women might have been able to send USD1.69 (nearly 29 percent of their wages) as remittances each week to Europe, leaving them 85 cents for clothing and amusements (Goldin 1990; Report on Condition of Woman and Child Wage-Earners in the United States 1910).

However, these numbers are estimates, and we have no detailed information on how many of these men and women were actually single, with a dependent family back in Europe, or even willing to send remittances. Women were more likely to start a family in the United States, and it remains unclear whether they were still willing to support their families of origin financially.

According to the 1910 US population census, about 1.57 million persons over the age of 13 born in the Habsburg Empire were making a living in the United States, namely 974,000 men and 596,000 women. We can further estimate that 90 percent of these men and about 25 percent of the women participated in the labor market, mostly as unskilled wage laborers or as domestic servants. Those 149,000 women expected a smaller income than their male peers. If all Habsburg migrant laborers were able to save USD25 for men or USD10 for women each month and transfer these sums back to families and relatives, the annual flow of remittances would have topped USD280 million.[1] In the daily practice of the late nineteenth and early twentieth centuries, most unskilled wage laborers did not have stable full-time jobs each month, never mind year-round. In 1926, for example, the Italian migrant Diego Delfino wrote a letter from Ohio to his daughter in Reggio Calabria: "Until now, it has not been possible for me to send the money for the board, given the dearth of work in this land, as I'm always waiting for the mines to reopen […] Here, if the miners don't work, money is hard to come by" (Cancian and Wegge 2016, p. 362).

In response to increasing political and public concerns about the negative effects of the growing numbers of Central and Southeastern Europeans arriving in the country, the US government formed the Dillingham Commission in 1907 (Benton-Cohen 2018). In that same year, this Commission estimated that all remittances transferred from the United States to Europe by migrants amounted to USD275 million, of which USD140 million were being transferred by banks owned by former European migrants (Dillingham 1911, p. 75).

However, from the perspective of the Austrian and Hungarian governments, of banks in the Habsburg Empire, and even of the population itself, migration to the United States was a financially positive development. In 1904, the Hungarian-born and New York-based US immigration inspector Marcus Braun interviewed the Bohemian-born and

[1] I want to especially thank James W. Oberly for putting together all this data and compiling the estimations.

Budapest-based banker Zsigmund Kornfeld on the economic and political significance of migration from the Kingdom of Hungary to the United States. According to Braun's report, Kornfeld said: "Let all go who can, earn all the money they can, learn the practical ways of the American laborer, and come home with both the money and experience thus gained" (Report of Immigrant Inspector Marcus Braun 1906, p. 12). Following his conversations with bankers in Budapest and Vienna, Braun estimated that the annual amount of remittances totaled USD50 million from the United States to the Kingdom of Hungary in 1904. Due to increasing demand for land by return migrants and those who received remittances in the Kingdom of Hungary, property prices began to increase (Report of Immigrant Inspector Marcus Braun 1906, p. 3). The 1907 report from the US Labor Department gives further information on remittances transferred via the international mail service:

> The most effective as well as the least expensive means is through the international and domestic mail service. Through this channel reliable information as to employment, wages, and location is given by the relative or friend in the United States to the intending immigrant before he leaves his native land. The relative or friend in the mine, factory, or work of construction knows if there is a shortage of labor or a place here for his relative or friend in Europe. The magnitude of the international mail and money-order business of the United States, together with the fact that the great mass of immigrants go unerringly to the States where wages are highest and their services in greatest demand, indicates the effectiveness of the system and the accuracy of the information. (Sheridan 1907, pp. 407–408)

Sending money through the US Post Office to the Austrian or Hungarian Post was popular with migrants, and from the mid-1880s onward, they took advantage of postal savings banks, where labor migrants could safely deposit their money and collect interest. By 1905, some 2 million people in the Austrian provinces had savings accounts with the post office, as did almost 0.6 million inhabitants of the Hungarian counties (Postal Savings Banks in Foreign Countries 1907, p. 21). Annual reports of the Postmaster General tracked the growth of remittances sent via international postal money orders to the Habsburg Empire. In 1897, the Post Office handled about 45,000 money orders on remittances, worth nearly USD750,000. Small savers made up the great bulk of users of this international money movement system, as the average money order was for less than USD20. The Slovak-speaking migrant Thomas Čapek reported that the postal savings bank in Košice/Kassa in the Kingdom of Hungary handled 6 million Crowns (about USD1.2 million) a year in savings from America. Čapek further cited information on remittances from one small village in Zemplín/Zemplén/Semplin County in which, in the 1890s, about 1100 people received an average of 35,000 Crowns (USD7000) per year from the United States (Čapek 1906, p. 157). The use of postal orders increased dramatically after 1900, meaning that by 1907 senders dispatched almost USD16 million to Austria-Hungary (Annual Reports of the Postmaster General, 1897 to 1914; Steidl et al. 2017, p. 287).

By 1908, the volume of international postal money orders going to the Kingdom of Hungary exceeded those bound for the Austrian part of the empire. Some of this intensified use of international postal money orders resulted from defaults, embezzlements, and other defalcations committed by private migrant bankers, especially during the economic slump of 1907/1908 (see, e.g., the case of Frank Zotti; Steidl et al. 2017, pp. 164–165). In the same year, the Postmaster General began reporting a reverse flow of international postal money orders. Transatlantic migration routes were never one-way streets, nor was the flow of money. While transatlantic migrants sent remittances to the Habsburg Empire, people in the empire also transferred money, although in much smaller amounts, to their loved ones in the United States. In 1908, some USD2.5 million were sent by individuals from Austria-Hungary to recipients in the United States, of which 60 percent (USD1.4 million) originated in the Kingdom of Hungary. Especially during economic crises and unemployment, some of that European money, no doubt, helped finance return migrations. In 1914, the US Post Office remitted USD19 million in international postal money orders to the Habsburg Empire, and received USD3.5 million in return (Annual Reports of the Postmaster General, 1897 to 1914). World War One disrupted the international mail service between the United States (which was neutral until 1917) and the Habsburg Empire. It also disrupted transmissions of international postal money orders, which declined in volume by two-thirds between 1914 and 1916.

Tracking the volume of remittances is never an easy task, neither in the records of the United States nor in surveys from the Habsburg Empire. One problem is the changing definition, as the US Treasury Department sometimes lumped church and non-profit benevolent donations together with remittance calculations. Also, the expenses of prepaid ocean passenger tickets or the tickets themselves were sometimes included. In the decades before World War One, the price for a one-way ticket was on average USD25, meaning this underwriting by US calculations represented millions of dollars expended by Habsburg migrants (Carter and Sutch 1997).

According to the contemporary economist Friedrich von Fellner, who published a series of volumes on national income in the Habsburg Empire and paid particular attention to the part remittances played in the economies of both parts of the empire, payments coming from abroad were an essential element of Imperial Austria's gross national product (GNP) as well as that of the Kingdom of Hungary. From 1911 to 1913 alone, migrants remitted more than 176 million Crowns to the Kingdom of Hungary (which is equivalent to the average purchasing power of about one billion Euros today) through mail and telegraph offices, money orders, postal savings bank checks, or via transfers made by local banking institutes. Von Fellner estimated the amount of remittances sent to Imperial Austria in 1910 at 146 million Crowns (equivalent to the average purchasing power of nearly 840 million Euros today) (von Fellner 1917, pp. 99 and 110).

Von Fellner went one step further and also estimated the amount of pocket remittances, meaning the savings from the United States taken back to Europe by return migrants. According to Hungarian statistics, nearly 18,000 return migrants carried on average about 2197 Crowns (equivalent to the average purchasing power of nearly 14,000 Euros today) in 1908/1909. Altogether, people returning to the Kingdom of Hungary arrived with about 39,000 Crowns (equivalent to the average purchasing power of more than 245,000 Euros today). In the years before World War One, on average 28,760 return migrants arrived in the Austrian part of the empire with about the same amount of pocket remittances as their Hungarian counterparts, amounting to about 63,000 Crowns each year (equivalent to the average purchasing power of nearly 379,000 Euros today) (von Fellner 1917, pp. 100 and 110). However, given the unknown numbers of unreported return migrants, pocket remittances, and the uncertain quantities of cash in private letters, such calculations have to be approached with caution.

A more recent study by Matthias Morys (2007) attempted to estimate the contribution of remittances, mainly from the United States, to economic developments in the Habsburg Empire. His work drew on reports by von Fellner and Franz Bartsch (1917), another Austrian economist working on the balance of payments for the Habsburg Empire before and during World War One. Based on this statistical data, Morys constructed a timeline of remittance payments from the United States of America to Austria-Hungary as well as to the Kingdom of Italy from 1880 to 1913. While Braun estimated remittances to the Kingdom of Hungary for 1904 at about USD50 million and omitted Imperial Austria, Morys calculated the sum of remittances for the whole empire in the same year at 208.6 million Crowns (about USD41.7 million in 1904 or equivalent to the average purchasing power of nearly 1.5 billion Euros today) and topping 262 million Crowns to Central Europe the next year (see Fig. 5.1). The amount remitted to the Kingdom of Italy in 1904 was much higher, with

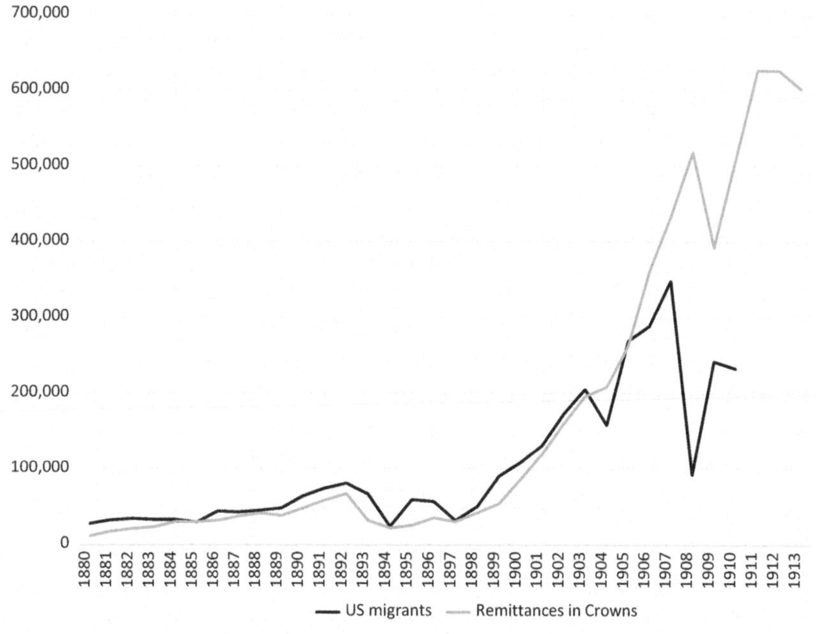

Fig. 5.1 Number of US migrants from the Habsburg Empire and remittances in Crowns, 1880–1913. (Source: Morys 2007 (accessed August 26, 2015); Chmelar 1973; Kön. Ungarisches Statistisches Zentralamt 1918. Note: No figures are available for US migrants from Imperial Austria between 1911 and 1913. For the purposes of comparison, the numbers of remittances in Crowns have here been divided by 1000)

about 584 million lire (an average purchasing power of more than 2.5 billion Euros today) (Morys 2007, pp. 16–17).

The figure shows the entire timeline that Morys constructed for the years 1880 to 1913 in comparison to the number of people from the Habsburg Empire who moved to the United States from 1880 to 1910 (detailed numbers for Imperial Austria are missing for the last three years). Remittances clearly grew in accordance with the number of migrants. A first peak of transatlantic migration was reached at the beginning of the 1890s, after which it declined sharply from 1892 to 1895 when an economic recession created unemployment and labor unrest in the United States. Habsburg citizens, therefore, postponed overseas movements to the second half of the 1890s. Those who arrived and worked in the United States up to the economic depression of the 1890s did send back their savings in accordance with their growing numbers. In 1892, the last year before the depression, migrants sent 67.4 million Crowns (equivalent to the average purchasing power of about 981 million Euros today) to the Habsburg Empire. The amount dropped to just 32 million Crowns the next year, and further to only 22 million Crowns in 1894. The biggest change came after the turn of the century, starting with a modest increase and then quadrupling between 1900 and 1914, in accordance with the much higher numbers of long-distance migrants. The peak years were 1905 to 1907, when a combined total of nearly 550,000 individuals departed the Kingdom of Hungary for the United States alone. By 1901, the Habsburg Empire received 119 million Crowns in remittances from the United States. A decade later, that number increased to 627 million Crowns. Again, the pattern depicted in the figure shows the impact of the economic slump in the United States on migrants and their remittances: the amount sent in 1909 was more than 100 million Crowns, down from the 1908 figure. Given the peak of unemployment in the United States in 1908, the number of transatlantic migrants from the Habsburg Empire fell dramatically. Accordingly, migrants from the Habsburg Empire and elsewhere lost their jobs, meaning that the savings they sent to Europe decreased the next year dramatically as well.

In the last years before the war, remittances were growing much faster than the number of Central Europeans arriving at US shores, which is a clear sign that former migrants eventually received better paying jobs in the United States, could save more funds, and accordingly were able to remit more of those savings to their families in the Habsburg Empire. According to David Good, who published widely on the economic growth of the Habsburg Empire, the increase in the volume of remittances after 1880 was a real economic change and not a reflection of inflation or currency changes. The empire's monetary system implemented the gold standard in 1892, and the Austrian and Hungarian Crown held its own against the Pound Sterling and the Dollar until wartime inflation started in 1915. Good found a pattern of price stability and steady, if unspectacular, economic growth in per capita income. He estimated that the annual growth rate of 1.63 percent in gross domestic production (GDP) per capita between 1870 and 1914 was due in part to remittances (Good 1994, p. 883). From 1910 to 1914, remittances made up 20 percent of asset flows in the balance of payments, easily outstripping the foreign income earned from transportation and tourism. A large balance-of-trade deficit in the years leading up to 1914 in both economies in the Habsburg Empire was thus partially offset by incoming remittances. Only the Kingdom of Italy had a comparable flow of remittances from its citizens who migrated to the United States, totaling between USD100 and USD150 million per year from 1905 through 1913 (Morys 2007, p. 17).

Conclusion

Between the 1880s and World War One, more than 3.7 million individuals moved in both directions between the Habsburg Empire and the United States. The motive for this historic migration was the search for better opportunities for themselves, but also for relatives and friends they left behind. Going abroad to earn higher wages and sending money to relatives and friends back home is thus hardly a new phenomenon. At the turn of the twentieth century, remittances were already part of a collective strategy that consisted in sending one or several members of the family abroad so that they could support those left behind. Furthermore, increasing globalization processes of the labor market modified transcontinental migration patterns from lifelong commitments to temporary limited stays and employment in the United States, and European migrants with the intention of returning based their decisions not only on their immediate and prospective circumstances in the host economy, but also on expected future returns in their countries of origin.

The amount of remittances sent from overseas to Central Europe can be estimated on the basis of reports by economists in the Habsburg Empire and the United States. While Braun's investigation found an amount of USD50 million sent from the United States to the Kingdom of

Hungary in 1904, von Fellner estimated the money sent in 1910 to have comprised on average USD40 million for the whole Habsburg Empire. In his constructed timeline, Morys cited a sum of USD42 million of remittances transferred in 1904 and more than USD102 million in 1910. Obviously, these estimates are far from perfect. Money was as well transferred via "invisible" informal channels, such as pocket remittances and private letters. Most estimates are based on the numbers of transatlantic migrants, but not all of these people were willing to support families in Central Europe, many had trouble keeping steady employment, and some, especially women, established their own families in the United States.

In 2019, remittances transferred from the United States all over the world exceeded USD71.5 billion (World Bank Group 2019). Adjusted for inflation, the 1911 remittances to the Habsburg Empire would have totaled about USD3 billion in today's US currency. The amounts sent were clearly less than those that migrant laborers send today to countries such as Mexico, Haiti, El Salvador, Guatemala, and Ecuador. However, the impact on the receiving country may be similar to that enjoyed by the population of the Habsburg Empire before World War One.

References

Adamic, L. (1932). *Laughing in the Jungle: The Autobiography of an Immigrant in America*. Harper & Brothers.

Annual Reports of the Postmaster General, 1897 through 1914 (Washington, DC). https://archive.org/details/annualreportsre00deptgoog. Last accessed April 26, 2023.

Anton Nemanich Papers. (1921). In *Digitizing Immigrant Letters*. https://ihrca.dash.umn.edu/dil/letters/anton-nemanich-letters/. Last accessed April 26, 2023.

Bartsch, F. (1917). Statistische Daten über die Zahlungsbilanz Österreich-Ungarns vor Ausbruch des Krieges. *Mitteilungen des k.k. Finanzministeriums*, 22, 1–159.

Benton-Cohen, K. (2018). *Inventing the Immigration Problem: The Dillingham Commission and Its Legacy*. Harvard University Press.

Cancian, S. & Wegge, S. A. (2016). "If It Is Not Too Expensive, Then You Can Send Me Sugar": Money Matters Among Migrants and their Families. *The History of the Family*, 21(3), 350–367.

Čapek, T. (1906). *The Slovaks of Hungary: Slavs and Panslavism*. The Knickerbocker Press.

Carter, S. B. & Sutch, R. (1997). Historical Perspectives on the Economic Consequences of Immigration into the United States. *NBER Historical Working Paper* 106(1997). http://www.nber.org/papers/h0106. Last accessed April 26, 2023.

Chmelar, J. (1973). The Austrian Emigration, 1900–1914. *Perspectives in American History*, 7, 275–378.

Colakovic, B. M. (1973). *Yugoslav Migrations to America*. Reed.

Deak, E. (1974). *Die Auswanderung aus Österreich im 19. und 20. Jahrhundert: Ein Überblick*. Institut für Österreichkunde.

Dillingham, W. P. (1911). *Reports of the Immigration Commission. Immigration Commission (1907–1910)*. Government Printing Office.

Dustmann, Ch. & Weiss, Y. (2007). Return Migration: Theory and Empirical Evidence from the UK. *British Journal of Industrial Relations*, 42(2), 236–256.

Esch, M. G. (2017). I.2 Migration: Transnationale Praktiken, Wirkungen und Paradigmen. In Hadler, F. & Middell M. (Eds.), *Handbuch einer transnationalen Geschichte Ostmitteleuropas. Band I. Von der Mitte des 19. Jahrhunderts bis zum Ersten Weltkrieg* (pp. 131–188). Vandenhoeck & Ruprecht.

Esteves, R. & Khoudour-Castéras, D. (2009). A Fantastic Rain of Gold: European Migrants' Remittances and Balance of Payments Adjustment during the Gold Standard Period. *Journal of Economic History*, 69(4), 952–965.

Evans Poznan, K. (2011). *Migrant Nation-Builders: The Development of Austria-Hungary's National Projects in the United States, 1880s–1920s*. PhD dissertation, College of William & Mary.

von Fellner, F. (1917). *Das Volkseinkommen Österreichs und Ungarns* (Sonderband der Statistischen Monatsschrift 21). Manz.

Feys, T. (2016). Transoceanic Shipping, Mass Migration, and the Rise of Modern-Day International Border Controls: A Historiographical Appraisal. *Mobility in History*, 7(1), 151–162.

Goldin, C. (1990). *Understanding the Gender Gap: An Economic History of American Women*. Oxford University Press.

Good, D. F. (1994). The Economic Lag of Central and Eastern Europe: Income Estimates for the Habsburg Successor States, 1870–1910. *The Journal of Economic History*, 54(4), 869–891.

Gould, J. D. (1980). European Inter-Continental Emigration: The Road Home. Return Emigration from the USA. *Journal of European Economic History*, 9(1), 41–112.

Grosjean, A. (2005). Returning to Belhelvie, 1593–1875: The Impact of Return Migration on an Aberdeenshire Parish. In Harper, M. (Ed.), *Emigrant Homecomings: The Return Movement of Emigrants, 1600–2000* (pp. 216–232). Manchester University Press.

de Haas, H. (2007). Remittances, Migration and Social Development: A Conceptual Review of the Literature. Social Policy and Development. Programme Paper

Number 34. https://www.unrisd.org/80256B3C005BCCF9/(httpAuxPages)/8B7D005E37FFC77EC12573A600439846/$file/deHaaspaper.pdf. Last accessed April 26, 2023.

John, M. (1996). Push and Pull Factors for Overseas Migrants from Austria-Hungary in the 19th and 20th Centuries. In Szabo, F.A.J. (Ed.), *Austrian Immigration to Canada: Selected Essays* (pp. 55–81). McGill-Queen's Press.

Keeling, D. (2013). *The Business of Transatlantic Migration between Europe and the United States, 1900–1914: Mass Migration as a Transnational Business in Long Distance Travel.* Cronos.

Kön. Ungarisches Statistisches Zentralamt, Ed. (1918). *Auswanderung und Rückwanderung der Länder der Ungarischen Heiligen Krone in den Jahren 1899–1913.* Ungarische Statistische Mitteilungen, new series(67). Pester Buchdruckerei-Aktiengesellschaft.

Krauss, M. (2001). Frauen und Migration: Eine einleitende Problemskizze. In Krauss, M. & Sonnabend H. (Eds.), *Frauen und Migration* (pp. 9–19). Steiner.

Mike Vukasinovich Papers. In *Digitizing Immigrant Letters.* https://ihrca.dash.umn.edu/dil/single-letters/mike-vukasinovich-letters-december-1-19xx/. Last accessed April 26, 2023.

Morys, M. (2007). Adjustment under the Classical Gold Standard (1870s–1914): How Costly did the External Constraint Come to the European Periphery? *Economics Series Working Papers*, 353. University of Oxford.

Postal Savings Banks in Foreign Countries. (1907). House Document 723, 59th Congress, 3rd Session.

Puskás, J. (1982). *From Hungary to the United States, 1880–1914.* Akad. Kiadó.

Puskás, J. (1990). Some Results of My Research on the Transatlantic Emigration from Hungary on the Basis of Macro- and Micro Analysis. In Puskás, J. (Ed.), *Overseas Migration from East-Central and Southeastern Europe 1880–1940* (pp. 43–58). Akad. Kiadó.

Report of Immigrant Inspector Marcus Braun. (1906). House Document 384, 59th Congress, 1st Session, 12.

Report on Condition of Woman and Child Wage-Earners in the United States. (1910). Vol. 5, Senate Document 645, 61st Congress, 2nd Session.

Sheridan, F. J. (1907). *Bulletin of the Bureau of Labor, 72* (September), 407–408.

Steidl, A. & Fischer-Nebmaier, W. (2014). Transatlantischer Heiratsmarkt und Heiratspolitik von MigrantInnen aus Österreich-Ungarn in den USA, 1870–1930. *L'Homme: Zeitschrift für feministische Geschichtswissenschaft*, 1, 51–68.

Steidl, A. et al. (2017). *From a Multiethnic Empire to a Nation of Nations: Austro Hungarian Migrants in the US, 1870–1940.* StudienVerlag.

Steidl, A. (2021). *On Many Routes: Internal, European, and Transatlantic Migration in the Late Habsburg Empire.* Purdue University Press.

U.S. Senate. (1910). Senate Document 645. Committee on Commerce. Report on Conditions of Woman and Child Wage-Earners in the United States, Vol. 5. 61st Cong., 2nd sess.

World Bank Group. (2019). *Migration and Remittances: Recent Developments and Outlook*. Migration Development Brief 31. https://www.knomad.org/sites/default/files/2019-04/Migrationanddevelopmentbrief31.pdf. Last accessed April 26, 2023.

Wyman, M. (1993). *Round-Trip to America: The Immigrants Return to Europe, 1880–1930*. Cornell University Press.

Zahra, T. (2016). *The Great Departure: Mass Migration from Eastern Europa and the Making of the Free World*. W. W. Norton & Company.

CHAPTER 6

Standing Waves: Remittances as Social Glue in Neo-Diasporic Communities

Marie Johanna Karner

Introduction: Diasporic Communities and Remittances

The technological innovations of the twenty-first century enable members of diasporic communities to share information, emotions, and money almost in real time. The resulting connections are decentered, lateral, and not solely "formed around a teleology of origin/return" (Clifford 1994, p. 306). Nevertheless, research on diasporic remittances often focuses on economic, social, cultural, and political relations along the origin-residence axis. Many studies tend to neglect multi-directional flows over time and their cohesive effects on diasporic communities.

Apart from this, remittance research indicates that remittance practices change (Meyer 2020), that the size of remittances depends on trust and intended use (Lianos and Pseiridis 2014), that remittances have moral dimensions (Simoni and Voirol 2020) as well as affective significance

M. J. Karner (✉)
Institute of Geography, Johannes Gutenberg University Mainz,
Mainz, Germany
e-mail: m.karner@geo.uni-mainz.de

S. Meyer, C. Ströhle (eds.), *Remittances as Social Practices and Agents of Change*,
https://doi.org/10.1007/978-3-030-81504-2_6

(Huennekes 2018), and that remittances partly mirror the social and political fragmentation of the homeland (Tabar 2014). The specifics are captured in framing "diasporic remittances" as "the outcome of a process of power struggle between home-bound actors *specific to the diaspora*" (Tabar 2020, p. 456, emphasis in original). Although these findings help to understand complex interdependencies, historical evidence is missing on the changing motivations of diasporic actors. Little is known about how their societal inclusion in their countries of residence influences diasporic remittances.

Despite multifaceted transformations, diasporic communities have not dissolved. Against this backdrop, a historical perspective on remittances based on the following questions enables a better understanding of bonding effects: which types of remittances are rather one-directional and which are reciprocal? Why do the types of remittances change over time? And how do remittances work as social glue or as a disruptive force in neo-diasporic communities? To answer these questions, I will here introduce the dynamic notion of *standing waves*, which provides a suitable metaphor of changing mutual and multi-directional material and immaterial remittance flows to analyze their impact on collective identity, group solidarity, shared practices, and emotionality. Taking into account the rhythm, amplitude, and directions of *standing waves*, I strive to characterize the dynamics of remittance transfers which seldom only increase or decrease over a period of time. *Standing waves* depict remittance transfer as a process, in constant interplay with financial support, material exchange, and emotional and social cohesion.

This chapter is divided into three parts: first, I will introduce the theoretical framework by conceptualizing the neo-diaspora as a "community of *standing waves*." Second, I will present my methodological framework and the research field. Finally, I will explore the historical dynamics of diasporic remittances circulating between Lebanon, Australia, and the USA as *standing waves*.

Theoretical Framework: Neo-Diaspora as a "Community of *Standing Waves*"

In view of the fundamental transformation of former ethnic groups, a new understanding of diaspora is useful to study the role of remittances. The theory of "neo-diasporic communities" (Karner 2021) stresses that their diffuse and permeable boundaries are defined by the understanding of knowledge orders, the adoption of emotional practices, the individual commitment to the community, the identification with collective (ethnic) identity elements, and shared interests. The neo-diasporic network often extends into different specialized fields of interaction potentially substituting homeland orientation. Thus, permanent transnational relations and one-directional remittances are not of crucial importance for a neo-diaspora. Likewise, the actual origin of a person is not decisive for belonging to a neo-diasporic community. Of significance is the commitment of individuals who establish institutions, occasions, and places for communication to enhance connectivity (Karner 2021, pp. 363–380).

To analyze diasporic remittances, it is useful to integrate a concept which abstracts the interaction of space and time in the digital age. The "space of flows" conceptualized by Castells (2004, p. 36) "is made of nodes and networks; that is, of places connected by electronically powered communication networks through which flows of information circulate and interact, which ensure the time-sharing of practices processed in such a space." The power system of a network is influenced by wider contexts and controlled by "programmers" determining the goals and "switchers" connecting different networks to share common goals (Castells 2004, pp. 31–34). These considerations can be applied to deterritorialized communities bound by common issues and orientations. This so-called translocal horizon of meaning reflects the connectivity of the local due to material and communicative flows that exceed national contexts (Hepp 2009, pp. 37–39). It is maintained by communication networks which exist transmedially through informal personal communication (e.g., chats) and self-produced media (e.g., magazines).

When combining "neo-diaspora" with the concept "space of flows," one should not just speak of "communities of flows" but, as the following analysis will reveal, more precisely of "communities of *standing waves.*" In physics, *standing waves* are produced by interference as a result of the superposition of two waves traveling in opposite directions. Their waveform does not move through space, but has nodes (zero amplitude) and antinodes (maximum amplitude) at fixed places without carrying energy away from the source. This metaphor is useful to illustrate that within neo-diasporic communities, certain material resources as well as normative structures (e.g., ideas, values, and beliefs), systems of practice (e.g., religious practices), and social capital, termed "social remittances" (Levitt

1998), are continuously and iteratively exchanged. Remittances circulate within multiple interlocking transnational networks, which is why the following analysis requires a "transnational gaze" (Levitt 2011, p. 12).

Methods and Context: A Multi-sited Approach and Historical Lens to Study *Standing Waves* Among Kfarsghabis

To better understand *standing waves* in their historical dynamics, I applied a multi-sited empirical approach. My empirical data was collected in the cities of Sydney (Australia), Easton (Pennsylvania, USA), Providence (Rhode Island, USA), and Dubai (United Arab Emirates) as well as in Kfarsghab, a Maronite village in the Wadi Qadisha (Holy Valley)[1] in the north of present-day Lebanon, to which most members of the selected case study relate their assumed common origin (see Fig. 6.1).

Fig. 6.1 The village of Kfarsghab with St. Mary's Church. (Photo taken by Karner, 2 July 2014)

[1] Since the late seventh century, the Holy Valley gave shelter to Maronites, an ethnoreligious group whose Eastern Catholic Church is in communion with Rome. During the reign of the Ottoman Empire, they stood under the protection of France and enjoyed special rights in the autonomous district of Mount Lebanon.

Emigration from Kfarsghab to the USA began in 1880, driven by poverty due to the fall in silk prices, poor harvests, and a massive population growth (Khater 2001). After the first family returned to Kfarsghab in 1884, further groups settled in New Orleans, Peoria, Pittsburgh, and St. Louis, sometimes via detours through Caribbean countries. Today, the majority of Kfarsghabis reside in Easton (approximately 350 families), where the first group arrived in 1901. Thirty years later, they opened their first Maronite Catholic Church as the centerpiece of community life to date. With at least 90 percent of the congregation claiming to be from Kfarsghab these days, some members founded the Kfarsghab Club in 2009. In Providence, by contrast, Kfarsghabis were only one of many Maronite groups that settled there. In 1911, they founded St. George Maronite Catholic Church in the Federal Hill district.

Emigration of Kfarsghabis to Australia started in 1887. After the first group found work in the Broken Hill mines, many followers earned their living as hawkers, (rail-)road construction workers, and agricultural laborers. After the outbreak of World War Two, many of them moved to Sydney, where other Lebanese immigrants had opened shops, department stores, and manufacturing plants as well as the first Maronite Catholic Church, built in Redfern in 1897. Between 1946 and 1955, the largest number of families from Kfarsghab arrived. Australia's open immigration policy caused a high population decline in the village. In 1952, the Australian Kfarsghab Lebanese Association Ltd. (AKLA) was founded in Sydney as the successor to a charitable organization which had become inactive. Additionally, the Mar Awtel Charity Fund was established in 1964.

Today, about 90 percent of Kfarsghabis live abroad. Their absolute number is estimated at between 16,000 and 20,000.[2] Those who migrated to countries like Brazil, the United Kingdom, and New Zealand did not establish organizational structures equivalent to those in Easton, Providence, and Sydney. In comparison to other Lebanese neo-diasporic communities, Kfarsghabis are considered one of the most loyal and economically successful.

In Lebanon, the Organization of Kfarsghab Solidarity (OKS) has implemented projects in Kfarsghab and Morh Kfarsghab since 1962. Morh Kfarsghab was acquired in the middle of the eighteenth century as winter dwelling in lower lands near the coast. This caused a seasonal migration

[2] In 1977, it was estimated that 8000 Kfarsghabians lived in Australia, 2000 in the USA, 500 in other countries, and 1000 in Kfarsghab itself (AKLA Silver Jubilee booklet, p. 11). This data is probably exaggerated, as the current e-mail list of the Australian Kfarsghab Association (AKA) covers only 1296 households.

between the two villages, where olive groves and orchards provide revenues for the majority of residents to this day. Currently, the government school in Morh Kfarsghab also educates the children of Syrian agricultural workers who brought their families when the Syrian civil war began in 2011.

I employed a historical lens to interpret the self-produced media collected at the locations introduced above and to analyze the information shared via digital communication platforms. Such sources can only be understood properly by integrating references to past contexts and local conditions. The magazine *AKLA News* (Australian Kfarsghab Lebanese Association News, AN), which was published between 1968 and 2000 up to three times a year in Sydney, constitutes the main source in this chapter. Most importantly, it compiled success stories about its members. I analyzed 43 out of 49 issues, as well as several jubilee and memorial booklets.[3] I gleaned further information from websites and blogs, which gained popularity in the 2000s, as well as from the following Facebook groups (FB), which I observed regularly and searched for keywords: Kfarsghab Lebanon (KL, founded on 2 May 2012, 1695 members), Australian Kfarsghab Association (AKA,[4] founded on 18 May 2012, 1774 members), and Our Lady of Lebanon Church—Easton (OLOL, founded on 18 August 2010, 1854 members). [5] This material is complemented by recorded qualitative interviews with 55 Kfarsghabis, 17 experts (e.g., priests and consuls), and 2 group interviews conducted between 2014 and 2018. When interview statements are referenced in the text below, the place of residence rather than the place of the interview is given in parentheses before the date to contextualize the statements. Moreover, formal speeches and communal practices were observed at more than 40 events and gatherings. Using a qualitative content analysis, I inductively generated seven main categories of remittances, which I further differentiated with the help of MAXQDA.

[3] The historical information cited here, unless otherwise indicated, is taken from *AKLA News*.

[4] The AKA originated as a merger of the AKLA and the Organisation of Australian Kfarsghab Solidarity (OAKS) founded in 1961. Many Kfarsghabians participated in the events of both associations.

[5] The mentioned membership figures refer to 23 January 2021.

Standing Waves over Time: "We Continue to Enjoy a Bond that is as Strong Today as When our Families Lived through Great Migration Adventures" (FB_KL, 6 April 2014)

The following analysis of financial and material resources as well as information, narratives, emotions, and visits exchanged among Kfarsghabis will help to understand why changes in the quantity and significance of remittances occur over time.

Remittance Money for Infrastructure: "Kfarsghab Will Become a Model Village" (AN, 1971/3, p. 16)

Donations for churches and cemeteries in Kfarsghab and Morh Kfarsghab have a long history. In 1927, two priests visited emigrants abroad to collect contributions for a new church in Kfarsghab. It is said that "most of the money was raised in one night" (AN, 1971/2, p. 17). Beyond that, the completion of St. Mary's Church was funded by visiting emigrants who also paid for the interior, including the altar, font, statues of saints, and pews (see Fig. 6.2). These donations were and are recognizable by donor plaques, stone engravings, and reports in *AKLA News*. In addition, numerous private functions like barbecues with up to 500 guests were organized to aid the churches. Further money was given to the parish of Kfarsghab in the form of inheritance, for example, A$254,000 in 1988 by a member who bequeathed the same amount to his Latin Church[6] in Sydney. To build a youth center in Kfarsghab, A$126,000 was sent by AKLA and OAKS in the year 2000. Between 1964 and 1998, Mar Awtel Charity spent the total amount of $327,954 for the restoration of churches, a church hall, and a hearse. A cooling system for a morgue was donated to allow burials to be postponed until relatives from abroad could arrive. Hence, the implementation of new technologies and investments in the built environment led to a transformation of customs and architecture in Kfarsghab. Simultaneously, they contributed to the visibility of spirituality and protected an active communal life, thus working as social glue.

Money was also invested in infrastructure in North Lebanon. In the 1920s and 1930s, Kfarsghabi emigrants backed the Qadisha Power

[6] Due to the White Australian policy dominant from the 1880s to the 1920s, many first-generation immigrants became members of Anglican or Latin Churches.

Fig. 6.2 The construction of St. Mary's Church in Kfarsghab, 1948. (Photo provided by James Haddad)

Company for hydroelectric energy, controlled by one of Lebanon's leading political families from their village, known as Estephan Family (Mokarzel 1933, p. 6). This resulted in electricity being introduced to Kfarsghab and Morh Kfarsghab relatively early. In later years, between

World War Two and the turn of the millennium, Kfarsghabis overseas financially and strategically supported the establishment of a post office, a public phone, generators, cable networks, and new streetlights. Moreover, the limestone terrain in situ required various strategies to supply drinking water to every house (e.g., drilling, reservoirs, pumps, or pipes). Farmland was upgraded with irrigation channels and with roads and bridges when agricultural improvements were viewed as "so vital to the livelihood of our relatives in Lebanon" (AN, 1987/1, p. 8).

These projects were managed by municipal and local councils as well as by the OKS, despite the administrative difficulties posed by the Lebanese civil war [7] from 1975 to 1990. Usually, successful projects were promoted by members in the diaspora in exaggerated terms. Yet, in some cases, they rated the project management as poor, accompanied by doubts about money leakage: "When they started the church hall, [the residents] said we need $300,000. After it was finished it cost $650,000. All the people who live abroad, they don't understand that. They have a very big question mark about that" (Mayor, Kfarsghab, 27 August 2014). The unrealistic perceptions of the emigrants and their accusations about the implementation processes, costs, and effects express misunderstandings and tensions between local leaders and donors from overseas.

Compared to the civil war years, remittance money for projects decreased after 2000. According to a young businessman who grew up in Kfarsghab before leaving Lebanon to study abroad and work in a Gulf state, this was not only due to the world financial crisis of 2007/2008:

> In the old days, money was sent much easier. Now there is always, you know, second guessing: 'Should we send? Do they really need it? Who is in charge?' [...] We've had lots of trust problems before. There have been many projects, but because there is no transparency, this is *the problem [emphasized]*, then suspicion appears and it becomes very complicated, because we are such a small community. (Anonymous, Kfarsghab, 18 July 2014)

[7] Clashes between the Phalangists, a Christian militia, with Palestinian factions over the latter's armed struggle against the Israeli occupation from Lebanese territory were followed by battles over the Lebanese state and its political system. Caused by several highly interconnected internal factors (e.g., Maronite hegemony as well as social and economic disparities) and external conditions (e.g., the question of Palestine), the alliances among Lebanese groups and external actors shifted constantly.

Apart from financial support, many early emigrants used their savings to buy property which expanded the village boundaries. The restoration of 65 old buildings and the construction of 72 new buildings between 1980 and 1994, some of which constituted palatial houses, was largely financed from abroad by members who thereby developed Kfarsghab "especially as a summer resort" (AN, 1974/2, p. 12). This trend continued until the mid-2000s, when recessions overseas sparked interest in the sale of land. To counteract this development, community leaders kept reminding members to register their children with the Lebanese embassies to enable the inheritance of land: "Kfarsghabis in Australia and USA, let's keep our flame bright! We encourage you to register as Lebanese to share Kfarsghab's magic with our future generations" (FB_KL, 18 September 2014).

Such appeals indicate that the preservation of Kfarsghab is a diminishing concern for future generations. Although the success of many community members as entrepreneurs (e.g., in the building sector and fruit trade in Sydney) and the number of high-level positions in all areas of employment (e.g., doctors and school directors) and society (e.g., politicians, judges, and priests) would allow for high future investments in infrastructure, remittance money is decreasing regardless of local needs. As I will show in the following, the (re-)construction of the neo-diasporic community has become detached from localities and transferred into the imaginary.

Knowledge, Medicine, and Sport: "Education in Lebanon is a Very Critical Tool" (AN, 1988/2, p. 31)

Education in Kfarsghab was highly dependent on remittances from Australia and the USA during the twentieth century. The first school for girls opened in Kfarsghab in 1931, followed by a girl's school in Morh Kfarsghab built in 1936 and later extended through donations (see Fig. 6.3). Moreover, emigrants decided to promote income opportunities and potential migration by paying teachers for English and sewing classes in Kfarsghab: "In Lebanon they will have had a basic training in skills which would enable them to pursue careers more promising than that of their forefathers; and if they decide to migrate, they will have proficiency in a language and skill training" (AN, 1970/1, p. 8). Training in sewing was only provided to girls and young women. This illustrates the gendered implications of remittances.

Fig. 6.3 School in Morh Kfarsghab with a "thank you" note for the committee in Australia, 1936. (Photo provided by Joseph Stephan)

In 1964, representatives of AKLA purchased a plot of land in Morh Kfarsghab for the construction of a secondary school. The plans were never realized despite their continuous enquiries to the Lebanese government and local council. With more success, they intervened in the 1970s when schools in Kfarsghab were to be closed. In the 1980s, money was even sent for textbooks and petrol to cover the inflationary transportation costs of teachers.

Members overseas tried to encourage tertiary education by monetary rewards for boys and girls with top marks in high school certificates in Kfarsghab and abroad. They also helped to pay for the college education of descendants of the Estephan family. As the only family from Kfarsghab who held a ministerial post and first represented North Lebanon in parliament in 1927, this support for the prestige of the honorable family receives special attention. The covering of tuition fees enabled the oldest son to graduate from the London School of Economics: "This was an opportunity for the community [overseas] to repay the family" (Scudder 2003). Until today, male descendants of the Estephan family are designated with the Arabic honorary title "sheikh" to acknowledge their present-day role as symbolic representatives of the Kfarsghabi community.

In 1969, AKLA bought a house in Kfarsghab to be used as a civic center. It was under the care of OKS until its sale in 1980 and provided a hall for up to 200 people, a health center, and an office. Its library was equipped with donations from Mar Awtel Charity and individual gifts "to provide the necessary books for the new generation of students in the town" (AN, 1996/1, p. 23). Books on law, politics, economics, journalism, and literature, as well as journals and periodicals, were intended to offer an integral education. The books as well as typewriters and photocopiers were moved to Morh Kfarsghab in the winter, as did the clinic established in 1971. Many of its medical supplies were brought by visiting emigrants. An ambulance was donated by a sponsor who promised to cover all future expenses. Furthermore, fundraisers for operations of two seriously sick girls were organized recently that raised $120,000 and $35,000, respectively.

"[T]o raise the status of Kfarsghab in Lebanon and overseas" (AN, 1972/1, p. 4), association services were also provided in Australia and the USA. Sponsorship, settlement assistance, and soft loans empowered immigrants arriving from Kfarsghab. In addition, the president of the AKLA established the Australian Lebanese Welfare Group of Parramatta in 1980 as a non-political and non-sectarian organization. He lobbied for resources, policies, and programs to enhance the integration of Muslims and Christians who arrived during the Lebanese civil war. Rising ethnic tensions and Lebanon's poor media image motivated leaders to "regain the solid reputation of the [Lebanese community in the] past" (AN, 1980/2, p. 11). With this in mind, they donated not only to aid organizations who looked after children with disabilities and needy people of their own community, but supported local churches, hospitals, and the cancer council in their countries of residence.

Sporting activities in country-specific disciplines are promoted in Australia and the USA as expressions of integration. In Sydney, the cricket club "AKA Crusaders" (founded in 1984) attracts many "non-Kfarsghabi" players these days, a fact that is highlighted to demonstrate the open and welcoming attitude of the Kfarsghabi community. Moreover, the AKA has organized a wide variety of annual tournaments (e.g., golf, touch football, cricket, netball, and the card game euchre) to date. In Easton, the Lebanese

American Athletic Association was founded in 1976 to hold yearly basketball tournaments. These activities are also transmitted to the youth in Kfarsghab. "[T]o promote sport in Kfarsghab" (AN, 1989/1, p. 21), donations were collected in Sydney during a function for the leading Kfarsghabi Rugby League hooker Benny Elias in 1989 after money had been sent in 1986 to purchase soccer equipment. In 2008, a basketball/ soccer pitch was opened in Kfarsghab on the initiative of the sheikh who mobilized Kfarsghabis overseas: "It was a real example of solidarity. Everybody came together, Kfarsghabis in Australia, USA, and Lebanon all came together for a project that was all-embracing, you know, it's for all the kids" (sheikh, Kfarsghab, 19 July 2014). The playground is used for sports, public screenings, and barbecues to this day.

Financial remittances to Kfarsghab remained relatively stable for many decades. One reason is the influx of new immigrants after World War Two, which revitalized social ties. Subsequently, transfers of money for infrastructure, education, medical care, and sport in the village temporarily increased, although many committed members had already successfully built their lives in the USA and Australia and encouraged the education of their children there.

Humanitarian Aid: "To Help Our Brothers and Sisters Abroad" (FB_KDF, 25 August 2020)

At the beginning of the Lebanese civil war, charitable projects were initiated "to aid the village community in Lebanon" (AN, 1975/2, p. 8). Financial remittances were sent by Mar Awtel Charity to buy staple foods and for medical treatments. Soon, humanitarian aid was extended to help over 500 refugees in Kfarsghab. In 1976, a special relief fund was created overseas to secure regular aid for food, clothing, and medicine in the village. In addition, money was given to Maronite institutions in Lebanon. To help persons with disabilities, orphans, and the elderly throughout the entire county, non-governmental organizations and foundations (e.g., the Lebanese Red Cross) were also supported. A national aid fund was also established by Kfarsghabis in 1985. This broader orientation to combat poverty and disease "irrespective of its origin throughout Australia and abroad" was formalized in the constitution of the AKA in 2001.

While humanitarian aid lost its urgency in the postwar decades, Lebanon's recent economic collapse calls for new initiatives. The Kfarsghab Diaspora Foundation (KDF) was founded on 5 June 2020 in response to the ongoing political, financial, and liquidity crisis in Lebanon, which has been compounded by the coronavirus. Altogether A$16,425 were collected through the crowdfunding platform GoFundMe to help families in Kfarsghab pay for electricity, pesticides, and food.

After the blast at the port of Beirut on 4 August 2020, members of the AKA in Sydney organized the freight of medicine and clothes donations. In Easton, the organization "Lehigh Valley for Lebanon" was initiated by a 23-year-old whose mother grew up in Kfarsghab. Backed by 18 Lebanese-owned businesses in the area who provided prizes for donors, she mobilized support for the victims of the disaster (see Fig. 6.4). Even Kfarsghabis in Lebanon distributed over 80 boxes of essential items and village products (e.g., olive oil) through the Maronite archdiocese of Beirut, despite their own crisis-related difficulties.

Material Objects and Symbols: "Just Make a Left into Paramatta Road When You Get to Kfarsghab" (AN, 1996/1, p. 24)

The local council of Kfarsghab decided to name the main road in the village Parramatta Road, on which the Parra Café is also located. These names refer to a western suburb of Sydney where many so-called Frozzies, a portmanteau of "Kfarsghabi" and "Ozzie" (Australian), live. A Parramatta councilor from Kfarsghab proposed this idea. The inauguration ceremony in Kfarsghab in 1995 was attended by Lebanese officials and nine Australian federal and state parliamentarians (see Fig. 6.5). In Easton, a street was named after Michael J. Khoury to honor a Kfarsghabi district judge and community leader in the USA.

Until today, the transnational lives of Kfarsghabis are accompanied by the permanent presence of national symbols. American and Australian flags wave over the roofs in Kfarsghab. In Sydney, Easton, and Providence, one encounters Lebanese flags in private spaces or hoisted at clubs and during Lebanese festivals. National flags are also wrapped around coffins to express the patriotic feelings of the deceased. In 2001, an Australian flag covered a coffin of a deceased community leader who passed away during his visit to Kfarsghab.

In their countries of residence, the respective national anthem is played at all formal gatherings, followed by the Lebanese one. Likewise, toasts are always given first to the respective head of state and second to the Lebanese president. Many present-day logos follow this principle, like the AKA emblem, which depicts the five stars of the Southern Cross on the top and

Fig. 6.4 The initiator of the organization "Lehigh Valley for Lebanon" (center, hands raised) with a group of participants of the larger "Stand up for Lebanon" demonstration in Centre Square in Easton, 9 August 2020. The posters blame political negligence for the explosion in the port of Beirut, call on the Lebanese government to resign, and express solidarity with the victims. The demonstrators' claims for justice correspond to the symbolism of the Soldiers and Sailors Monument in the background, which is transformed into the allegedly world's largest Peace Candle each year during the Christmas season. (This image is used with the permission of Ally Karam, 9 August 2020)

a cedar on the bottom. Earlier illustrations, like the cover of an issue of *AKLA News* from 1970, express a strong emotional connection to Kfarsghab (see Fig. 6.6). Such images became dominant in the 1970s when multicultural policies and antiracist discourses arose. They also reflect the fear of losing one's identification, norms, and values. Elderly members saw their lifestyle threatened by the permissive environment influencing the youth: "If we do not take enough care, we will gradually lose our tradition and national identity in our new environment of excessive individual freedom" (AN, 1975/2, p. 3).

Fig. 6.5 The inauguration ceremony of Parramatta Road in Kfarsghab (top) and the sign today (bottom). (Top photo provided by Antonio Jabbour from Joe Barakat's personal archive, bottom photo taken by Karner, 9 July 2017)

Before electronic communications prevailed, *AKLA News* was received by association members worldwide and praised as "undoubtedly something very valuable in its attempt to keep the people of Kfarsghab, in Lebanon and abroad, informed and in touch with each other" (AN, 1970/3, p. 19). Jubilee booklets about the achievements of Kfarsghabis were also handed out to government officials to advance the members' lobbying efforts in Australia and the USA. They were even given to

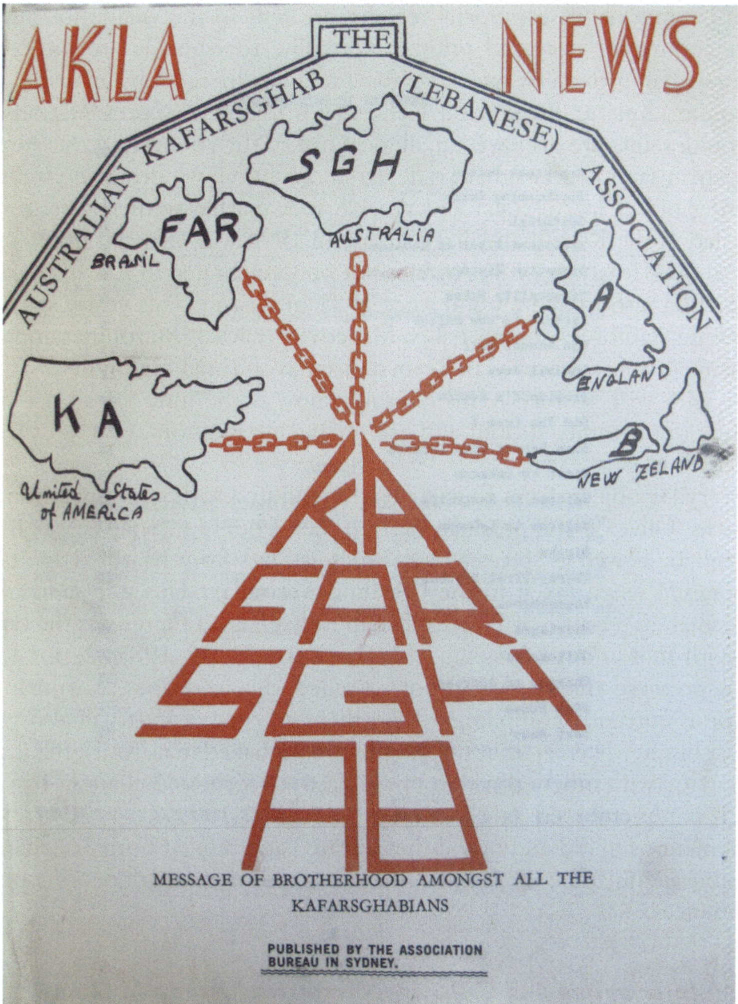

Fig. 6.6 Cover of *AKLA News*, 1970. (Magazine provided by Ray Abraham, photo taken by Karner, 23 December 2014)

newspaper editors to counter defamatory articles in the local press. If such articles were reprinted in *AKLA News*, which is rather rare, their non-representativeness and the damage they inflict on the community was severely criticized in the framing remarks.

In exceptional cases, mortal remains are sent to the village for burial, most commonly deceased priests. Normally, Kfarsghabis are buried in close spatial proximity overseas, for example, in sections named after Maronite saints at Rookwood Cemetery in Sydney. Representations of Maronite saints are displayed at all locations of the community. St. Awtel, the patron saint of Kfarsghab, is depicted on church windows and walls of meeting places in Australia and the USA. A marble statue of St. Awtel unveiled in the Kfarsghab village square in 1996 was financed by a family abroad. The feast day of St. Awtel is not only celebrated in Kfarsghab, but since 1964 also in Sydney and since 1981 in Easton. This yearly spiritual gathering reinforces commonality. Moreover, relics of Maronite saints are exchanged transnationally and experienced as spiritual highlights: "To all those who wish to receive his blessings, now is the time for a once in a lifetime opportunity to join and ask for his intercession" (FB_OLOL, 9 March 2016).

Everyday objects from Kfarsghab are attributed with symbolic meaning overseas. Olive oil and products derived therefrom (e.g., soap), Arak from Kfarsghab, as well as spices and Lebanese sweets from nearby Tripoli are reappraised when taken to the USA and Australia: "This gift, ladies and gentleman, is a bottle of arak distilled in Kfarsghab. It represents the binding spirit that unites Kfarsghab with Parramatta" (AN, 1988/2, p. 12).

To preserve the knowledge of so-called village recipes, a woman in Easton is currently compiling a Kfarsghabian cookbook. It will also contain dishes newly created in the diaspora (e.g., baked macaroni), thanks to interaction with other ethnic groups in Easton's former "Lebanese Town," which is remembered as a "melting pot" (AN, 1999/1, p. 20). These combinations of old and new dishes, created and refined both in Lebanon and abroad, illustrate the circular, hybrid operation mode of neo-diasporic remittances.

Information and Collective Narratives: "News and Gossip of the Community at Large" (AN, 1999/1, p. 24)

Kfarsghabis used to exchange information via letters, telegrams, telephones, recorded cassettes, photographs, and videos, except during episodes of war, when communications services stopped. For many decades, *AKLA News* did not only inform about community news, events (e.g., debutante balls or "haflis"), and projects, but listed newlyweds, parents of newborns, graduates, and deaths in Australia, the USA, and Lebanon:

"The Kfarsghabi magazine is the news link and the bearer of greetings and love among the Kfarsghabi people in the homeland and abroad" (AN, 1974/3, p. 3). Produced in Australia, the magazine reaffirmed conventions and commonalities among its readers worldwide without obscuring differences in lifestyle: "It softens the edges and allows the American reader to glimpse the life of a transplanted community very much like his or her own, yet significantly different in ways that pertain to social customs and institutions" (AN, 1998/1, p. 31).

Early issues reconstructed the history of both villages and of the "five founding families." The migration history from Kfarsghab included lists of emigrant groups and personal anecdotes. General information on Lebanon was added with the outbreak of the civil war, particularly glorifying the historical achievements of Maronites. In addition to the magazine, lectures about Kfarsghab and Lebanon began to be held in the 1970s. On this foundation, members in the USA and Australia discussed war incidents and village issues with visitors from Lebanon: "[T]he visitors expressed their views on what they regard to be the most important project for Kfarsghab" (AN, 1973/1, p. 15). Exhibitions on the achievements of Kfarsghabis were organized in Sydney in 2007 and 2012, followed by a historical display on Lebanese immigrants in Northampton County in Easton's Sigal Museum in 2019.

Text extracts of *AKLA News* are reused on websites and in social media to this day, illustrated with historical pictures, documents, and newspaper clippings. The administrators of the Kfarsghab Lebanon Facebook group reside in Kfarsghab, Sydney, and Easton. By portraying successful individuals in business, sports, politics, science, and the clergy, they (re-)construct role models in a similar manner to magazines and exhibitions. One example is a real estate investor who was also a columnist for the Arabic-language daily *Al-Hoda* in New York City. The many appreciative comments reflect communal pride: "[H]is experiences, his stories, his knowledge and his contacts were vast. He was widely loved and always will be" (FB_KL, 24 April 2014). In general, the deceased are idealized by reference to their commitment to family, integration, hospitality, and other traits: "Our uncle […] was a true pioneer. He migrated to Australia in 1922 at the age of 19. He worked extremely hard and achieved great success in his business ventures. He was well known for his generosity and strong faith" (FB_KL, 29 May 2015). By contrast, counter-narratives about Kfarsghabis are mainly told face-to-face and only hinted at in social media: "A controversial figure for several reasons but also a highly successful one, in business at least" (FB_KL, 3 July 2015).

Personal strengths are ascribed to one's believed descent from Kfarsghab bearing witness to its unique location: "He was born in Kfarsghab and breathed vitality from its breezes and drank from its waters strength and tenacity" (AN, 1984/1, p. 14). To reconstruct the lineages of the founding families, the Kfarsghab Australian Family Tree Association (KAFTA) was founded in 2012: "I'm fascinated by the history of the village, by the notion of the five families. It's who we are, it's our roots. And if you don't write it down, it's gone. And it's gone forever" (Founder Kfarsghab Club, Easton, 28 July 2015). KAFTA provides an online portal to enter and search for genealogical data (10,460 entries, 23 January 2021). The database functions to verify the central collective narrative of a common origin with the help of modern technology and pseudo-scientific methods.

In pre-digital information sources, conventional values linked to ancestors were framed as essential for integration: "We have a moral obligation to transmit the values and customs [...] which our forefathers struggled to give us. [...] He who rejects his origin and background is not likely to be faithful to his new adopted country and human values, especially religious ones" (AN, 1975/2, p. 3). In the past two decades, appeals became louder to counter the increasing number of family breakups, whereas before, members were predominantly asked to eliminate disunity and personal conflicts. The following moral imperative is constantly stressed: "We shall [...] remain loyal to our new country. We shall respect and uphold the constitutions, laws and traditions" (AN, 2000/1, p. 30).

Emotions: "Joy Shared is Joy Multiplied. Grief Shared is Grief Divided" (FB administrator, Sydney, 21 August 2015)

Joyful events are occasions to experience solidarity and commonality: "The laughter, smiles, hugs, kisses, and pure joy on people's faces were priceless. What a great festival!!!" (FB_KL, 6 August 2018). Especially when performing the folk dance Dabke at weddings and festivals, a group feeling is mobilized due to the physical closeness and synchronous sequence of steps.

Social cohesion is also strongly felt during condolences, funerals, and at the annual mass for the souls of all deceased Kfarsghabis. In cases of death, up to three requiem masses are celebrated by relatives living in different locations: "A lot of us still have those same common roots. And like I said, a death there is just like a death here" (student, Easton, 2 August 2015). Today, obituaries are shared via the communities' Facebook groups and receive numerous sympathy comments and grief-expressing emojis. This emotional care among members existed before Web 2.0: "My sincere thanks again especially to those abroad, who sent us telegrams, letters, cards and telephone calls of comfort" (AN, 1977/1, p. 34). Expressing condolences, caring for the sick, and congratulating on weddings, births, and baptisms are linked to the social norm of "wejbet," meaning, in the words of one interview partner: "You have to do your duties!" (motel owner, Sydney, 11 August 2014). Although solidarity practices are based on reciprocity, occasional or temporary and even permanent or long-term abandonment are nowadays accepted, so that (re-)joining the community is possible at any time.

Moreover, feelings of appreciation, gratitude, and responsibility are linked to patriotism and are exchanged among members. As early as 1919, emigrants acknowledged the sheikhs as prominent advocates of Kfarsghab with the following lines:

> No one who has watched closely the untiring efforts and never-failing kindness, hospitality, and consideration can entertain a doubt that they are competent, efficient, and zealous, and always ready to help their fellow-townsmen, morally and financially, and they are worthy of our confidence and esteem. (Display at Beit Estephan)

Decades later, demonstrations were held in the USA and letters were sent to Lebanese authorities and the UN to end the civil war. Furthermore, members abroad expressed appreciation to the El-Marada militia for fighting "for a free democratic Lebanon" (AN, 1976, p. 19). The patriotic and financial support from overseas was acknowledged by residents in Kfarsghab, who implicitly expressed their expectation of its continuation: "We appreciate the quick response to our plight [...]. We always feel confident in your determination and co-operation to assist your brothers in your birth place every time we face a problem or crisis" (AN, 1994/1, p. 11).

In Easton, Providence, and Sydney, Kfarsghabis express their gratitude for the opportunities received and credit local politicians for supporting their projects. Moreover, they praise God for being blessed with happiness, success, and health, and thank St. Awtel for protection. Associated with this, Kfarsghabis share a feeling of being privileged: "I definitely feel a very strong sense of pride and a deep connection to come from this village" (banker, Sydney, 19 July 2014).

Visitors: "[A] Most Pleasant Holiday and Happy Reunion with their Relatives and Friends" (AN, 1972/2, p. 18)

In the 1960s and 1970s, invitations were sent by the OKS hoping that Kfarsghabis would "come and enjoy the hospitality and generosity of [their] beautiful homeland" (AN, 1974/1, p. 13). Functions and picnics have been organized for visitors ever since. In 1977, a Kfarsghabi world traveler visited the village, which had been completely spared by the civil war:

> I had only planned to stay an afternoon. I never left Kfarsghab for 21 days. Kfarsghab became one of the best times of my travels. I was tired, and sick, and starving, and had almost no money. They looked after me like a father and a mother. I fattened up on the best food I have ever eaten. (AKA Exhibition, 2012)

In the first decade after the war, the visitor numbers grew to 200 annually as the perception of Lebanon as a battleground diminished: "Every year was like multiplying, multiplying, but due to all the geopolitical problems we had, people have hit the brakes" (sheikh, Kfarsghab, 19 July 2014). Visitors not only stay in Kfarsghab with their relatives and friends, but visit churches and monasteries, historical sites, "souks" (markets), and shopping malls, and enjoy the northern beaches and nightlife in the coastal cities Batroun, Byblos, Jounieh, and Beirut. However, spiritual and social activities in the refreshing summer village stand out for all the visitors: "Including myself, the people of Kfarsghab feel at ease when they are praying. [...] Kfarsghab also holds many different activities and events. [...] These occasions make us become very social with one another" (FB_KL, 2 October 2014).

Visits to Kfarsghab enhance the identification of young and new members: "Each trip rewards me with new friends (and, inevitably, new branches on the family tree), a few local words to add to my limited vocab, and a renewed sense of belonging" (blogpost, 28 July 2015). Ostensibly "centuries-old traditions" (FB_KL, 25 August 2014) attract visitors to Kfarsghab, who celebrate the annual feast day "in the Lebanese style with 'tubble and zammer' [the drum and the horn] and folk dance" (AN,

1973/3, p. 24). With the motto "one village, many stories," the first annual dinner in honor of Kfarsghab's diaspora was held in 2018 by the municipality, which was intended to reinforce bonds: "It is vital for us. [...] The second, third and fourth generation is not interested in coming back to Lebanon. They know nothing about it" (mayor, Kfarsghab, 27 August 2014). While the popularity of visits to Kfarsghab is decreasing, the place is increasingly envisioned as sacred and paradisiacal: "[T]hat beautiful village clinging to the cliffs of the holy valley of Kadisha and so near to the eternal Cedars of Lebanon" (AN, 1995/1, p. 6).

When traveling became an accessible activity, Kfarsghabis also flew between Easton, Providence, and Sydney for their honeymoons and to attend weddings, funerals, and other significant events. In the past, transnational travels were meticulously documented in *AKLA News*, whereas today photos and live videos on Facebook and Instagram fulfill this function. In 2000, a Kfarsghabi reunion was organized in Lincoln, Rhode Island. This event was not repeated, by contrast to the Lebanese Heritage Days that have taken place in Easton since 1978: "Every year visitors to the celebration come from as far as California to Florida, Lebanon and Australia" (FB_OLOL, 28 July 2017). Visitors between Australia and the USA exchange views on the challenges faced by their local communities. During their visits, they also used to convince relatives to contribute to large infrastructure projects in Kfarsghab when these were funded on a large scale.

Banquets, parties, and receptions are held to welcome community representatives (e.g., presidents of associations, sheikhs, and mayors), politicians, Christian clergymen, nuns, as well as influential businessmen. Early festive dinners date back to 1928, when the later Member of Parliament Sheikh Youssef Estephan was delegated to visit the Lebanese emigrants for a report entitled "Number of emigrants, their intellectual advancement and their habits" (AKA Exhibition, 2012) (see Fig. 6.7). After his death in 1947, community leaders from Australia and the USA established closer relationships to political leaders from the neighboring Zgharta District when they visited Lebanon: "[The AKLA ex-president] had an official meeting with the President, Suleiman Frangieh, and thanked him for supporting the projects under construction in Kfarsghab" (AN, 1975/2, p. 7). Personal relations with decision makers ("wasta") are crucial to securing approvals and government funds. Lebanon's political system is based on clientelism, which is why political parties even fly supporters to Lebanon to partake in elections (Tabar 2014, p. 453).

Fig. 6.7 Dinner in honor of the Member of Parliament Youssef Estephan from Lebanon, Book Cadillac Hotel Detroit, 1928. (Picture displayed at Beit Estephan in Kfarsghab, photo taken by Karner, 16 July 2014)

Conversely, Australian and American politicians and state representatives with and without Lebanese ancestry attend community functions in Sydney, Easton, or Providence. They even travel to selected villages in Lebanon to appeal to voters with Lebanese ancestry in their electoral districts. In 1980, the Australian Commissioner for Community Relations published an article in *The Australian* after his visit to Lebanon explaining that Kfarsghab "boasts the largest proportion of Lebanese immigrants to Australia than any other place in Lebanon" (AN, 1980/2, p. 27). These days, potential voters are informed by politicians via brochures and social media posts: "In Kfarsghab I met [the] Mayor and many members of the community and visited the local bakery next to the church. The holy valley of Qadisha was home to many local people" (Finn 2016, p. 2).

Conclusion: *Standing Waves* as Social Glue in Neo-Diasporic Communities

The diverse orientation, persistence, and meaning of remittances in neo-diasporic contexts require a new and accurate conceptualization. Different types of remittances move continuously and iteratively in opposite and multiple directions. This creates superpositions of *standing waves* that uninterruptedly reach and connect members. Even if certain types flow rather in one direction, the reciprocal and multi-directional exchange of other types makes the notion of the imagined place of origin as a dependent location obsolete. *Standing waves* not only exist along the origin-residence axis, but potentially between and within all locations where members reside.

In everyday lived experience, the wavelength (or rhythm) and amplitude of reciprocal waves vary over time, meaning that the regularity and amount of money, (practical) knowledge, medicine, humanitarian aid, objects, symbols, information, narratives, norms, ideas, emotions, and visitors differ. Flags and signs are visible indicators of prevailing or past *standing waves*, whereas information and stories are rather invisible indications. They are shared via magazines, social media, and personal communication, and locally through seminars and exhibitions. Patriotic symbols, everyday goods, and practical knowledge transcend the boundaries of nation states and express hybrid, transnational lifestyles, and belongings.

Not only the rhythm and amplitude of *standing waves* changes, but also the dominance and orientation of material and immaterial resources. The composition depends on the economic and politic (in-)stability in the country and place of origin, the degree of societal inclusion in the country of residence, local, and global crises, as well as the communicative connectivity of members and the commitment of individuals. The findings of my research show that decreases in financial remittances to Lebanon are caused by a complex interplay of an assumed lower demand, as well as a lack of transparency, trust, and fewer initiatives. This is linked to the tendency that the material existence of the imagined place of origin loses importance for members who never physically stayed there, which goes hand in hand with its attribution as a "sacred location" (Escher 2008, p. 23). In addition, money is increasingly used to build and expand meeting places in the countries of residence. Clubs and churches are reproduced structures of the imagined origin that allow for bonding and spiritual and transcendent experiences overseas.

The historical perspective further discloses that certain flows have always moved in multiple directions. Nevertheless, the speed at which material and immaterial resources are transmitted has changed. Thanks to innovations in technology, money, information, and emotions can reach the recipient almost in real time. The features of social media platforms allow for immediate communication, which has strengthened the ties among members. Moreover, diasporic remittances are based on moral obligations, but follow a rather voluntary principle compared to familial remittances. This means that commitment to the community is rewarded by recognition, while individual temporary, occasional, long-term, or permanent restraints from solidary practices are accepted. This permits (re-) integration into the community at any time.

While customs are being revived abroad, the popularity of country-specific sports has been transferred to Kfarsghab. Simultaneously, this place is idealized as authentic and untouched by members overseas although there, as well, social conventions, norms, and values are fading. To meet the expectations of visitors who aim to deepen their understanding of traditions, certain cultural practices (e.g., cooking and dancing) are being revived in modified ways or newly introduced. Such traditionalizing effects on the village are not accepted uncritically especially by those local residents who want to be perceived as innovative and future-oriented.

The concept "space of flows" (Castells 2004) is useful to disclose the dynamic power system and tensions within neo-diasporic communities. If leaders in the imagined place of origin seem not dedicated enough, it is not uncommon that members abroad try to become "programmers." They take decisions on how to improve the conditions for the residents who are expected to manage the projects on site. In the digital world, communication flows can emanate from all members independent of their financial means. Hence, the internet has empowering effects and enables the emergence of new "programmers." These respected leaders use their social, cultural, and economic capital to engage with local decision makers hoping for a faster realization of projects. If they implement goals and increase resources through cooperation, they function as "switchers" and generate benefits beyond their community. In their countries of residence, they participate in all sectors of society. They are committed to reducing racist discrimination, stereotypes, and obstacles to integration, while attempting to enhance tolerance and prestige. However, both interaction and diasporic remittances partly reflect social and political frictions in the homeland with a tendency of re-remitting divisions and conflicts. Conversely, tours by politicians through countries of origin of former migrants mainly have the strategic intention to gain voters from neo-diasporic communities in their electoral districts.

Standing waves and thus the rhythm of remitting are essential for the (re-)construction of collective identities and to counteract the loss of norms and values. Stories about role models and communal advancements emphasize themes like ambition, success, faith, pride, and mutual support. Thereby, hospitality, family orientation, generosity, loyalty, and law abidance are mediated as the basis for similarities in everyday life, socialized or learned group solidarity, and integration. Important occasions to experience joy, grief, cultural reaffirmation, and spiritual commonality are festivities which take place at all locations. The expression of sympathy has a high significance and is communicated face-to-face and digitally with the help of emojis. Today, gratitude is expressed mostly for emotional support and rarely for financial assistance to the imagined place of origin, which over time was subject to sacralization. This is accompanied by the diminishing importance of its material existence for members in the diaspora.

Overall, the transformation of a diaspora into a neo-diaspora bound by an imagined ethnic identity is expressed in emotionality, solidarity, spirituality, shared practices, and interests as well as local business and political ties. This transformation explains changes in the dominant type of remittances. Especially symbols, information, collective narratives, and emotions determine *standing waves* between and within the locations of a neo-diaspora. The omnipresence of waves functions as social glue in neo-diasporic communities, while the imagined place of origin becomes a sacred place for the majority of members: "Kfarsghab is not the stone and mortar, it is the spirit and the people" (AN, 1996/1, p. 27).

Acknowledgments I would like to thank the German Research Foundation (DFG) for financing the project "Lebanese Global Villages: Practices of Reproduction and Constitution of Global Communities." My sincere gratitude goes to my interview partners, who provided access to documents and social media platforms of their communities.

References

Castells, M. (2004). Informationalism, Networks, and the Network Society: A Theoretical Blueprint. In M. Castells (Ed.), *The Network Society: A Cross-Cultural Perspective* (pp. 3–45). Elgar.

Clifford, J. (1994). *Diasporas. Cultural Anthropology, Further Inflections: Towards Ethnographies of the Future, 9*(3), 302–338.

Escher, A. (2008). The Arab American Way: The Success Story of an American Family from a Syrian Village in Global Diaspora. *American Studies Journal, 52.* www.asjournal.org/archive/52/152.html.

Finn, J. (2016, July). A Newsletter from Julia Finn MP, Your State Member for Granville. Community Delegation Goes to Lebanon, Special Issue. Granville Gazette.

Hepp, A. (2009). Digitale Medien, Migration und Diaspora: Deterritoriale Vergemeinschaftung jenseits nationaler Integration. In U. Hunger & K. Kissau (Eds.), *Internet und Migration: Theoretische Zugänge und empirische Befunde*. Medien—Kultur—Kommunikation (pp. 33–51). VS Verlag für Sozialwissenschaften.

Huennekes, J. (2018). Emotional Remittances in the Transnational Lives of Rohingya Families Living in Malaysia. *Journal of Refugee Studies, 31*(3), 353–370.

Karner, M. J. (2021). *Neo-diasporische Gemeinschaften: Blouzaniyye in Sydney, Australien*. Franz Steiner Verlag.

Khater, A. F. (2001). *Inventing Home: Emigration, Gender, and the Middle Class in Lebanon, 1870–1920*. University of California Press.

Levitt, P. (1998). Social Remittances: Migration Driven Local-Level Forms of Cultural Diffusion. *The International Migration Review, 32*(4), 926–948.

Levitt, P. (2011). A Transnational Gaze. *Migraciones Internacionales, 6*(1), 9–44.

Lianos, T. P., & Pseiridis, A. (2014). I Trust, Therefore I Remit? An Examination of the Size and Motivation of Remittances. *Journal of Ethnic and Migration Studies, 40*(4), 528–543.

Meyer, S. (2020). "Home Is Where I Spend My Money": Testing the Remittance Decay Hypothesis with Ethnographic Data from an Austrian-Turkish Community. *Social Inclusion, 8*(1), 275–284.

Mokarzel, S. A. (1933, November 24). Qadisha Power Now in Trouble. *The Syrian World*, 6.

Scudder, G. (2003, January 19). Easton Church Meets Student it Supported. *The Morning Call.*

Simoni, V., & Voirol, J. (2020). Remittances and Morality: Family Obligations, Development, and the Ethical Demands of Migration. *Journal of Ethnic and Migration Studies*, 1–21.

Tabar, P. (2014). "Political Remittances": The Case of Lebanese Expatriates Voting in National Elections. *Journal of Intercultural Studies, 35*(4), 442–460.

Tabar, P. (2020). Transnational is Not Diasporic: A Bourdieusian Approach to the Study of Modern Diaspora. *Journal of Sociology, 56*(3), 455–471.

PART II

Migrants as Game Changers: Rethinking Collectivity and Agency of Remittances

Aside from individual earmarking, remittances represent collective aspirations on an economic, social, and political level. Migrants are game changers and by sending money, ideas, health advice, and objects for daily use, they change more than their own household and family life in both their places of origin and residence (Glick Schiller 2010; Grabowska et al. 2017; Pitkänen et al. 2012). We therefore have to rethink the dynamic and transformative workings of remittances, especially on a collective level. On a micro-level, transformation occurs in "bundles," meaning that individual changes in practice are embedded in deeper values and attitudes and thus foster social change through their symbolic significance (White and Grabowska 2019). This section shows how remittance practices are influenced not only by individual senders and receivers but also by collectives, the nation state, and religious communities. Remitting is more than an individual choice, it is a social practice (Page and Mercer 2012). In looking at past and present remittance behaviors on multiple levels, we can also derive assumptions about the future of transnational networks, for example challenging the remittance decay hypothesis and replacing it with a more nuanced analysis of senders and receivers in their collective social contexts (Carling 2008; Meyer 2020; Orozco 2013). One of those contexts is Islamic charity: In her chapter, Marta Bivand Erdal analyzes how remittances and charity money overlap. What kind of money pays to take care of elders in transnational Muslim communities? Is it remittance money or *zakat*, the compulsory alms which Muslims are prescribed to offer annually? In Erdal's analysis, the confluence of remittances and transnational Islamic charity reveals the salience of relational, emotional, and material aspects. She thereby shows that space transcends not just the borders of nation states, but also between this world and the hereafter.

Collectivity is further represented in the form of the nation state in Hasan Mahmud's chapter. He examines the processuality, dynamics, and ambiguity of remittances, focusing on the transformation of sending practices by looking at the role of the destination state. Japan's restrictive immigration regime led to permanent settlement of migrants from Bangladesh but also family separation across borders. Subsequently, migrants remitted half of their earnings back home. By contrast, Bangladeshi migrants in the USA found themselves in a more inclusive environment, fostering permanent settlement, family reunification, and integration, leading to the portion of savings sent to Bangladesh being reduced to one-third of their income. Although ever more people live and work across borders, the nation state thus remains a powerful and decisive reference frame.

Remittances also have implications on an individual, household, and community level. This influence can be measured in social resilience and community projects relating to health and education, as the contributions by Eric Bayala and Eveline Odermatt show. Positive and negative effects of remittances are addressed here: While remittances promote social networks and participation, they can also weaken institutional structures and lead to dependencies along neocolonial lines. Health organizations distribute not just health infrastructure and knowledge in the countries of origin, but also function as pervasive neoliberal assemblages (Levitt and Rajaram 2013). Collective remittances are further earmarked with the motivation to engage in transnational support strategies. Drawing on interviews with Moldavian migrants in seven European countries, Odermatt carves out the multilayered motivations to remit, from social positioning and the feeling of being part of the host land through to past and current visions of Moldova, especially aiming to overcome the communist past through collective remittance practices. Thereby, the migrants have demarcated themselves from professional development aid, coining their contributions as acts of solidarity rather than charity and thus challenging the migration-development nexus.

Eric Bayala's chapter functions as a complement to Odermatt's study, exploring how collective remittances from abroad affect the places of origin and how they are perceived by the locals left behind. He shows the multilayered, connective, as well as disruptive effects of health infrastructure projects, which were initiated in the Centre-Est Region of Burkina Faso by diaspora hometown associations in Italy. Overall, access to healthcare improved, with women benefitting particularly. Remittances strengthened community resilience, but also increased dependency on the diaspora in Europe and decreased self-determined initiatives in situ.

Overall, these chapters carve out the ambiguity, transformability, and collectivity of remittances, conflating individual and collective perspectives in places of residence as well as origin. Remittance actors—meaning migrants, non-migrants, institutions, and governments—are agents of social change and contribute to better life conditions. At the same time, however, they drive restrictive migration regimes, thus fostering neocolonial and neoliberal tendencies of global inequality and (self)exploitation.

References

Carling, J. (2008). Toward a Demography of Immigrant Communities and Their Transnational Potential. *International Migration Review*, 42(2), 449–475. https://doi.org/10.1111/j.1747-7379.2008.00131.x

Glick Schiller, N. (2010). A Global Perspective on Migration and Development. In N. G. Schiller & T. Faist (Eds.), *Critical Interventions. Migration, Development, and Transnationalization: A Critical Stance* (pp. 14–37). Berghahn Books.

Grabowska, I., Garapich, M. P., Jaźwińska, E., & Radziwinowiczówna, A. (2017). *Migrants as Agents of Change*. Palgrave Macmillan UK. https://doi.org/10.1057/978-1-137-59066-4

Levitt, P., & Rajaram, N. (2013). Moving toward reform? Mobility, health, and development in the context of neoliberalism. *Migration Studies*, 1(3), 338–362. https://doi.org/10.1093/migration/mnt026

Meyer, S. (2020). 'Home Is Where I Spend My Money': Testing the Remittance Decay Hypothesis with Ethnographic Data from an Austrian-Turkish Community. *Social Inclusion*, 8(1), 275–284. https://doi.org/10.17645/si.v8i1.2435

Orozco, M. (2013). Migrant Remittances and Development in the Global Economy. Diasporas in World Politics. Lynne Rienner Publishers Inc.

Page, B. & Mercer, C. (2012). Why Do People Do Stuff? Reconceptualizing Remittance Behaviour in Diaspora-Development Research and Policy. *Progress in Development Studies* 12(1), 1–18.

Pitkänen, P., Içduygu, A., & Sert, D. (Eds.). (2012). International Perspectives on Migration: Vol. 3. Migration and Transformation: Multi-Level Analysis of Migrant Transnationalism. Springer.

White, A., & Grabowska, I. (2019). Social Remittances and Social Change in Central and Eastern Europe: Embedding Migration in the Study of Society. *Central and Eastern European Migration Review*, 8(1), 33–50. https://doi.org/10.17467/ceemr.2019.05

CHAPTER 7

The Confluence of Remittances and Transnational Islamic Charity

Marta Bivand Erdal

Introduction

The flows of remittances from migrants back to the societies and families in their places of origin have received substantial attention, not least as a result of interest in the migration-development nexus (Nyberg-Sørensen et al. 2002; Sørensen 2012; Maimbo and Ratha 2005). By contrast, the similarly large-scale flows of "transnational Islamic charity"—which also constitute private funds sent by migrants back to their communities and families, as voluntary or prescribed Islamic alms—have received far less attention both in academic and development circles in the Global North (notable exceptions include Benthall and Bellion-Jourda 2003; Benthall 2016).

This chapter explores this paradox and the underlying question about the confluence of migrant remittances and transnational Islamic charity. Are the two in fact the same flows of money, just called by different names? Are they distinct only in the eyes of the individuals involved, on the basis

M. B. Erdal (✉)
Peace Research Institute Oslo, Oslo, Norway
e-mail: marta@prio.org

S. Meyer, C. Ströhle (eds.), *Remittances as Social Practices and Agents of Change*,
https://doi.org/10.1007/978-3-030-81504-2_7

of religious motivations and obligations? Or are these two overlapping yet distinct sets of transnational financial flows? Moreover, what are the temporal dimensions at play here, when the transcendental is recognized? If migrant remittances are expected to "decay" over time as family ties wane, what would be the parallel expectation for transnational Islamic charity? Might there be cases of transformation from remittances decay toward engagement in transnational Islamic charity, within the same transnational social fields?

Migrant remittances are defined as the money migrants send back home to their immediate family and beyond (Lindley 2010; Stark and Lucas 1988). The volume of registered remittances has increased substantially since the early 2000s as a result of more accurate measurements and the growing amounts of money being sent. The officially reported figures of remittance inflows are usually based on reports from state banks. Official records cannot account for transfers made informally, such as when migrants visit and bring back cash with them. Meanwhile, the common conception of what migrant remittances are seems fairly well-established (Maimbo and Ratha 2005).

In Muslim societies—and among migrants from Muslim societies—Islamic charity is an equally well-understood part of the conceptual and moral universe (Benthall 1999). Transnational Islamic charity refers to the transnationalization of Islamic charity as a result of migration, whereby religious practices have been stretched across social and geographic space (Erdal and Borchgrevink 2017; Borchgrevink and Erdal 2017). Islamic charity is defined as one of the five pillars of Islam, *zakat*, the compulsory alms which Muslims are prescribed to offer annually, amounting to 2% of the value of personal assets. Islamic charity is also part of a broader religious teaching about society, poverty, and human interaction, and includes a number of other specific prescribed and voluntary religious practices (Benthall 1999; Kochuyt 2009; Carre 1992). Within Islam—among scholars as well as believers—there are different interpretations as to the role of charitable practices as vehicles of redistributive justice in society (Kroessin 2008). The role of *zakat* is central here, but Islamic charity involves other forms of charitable practices and rituals which are relevant for a discussion on the confluence with remittances, such as *zakat-ul-fitr* which is given during the month of Ramadan, the ritual sacrifice, *qurbani*, and voluntary alms and good deeds, *sadqa*.

I will here draw on the concept of remittance scripts (Carling 2014) as an analytical tool to explore the extent to which remittances and transnational Islamic charity are the same cross-border money flows called by different names, or how they are distinct. I argue that migrants draw on a range of remittance scripts in performing transnational Islamic charity, often distinguished by whether the receiver knows whether the transfer was charitable or not. Some transfers may thus be scripted as a donation or help, others as an obligation, allowance, or gift. In yet other cases, transfers scripted as investment might still be considered charitable, reflecting the composite nature of scripts—depending on the various interacting motivations driving these actions.

By unpacking the conflated monetary flows of remittances and transnational Islamic charity, this chapter offers a new theorization of remittances. First, segmented and layered remittance scripts offer alternative temporalities when seen explicitly in relation to religion and faith-based motivations for actions. Here, the future extends not only within one's lifetime, but also to the hereafter. Second, by paying analytical attention to the confluence of remittances and transnational Islamic charity, new light is shed on remittance dynamics within the migration-development nexus, moving beyond economic perspectives to complement our understanding of transnational relational dynamics. Third, the universality of the remittance decay hypothesis is questioned, as religious motivations for transnational monetary flows foreground alternative generational and temporal dynamics, suggesting that remittance decay may in some instances be replaced by transnational Islamic charity.

I will begin by setting out the analytical approach taken to remittances and transnational Islamic charity, before presenting the methods and data. The analysis section presents the data and discusses the confluence of migrant remittances and transnational Islamic charity based on 12 scripts which might be mobilized by migrants (and their relatives) to motivate, justify, or make sense of financial transfers. The conclusion reflects on the question of how it might matter whether there exists a confluence of sorts between migrant remittances and transnational Islamic charity.

Approaching Remittances and Transnational Islamic Charity Analytically

Over the past two decades, interest in religion has reemerged in the social sciences (Kong 2010; Ammerman 2014), including in migration studies (Levitt 2003; Bowen 2004; Levitt 2007; Pasura and Erdal 2016; Pasura

2012; Saunders et al. 2016). However, this interest has only been taken up in the context of the migration-development nexus to a limited extent (de Haas 2010; Page and Mercer 2012; Brinkerhoff 2012). Thus, while questions about the motivations for remittance-sending, often framed around the altruism versus self-interest dichotomy (increasingly viewed as a continuum), have been central, religion and faith-based motivations have only to a very limited extent been engaged with explicitly (exceptions include Kelly and Solomon 2009; Unheim and Rowlands 2012; Oommen 2020; Roman and Goschin 2011).

Broadly speaking, there is an acknowledgment that religion in its various manifestations matters within transnational social fields (Wuthnow and Offutt 2008; Levitt 2003; Levitt 1998; Levitt 2004). Yet studies that address religion and remittances are relatively few and increasingly refer to social remittances (Isaakyan and Triandafyllidou 2017; Vari-Lavoisier 2016) or emotional remittances rather than remittances as a monetary transaction. Among studies which address monetary remittances and religion head-on, some specifically consider "sacred remittances" (Garbin 2019) as money sent in the context of institutionalized religion, such as within a transnational African church (see also Garbin 2014). A relevant approach in the context of the confluence of migrant remittances and transnational Islamic charity is to recognize how remittances—as monetary transfers—are inextricably also social (Carling 2014; Erdal 2014; Rahman and Fee 2012). It subsequently needs to be recognized that the social and religious at times interact, conflate, or complement each another, including with regard to the motivations driving these transnational financial flows.

I will now turn to some specific approaches which support the analytical engagement with the confluence of remittances and transnational Islamic charity. First, I will define what is meant by transnational Islamic charity and justify why a lived religion approach is analytically appropriate. Second, I will discuss the notion of "remittance scripts" (Carling 2014) and suggest that an interrogation of transnational Islamic charity in relation to migrant remittances allows this notion to be pushed further. Finally, I will discuss analytical approaches to time which are crucial to the subsequent analysis of remittances, as both the same and distinct from transnational Islamic charity.

Lived Religion and Islamic Charity

As discussed above, Islamic charity refers to both voluntary and prescribed practices of charity within Islam (Benthall and Bellion-Jourda 2003; Benthall 1999). In a migration context, Islamic charity may be understood in terms of how "people practice Islamic charity as everyday rituals locally and transnationally [which] the individuals involved in these social practices ascribe religious significance to" (Erdal and Borchgrevink 2017, p. 134). When asking whether it is in fact the same money that is being measured and discussed and when referring to remittances and Islamic charity, it is necessary to consider how this might be ascertained. Does the difference lie in the motivations of the senders or receivers, does it lie in the nature of the transaction and who the receivers are? Or does it come down to senders and/or receivers believing that a third and divine actor might be party to the transaction in a spiritual sense? Basic knowledge about Islamic charity would suggest that migrant remittances and transnational Islamic charity indeed overlap, but are at times also distinct. Moreover, whether particular types of prescribed and voluntary Islamic alms are mutually replaceable transactions or not, relates specifically to whether these constitute *zakat*, *sadqa*, *qurbani*, or Ramadan offerings.

It is important to try to understand not just what people do and why, but also how they themselves ascribe meaning to their actions, a meaning which they may or may not articulate explicitly to their counterparts within the transnational social field. This approach borrows from the "lived religion" tradition in the sociology of religion, but also draws on theory of practice and attention to everyday experiences and people's own sense-making therein (Ammerman 2007, 2014; Page and Mercer 2012). Understanding remittances and transnational Islamic charity as international monetary flows—as "compound and variable" (Carling 2014, p. 251) everyday practices—means approaching them in terms of lived experience and not essentializing the religious, but also moving beyond reducing it to a generic sociocultural category (Bolognani and Mellor 2012).

The lived religion perspective helps us grasp and take seriously how religion is important for immigrants outside of religious organizations in social institutions (Cadge and Ecklund 2007). It thus creates space to seek to understand the ways in which "[f]aith guides how they live their everyday lives, whom they associate with, and the kinds of communities they belong to, even among people who say they are not religious" (Levitt

2007, p. 15). This is significant in the context of exploring the conflation—as well as interaction or divides between—remittances and Islamic charity and necessitates attention to intentions and normative grounds for action. In other words, attention needs to be paid to the too often implicit, the unspoken, and deeply personal motivations for actions. In engaging with the confluence of remittances and Islamic charity, people's motivations and how they ascribe meaning to their actions conflate the religious, cultural, and social. Nevertheless, an analysis of this conflation can be instructive for a better understanding of the motivations that drive one or both of these financial flows.

Remittance Scripts

Using remittance scripts as a tool, it is possible to unpack the motivations underlying interpersonal and composite transactions as well as social positions within a given transnational social field (Carling 2014; Meyer in this volume). This reflects a similar recognition to that found in the lived religion approach, through which everyday life is acknowledged as a relevant empirical domain within which to understand the motivations underlying human actions. Motivations are here rendered in the plural, in recognition of the multiple normative repertoires which may be drawn on, such as interpersonal, cultural, ideological, or religious. Thus, "[t]he notion of scripts implies that many aspects of behaviour are routinized. But this observation does not preclude improvisation, negotiation, and contestation; scripts are not reducible to programming" (Carling 2014, p. 221).

The 12 scripts identified by Carling (2014) based on an in-depth review of empirical studies of remittances are compensation, repayment, authorization, pooling, gift, allowance, obligation, sacrifice, blackmail, help, investment, and donation. Each of these has its particular relational underpinnings and might appear together with other scripts, either simultaneously or in sequence. These relational underpinnings are described in terms of the "transnational relationships" of which they are constitutive:

> The same money can, in some situations, play sequential roles in multiple scripts. This form of layering occurs when recipients are instructed to spend the money in particular ways. For instance, migrants may refrain from making religious donations or offering gifts directly, but instead earmark remittances to family members for these purposes. The money then follows the authorization script in the sense that it never becomes the recipients'

> property. However, the arrangement bestows prestige or virtue upon the family members when they make donations (James 1997). The transaction could therefore simultaneously conform to the repayment or obligation script, with the twist that migrants bestow prestige rather than money upon the recipients. (Carling 2014, p. 249)

Drawing on remittance scripts as an analytical tool for exploring the confluence of remittances and transnational Islamic charity allows for a focus on both potential overlaps and distinctions. A pertinent question appears to be: Are there remittances sent by Norwegian-Pakistani Muslims that cannot also be conceptualized as transnational Islamic charity and, if so, which scripts are characteristic of such remittances, by contrast to those where a confluence with transnational Islamic charity may easily be assumed? Simultaneously, as I also explore below, how do scripts layer in the production of what can be described as transnational Islamic charity, where single scripts making up a composite transaction in full might not alone be described as transnational Islamic charity?

The point of this disaggregation is notably not to define in unequivocal terms which scripts are or are not mobilized by different actors in relation to a given transaction, but rather, using the somewhat different logic of transnational Islamic charity, to push the relational underpinnings of the notion of remittance scripts further. I suggest that the temporal perspectives which religious motivations introduce, which operate with a different logic—spanning the here-and-now and the hereafter—may be instructive.

Temporal Perspectives

What can be described as a temporal turn is evident in migration studies (Cwerner 2001; Griffiths 2014; Robertson 2015). This includes different dimensions, from a demographic attention to generations and the role of age and life-cycle stage, to the empirical concern with different effects of experiencing time—such as in the context of waiting for asylum decisions or deportation—and a more general openness to the analytical inclusion of the temporal alongside both the spatial and the economic, political, or social. Temporal perspectives include paying attention to the experience of time and its passage, as well as a recognition of the existential dimensions of time and the human condition of being placed finitely within a lifetime (Ryan and D'Angelo 2018; Erdal and Borchgrevink 2017). This latter point is relevant to the study of lived religion and people's experiences of their own lives as set within time, in existential terms, and the ways in which faith or religion may or may not impact this experience.

The relevance of temporal perspectives to this chapter is twofold. First, it relates to the well-known "remittance decay hypothesis" (Grieco 2004; Meyer 2020; Arun and Ulku 2011) and, second, it relates to this existential perspective of time, where how we approach people's ways of making sense of or ascribing meaning to their actions may be curtailed if we do not recognize the possibility of also including a perspective which allows for the salience of what might extend beyond a person's own lifetime (Westerhof 2010; Shoeb et al. 2007; Rahman 2019).

The "remittance decay hypothesis" posits that remittances typically decay over time, as migrants' ties with family weaken, perhaps as migrants' parents pass away, and their children are born and later come of age in countries of settlement, requiring financial priorities to shift geographically, too (Makina and Masenge 2015; Amuedo-Dorantes and Pozo 2006). The remittance decay hypothesis overall finds support over time, though with significant variations across contexts of origin and settlement, and in relation to varying types of migration trajectories among family members (Arun and Ulku 2011). Nevertheless, from the point of departure that migrants remit money to support family members back home, in many cases, such support to family members in countries of origin does decrease over time. An interesting question, however, is whether these transnational support mechanisms then stop—or whether, how, and in which cases, transnational support mechanisms are perhaps maintained but take on new forms.

The second and more existential way in which temporal perspectives matter in this chapter pertains to the timeframes within which we seek to analyze human actions and their underlying motivations. If the hereafter, as well as the possibility of divine actors having a meaningful presence in people's lives, is assumed to be irrelevant, simply ignored, or left aside as a religious artifact, then it might become impossible to analyze the dynamics of human action as actors themselves might give these meaning. Meanwhile, it is noteworthy that such existential dimensions to life—which are after all intrinsically human—are far better researched in the context of refugee experiences than with other migrants (Saunders et al. 2016; Fiddian-Qasmiyeh 2011; Ager et al. 2015). Perhaps this is connected to such circumstances more often being characterized by extreme uncertainty and loss, sensitizing researchers to existential dimensions spanning beyond the here-and-now.

The 12 remittance scripts discussed above foreground the relational dynamics of transnational exchanges often set within family networks. These are applied as analytical tools in this chapter, adding a temporal lens which includes the past, present, and future, also allowing for the hereafter and existential dimensions of time to be included where these are relevant to the analysis of how actions are given meaning. The remittance scripts are utilized in order to approach and unpack the confluence of migrant remittances and transnational Islamic charity.

Methods, Data, and Context

The empirical context from which the data for this chapter is drawn is the transnational social field spanning Pakistan and Norway. Such fields are co-constituted by interpersonal relationships stretching across generations over time, involving multiple mobilities, including emigration and immigration, return mobilities, and visits (see, e.g., Erdal 2012; Abdin and Erdal 2016; Erdal 2014; Erdal 2016). This transnational field stretches not only between an area of origin and an area of settlement in two different countries: within the origin context, there are multiple locations where family and kin live, while the context abroad includes various places in Norway and in different countries around the world where family members might be scattered.

The data this chapter builds on consists of 97 semi-structured interviews with Norwegian-Pakistani migrants and descendants, as well as focus groups with 52 participants, conducted between 2008 and 2014 in Norway and Pakistan. The data was collected by the author and by research assistants in Norway mainly using Norwegian and in Pakistan using English, Urdu, or Punjabi. The interviews and focus groups explored remittances, other transnational ties, and Islamic charity practices, and were collected in the context of three different research projects: *Remittances from Immigrants in Norway* (2007–2012); *Possibilities and Realities of Return Migration* (2010–2016); and *Private Islamic charity and Approaches to Poverty Reduction* (2011–2015), all funded by the Research Council of Norway. As I return to, for the purposes of this chapter the data set was pooled, but attention was paid to the ways in which the different project's framings might have affected the data in relation to the question of the confluence of migrant remittances and transnational Islamic charity.

Remittances and/or Transnational Islamic Charity?

The data analyzed in this chapter was collected in the context of research on remittances and on transnational Islamic charity among migrants. Their confluence is explored through an analysis of the remittance scripts mobilized by the migrants. I also acknowledge that remittance scripts are often segmented and may well differ depending on whether they are evaluated by the sender or receiver, that they may also differ over time, and that especially the form of Islamic charity *sadqa* is a flexible concept, which can easily overlap with remittance transactions, depending on context and narration.

This analysis section starts with a presentation of the data and a discussion of the motivations for sending remittances and giving Islamic charity transnationally, focusing on the motivation interface of the confluence. The second part of the analysis takes the twelve remittance scripts as a point of departure, where I will review the types of remittance scripts mobilized for four kinds of Islamic charity in the overall dataset (*zakat, zakat-al-fitr, qurbani,* and *sadqa*), before turning to a discussion of the ways in which transnational Islamic charity is often part of segmented remittance scripts.

It is worth noting, first, that there clearly is a spectrum whereby some transfers of transnational Islamic charity are seen as distinct from remittances set within family obligations and exchange relationships, whereas some remittance transactions would hardly be described as charity. Meanwhile, in a predominantly Muslim context and within a transnational social field where culture, faith, and tradition tend to mesh, the gray zone is where most transactions are located, and as such might be construed both as remittances and as transnational Islamic charity. The lived religion approach taken in this chapter reveals this to be especially true as many Muslims practice their faith in ways which theologians would not define as correct or entirely according to scripture. In their own eyes, however, certain remittance transactions may acquire a religious meaning, even if they do not fully align with religious teachings. Second, as noted, the data this chapter draws on was collected in the context of research projects about both remittances and transnational Islamic charity. Faith-based motivations for financial transfers were discussed in the context of both projects, to varying degrees, and with different types of reflection, but no clear differences were identified regarding which project the interviews were conducted within.

Sending Money Home: A Confluence of Motivations?

Motivations are a key theme in remittance research. When speaking with migrants about their financial transfers to people in their communities of origin and the reasons they send money, responses like Raheela's [1] below were common:

> Marta: Do you send money to Pakistan sometimes?
> Raheela: Yes, yes of course. Well, the zakat is sent there. And then if there are emergencies in the family. Well, and gifts for weddings.. If my parents ask me to help someone specific. […] I also pay school fees for a nephew. And a second cousin with small children became a widow, I try to help her.

Raheela's summary of the types of situations where she sends money mentions *zakat* specifically as one type of transfer, and then goes on to list both specific situations and events as well as long-standing arrangements and life circumstances that explain her actions and her respective motivations. Within Islamic charity, and for *zakat*, specifically assisting widows is an important responsibility, not least when there are widows within one's own family. Thus, her relationship to her second cousin may be closer or more distant, but the religious responsibility for providing assistance is also relevant.

Ahmed's words below reflect another approach to obligation and responsibility in the context of remittance-sending and/or transnational Islamic charity:

> I gave it because my sister needed it and not because it was sadqa or anything. They asked me so I had to give, and that's that, but in the aftermath, they will think that it was a good deed and that it is good, and it is!

On the one hand, the family asked Ahmed for assistance, he provided it, and "that's that." On the other hand, however, he also mentioned how in the aftermath—with reference to the hereafter—this will be seen as a good deed. Thus, while the motivation for Ahmed's action was not religious in principle, further meaning can be added in retrospect. One interpretation might be that Ahmed was asked for familial support, but that this could include religious aspects, as motivations intertwine. A further dimension is related to expectations toward migrants, where "the burden

[1] All names are pseudonyms.

of remittances" is a well-known experience (Akuei 2005; Lindley 2010), but where such expectations might also take on a religious layer, whereby the "good migrant" could potentially be equated with the "good Muslim."

In interviews about transnational Islamic charity, references to global solidarity and humanism surfaced, such as with Ifthikar (whose parents migrated from Pakistan to Norway):

> Looking at it from a human rights perspective or from a human perspective, I feel it is a common understanding and that also with our belief as Muslims [...] it's an obligation to support your fellow humans, it's a duty, it's a must, and I think that's what triggers and motivates.

As such, motivations to assist are anchored in a sense of duty toward fellow human beings, whereas duty is also a key to remittance-sending, whether in relation to children and parents, or other relationships of obligation connected with varying expectations. In both interviews focusing on remittances and on transnational Islamic charity, the fact of being a migrant was a common theme connected with motivations and all the more so an obligation to contribute financially, as Rabeea (whose parents migrated to Norway) described:

> I have been given enough resources, I feel I have to share a bit with those who are in need of it, so I think that would be the motivation.

Rabeea describes her motivations for sending remittances to family members in markedly similar terms to that of practicing Islamic charity transnationally. Thus, remittances sent in the context of a wealth gap between the sending and receiving context are perhaps particularly likely to converge with or take on aspects of transnational Islamic charity. When asked to explain what Islamic charity refers to, Zulfiqar responded that it:

> refers to helping others, poor, there are different ways to understand this, many of the prophets have said that a smile is sadqa, My definition of sadqa is that you give money to someone who needs it or to whomever, whenever in a way, so every time I had sent money to Pakistan that would have resulted in sadqa, so everything that isn't zakat is sadqa, as long as it is money that goes from my pocket to someone else.

For Zulfiqar, there is an almost one-to-one relationship between remittance-sending and transnational Islamic charity, and he distinguishes between different forms of charity within his financial transfers to Pakistan. However, for Raheela, when confronted with this question, some distinctions mattered:

> Marta: In your opinion, is sending money to your family and giving Islamic charity the same or different? How?
> Raheela: Well, first of all you have to distinguish between who is or isn't entitled to receive zakat, or even with sadqa, you have to think about this.

Raheela also referred to the distinction between *zakat* and *sadqa* according to Islamic teaching and who is entitled to receive *zakat* on which grounds. However, she also stressed that even with *sadqa*, there are things to think about before a financial transfer to family can be described as *sadqa*. These are clearly personal as well as spiritual reflections for Raheela, as well as for other interviewees. Mariam raised another dimension which was evident in interviews starting with remittances and with transnational Islamic charity:

> The giving part of the culture is very visible during Ramadan, because then you will see that people will give money, but also food and drinks and things like that.

She mentioned a culture of giving in general and tied to distinct moments in a religious annual cycle. A general culture of giving in Pakistan is sometimes seen as a culture of charity and associated with upholding unequal structures, where some are entitled to give and others are left waiting for alms. Religion might also be seen as a force for good, helping people see beyond the needs of themselves and their closest family. Meanwhile, the significance of the calendar and of particular moments of giving are hard to overestimate—for both Eid-specific practices of charity—*zakat-al-fitr* and *qurbani*—are upheld also by migrants who describe themselves as more cultural than practicing Muslims.

In discussing the motivations for financial transfers to and transactions with relatives and others in Pakistan, migrants living in Oslo often describe motivations while simultaneously mentioning who receives money and providing reasons why this is necessary or desirable. These may or may not align with the motivation itself and/or with the expectations of others, which in turn may affect both the motivations and narrations thereof. As with general references to culture or tradition, to religious duty specifically, or to the wealth gap which obliges migrants to contribute, Masooda's reflections below on her caring responsibilities for her mother are echoed in similar statements across the dataset:

> Masooda: Then I also have, my mother is now very old and there isn't anyone there who can take care of her … so there are a few ladies who help out with washing her clothes and help her … and when I have money, I will send it to them … because they … when I am not there and I can't help my mother … it's my responsibility to help the women who are helping my mother …
> Marta: Is it like, you pay them, or?
> Masooda: No, I don't pay them … because their wage, they receive that either from my mother or someone else … I count it as zakat.

The duty Masooda feels to support her mother is set within a particular context, where her brothers will feel the formal duty to do so, whereas Masooda's caring responsibility is more on an emotional level, as a daughter living far away. However, this is also reflective of the fact that cultural codes are often not as absolute as they may appear. Daughters do support their parents, but how this is done will depend on how their brothers relate to this and will often not be public. So Masooda, for example, supports the women who work for her mother not by employing them or paying part of their salary, but rather through her *zakat*.

Noman's reflections on the confluence of remittances and transnational Islamic charity were instructive: he recounted how he and his wife send money to Pakistan, helping relatives, those working for relatives, and others. He underlined the significance of religious duty—but in the sense of Islam being a way of life. The examples he gave were of him and his wife putting off a bathroom renovation when floods hit Pakistan in 2010 to rather help; how he and other Muslims give more when they go through difficult times; how Muslims give more in the holy month of Ramadan; how he and his wife give more when something good happens, in gratitude—sometimes to organizations, but most often through informal networks to family.

The above interview extracts and discussion point very clearly to a confluence of motivations—sometimes implicit, other times explicit—between remittances and transnational Islamic charity. It might thus seem that in the case of Pakistani migrants sending money to their relatives, the question of whether this constitutes remittances or transnational Islamic charity and whether these are the same or different financial flows is redundant. However, this question can be further interrogated through applying the 12 remittance scripts to evaluate which ones are mobilized in the context of different forms of transnational Islamic charity, and which are not.

Remittance Scripts and Transnational Islamic Charity

Recalling the 12 remittance scripts introduced by Carling (2014), namely compensation, repayment, authorization, pooling, gift, allowance, obligation, sacrifice, blackmail, help, investment, and donation. Several were already mentioned explicitly in the analysis above, especially duty and responsibility (Ahmed, Ifthikar, Rabeea, Masooda, and Noman), which featured centrally as core scripts in financial transfers from migrants or their descendants to their family and relatives in places of origin. This script appears to apply similarly to remittances and Islamic charity, while at the same time also having a specific resonance with particular forms of Islamic charity, notably with zakat (Raheela and Masooda).

Migrants or their descendants can also draw on scripts where transnational Islamic charity is inherent, such as help and donation. However, these scripts do not make Islamic charity mutually exclusive from remittances, but rather underscore the spirit of Islamic charity in relation to providing assistance, as a potential frame for many transnational financial transfers (Raheela and Masooda). Furthermore, multiple scripts which have a specific role at a given point in time (compensation, repayment, gift, and allowance), but which are subsequently also re-scripted as a particular form of transnational Islamic charity (Mariam, Masooda, Zulfiqar, and Noman), can be drawn on. Finally, scripts which do not consciously have anything to do with transnational Islamic charity, may be drawn on, enabling performance of Islamic charity without the receiver knowing about it. In several of these scenarios, the scripts may be segmented and/or reassigned over time, and/or the sender and receiver may have different perspectives on (and information about) which scripts are being mobilized in relation to particular financial transfers.

Table 7.1 depicts which scripts were found in the dataset overall in relation to the four different types of transnational Islamic charity. As the interview extracts above illustrate, there are often segmented uses of scripts, which (may) result in the confluence of remittances and transnational Islamic charity.

Table 7.1 Scripts mobilized in relation to four types of transnational Islamic charity

Scripts	***Zakat*** *(the prescribed 2.5% of annual assets to defined receivers)*	***Zakat-al-fitr*** *(prescribed at the end of Ramadan)*	***Qurbani*** *(the prescribed religious ritual slaughter)*	***Sadqa*** *(voluntary offerings and good deeds)*
Compensation	x			x
Repayment				x
Authorization	x			x
Pooling	x		x	x
Gift	x	x	x	x
Allowance	x			x
Obligation	x	x	x	x
Sacrifice				
Blackmail				
Help	x	x	x	x
Investment	x			x
Donation	x	x	x	x

Two scripts were not found in the interviews which referred to transfers as Islamic charity: blackmail and sacrifice (in the sense of migrants making a sacrifice for family members). The reasons why are fairly intuitive, as religious alms would typically not be associated with blackmail, and if any sacrifice was involved, this would not be openly reported in the context of Islamic charity by the giver. By contrast, there are four scripts which dominate in relation to transnational Islamic charity, namely: gift, obligation, help, and donation. These four are common across the spectrum of different forms of Islamic charity *zakat, zakat-al-fitr, qurbani*, and *sadqa*.

Some scripts are mobilized only in conjunction with particular forms of Islamic charity. Compensation, authorization, allowance, and investment scripts are mobilized in the context of *zakat* and *sadqa*, but not *zakat-al-fitr* or *qurbani*, as the latter are linked with the specific regulations of Islamic charity connected with the Islamic calendar. Finally, pooling is associated with *zakat*, *qurbani*, and *sadqa*, whereas repayment is mobilized as a script in connection with *sadqa*. Thus, different scripts across the dataset appeared to be mobilized with regard to how migrants narrated their financial transfers as linked to Islamic charity, to different extents, and in conjunction with particular forms of Islamic charity, while some were not mobilized at all.

Interrogating the Confluence

In interrogating the confluence of remittances and transnational Islamic charity, the narratives of migrants or their descendants become central. Does the confluence occur in narrative terms, in the ways in which these financial transfers are spoken about? Or is there a distinction in substance? Islamic charity may be seen as practice, but it is also part of a worldview and a resource that human beings draw on to make sense of their lived experiences, including for motivating and justifying their own actions. Yet the question remains whether a distinction between remittances and transnational Islamic charity makes sense and, if so, why, how, and for whom.

First, when migrants send Islamic charity internationally, this involves a transfer mechanism (a bank, a friend traveling, or a Money Transfer Operator), and it may involve an intermediary who passes on the charity to the ultimate recipient, an individual, a family, a mosque, or an organization. Islamic charity is altered by migration in the same ways as intra-family assistance, which is transformed into remittances as a result of migration. Money which may well have changed hands in any instance now changes hands across international borders.

Second, there is a spatial and emotional distance involved, which affects those giving charity. In the context of Pakistani migration to Norway, the inherent wealth gap is a constant potential reminder of those in need in the communities left behind in Pakistan. For migrants, the geographic distance, combined with an emotional closeness to their communities of origin in Pakistan, arguably affects how they relate to both Islamic charity and sending remittances to family, both of which are often anchored in a faith-based universe of meaning.

Third, exposure to new societies might affect migrants' Islamic charity, whether in terms of their ideas about poverty and development, or with regard to how migrants' descendants in due course approach Islamic charity as Muslims with hyphenated identities, such as in the case of Norwegian-Pakistani youth and adults. The relationship between remittances and Islamic charity may also change, shifting the balance more in the direction of one or the other, and increasing or decreasing the degree of conflation for different individuals.

Fourth, migration also affects the ways in which Islamic charity is organized in diaspora communities, both in that these most often take on transnational forms, as cross-border practices to their country of origin, or third countries, albeit with very different organizational forms. These organizational forms include religious networks, organized diaspora development engagements, organized mosque activities, multiethnic Muslim organizations, informal collections, and—as focused on here—initiatives and efforts by individuals, loose networks, and family.

Further analyses could be done focusing on collective remittances, although compared with the volume of individual or family-level remittances, the volume of organized collective remittances remains rather meager. Certainly, when considering collective remittances, a distinction between migrant-led initiatives that are or are not faith-based is not always easy to make (Borchgrevink and Erdal 2017).

Conclusion

As shown through the analysis of overlapping motivations, which used remittance scripts to unpack often segmented transfers, and considering the impact of migration on transfers (both in families and as charity), the confluence of remittances and transnational Islamic charity becomes apparent. The difference between the two matters for some in religious terms—what is and is not charity of a particular form—and for others in familial terms, where support is offered not out of religious obligation. However, the gray zone appears to dominate, where chances are that religious meaning may be ascribed to financial transfers otherwise referred to as migrant remittances, more often than not by the sender, and sometimes by an intermediary or even the recipient, too.

What does exploring the confluence of remittances and transnational Islamic charity add, and to which academic debates? Three insights are worth sharing. First, a challenge when studying the role of religion in relation to social, cultural, or economic phenomena is how to approach what is or is not religious, whether to stay at a perhaps superficial external level—observing rituals or practices which are unquestionably religious, or whether to ask people to share, explain, and reflect on religious meaning, on their faith, and how it guides their ideals and actions in everyday life. There are caveats to both approaches. Nevertheless, it seems that there continues to be space within migration studies to seek to understand the role which faith may play as a factor co-constituting people's desires and motivations, their choices and actions, and how they choose to narrate their stories. Paying careful analytical attention to the role which faith may play enables us to avoid both an essentialization and an instrumentalization of religion.

Second, in order to understand and theorize remittance-sending motivations, applying remittance scripts to the confluence of remittances and transnational Islamic charity not only underscores the salience of relational, emotional, and material aspects, but also contributes temporal dimensions. These temporal dimensions, due to their religious logic spanning from the here-and-now into the hereafter, operate differently from more common temporal dimensions included in analyses, such as the passage of time since migration, the length of visits, the passage of time after visits, or age and life stage, as well as the age of family members, and eventually the passing away of parents, siblings, and others. In addition to these salient—often highly relational—temporal dimensions, the addition of the hereafter radically opens up the relevant time horizons for understanding human actions. If financial transfers are sent with a motivation of reward in the hereafter, by God—not in the present or near future, and from the receiver—this alters how we can make sense of the transactional logic of exchange which is so often applied (Fokkema et al. 2013; Åkesson 2011; Cliggett 2005).

Finally, paying attention to both the long-term perspective and religion allows for a fresh perspective on human action, which encompasses transcendental considerations as well as intergenerational change. This chapter also draws on interviews with descendants of Pakistani migrants born in Norway. They did not have the same remittance obligations as their parents and financial transfers often focused rather on transnational Islamic charity of different forms. It might therefore be hypothesized that there may be a process where (intra-familial) remittance decay morphs into transnational Islamic charity (targeting broader communities) (see also Adugna Zewdu 2019; Meyer 2020). Thus, considering religious motivations for financial transfers at the intersection of remittances and transnational Islamic charity might challenge the remittance decay hypothesis, *if* the generations that follow on from the migrant generation, instead of stopping financial transfers, shift these toward charitable forms—in the case of Muslims, as transnational Islamic charity.

References

Abdin, Z. U. & Erdal, M. B. (2016). Remittance-sending among Pakistani Taxi-Drivers in Barcelona and Oslo: Implications of Migration Trajectories and the Protracted Electricity Crisis in Pakistan. *Migration and Development,* 5(3), 378–393.

Adugna Zewdu, G. (2019). Remittance Flows, Remitting Behavior and Utilization Patterns: The Case of Ethiopia. *Social & Cultural Geography*, 1-21. DOI: https://doi.org/10.1080/14649365.2019.1685677

Ager, J., Fiddian-Qasmiyeh, E. & Ager, A. (2015). Local Faith Communities and the Promotion of Resilience in Contexts of Humanitarian Crisis. *Journal of Refugee Studies*, 28(2), 202–221.

Åkesson, L. (2011). Remittances and Relationships: Exchange in Cape Verdean Transnational Families. *Ethnos*, 76(3), 326–347.

Akuei, S. R. (2005). *Remittances as Unforeseen Burdens: The Livelihoods and Social Obligations of Sudanese Refugees.* Global Commission on International Migration. Geneva.

Ammerman, N. T. (Ed.). (2007). *Everyday Religion: Observing Modern Religious Lives.* Oxford University Press.

Ammerman, N. T. (2014). Finding Religion in Everyday Life. *Sociology of Religion*, 75(2), 189–207.

Amuedo-Dorantes, C. & Pozo, S. (2006). The Time Pattern of Remittances: Evidence from Mexican Migrants. *Well-being and Social Policy*, 2(2), 49–66.

Arun, T. & Ulku, H. (2011). Determinants of Remittances: The Case of the South Asian Community in Manchester. *The Journal of Development Studies*, 47(6), 894–912.

Benthall, J. (1999). Financial Worship: The Quranic Injunction to Almsgiving. *Journal of the Royal Anthropological Institute*, 5(1), 27–42.

Benthall, J. (2016). Have Islamic aid agencies a privileged relationship in majority Muslim areas? The case of post-tsunami reconstruction in Aceh. *In Islamic charities and Islamic humanism in troubled times*. Manchester University Press.

Benthall, J. & Bellion-Jourda, J. (2003). *The Charitable Crescent: The Politics of Aid in the Muslim World.* I.B. Tauris.

Bolognani, M. & Mellor, J. (2012). British Pakistani Women's Use of the 'Religion versus Culture' Contrast: A Critical Analysis. *Culture and Religion*, 13(2), 211–226.

Borchgrevink, K. & Erdal, M. B. (2017). With Faith in Development: Organising Transnational Islamic charity. *Progress in Development Studies*, 17(3), 214–228.

Bowen, J. R. (2004). Beyond Migration: Islam as a Transnational Public Space. *Journal of Ethnic and Migration Studies*, 30(5), 879–894.

Brinkerhoff, J. M. (2012). Creating an Enabling Environment for Diasporas' Participation in Homeland Development, *International Migration* 50(1), 75–95.

Cadge, W. & Ecklund, E. H. (2007). Immigration and Religion. *Annual Review of Sociology*, 33(1), 359–379.

Carling, J. (2014). Scripting Remittances: Making Sense of Money Transfers in Transnational Relationships. *International Migration Review*, 48(1), 218–262.

Carre, O. (1992). Religion and Development in Islamic Countries: Elements of Islamic Economics. *Social Compass,* 39(1), 55–65.

Cliggett, L. (2005). Remitting the Gift: Zambian Mobility and Anthropological Insights for Migration Studies. *Population Space and Place,* 11(1), 35–48.

Cwerner, S. B. (2001). The Times of Migration. *Journal of Ethnic and Migration Studies,* 27(1), 7–36.

de Haas, H. (2010). Migration and Development: A Theoretical Perspective. *International Migration Review,* 44(1), 227–264.

Erdal, M. B. (2012). 'A Place to Stay in Pakistan': Why Migrants Build Houses in their Country of Origin. *Population, Space and Place* 18 (5), 629–641.

Erdal, M. B. (2014). The Social Dynamics of Remittance-Receiving in Pakistan: Agency and Opportunity among Non-migrants in a Transnational Social Field. In M. Rahman, T. T. Yong & A. K. M. A. Ullah (Eds.), *Migrant Remittances in South Asia Social, Economic and Political Implications* (pp. 115–134). Palgrave Macmillan.

Erdal, M. B. (2016). Juxtaposing Pakistani Diaspora Policy with Migrants' Transnational Citizenship Practices. *Geoforum,* 76, 1–10.

Erdal, M. B. & Borchgrevink, K. (2017). Transnational Islamic charity as Everyday Rituals. *Global Networks,* 17(1), 130–146.

Fiddian-Qasmiyeh, E. (2011). Introduction: Faith-Based Humanitarianism in Contexts of Forced Displacement. *Journal of Refugee Studies,* 24(3), 429–439.

Fokkema, T., Eralba C. & Ambrosetti, E. (2013). Giving from the Heart or from the Ego? Motives behind Remittances of the Second Generation in Europe. *International Migration Review,* 47(3), 539–572.

Garbin, D. (2014). Regrounding the Sacred: Transnational Religion, Place Making and the Politics of Diaspora among the Congolese in London and Atlanta. *Global Networks,* 14(3), 363–382.

Garbin, D. (2019). Sacred Remittances: Money, Migration and the Moral Economy of Development in a Transnational African Church. *Journal of Ethnic and Migration Studies,* 45(11), 2045–2061.

Grieco, E. (2004). Will Migrant Remittances Continue Through Time? A New Answer to an Old Question. *International Journal on Multicultural Societies,* 6(2), 243–252.

Griffiths, M. (2014). Out of Time: The Temporal Uncertainties of Refused Asylum Seekers and Immigration Detainees. *Journal of Ethnic and Migration Studies,* 40(12), 1991–2009.

Isaakyan, I. & Triandafyllidou, A. (2017). 'Sending so Much More than Money': Exploring Social Remittances and Transnational Mobility. *Ethnic and Racial Studies,* 40(15), 2787–2805.

James, K. (1997). Reading the Leaves: The Role of Tongan Women's Traditional Wealth and Other 'Contraflows' in the Process of Modern Migration and Remittance. *Pacific Studies,* 20(1), 1–27.

Kelly, C. S. & Solomon, B. (2009). The Influence Of Religion On Remittances Sent To Relatives and Friends Back Home. *Journal of Business & Economics Research*, 7(1), 91-102.
Kochuyt, T. (2009). God, Gifts and Poor People: On Charity in Islam. *Social Compass*, 56(1), 98–116.
Kong, L. (2010). Global Shifts, Theoretical Shifts: Changing Geographies of Religion. *Progress in Human Geography*, 34(6), 755–776.
Kroessin, M.R. (2008). *Concepts of Development in 'Islam': A Review of Contemporary Literature and Practice*. Religions and Development Research Programme.
Levitt, P. (1998). Local-Level Global Religion: The Case of US-Dominican Migration. *Journal for the Scientific Study of Religion*, 37(1), 74–89.
Levitt, P. (2003). 'You Know, Abraham Was Really the First Immigrant': Religion and Transnational Migration. *International Migration Review*, 37(3), 847–873.
Levitt, P. (2004). Redefining the Boundaries of Belonging: The Institutional Character of Transnational Religious Life. *Sociology of Religion*, 65 (1), 1–18.
Levitt, P. (2007). *God Needs No Passport: Immigrants and the Changing American Religious Landscape*. The New Press.
Lindley, A. (2010). *The Early Morning Phone Call: Somali Refugees' Remittances*. Berghahn Books.
Maimbo, S. M. & Ratha, D. (Eds.). (2005). *Remittances: Development Impact and Future Prospects*. The World Bank.
Makina, D. & Masenge, A. (2015). The Time Pattern of Remittances and the Decay Hypothesis: Evidence from Migrants in South Africa. *Migration Letters*, 12(1), 79–90.
Meyer, S. 2020. 'Home Is Where I Spend My Money': Testing the Remittance decay hypothesis with Ethnographic Data from an Austrian-Turkish Community. *Social Inclusion*, 8 (1), 275–284.
Nyberg-Sørensen, N., Van Hear, N. & Engberg-Pedersen, P. (2002). The Migration-development nexus: Evidence and Policy Options. State-of-the-Art Overview. *International Migration*, 40(5), 3–47.
Oommen, G. Z. (2020). Gulf Migration, Remittances and Religion: Interplay of Faith and Prosperity Amongst Syrian Christians in Kerala. In S. I. Rajan & G. Z. Oommen (Eds.), *Asianization of Migrant Workers in the Gulf Countries* (pp. 247–266). Springer.
Page, B. & Mercer, C. (2012). Why Do People Do Stuff? Reconceptualizing Remittance Behaviour in Diaspora-Development Research and Policy. *Progress in Development Studies*, 12(1), 1–18.
Pasura, D. (2012). Religious Transnationalism: The Case of Zimbabwewan Catholics in Britain. *Journal of Religion in Africa, 42*(1), 26–53.
Pasura, D. & Erdal, M. B. (2016). Introduction: Migration, Transnationalism and Catholicism. In D. Pasura & M. B. Erdal (Eds.), *Migration, Transnationalism and Catholicism* (pp. 1–20). Palgrave Macmillan.

Rahman, F. (2019). 'I Find Comfort Here': Rohingya Women and Taleems in Bangladesh's Refugee Camps. *Journal of Refugee Studies* doi.org/10.1093/jrs/fez054

Rahman, M. & Fee, L. K. (2012). Towards a Sociology of Migrant Remittances in Asia: Conceptual and Methodological Challenges. *Journal of Ethnic and Migration Studies,* 38(4), 689–706.

Robertson, S. (2015). The Temporalities of International Migration: Implications for Ethnographic Research. In S. Ozkul Castles & M. Cuba (Eds.), *Social Transformation and Migration: National and Local Experiences in South Korea, Turkey, Mexico and Australia* (pp. 45–60). Palgrave Macmillan.

Roman, M. & Goschin, Z. (2011). Does Religion Matter? Exploring Economic Performance Differences Among Romanian Emigrants. *Journal for the Study of Religions and Ideologies,* 10 (30), 183–212.

Ryan, L. & D'Angelo, A. (2018). Changing Times: Migrants' Social Network Analysis and the Challenges of Longitudinal Research. *Social Networks,* 53, 148–158.

Saunders, J. B., Snyder, S. & Fiddian-Qasmiyeh, E. (2016). Introduction: Articulating Intersections at the Global Crossroads of Religion and Migration. In J. B. Saunders (Ed.), *Intersections of Religion and Migration* (pp. 1–46). Palgrave Macmillan.

Shoeb, M., Weinstein, H. M. & Halpern, J. (2007). Living in Religious Time and Space: Iraqi Refugees in Dearborn, Michigan. *Journal of Refugee Studies,* 20 (3), 441–460.

Sørensen, N. N. (2012). Revisiting the Migration–Development Nexus: From Social Networks and Remittances to Markets for Migration Control. *International Migration,* 50 (3), 61–76.

Stark, O., & Lucas, R. E. (1988). Migration, Remittances, and the Family. *Economic Development and Cultural Change,* 36(3), 465–481.

Unheim, P & Rowlands, D. (2012). Micro-Level Determinants of Remittances from Recent Migrants to Canada. *International Migration,* 50 (4), 124–139.

Vari-Lavoisier, I. (2016). The Economic Side of Social Remittances: How Money and Ideas Circulate between Paris, Dakar, and New York. *Comparative Migration Studies, 4* (1). doi.org/10.1186/s40878 .

Westerhof, G. J. (2010). 'During my Life so Much Has Changed that It Looks like a New World to Me': A Narrative Perspective on Migrating in Time. *Journal of Aging Studies,* 24 (1), 12–19.

Wuthnow, R. & Offutt, S. (2008). Transnational Religious Connections. *Sociology of Religion, 69* (2), 209–232.

CHAPTER 8

Remittances and the Destination State: A Comparison of Bangladeshi Migrants in Japan and the USA

Hasan Mahmud

Introduction

Remittances are one of the most celebrated aspects in the discourses of migration. While migrants endure various kinds of uncertainty, hardship, and suffering on their way to their destinations as well as in their new residences and workplaces, their remittances considerably improve the lives of those they left behind—the family and community in their places of origin. Researchers have documented how remittances allow access to better education, health, and nutrition for the members of the migrant's family (Amega 2018; Lu 2012; Thow et al. 2016), help develop local infrastructure, and boost economic activities (e.g., Redehegn et al. 2019). Moreover, remittances contribute significantly to GDP and help stabilize the national balance of payments for a number of origin countries (Meyer and Shera 2017). These macroeconomic impacts entice many countries in the Global

H. Mahmud (✉)
Northwestern University in Qatar, Doha, Qatar
e-mail: hasan.mahmud@northwestern.edu

S. Meyer, C. Ströhle (eds.), *Remittances as Social Practices and Agents of Change*,
https://doi.org/10.1007/978-3-030-81504-2_8

South (Guevarra 2010; Iskander 2010; Rodriguez 2010) as well as international organizations (e.g., the International Organization for Migration, the International Fund for Agricultural Development, and the World Bank) to enthusiastically praise remittances as a source of funding development (Kapur 2004).

Contrarily, there are anti-immigration narratives that are built on a perceived fear and hatred of migrant populations among the conservative factions in destination countries. In fact, the growing right-wing political parties and their media front construct migrants as scapegoats for a number of structural problems in their native countries (Hogan and Haltinner 2015). A common focus in these discourses is the economic and social problems in the destination countries and the more or less subtle claims—almost always supported with fabricated evidence—that migrants are responsible for those problems. Consequently, calls for expelling migrants who are already inside the destination countries and stopping potential migrants at the borders are central issues in right-wing political activism. In Europe, public discourse on migration has substantially turned its focus on the recent "migration crisis," feeding into pre-existing anti-immigration discourses and political actions (Dennison and Geddes 2018). Anti-immigration fervor in the destination countries also affects remittances, the lifeline of over 250 million migrants and their families in poorer countries (IOM 2020). In this context, it is important to understand the role of the destination state in the different discourses and regimes of migration. In this chapter, I argue that the different migration policies of the destination states have immediate effects on remittance-sending. I will explore this hypothesis with comparative data from Bangladeshi immigrants to Japan and the USA.

I will begin by briefly reviewing the literature on the role of the destination state in shaping migrants' remittances and discussing their experience with the destination state. I will then present the methodology of this study. This will be followed by the case studies of Bangladeshi migration to Japan and the USA and the data analysis showing how the destination states shape Bangladeshi migration to these countries. Finally, I will analyze the influence of the destination state on remittances by focusing on the remittance decay hypothesis.

Earlier Approaches to the Role of the Destination State in Remittance Research

Remittances are defined as personal financial transactions whereby migrants send a part of their income to family overseas. Due to an inherent subject orientation in the social sciences and in contemporary migration research, the scholarly focus today mainly lies on the migrants and their families, which leaves the role of the state underexposed and under-researched. Interestingly, there was academic interest in the role of the destination state in remittances in the 1970s, long before the emergence of the remittance-and-development discourse of the late 1980s (De Haas 2010). In his study on the migrant workers in the mining sector in South Africa and those in agriculture in California, Michael Burawoy observed that the destination state deployed legal instruments such as "the influx control" and "the pass law" to give urban residence only to those employed (i.e., male workers) while keeping others in the reserves or Bantustans and surrounding black territories (Burawoy 1976, p. 1060). These laws required the workers to return home if their employment contract ended without a subsequent contract or if they became unemployed due to retirement, disability, or simply a scarcity of employment opportunities. The lack of a legal right for the migrant to permanently reside in the destination state compelled them to maintain contact with their families in the reservations, or the black territories. The families also needed the migrants' financial support to subsist because of hardships in the local economy. This strong interdependence between migrants and their families is evident in remittance practices that facilitate family cohesion and belonging (p. 1062).

We can thus clearly see how the destination state influences remittances. It plays a decisive role in rendering the migrants' entry and stay in the destination country conditional upon their employment and in keeping them apart from their families in their place of origin. Thus, the destination state makes the productive migrant functionally dependent on the reproductive family by the deploying state institutions. This link between the motivation to migrate and to remit to the family was theorized in the mid-1980s in the New Economics of Labor Migration (NELM). Lucas and Stark (1985) published the first empirical study on remittances in Botswana, which conceptualized migrants as rational actors who enter into a contractual arrangement with their family whereby the family sends the migrants abroad to earn additional income and the migrants reciprocate accordingly. While we owe much to the approaches of NELM, it has generated criticism as well, for example that, based on household surveys, remittance motivation is analyzed much more from the receivers' than the senders' point of view (Mahmud 2020).

Turning back to the destination state as a research interest, a number of scholars have identified the state's role in facilitating international migration as a strategy for earning foreign income. For instance, Rodriguez recognized what she called "migrant citizenship" through which the Philippine state reconfigures nationalism by drawing migrants into the rhetoric of filial piety (pp. 86–87) and thereby encourages them to remit (p. 185). Guevarra (2010) argued that the Philippine state works with a gendered and racialized moral economy, which bases the ideal behavior of migrant workers on remittances. Iskander (2010) was even more explicit in recognizing the state's role in remittances. By adopting what Iskander called an "interpretative engagement," the states of Morocco and Mexico formulated policies that channel remittances for investment in community development. They thus enhance the migrants' efforts to improve the lives of their families and communities and, more broadly, their nation. Clearly, these studies establish the role of the origin state in shaping migrants' employment abroad and sending remittances home, thereby demonstrating the need to move beyond the individualistic perception of remittances inherent in the dominant NELM perspective. Similarly, scholars recognize the active role of the destination state in regulating migration (Hollifield 2004), which inevitably affects the migrants' employment abroad and their transnationalism, including their remittances.

Remittances undergo noticeable changes over time and according to the personal situations and living conditions of migrants. The decline of money transfers in particular has been analyzed with the model of the remittance decay hypothesis. According to this hypothesis, remittance flows are influenced by the timespan during which migrants live abroad: the longer they live in their destination state, the less money they send. Remittances also decline when the family joins the migrant, and the death of parents also contributes to remittance decay (Carling 2008; Lucas and Stark 1985; Makina and Masenge 2015; Meyer 2020; Rapoport and Docquier 2006). Other factors like plans for return migration and the closeness to the remittance recipients also influence the amount of remittances sent home. What has not been added to this equation so far is the factor of the destination state and its immigration policies. In this chapter, I will address this question with a comparison of immigration to Japan and the USA, the conditions of settling in those countries, and the consequences those conditions have on remittances.

Encountering the Destination State

Migrants inevitably encounter the destination state at its border, where it exercises sovereign authority over who is allowed in (Hollifield 2004; Zolberg 1999). Due to a lack of income opportunities at home, migrants go abroad for employment. While migration might be motivated economically, transnational practices including remittances are also conditioned by destination state policies. For example, Hollifield (2004) argued that the destination state is becoming inherently interested in regulating migration as much as maintaining the security of the state and the well-being of its citizens. Burawoy (1976) observed how the destination state directly engages in regulating migration by separating employable males from their families and defining the migration as temporary. Thus, remittances become an essential relation: the families depend on the migrants' remittance for subsistence while the migrants need to maintain their membership in the family to which they must return due to the inability to settle permanently in their destination country. In the Middle East and East Asia, destination countries use immigration laws to keep the migrants in certain labor market sectors by attaching them to a particular employer or job, housing them in workers' colonies, and restricting their labor market mobility, while rigid immigration controls (for instance frequent raids and strict security checks) prevent them from overstaying their visas (AlShehabi et al. 2015; Seol and Skrentny 2009; Shipper 2002; Tseng and Wang 2011).

Empirical studies have documented how the destination states exert control over the foreign populations through various legal mechanisms. For instance, destination states put in place extensive immigration and border control policies and practices that define the migrants either as "permanent residents" who are allowed to settle in the country, as "temporary workers" or short-term "visitors" who are allowed to stay for a certain period, or as "undocumented" foreigners who must evade the legal procedures upon entry (Castles 2011; Munck 2008; Neumayer 2006). Quantitative studies on remittances have shown how these different legal statuses affect migrants' income and remittances. For example, Glytsos (1997) found that remittances from temporary Greek immigrants in Germany and Australia constituted an obligation to their families back home, whereas remittances from permanent immigrants were voluntary and followed the gift script (p. 429; on scripting remittances, see Carling 2014). Thus, the ability to settle permanently affects remittance behavior, specifically reducing the likelihood to send remittance (Markova and Reilly 2007). Perhaps this explains why temporary migrants send higher proportions of their earnings compared to permanent immigrants (Mahmud 2016), as Pinger (2010) explained by reference to their plan to return home. This conclusion is further supported by the fact that the transition from undocumented status to permanent legal status and family reunification reduces the migrants' propensity to send remittances (Amuedo-Dorantes and Mazzolari 2010).

The destination state also shapes remittances indirectly. For instance, the USA sometimes adopts policy measures for undocumented migrants to legalize their stay by allowing them legal permanent residency (e.g., the IRCA of 1986), which substantially increases the migrants' labor market position and bargaining power (Kossoudji and Cobb-Clark 2002). The state also sets up mechanisms for these migrants to acquire citizenship that further improves their bargaining power and expands their rights and privileges (DeVoretz and Pivnenko 2005). In these circumstances, the migrants' income opportunities as well as their capacity to save in their destination country increases. If migrants acquire a legal status that increases their earnings and savings, but cannot settle permanently in their destination state, they ate more likely to send remittances. As I have showed, multifaceted indicators can lead to an increase or decay of remittances. In this chapter, I will elaborate on these processes in the context of Bangladeshis' remittances from Japan and the USA.

Methodology and the Two Fields of Research

This chapter is based on an ethnography of migrants' remittances from Japan and the USA to Bangladesh, focusing on the role of the destination state therein. I selected these two destination states because of their opposing approaches toward migration policies—inclusive in the USA and exclusionary in Japan—to see how they affected remittances differently. To this end, I conducted ethnographic fieldwork in Tokyo and Los Angeles between 2012 and 2015, which I followed up with short field visits in 2017 and 2018. In both cities, I conducted small, purposive surveys, based on a sample of 120 migrants in Tokyo and 200 migrants in Los Angeles, and used this quantitative data to assess general patterns of remitting. Further in-depth interviews with 42 respondents in Tokyo and 45 in

Los Angeles were conducted and analyzed along with ethnographic field notes to explore the social mechanisms of remittance practices. For the purpose of maintaining the interview partners' confidentiality, I used pseudonyms and fabricated personal information throughout.

During my fieldwork, there were about 10,000 Bangladeshi migrants in Japan, most of whom had come as laborers and lived in and around metropolitan Tokyo. Despite some migrants' willingness and active initiatives to stay longer and settle permanently, Japan compelled all migrants to return to Bangladesh after some time, or to remigrate to another country for a certain period of time (Mahmud 2014, 2017; Oishi 2012). Thus, the ebbs and flows of migration from Bangladesh to Japan as well as the migrants' experiences in everyday life, including remittances, were inevitably affected by Japan's policies toward the migrants (Mahmud 2013).

Turning to the research field in the USA, the Bangladeshi consul general in Los Angeles estimates that the total number of Bangladeshis falls somewhere between 20,000 and 30,000 in Los Angeles and some 80,000 in California generally, making the region the nation's second-largest home to Bangladeshis after New York. These immigrants are mostly concentrated in the neighborhood called "Little Bangladesh" within Koreatown. The first Bangladeshi business—a restaurant-cum-ethnic store—was established in Koreatown in 1993. Today, there are six Bangladeshi restaurants and ethnic stores, two afterschool prep centers, and two video stores in Little Bangladesh, as well as about 300 liquor stores and gas stations owned by Bangladeshis all over Los Angeles.

The contexts and conditions for migrants settling reveal a number of differences between Tokyo and Los Angeles. First, Bangladeshi migrants in Tokyo found their stay in Japan to be temporary and their return inevitable, whereas those in Los Angeles saw the USA as their ultimate home for permanent settlement. This contrast was explicit in the continuous development and growth of the Bangladeshi immigrant community in Los Angeles, compared with the gradual diminution in the size of their counterpart in Japan. Beginning with a few hundred Bangladeshis in Los Angeles in the 1980s, the community grew to over 50,000 immigrants by 2010. By contrast, the number of Bangladeshis in Japan continued to dwindle from over 50,000 in the early 1990s to about 10,000 during my initial fieldwork in 2013.

Second, most Bangladeshis entered Japan as tourists and overstayed their visas, or entered under the pretext of being college students, earning an income illegally. By contrast, nearly all Bangladeshis in the USA entered the country as legal permanent residents, eligible to work full time, or with a genuine intent to study, finding employment after graduating. This meant that the majority of Bangladeshi migrants in Tokyo worked in unskilled and part-time jobs, evading law enforcement, whereas Bangladeshis in Los Angeles were legally employed in both unskilled and professional jobs.

Third, almost all Bangladeshis migrated to Japan alone, regardless of their marital status. The temporary migration opportunities were open only to male migrants, who would have to return to Bangladesh to raise a family, whereas the USA allowed and even encouraged migration with family and permanent settlement in the USA. These differences in the destination states' immigration policies and practices affected the migrants' choices and their relationships with their families, communities, and states, all of which shaped their transnational practices, including remittances.

A comparison between the cases of Bangladeshi migrants in Tokyo and Los Angeles allows for a comparison of both South-South and South-North migration and of corresponding remittances. In addition, there was a practical concern in choosing these two field sites: having been a Bangladeshi graduate student in both Tokyo and Los Angeles, I was familiar with these migrant communities through networks of friends and acquaintances. Thus, gaining access to interview partners was relatively easy and we quickly built a foundation of trust.

The Destination State in Bangladeshi Migration to Japan and the USA

According to Bangladesh Bank statistics, the total amount of remittances Bangladesh received from Japan and the USA in 2019/20 were USD49.35 million and USD2403.40 million, respectively.[1] While the government engages in the management of Bangladeshi migration to a number of countries in the Middle East and Southeast Asia, the state has very limited—if any—influence on migration to Japan and the USA. Rather these two migration flows are primarily driven by the policies of the destination states. As I discuss below, the opportunity to migrate to Japan was limited to the rural communities of a few districts due to the heavy dependence of this migration on migrant networks, while migration to the USA was relatively open.

[1] Source: https://www.bb.org.bd/econdata/wagermidtl.php (accessed July 22, 2020).

Japan

Japan is known for its restrictive immigration policies, particularly toward low-skilled migrant workers. In the 1980s, Japan saw a strong economic boom coinciding with an acute labor shortage. Japanese employers, particularly small- and medium-sized entrepreneurs, were in such a dire situation that up to 50 companies would go bankrupt every week because they could not process orders due to the lack of workers on their factory floors (Goodman 2004). Therefore, Japan adopted a number of policies to promote labor migration while at the same time minimizing the possibility of permanent settlement of the foreign population. The conservative bureaucracy, unwilling to allow a large number of migrant workers into the country, offered visas on arrival to visitors from Iran, Pakistan, and Bangladesh (Higuchi 2007; Okabe 2011). These visitors would immediately take up employment in Japanese companies and frequently overstayed their visas. Some enterprising individuals in Bangladesh found earning opportunities by migrating to Japan and some established businesses that arranged migration to the country for others.

As Mahmood (1994) observed, the number of Bangladeshis in Japan jumped from a few hundred to over 34,000 between 1987 and 1990. Two-thirds of these migrants had been employed or self-employed before their migration, and only one-fifth were students. This first period of Bangladeshi migration included middle- and lower-middle-class men from a few villages. It is estimated that more than three-fourths of them came from Munshiganj District, south of Dhaka. They were quite young, with some coming right after college graduation (Higuchi 2007). Since Japan did not allow low-skilled and unskilled foreign workers, Bangladeshis used informal networks of co-ethnics who helped them to enter Japan as visitors, tourists, or students (Rahman and Fee 2011). This migration abruptly stopped due to Japan's immigration policy reform in 1990, when the government rescinded the visa-waiver program in response to a combination of pushback from Japanese society against a rapidly growing foreign population, the unwillingness of the bureaucracy to allow the incorporation of migrants, and the discovery of another source of cheap labor in Latin America.

Migration to Japan had a good reputation in Bangladesh due to paying the highest salaries for low-skilled jobs and enabling the largest amounts of remittances compared to any other destination country of Bangladeshi migrants (Mahmud 2016). The cancelation of the port-entry visa facility for Bangladeshis caused a halt in new arrivals from Bangladesh. Anti-immigration measures, particularly police raids in workplaces and immigrant neighborhoods, resulted in massive numbers of arrests and deportations of Bangladeshis in the early 1990s. However, the awareness of high-earning opportunities and the presence of relatives and friends in Japan continued to attract new aspirants from Bangladesh, who would look for alternative ways to migrate to Japan and earn their fortune. Entering as a student emerged as the alternative they were looking for. In 1984, the Japanese government had inaugurated policies to internationalize higher education (Liu-Farrer 2009, p. 2011). With Japan's cancelation of visas on arrival and the deportation of undocumented migrants, acquiring a student visa as a self-funded language student became the primary route of entry. With the help of relatives as well as professional migration agents, aspiring Bangladeshis obtained information about admissions, courses, fees, etc., procured the documents, such as the certificate of eligibility issued by the immigration department in Tokyo, and found accommodation and jobs once they arrived in Japan. Although these migrants held student visas, they were qualitatively different from student migrants in the USA, the UK, and Australia, in that these migrants in Japan used student visas for legal entry while they spent all of their time earning, saving, and remitting money. Empirical studies have recognized that these self-funded students frequently violate the 28-hour work limit set by their visa category and work as long as—sometimes longer than—a full-time employee (Liu-Farrer 2009; Mahmud 2014). The most recent immigration policy revisions in Japan also recognized international students as a pool of part-time workers (Milly 2020).

The USA

Bangladeshi migration to the USA was very meager until the introduction of the Diversity Visa (DV1) lottery in the early 1990s, when Bangladeshis began to enter the USA in their thousands. The statistical yearbooks for the US Immigration and Naturalization Service documented only 154 Bangladeshis in 1973 and 787 in 1983. Then, in 1990, the introduction of the OP1 visa lottery (the predecessor of the DV1 visa lottery) resulted in the admission of 10,676 immigrants from Bangladesh (Aswad and Bilge 1996, p. 159). Thereafter, the immigrants entering through this visa lottery program outnumbered those entering the USA by other means. Each year, several thousand Bangladeshis entered the USA through this diversity visa lottery, until they reached the numerical threshold that excluded Bangladesh from the program in 2012.

Despite this exclusion from the government-sponsored DV1 visa lottery program, immigration from Bangladesh to the USA continued to grow. Thanks to the US family unification policy, those with family members and close relatives who are US citizens can still enter the USA as immigrants. According to US Department of State statistics, 14,946 Bangladeshis entered the USA with immigration visas in 2018. Almost all of these immigrants (14,818 or 99 percent) obtained their visas through the sponsorship of immediate family members or close relatives. State Department statistics show that from 2012 to 2018, the total number of immigrants from Bangladesh remained over 12,000 per year. Vaughan and Huennekens (2018) observed that between 2000 and 2016, the Bangladesh chain migration multiplier was 4.44, higher than the most recent worldwide average chain migration multiplier of 3.45.

US policy toward foreign students offered another avenue for Bangladeshis to enter the USA. The US ambassador to Bangladesh reported 7143 Bangladeshi students in the USA at the graduate level in 2018, making Bangladesh ninth among the top 25 student-sending countries. The US embassy in Bangladesh eased student visa processing in 2012, which caused a significant increase in the flow of Bangladeshi students to the USA. Between 2012 and 2017, the number of Bangladeshi students in the USA increased by 53.5 percent, with a 9.7 percent increase in 2017 compared to the previous year, while the international average increased by only 3.4 percent according to the 2017 Open Doors Report on International Educational Exchange. After graduation, these students usually find professional employment and acquire permanent residency and citizenship, thereby facilitating further migration of their close relatives through the family unification policy. Members of the Bangladeshi diaspora community are more likely to have a university degree than the average population of the USA and have a higher household income than the US median (MPI 2014).

Finally, unlike in Europe, where most Bangladeshis enter by crossing the Mediterranean (Qayum 2017), they very rarely number among the undocumented migrants in the USA. Perhaps this is due to the vast geographical distance between the two countries and the absence of transnational underground networks like those serving other well-known migrant groups. Nevertheless, there is a small but significant number of undocumented Bangladeshi migrants in the USA, who entered as tourists or visitors and then overstayed their visas. The majority manage to legalize their stay through marriage or applying for political asylum, while a few remain undocumented.

Remittance Decay in the Context of the Destination State

Although the governments of both Japan and the USA play a decisive role in Bangladeshi migration to these countries, they pursue their policies from different motivations, resulting in exclusionary and receptive destination contexts respectively. These, in turn, have divergent impacts on remittance behaviors.

Japan: Temporary Migration without the Family and Remittances

Japan is known as an exceptionally restrictive immigration destination among all the liberal democratic countries (Oishi 2012). Nevertheless, the total non-citizen population in Japan increased by about 20 percent between 2007 and 2017, from about 2.1 million to nearly 2.6 million. Together with various government programs to bring in foreign workers, this rising number indicates an opening of the Japanese border for migrants. However, Japan is maintaining its policy not to allow permanent settlement by adopting various direct and indirect mechanisms (Mahmud 2014; Okabe 2011; Tarumoto 2019).

It is obvious from the formal immigration policies and practices that Japan wants foreign workers to enter and work for a certain number of years, and then leave Japan. My interview partners who entered Japan as short-term visitors or as self-funded students confirmed this assumption. For instance, Rahman (a 54-year-old community leader and permanent resident through marriage) stated:

> While it was easy for us to enter Japan and find highly paying work [compared with work in Bangladesh], we all knew that we would have to go home. Also, living on construction sites or in factories in remote areas was difficult. Moreover, the fear of being arrested and deported was always there. So, we would spend all of our time working and earning so that we could earn as much as possible and leave Japan with 'big' money.

The first influx of foreign workers to Japan occurred when the port-entry visa policy for citizens of Iran, Pakistan, and Bangladesh was introduced in 1987. The rapid increase of Bangladeshi migrants in Japan between 1987 and 1990 noted by Mahmood (1994) primarily consisted of undocumented migrants who entered Japan as tourists with permits for 15 to 30-day stays, but who would take up employment and overstay their visas. With new immigration policies adopted in 1990, the Japanese government started to arrest and deport many of those migrants. Scholars have argued that Japan changed its position regarding those visa-overstayers because a large population of migrants of Japanese descent were identified living in Latin America, whom the Japanese government actively pursued to bring back to replace the undocumented Asian migrants.

Studies have observed a similar reluctance by the Japanese government concerning self-funded students violating the immigration law. While there is a 28-hour weekly work limit for students to engage in part-time jobs, most students take multiple jobs and work much longer hours to maximize their earnings. These student migrants conceal their violation of the legal work-hour limit by maintaining multiple bank accounts and getting paid in cash. The immigration authorities turn a blind eye and rarely investigate the students' entire banking transactions to detect their violation of the work limit. Moreover, several language schools developed a reputation for selling student visas, whereby students would enroll to maintain their student status while working in multiple part-time jobs for longer than full-time employment. Inspections by the immigration authorities and corresponding restrictive measures were temporary and would eventually be lifted, thus allowing these schools to bring in more student migrants. However, Japan strictly enforces the rule for maintaining student status for these migrants to stay on. Given that the studentship ends after four to six years, the migrants have to leave Japan and return home. As Kamal (27 years old, single with a student visa, four years in Tokyo) shared:

> I would have stayed here for a few years more. But my education does not help me to get a job that would make me eligible for work visa. It is also impossible to overstay, as there are police everywhere, you know. So, I have to return home despite opportunities to earn high amounts of money really fast. You know how it feels! I have come here to earn money, and there are plenty of jobs. Yet, I cannot stay.

I observed that entering Japan as a self-funded student in Japanese language schools emerged as the most common way for Bangladeshis to migrate after the visa-on-arrival scheme ended. This migration was more selective than the previous one due to the higher costs and bureaucracy involved in getting admission into language schools, preparing paperwork for various institutions to process the visa, and arranging for housing and other daily necessities once in Japan. The legality of their stay allowed the migrants to live in metropolitan Tokyo and other large cities and work in better-paying restaurants, unlike their counterparts among the visa-overstayers. The opportunity to earn through multiple part-time jobs, the necessity of sending money home, and the inability to find professional jobs due to not studying enough make these migrants' return to Bangladesh inevitable.

Similar observations can be made about those Bangladeshis entering Japan through the newly enacted Technical Intern Training Program (TITP) that requires the interns to return to their home at the end of their five-year stay. While originally conceptualized as a temporary training program through which Japan contributed to the origin country, the recent change in this program (adopted in 2017) allows the interns to extend their stay by up to five years, with some eventually able to acquire permanent residency and citizenship, thereby revealing the true motivation of Japan to use the TITP as a way of recruiting migrant workers. Representatives of the Japanese government signed a Memorandum of Cooperation with Bangladeshi government representatives on August 27, 2019, which specified 14 sectors in which Japan will recruit migrant workers from Bangladesh. Although interns in a few specific sectors are allowed to renew their visas multiple times and acquire permanent residency and even citizenship, the number of naturalizations is negligible compared to the total number of migrants who have to leave Japan. Thus, Japan constructs migration primarily as temporary, whereby it allows foreigners to enter and work, but only for a certain period.

In sum, Bangladeshi migration to Japan began with the visa-waiver program adopted by the Japanese government and was shaped thereafter by successive changes in Japanese immigration policies. This partly explains why the number of Bangladeshis in Japan continuously declined, from its peak at over 50,000 in the early 1990s down to approximately 16,000 in

2018 (according to the Japanese Ministry of Foreign Affairs).[2] I argue that this inability to stay permanently and raise a family in Japan causes Bangladeshi migrants to send a large portion of their income to Bangladesh for family maintenance, investment, and savings. I enumerated from a purposing sample survey that these migrants sent about 60 percent of their income in remittances to Bangladesh for family maintenance as well as to realize their future plans including investing in income-generating activities and savings in their country of origin. This finding also suggests that remittances from Japan—and other destination countries characterized by temporary visa status and family separation—will remain high. Most importantly, these findings show that the destination state shapes remittances by requiring family separation and denying permanent settlement.

The USA: Permanent Settlement, Family Unification, and Remittances

In contrast to Japan, the US immigration policy welcomes specific groups of migrants to enter and permanently settle in the USA through its DV1 lottery program, family-sponsored immigration, and employer-sponsored immigration, among several other programs. The US government's interest in keeping migrants in the USA is also manifested in its occasionally adopted Temporary Permanent Status (TPS) programs. Moreover, the government runs various programs to support the naturalization and settlement of new immigrants and provides fund to civil society organizations to offer supporting services to the new immigrants. According to the US Citizenship and Immigration Services (USCIS) department, a total of 834,000 new citizens were naturalized and nearly 577,000 individuals were granted permanent residency in 2019.

Permanent settlement defines Bangladeshi migration to the USA. From the very beginning, all of my interview partners reportedly knew that they were going to leave Bangladesh to settle permanently in the USA. The US immigration policy of allowing family unification led to the migration of entire families to the USA. Consequently, Bangladeshi immigrant neighborhoods have sprung up in most large US cities, including New York, Los Angeles, Detroit, Atlanta, Dallas, Houston, Boston, Indianapolis, and Chicago.

[2] https://www.mofa.go.jp/region/asia-paci/bangladesh/data.html (accessed July 5, 2023).

Despite fostering a national tradition of immigration, scholars have also recognized racism in US immigration policies and practices (Tourse et al. 2018; Valdez 2016), especially during the Trump administration from 2016 to 2020. Nevertheless, and contrary to my expectations, my interview partners shared very positive impressions of the USA as a migration destination and of their new permanent home. The increase in anti-immigration rhetoric and discrimination under the Trump administration did not cause any significant change in this perception, as demonstrated in the continuously high number of new immigrants from Bangladesh. My interview partners would often cite their lives full of uncertainty and insecurity in Bangladesh to support their claim of having a better life in the USA, and they praised a range of support services from the US federal government and local governments. These include subsidized English language classes and vocational courses with stipends from the government, free or subsidized health insurance, low-income housing, and tax refunds. Moreover, these immigrants can send their children to public schools for free. Finally, there are other employment-related services for new arrivals. While some questioned the adequacy of these services, they presented these as evidence of the US government's welcoming stance toward the new immigrants and their permanent settlement.

My interviewees experienced both economic and social security after migrating to the USA. They found opportunities for upward mobility—though limited—not only for themselves but also for the next generation, opportunities that they had not experienced in Bangladesh. They were able to establish their own ethnic neighborhoods, which provided them with familiar public spaces in the foreign land. Although they still belonged to a minority, the Bangladeshi diaspora community was well integrated into the labor market and social life in the USA. While low-paying jobs enabled the first generation to survive, their emphasis on higher education for their children, who were able to accompany them to the USA, facilitated a quick improvement in social status for many in the second generation, as is substantiated by numerous instances of highly educated Bangladeshi youth coming out of working-class families. In a way, they lived the American Dream at a time when many Americans had lost sight of it. Settling permanently and sponsoring immigration of their close relatives was one of the main goals of the migration project, as Ataur (a former schoolteacher in Bangladesh who entered the USA on a diversity visa in 2011 and is now a cashier in a gas station) stated:

> My work is very painful. I have to stand behind the cash register for the whole period of eight to ten hours each day for six days a week. This causes severe pain in my back and legs. But I cannot leave the job because I need money to send home for my family. Therefore, I take pain medicine so that I can endure the pain. It is just for a few years until my family joins me here [he smiled, giving an optimistic impression]. I'm working here because I will be able to bring my parents and younger brothers to the USA. This is an unimaginable success for a school teacher like me.

This statement supports the idea that migrants persevere in back-breaking jobs to earn and send remittances to their family in their country of origin (Ahsan 2011; see also the remittance script "sacrifice," Carling 2014). However, it also clearly shows that Ataur's financial bond with the homeland has a time limit and that remittances for family support will stop once the family reunites in the destination country. Finally, as family unification is regulated by the state, this case demonstrates that state policies have a considerable influence on remitting.

I enumerated from a purposive sample survey that the migrants send about one-third of their income in remittances to Bangladesh. Once their families reunite in the USA, living expenses increase and there is less money available to send to their places of origin. However, my interview partners recognized that even their small savings translated into large enough amounts to invest in assets in Bangladesh that would bring them both income and prestige. They also talked about helping their relatives and neighbors in times of need as well as charitable spending for schools, religious institutions, and so forth. Nevertheless, these remittances tend to be significantly smaller and mostly occasional compared to remittances for family support. Thus, I recognized declining patterns of remittances among Bangladeshi migrants in the USA, which support the remittance decay hypothesis. More precisely, remittances not just declined but also transformed: from regular family support toward unsteady investments and charity. The migrants' permanent settlement and family unification in the destination country causes remittances to gradually decline. Yet greater economic opportunities as well as the presence of kin and other relatives in the origin country are likely to encourage migrants to send remittances, although less frequently and in smaller amounts.

Conclusion

Contrary to the individualized conceptualization of migration, I found that the destination state plays a decisive role in shaping international migration and remittances. Both Bangladeshi migrations to Japan and the USA are primarily shaped by the destination states' immigration policies. Japan not only regulates Bangladeshi migrants' entry to the state, but also their stay in and departure from the country, which is most clearly observed in the case of self-funded language students. Japan allows these de facto migrant workers as international students and overlooks their unauthorized extended work hours in multiple part-time jobs at restaurants. Yet Japan strictly enforces the conditionality of maintaining studentship and ensures their return home when their student status runs out. Given that these migrants do not earn credentials nor work experience that would allow them to access professional jobs and stay longer, they solely focus on earning as much as they can and remit most of their income to Bangladesh. This illustrates how transnationalism—or maintaining cross-border connections and sustaining these through various practices including remittances—is strongly linked to the state's policies and practices. Furthermore, I observed a perception of Japan as forever foreign among most Bangladeshi migrants, which potentially influences their high propensity to engage in transnational practices like remitting.

Like the case in Japan, US immigration policy plays a central role in Bangladeshi migration. As discussed above, Bangladeshi migration to the USA until 2012 depended primarily on the DV1 program. Nowadays, nearly all Bangladeshis migrate through the family unification policy. Unlike Japan, the USA offers various forms of support for immigrants to settle permanently. These immigrants not only settled with their respective families but also sponsored the immigration of their parents and siblings: All of my respondents among the low-income families and most of those among the professional immigrants reported applying for the immigration of their parents and siblings as soon as they got US passports. Settling permanently and sponsoring close relatives became so common that these behaviors would influence almost all aspects of their lives after migration, especially remittances.

My analysis show, Japan allows migrant workers to enter and stay for a few years, but maintains that they should not settle permanently and raise families in Japan. Therefore, migrants in Japan always need to send remittances for various purposes including family maintenance, investments, and savings. By contrast, the USA not only allows immigrants and their families to settle permanently, but also offers various means of support to this end. Consequently, remittances have gradually declined as they do not need to send money for family maintenance. Nevertheless, these migrants still send remittances in order to invest or to give to charity.

Migrants' motivations for sending remittances are well established in the current literature. Some scholars have also convincingly demonstrated the role of the origin state in shaping remittances. What lacks attention is the respective impact of the destination state. This chapter contributes to closing this gap by recognizing the role of the Japanese and US governments in shaping Bangladeshi remittances. Remittance decay depends not just on the time period migrants spend abroad, but also on a bundle of legal factors, such as immigration policies and visa regulations. Further studies are necessary, for example looking at successive generations of migrants in various destination countries characterized by different immigration policies.

References

Ahsan U. (2011). Dynamics of Remittance Practices and Development: Bangladeshi Overseas Migrants. *Development in Practice*, 21(8), 1153–1167.

AlShehabi, O., Hanieh, A. & Khalaf, A. (2015). *Transit States: Labour, Migration and Citizenship in the Gulf.* Pluto Press.

Amega, K. (2018). Remittances, Education and Health in Sub-Saharan Africa. *Cogent Economics & Finance*, 6(1). DOI: https://doi.org/10.1080/23322039.2018.1516488

Amuedo-Dorantes, C. & Mazzolari, F. (2010). Remittances to Latin America from Migrants in the United States: Assessing the Impact of Amnesty Programs. *Journal of Development Economics*, 91, 323–335.

Aswad, B. C. & Bilge, B. (1996). *Family and Gender among American Muslims.* Temple University Press.

Burawoy, M. (1976). The Functions and Reproduction of Migrant Labor: Comparative Material from Southern Africa and the United States. *American journal of sociology*, 81(5), 1050–1087.

Carling, J. (2008). The Determinants of Migrant Remittances. *Oxford Review of Economic Policy*, 24(3), 581–598

Carling, J. (2014). Scripting Remittances: Making Sense of Money Transfers in Transnational Relationships. *International Migration Review*, 48(4), 218–262.

Castles, S. (2011). Migration, Crisis, and the Global Labour Market. *Globalizations*, 8(3), 311–324.

De Haas, H. (2010). Migration and Development: A Theoretical Perspective. *International Migration Review*, 44, 227–264.

Dennison, J. & Geddes, A. (2018). A Rising Tide? The Salience of Immigration and the Rise of Anti-Immigration Political Parties in Western Europe. *The Political Quarterly*, 90 (1), 107-116.

DeVoretz, D. J. & Pivnenko, S. (2005). The Economic Causes and Consequences of Canadian Citizenship. *Journal of International Migration and Integration*, 6, 435–468.

Guevarra, A. R. (2010). *Marketing Dreams, Manufacturing Heroes: The Transnational Labor Brokering of Filipino Workers*. Rutgers University Press.

Glytsos, N.P. (1997). Remitting Behaviour of "Temporary" and "Permanent" Migrants: The Case of Greeks in Germany and Australia. *LABOUR*, 11, 409–435. https://doi.org/10.1111/1467-9914.00043

Goodman, R.(2004). Review Works. *The Journal of Japanese Studies*, 30(2), 465–471.

Higuchi, N. (2007). Remittances, investments and social mobility among Bangladeshi and Iranian returnees from Japan. In *Proceedings for the 8th Asia and Pacific Migration Research Network Conference on Migration, Development and Poverty Reduction*.

Hogan, J. & Haltinner, K. (2015). Floods, Invaders, and Parasites: Immigration Threat Narratives and Right-Wing Populism in the USA, UK and Australia. *Journal of Intercultural Studies*, 36(5), 520–543.

Hollifield, J. (2004). The Emerging Migration State. *International Migration Review*, 38(3), 885–912.

International Organization for Migration (2020). World Migration Report 2020. https://publications.iom.int/system/files/pdf/wmr_2020.pdf

Iskander, N. N. (2010). *Creative State: Forty Years of Migration and Development Policy in Morocco and Mexico*. Cornell University Press.

Kapur, D. (2004). Remittances: The New Development Mantra? G-24 Discussion Paper Series, 29. https://unctad.org/system/files/official-document/gdsmdpbg2420045_en.pdf

Kossoudji, S. A. & Cobb-Clark, D. A. (2002). Coming Out of the Shadows: Learning about Legal Status and Wages from the Legalized Population. *Journal of Labor Economics*, 20, 598–628.

Liu-Farrer, G. (2009). Educationally Channeled International Labor Mobility: Contemporary Student Migration from China to Japan. *International Migration Review*, 43, 178–204.

Lu, Y. (2012). Household Migration, Remittances and their Impact on Health in Indonesia. *International Migration*, 51(S1): 203—215.

Lucas, R.E.B. & Stark, O. (1985). Motivations to Remit: Evidence from Botswana. *Journal of Political Economy*, 93(5), 901–918.

Mahmood, R. A. (1994). Adaptation to a New World: Experience of Bangladeshis in Japan. *International Migration*, 32(4): 513–532.

Mahmud, H. (2013). Enemy or Ally: Migrants, Intermediaries and the State in Bangladeshi Migration to Japan and the United States. *Migration and Development*, 2, 1–15.

Mahmud, H. (2014). It's My Money: Social Class and Perception of Remittance among Bangladeshi Migrants in Japan. *Current Sociology*, 62(3), 418–430.

Mahmud, H. (2016). Impact of the Destination State on Migrants' Remittances: A Study of Remitting among Bangladeshi Migrants in the USA, the UAE and Japan. *Migration and Development*, 5(1), 79–98.

Mahmud, H. (2017). Social Determinants of Remitting Practices among Bangladeshi Migrants in Japan. *Sociological Perspectives*, 60(1), 95–112.

Mahmud, H. (2020). From Individual Motivations to Social Determinants: Towards a Sociology of Migrants' Remittances. *International Social Science Journal*. DOI: https://doi.org/10.1111/issj.12247.

Makina, D. & Masenge, A. (2015). The Time Pattern of Remittances and the Decay Hypothesis: Evidence from Migrants in South Africa. *Migration Letters*, 12(1), 79–90

Markova, E. & Reilly, B. (2007). Bulgarian Migrant Remittances and Legal Status: Some Micro-Level Evidence from Madrid. *South-Eastern Europe Journal of Economics*, 5, 55–69.

Meyer, D. & Shera, A. (2017). The Impact of Remittances on Economic Growth: An Econometric model. *EconomiA*, 18(2), 147–155.

Meyer, S. (2020). "Home Is Where I Spend My Money": Testing the Remittance Decay Hypothesis with Ethnographic Data from an Austrian-Turkish Community. *Social Inclusion*, 8(1), 275–284.

Milly, D. J. (2020). Japan's Labor Migration Reforms: Breaking with the Past? *Migration Policy Institute*.

Migration Policy Institute (2014): The Bangladeshi Diaspora in the United States. https://www.migrationpolicy.org/sites/default/files/publications/RAD-Bangladesh.pdf

Munck, R. (2008). Globalisation, Governance and Migration: An Introduction. *Third World Quarterly*, 29, 1227–1246.

Neumayer, E. (2006). Unequal Access to Foreign Spaces: How States use Visa Restrictions to Regulate Mobility in a Globalized World. *Transactions of the Institute of British Geographers*, 31, 72–84.

Oishi, N, (2012). The Limits of Immigration Policies: The Challenges of Highly Skilled Migration in Japan. *American Behavioral Scientist*, 56(8): 1080–1100.

Okabe, M. (2011). The "Outside-In": An Overview of Japanese Policy from the Perspective of International Relations. In E. Guild & S. Mantu (Eds.), *Constructing and Imagining Labour Migration: Perspectives of Control from Five Continents* (pp. 189–204). Ashgate.

Pinger, P. (2010). Come Back or Stay? Spend Here or There? Return and Remittances: The Case of Moldova. *International Migration,* 48, 142–173.

Rahman, M. & Fee, L. K. (2011). The development of migrant entrepreneurship in Japan: Case of Bangladeshis. *International Migration and Integration,* 12, 253–274.

Qayum, N. (2017). Chasing the Dubai Dream in Italy: Bangladeshi Migration to Europe. *Migration Information Source.* MPI. https://www.migrationpolicy.org/article/chasing-dubai-dream-italy-bangladeshi-migration-europe

Rapoport, H. & Docquier, F. (2006). The Economics of Migrants' Remittances. In S. C. Kolm & J. M. Ythier (Eds.), *Handbook of the Economics of Giving, Altruism and Reciprocity* (Vol. 2, pp. 1135–1198). Elsevier.

Redehegn M. A., Sun D., Eshete A. M. & Gichuki C. N. (2019). Development Impacts of Migration and Remittances on Migrant-Sending Communities: Evidence from Ethiopia. *PLoS ONE, 14*(2).

Rodriguez, R. M. (2010). *Migrants for Export: How the Philippine State Brokers Labor to the World.* University of Minnesota Press.

Seol, D. H., & Skrentny, J. D. (2009). Why is There so Little Migrant Settlement in East Asia? *International Migration Review*, 43, 578–620.

Shipper, Apichai (2002). The Political Construction of Foreign Workers in Japan. *Critical Asian Studies,* 34(1), 41–68.

Tarumoto, H. (2019). Why Restrictive Refugee Policy can be Retained? A Japanese Case. *Migration and Development*, *8*(1), 7–24.

Thow A. M., Fanzo J., Negin J. (2016). A Systematic Review of the Effect of Remittances on Diet and Nutrition. *Food and Nutrition Bulletin*, 37(1), 42–64.

Tourse R. W. C., Hamilton-Mason J., Wewiorski N. J. (2018). Immigration through the Lens of Systemic Racism. In: *Systemic Racism in the United States.* Springer.

Tseng, Y. & Wang, H. (2011). Governing Migrant Workers at a Distance: Managing the Temporary Status of Guestworkers in Taiwan. *International Migration*, 51(4), 1–19.

Valdez I. (2016). Punishment, Race, and the Organization of U.S. Immigration Exclusion. *Political Research Quarterly*, 69(4), 640–654.

Vaughan, J. & Huennekens, P. (2018). Bangladesh: A Case Study in Chain Migration. Center for Immigration Studies. https://cis.org/sites/default/files/2018-01/vaughan-bangladesh.pdf

Zolberg, A. R. (1999). The Politics of Immigration Policy: An Externalist Perspective. *American Behavioral Scientist*, *42*(9), 1276–1279.

CHAPTER 9

"We Do Solidarity, Not Charity": The Collective Remittance Practices of Moldovan Migrants

Eveline Odermatt

Introduction

Since the late 1990s, international organizations, European state development agencies, and NGOs have viewed increasingly migrants as potential drivers of and "investors" in development in their countries of origin. As a leitmotiv of this discourse, migrants are portrayed as agents of development via their associations and remittance practices or through their return (CIM/GIZ 2012; IOM and MPI 2012). The optimistic policy framing of the migration-development nexus, referring to a set of multifaceted interdependencies between the two complex social phenomena, has also provoked a growing academic interest in migrants' transnational practices of giving and their potential to alleviate poverty in their countries of origin. Nevertheless, it remains difficult to single out the effect of various forms of remittances on transformative social change in the countries of origin

E. Odermatt (✉)
University of Fribourg, Fribourg, Switzerland
e-mail: Eveline.Odermatt@unifr.ch

S. Meyer, C. Ströhle (eds.), *Remittances as Social Practices and Agents of Change*,
https://doi.org/10.1007/978-3-030-81504-2_9

(Isaakyan and Triandafyllidou 2016; Lacroix et al. 2016; Page and Mercer 2012). While the overwhelming majority of research on the topic has focused on financial flows at the macro level, the micro-level power dynamics of migrants' collective involvement in concrete transnational aid practices has so far attracted less attention.

This chapter provides an insight into how the discourse of migrants' contributions to developmental transition is put into concrete practice in the case of Moldova. More precisely, I highlight Moldovan migrants' subjective motivations to engage in collective transnational aid efforts, understood as transnational practices, in the same vein as other transnational activities, such as return visits and cross-border communication. This encompasses both financial transfers and other forms of remitting practices, commonly known as social remittances, such as the transfer of ideas, behaviors, values, norms knowledge, and qualifications between migrants' destination countries and places of origin (Levitt 1998).

Whereas most studies of remittances focus on the practices that individual migrants transfer to their countries of origin, this chapter provides an insight into the performances of migrant organizations. It thus highlights aspects of collective remittances, which are exchanged by migrants in their role as organizational members in settings such as migrant associations, church groups, and political parties (Levitt and Lamba-Nieves 2011).

The main argument here is that collective remittance practices emerge from both migrants' personal everyday lives, connecting multiple localities, and their past and current visions of their home country. Thereby, the chapter aims to contribute to the broader theoretical discussion on linkages between patterns of remittance as social practices of Eastern European migrants living in EU countries and the development transition in the Eastern European "neighborhood."

I will begin by setting out the theoretical and geographical terrain of the study. I will then identify four types of migrants' motivations for taking part in aid practices directed toward Moldova (e.g., support of local hospitals and schools). The first two categories of motivations relate to migrants' individual opinions and attitudes, which are strongly interwoven with their multi-sited social lives and migration experiences, including their integration in different social and spatial contexts and experiences of deskilling, understood as being highly qualified but employed in low-status and low-paid jobs. In section three, I will introduce two patterns of aid practices that are shaped by the home country context—by Moldova's communist past and the country's marginalized place within the socio-spatial configuration of Europe today. I will conclude with a sketch of migrants' personal reflections of their remitting practices in relation to the aid practices performed by mainstream development agencies. This will demonstrate that significant differences of opinion exist between migrants and development agencies concerning the nature of cross-border aid practices. Of particular note in this context is the migrants' rejection of top-down approaches and the professional "charity practices" performed by aid agencies.

Setting the Scene: The Theoretical and Geographical Terrain

The 2000s witnessed a boom in studies on the impact of migration on various social, political, and cultural outcomes. This body of literature established that besides monetary flows, which imply multifaceted practices, exchanges, and social consequences that reach far beyond the economic realm, non-monetary flows, such as the circulation of ideas, also influence the sociopolitical environment of migrant countries of origin (Boccagni et al. 2016; Lacroix 2014; Piper 2009). In addition, since the transnational turn in the 1990s, migrant associations have increasingly been considered as members of "transnational civil society," or as actors within transnational spaces (Faist 2000). They have since become a familiar motif in debates within different disciplines where a spatial framework that privileges the transnational is commonly deployed (Mullings 2012). For these reasons, a range of international development agencies have launched migrant association-led programs aiming at maximizing their development potential through financial and technical support, and at bringing the associations' activities implemented in migrant-sending countries, including Moldova, into the development establishment (IOM and MPI 2012). So far, however, the academic literature on the topic of the diffusion of transnational collective practices has heavily concentrated on Western European countries and the USA on the one hand and African, Caribbean, and Asian countries on the other (Grabowska and Garapich 2016). Although in the past few years, the body of literature on patterns of intra-European remittance practices has been growing, the social practices contributing to the transformation in migrants' countries of origin within Europe have received less attention (Sinatti and Horst 2015). Yet, as Castles stressed: "The notion of social transformation signifies profound structural modifications of social relations" (2016, p. 19). The transformation in Central and Eastern European countries from communist and centrally planned economies to democratic systems with free market conditions has not only been geographically uneven, with some leftovers from the communist era, and with delayed convergence with Western democratic countries in many spheres of life, but has also profoundly changed social relations. These conditions sometimes create context-dependent gaps for social remittances that can be captured in transnational social spaces (Faist 2000) or transnational social fields (Glick Schiller 2005), for instance within the Moldovan migrant community in Western European countries.

Turning to the geographical background of this study, the small Republic of Moldova—situated between Romania and Ukraine—is one of Europe's lesser-known countries. Yet, with its intense recent experience of migration, it presents a fertile territory for an in-depth study of intra-European migration-transformation dynamics, with special emphasis on the role of migrant associations. Since Moldova achieved independence in 1991, the country has witnessed out-migration on a large scale. Estimates of the number of migrants range up to 50 percent of the economically active population, or one-third of the total population (UNDP 2019). Financial remittances account for 43 percent of the country's GDP (IMF 2015), which makes Moldova one of the world's top recipients of financial remittances per capita. The country's large-scale emigration has been accompanied by a rise in formal and non-formal organizational activities aimed at Moldova, as well as a grouping of activities under umbrella schemes in migrant destination countries (Cheianu-Andrei 2013). However, most migrant associations are small and volunteer-run, and their role in Moldova's development remains modest due to shortcomings in their organizational and financial capacities. Furthermore, according to migrants, the morphological transformation of their community toward becoming a "Moldovan community of transnational aid practices" is still in the making due to the relatively recent emigration of Moldovans toward Western Europe and the migrants' rather weak social integration in their host societies (Odermatt 2017).

The policy discourse of migrants' involvement in development raises a couple of questions: What are Moldovan migrants' subjective motivations for participating in collective transnational giving? And what are the migrants' own reflections on their patterns of remittance practices? I have here opted for a transnational lens in order to answer these questions, taking into account that migrants' border-crossing aid practices refer to multiple social spaces and reflect different senses of belonging (Glick Schiller et al. 1999). This has allowed me to see how migrants' ways of being and their ways of belonging affect their collective practices of aid-giving in a reciprocal process. Additionally, as mentioned above, I also deploy a transnational social field approach (Amelina and Faist 2012; Faist 2010). I here conceptualize migrant civil society as a transnational social field in which "transnational spaces comprise combinations of ties and their substance, positions and networks of organizations that cut across the borders of at least two nation states" (Faist 2010, p. 21). This means that I will here trace the transnational social field within which migrants appear not as foreigners to be differentiated, or natives in a specific geographical context, but as actors that connect one another through their collective engagement. Simultaneously, I will analyze field-specific symbolic, organizational, and economic resources. These resources include, for example, the ability of individuals, such as migrants and their associations, to participate in multiple localities (Amelina and Faist 2012). By applying this notion of a transnational field, I seek to delineate the genesis of Moldovan migrant associations as transnational social formations, as well as the particular macro-societal context in which these associations operate, such as the international development aid system. Accentuating the relationships that unfold across several receiving countries has allowed me to access a core group of active migrant leaders living in different countries, who maintain strong transnational social networks across several migrant host countries and with Moldova. For the investigation of the internal logic of interpretations and performances around migrants' collective performance, I engaged with Bourdieu's *Theory of Practice* (1985) and subsequently define the "Moldovan migrant community" as "a community of practice and everyday lives."

The data collection took place over a period of one year, as part of my multi-sited doctoral research (Odermatt 2017). Employing Marcus's approach (1995), I followed the "discourse on migrants' contribution to development" within the transnational social field of migrant civil society and within the transnational field of development organizations across seven European countries: Belgium, France, Germany, Italy, Moldova, Switzerland, and the UK. In total, I conducted 84 in-depth interviews with a heterogeneous sample of migrants of various ages, genders, migratory experiences, and occupational backgrounds (low-skilled and high-skilled occupations) and with a variegated group of aid professionals.

Additionally, I participated in a wide range of events addressed to migrants and development actors, and drew on a set of further ethnographic fieldwork methods, such as different visual methods and ethnographic walks. Finally, I applied a matched sample approach (Mazzucato 2009) that consisted of four development project settings applied as in-depth transnational case studies.

On Channeling the Good Spirits: Migrants' Personal Migration Experiences as a Motivation for Collective Remitting

In this section, I will introduce the forms of aid practice that emerged as a result of the lack of sociocultural integration in Moldovan migrants' host societies and their deskilling. Besides impacting upon migrants' collective commitments toward Moldova, these migration characteristics are all typical of the complex and dynamic intra-European East-West migration currently taking place, but have to date not been widely examined in the majority of studies on Moldovan migration (Odermatt 2017). I will here analyze the impact of these migration characteristics on the social process of creating a "Moldovan community of transnational collective practice." To this end, I opted for a processual conceptualization of the migrant transnational community, as "a process in which space, place and time are not static but continuously used, imagined, and negotiated in the construction of both bounded and unbounded identities, communities, and nation-states" (Mavroudi 2007, p. 473). I here investigate migrants' views on power relations, inclusion and exclusion in the process of their transnational migrant civil society formation, and their definitions of connectedness to Moldova. Finally, I will highlight how within the *field logic* (nomos), specific categories of practice arise, based on different field-specific symbolic, organizational, and economic resources (Bourdieu 1985).

Belonging and Self-Representation

One particularity of the Moldovan migrant community, compared to other migrant groups, is that the chairpersons of migrant associations are not necessarily highly integrated in their host societies (Lacroix 2011 on Polish migrant organizations in the UK, see Odermatt 2017). According to the core group of migrant leaders, the rather weak social inclusion of many Moldovan migrants in their host countries presents a serious impediment to becoming a "Moldovan community of transnational aid practices." In their opinion, migrants mostly get involved in local activities because "they feel lonely." The associations provide them with a place abroad that feels warm and familiar. In the migrant leaders' opinion, community-related activities with the sole aim of meeting up with other co-citizens and to spend quality time in Paris, Rome, or elsewhere, are unacceptable collective practices. They do not fit into the common shared understanding of development-oriented performances directed toward Moldova. Moreover, these engagements are even regarded as an "ethnic mobility trap" in migrants' host countries that can hinder the advancement of Moldovans' collective activities toward transnational humanitarian practices. As Ion (translator and writer, 34, Paris) stated:

> Most migrants are not well integrated, because they think they will go back one day, and they feel lonely. That's why they create associations, so that they feel less isolated. But they have not yet understood that you don't need to create an association to organize a barbeque or picnic [laughs]! That's ridiculous, and that's why our activities remain so communal, and we don't develop in a professional way.

While living physically isolated in the spatial and material peripheries of European centers, in Paris, London, or Rome, some migrants aspire to claim a place in the heart of the transnational migrant civil society. Thus, the participants' overriding motivation to engage in this type of collective remitting is a "performative act of belonging" (Fortier 2000). Put differently, the *field logics* of these practices is the quest to belong in the migrants' transnational field.

Another reason why the majority of migrant leaders consider their community morphology as still being too inward-oriented is that cultural activities (such as festivals and concerts) are perceived as too dominant in relation to other practices such as transnational activities directed toward Moldova. In general, the relevance of the leisure side of migrant associations is well recognized, as cultural activities can provide migrants with a welcome distraction from the everyday hardships many of them face abroad (Boccagni 2017). Furthermore, these can also generate much-needed emotional support, a means to escape from their loneliness and isolation, which most migrants do not receive in the local social environments of their domiciles. Christina (housewife, 29, London) commented on the need felt by some research participants for more opportunities in this area:

> We would like to have more cultural events for us, events where we can dress up nicely. Real evenings out, where we can forget about our everyday worries. Something nice for us, our community, not only charity events for people in Moldova. We are missing these kinds of events, because we are not fully integrated into British society.

Simply put, and contrary to the above-mentioned statements of migrant leaders, Christina seeks “community” and not “transnational solidarity” in the common understanding of cross-border development practices as expressed by migrant leaders. Although some migrant associations try to combine these two aspects, for instance by organizing fundraising events in restaurants or bars, often in combination with concerts, plays, or lectures performed by Moldovans. Nonetheless, throughout this study, narratives surrounding cultural activities emerged as concise examples of struggles within the migrant space over shared commitments to the value of their common associative practices (Schatzki 2001).

Lastly, an engagement in the diaspora can also provide some participants with a space for self-performance and publicity, which most of them cannot achieve in their destination countries because of their geographically and socially marginalized positions. Once again, this attitude is criticized by other interviewees, who see this as a cult of self-positioning, as a possibility to become, via development interventions, the center of attention in the local or transnational migrant space, and in the Moldovan media. As Rosa (entrepreneur, 43, London) stated:

> Every charity activity, even the smallest events, very quickly do the rounds in our diaspora and on the internet. Everybody is always extremely keen that the other leaders see pictures of their events and of the celebrities they invite in the Moldovan media.

In summary, the Moldovan migrants’ rather weak social integration in their destination countries can reinforce the need to belong either to the local migrant community abroad or to the transnational migrant civil society, encompassing several destination countries as well as Moldova. According to migrant leaders who are highly engaged in aid activities directed toward Moldova, however, the motivation to engage in collective aid practices in order to belong to a community is not an accepted motive for a collective engagement. In their opinion, it prevents the capacity-building of migrant cross-border humanitarian interventions in Moldova.

On Becoming a Person Again: Remittance Practices Shaped by Migrants' Professional Skills

Moldovan migrant leaders exhibit similar characteristics across all the countries studied here. They have a high level of education—most chairpersons of associations have a university-level education—and a high level of networking capacities. They are described by migrants as a "specific type of leader personality" with strong ties to Moldova. Yet, in contrast to other migrant groups, a specific feature of Moldovan leaders is that only a few of them pursue high-skilled or medium-skilled jobs abroad (compare Pirkallainen et al., 2013 by reference to Somali associations in Finland). The majority of Moldovan migrant leaders are high-skilled migrants pursuing low-skilled jobs. This current phenomenon of deskilling among Moldovan migrants living in the Western European countries studied here proved to be a determining motive for participants to engage in development-oriented practices. For many high-skilled migrants working in low-skilled jobs, transnational collective volunteer efforts toward Moldova present a welcome opportunity to apply their individual skills and resources, which they cannot use in their downgraded professional occupations. In other words, they have the freedom to share their passions. The underlining mission of this category of practice is to overcome discrepancies between migrants' competences and social positions in the host countries as well as a temporal restoration of their professional skills and identities. As Anna (translator/writer, 45, Rome) stated:

> We conduct our activities not only for people in Moldova, but also for ourselves, for all of us who are not able to draw on our full professional and individual potentials and our passions, because all of these resources are not in demand in our jobs.

Boccagni (2017) maintained that while the immigrant condition itself is for many migrants a source of lesser social status, over time there seems to be a cognitive adaptation. This is also the case for Anna. For her, a transnational engagement can be understood as a coping strategy to counter the downward socioeconomic mobility that she experienced through migration—from a university lecturer with a national reputation in Moldova to an anonymous care worker in Italy—and to restore her social status.

To sum up, Moldovan migrants' collective remittance patterns emerge from a complex interplay of mostly understudied migration experiences, such as migrants' rather weak sociocultural integration in their host societies or their experienced deskilling. Thus, similarly to other migrant groups, Moldovans' underpinning motivations to engage in collective transnational aid efforts are multifaceted and integrated into different aspects of their everyday lives and biographical projects (Erdal and Borchgrevink 2016).

National Historic Determinants and Core-Periphery Dynamics of the Home Nation

In this section, I will present two aspects that influence Moldovan migrants' collective remitting, which I argue have not been sufficiently materialized in the academic debate. These are Moldova's national historical context and the broader geographical core-periphery dynamics of the sending nation.

Overcoming the Soviet Past: Regaining Confidence Through Collective Remittance Practices

The rather negative stance of migrants toward their home country's Soviet past proved to be an important determinant for cultivating collective aid-oriented links with Moldova. According to Montanari (2001), a dominant national discourse in Romania and Moldova is a resignation and passivity toward their fate—a sort of suffering without rebellion, which is present in national myths and popular art. History has taught Moldovans to be patient, because every savior in the past turned out to be an exploiter, from the Hungarians and the Turks to the Russians (Ammassari 2001). This historical and cultural legacy of oppression in the past is strongly present in the narratives on migrants' experiences during the Soviet Republic of Moldova. Thus, for some migrants, transnational migrant civil society offers a welcome space for rising from their felt oppression by the Russians, or as a meaning-making resource to leave the past behind and to regain confidence. The following quote by Vasili (physicist, 39, Paris) illustrates that individually perceived oppression is still deeply rooted in

Moldovan migrant biographies, even if they consider themselves professionally successful and well-integrated:

> My personal motivation for my associational engagement toward Moldova is to take a sort of revenge. Ehm, not a personal revenge, but ehm a revenge for my country, because Moldovans have been badly treated for a long time. We were always seen as second-class citizens, and I want to show that this is not true, that we are capable of doing things, and that we are capable of doing these things well.

The interviewees not only stressed that Soviet imperialism had diminished their self-esteem, but also highlighted that some of their co-citizens compensated for their negative experiences in the past through collective giving, for instance via their own self-seeking practices. The narrative account by Oleg (44, project coordinator, Padova) reflected this motivation:

> We are like the typical character in Gogol's stories, the simple-minded peasant, the small man who wants to gain more dignity after years of oppression. I think this is the reason why so many organizations have been established. Migrants are committed to gaining personal advantages over others, because of their inferiority complex vis-à-vis the Russians, who marked us as second-class citizens. Ehm, how can I say this, by having their own associations, and their projects, and by calling themselves 'presidents,' they boost their low self-esteem.

Moreover, memories of the Soviet past can push migrants' aspirations to move beyond the above-mentioned cultural activities carried out in the host countries toward more transnational practices. As Dragomir's (construction worker, 48, Paris) stated:

> We need to show others that we are able to organize development activities back home, activities that go beyond festivals. We need to show them that we are not here to sing and dance. It would be catastrophic to only do that, because it would mean that those who put us down are right; those who held us back from developing and from having a normal life for many years.

Evidently, migrants' aspirations to (re-)gain confidence by means of aid-oriented engagements as a pattern of transnational giving illustrates the importance of understanding the ways in which the past is culturally constructed and selectively applied in migrants' contemporary transnational social practices (Verdery 2005). Viewing migrants' transnational efforts as an articulation of dealing with their own Soviet past goes beyond the few well-known assumptions about collective practices of post-socialist migrant communities in Western Europe, such as their lack of institutional trust or the expected symbolic practices of an elusive "Communist nostalgia" (Slavoka 2017). Therefore, I argue that there is more to individual and collective memory than the conceptual fuzziness surrounding nostalgification in post-socialist studies, which often erases the complexity and ambiguity of memory practices.

Putting Moldova Center-Stage: (Re-)Connecting Moldova with Europe Through Collective Remittance Practices

A last important aspect of collective transnational aid practices among Moldovan migrants is their home country's marginalized place within today's Europe. The Republic of Moldova at the presumed margins of Europe, wherever we claim to fix its eastern borders, is not what one would call a press darling, nor is it a transnational hub. The capital city Chisinau stands in sharp contrast to busy "Eurocities" such as Paris or London, woven with international relations, attracting and hosting the world. It is precisely this spatial European core-periphery dynamic that for some Moldovan migrants presents a motivation for becoming engaged in cross-border activities. These migrants' incentives to engage in activities in Moldova is that they consider their engagement a form of regaining space or (re-)connecting their marginalized home country with Europe.

First, some of the interviewees are generally optimistic about the country's prospects and confident in their ability to contribute to positive change in Moldova through their collective transnational remittance practices, although their home country is also marginalized in international funding programs. As Kiril (IT engineer, 38, Paris) stated:

> Even if we are not yet a member of the EU, I want to show the members that we have things to share, like ehm our rich cultural heritage and our multiculturalism. Our country is still left out in many European programs for NGOs. But I want to show Europe that we exist. Yes, that's my aim. With our activities, I want to show that it's not only political or geo-political ideology that creates a country, but also culture, and ehm grassroots projects, like we do. And that we can move things together.

Second, the fact that Moldova is not a press darling in the migrant-receiving countries studied here has generated two trends. First, the little attention the country receives in public discourse can foster specific forms of relationships between Moldovan migrant associations and Western European NGOs. Liliana (34, freelancer, Paris) touched on this point:

> I' not exaggerating, but we have done consulting for French development NGOs who wanted to get engaged in Moldova, and they really don't know anything about our country. One was a big international NGO and people there knew everything about Africa, but when it came to Moldova, all of a sudden there was a big silence. Ehm, that's why I think our association could create more links and connect NGOs here better with Moldova.

This quote shows that Moldova's unpopularity can motivate migrants to become bridge-builders for development NGOs in their countries of residence and to bring Moldova to international attention. The role of migrant associations is, however, not restricted to connecting development NGOs with Moldova. Collective aid practices are also seen as a means of (re)-connecting their home country with Europe more broadly. Here, the motivation of migrants for creating transnational links with Moldova is to belong to Europe, which is regarded by the majority of interviewees as a territory of "progress" or "open-mindedness."

The second narrative theme emerged with regard to the core-periphery dynamics of the origin country, namely migrants' frustration about Western Europeans' general disregard vis-à-vis their home country. The perception of Moldova as "isolated outsiders" at the territorial edge of the EU is viewed by some leaders as (re-)enforcing parochialism rather than helping to improve the socioeconomic situation in Moldova. In their opinion, the public neglect of Moldova and its attributed backwardness preserves provincial practices in Moldova. This impairs the capacity-building of migrant associations in promoting transformative change in Moldova. Svetlana (journalist, 54, Geneva), a migrant leader, expressed her frustration with Europe's view of Moldova as a remote eastern flank:

> We are a territory in Europe, but we are talking about a country that has never had a say, and as long as Europe treats us as some sort of province, without a genuine interest in us, the backward provincial practices in Moldova and in our diaspora will continue. I don't think there will be positive changes like this. Some of our migrant leaders will just continue to create associations for their own self-seeking interests, like politicians pursue

> their own interests in Moldova, because nobody pays the country any attention.

Similarly, some interviewees viewed the emphasis on Moldova's "otherness" by mainstream development actors as unprofessional. Consequently, they rejected their development interventions in the country and were not interested in teaming up with aid agencies. Svetlana (factory worker and artist, 55, Munich) voiced a typical view on this issue:

> We often visited German development programs near the hospital that our organization supports. One was a training seminar by the German ministry on how to write job applications. I was standing there and I thought: Do I see this right? This is very unprofessional. It doesn't work like that in Moldova at all. This is all nonsense! You can't teach people how to apply 'European-style' there. It's a completely different system.

By contrast, other migrants engage in activities aimed precisely at supporting development NGOs to enhance their understanding of the "Moldovan way of functioning," for instance by matching them with potentially trustworthy and reliable Moldovan counterparts. As Natasha (shop-assistant, 48, Paris) stated:

> Most of the Western NGOs don't know how to judge our people, because they don't know the system. And sometimes, they don't even know that you need to check, double check and triple check with whom you want to work in Moldova. And we want to help them with that.

Natasha's account is an illustrative example of how migrants negotiate meanings of their home country's sociopolitical place in today's world in their transnational collective activities. These forms of transnational aid engagement can be understood as a mixture of migrants' compensation for an experienced "backwardness" and a growing malaise about their home country's image as an out-of-the-way place.

"We Don't Do Charity [...]. We Do Real Things": Migrants' Understanding of Development Practices in Relation to Mainstream Aid-Giving

In this last section, I will address the migrant leaders' self-reflections on their forms of collective remittance contributions, emphasizing the differences which emerged in relation to the development establishment's ways of doing development.

Most migrants have a positive attitude toward foreign aid investments in Moldova. However, their appreciation of the development industry's investments in Moldova does not necessarily mean that they also endorse the latter's development practices. On the contrary, migrant leaders' understanding of aid practices can significantly differ from those performed by the formal development establishment, including governmental organizations or international organizations. Some interviewees even expressed a rather negative stance toward mainstream aid mechanisms and questioned the development establishment's contemporary practices. They portrayed the "development set" as being too bright and noble, highlighting that aid workers travel too much, use posh words, and spend their funds on fancy hotels instead of on people in need. Consequently, they distance themselves from the help industry's professional practices. As Anastasia (tour guide and translator, 46, Berlin) stated:

> In Chisinau, you see the development people driving around in their expensive jeeps. That's what they call charity. That's not what we do. We don't do charity. I don't even like the word charity. We do real things, the most natural things, we help the poor and vulnerable. It's more, ehm, solidarity.

For interviewees like Anastasia, sending individual or collective remittances to non-migrant kin is constructed as a way of respecting "natural things" (i.e., helping "the poor and vulnerable"), something migrants view as a duty, regardless of the nature of their remitting practices. Additionally, the quote reveals that some participants associate the concept of "charity" with the development industry's practices, while their own practices are regarded as "solidarity." Most interviewees interpreted the "charity practices" performed by development actors in a rather limited way as top-down structural support, while the main function of their own "solidarity practices" lies in a bottom-up approach to aid provision. Therefore, an important issue that emerged in terms of migrants' dissociation from mainstream development practices is the migrants' self-reflections on their development interventions as doing "real things," understood as "people-to-people solidarity" as opposed to doing "charity."

Furthermore, some engaged migrants do not agree with the contemporary practice of professional charity because of their professional nature. Professionally run practices do not fit into their understanding of loyalty toward Moldova as coming from the migrants' hearts, or as an emotional engagement. Particularly those migrants for whom altruism is their main motivation for humanitarian interventions are reluctant about professionally run organizations, be they aid agencies or migrant organizations. They simply do not aspire to a developing professionalization of their own associations. Instead, they wish to keep their collective activities voluntary. Ion (translator, 34, Paris) represents the opinion of those migrants who see the development professionals or migrants engaged in professional activities as solely pursuing their self-interests by earning their living through aid interventions. Like numerous non-migrant-led alternative development NGOs, migrants like Ion aim to pursue their associative activities as independent NGOs outside the official development industry. As he stated:

> I don't want our association to become professional, because it would mean that I would do my activities just for money. But I am myself interested in the Moldovan community here, that's why it is a personal interest. There are people who do it professionally, and they get grants. I don't believe in this kind of people, because they are not genuinely interested in the migrants, nor in the beneficiaries in Moldova. They just want to earn money.

Lastly, and very broadly, obstacles and struggles over definitions of the "collective productive use" of material, social, and financial remittances were found in this study. Migrants reported that the practice of sending material goods to partner institutions, such as medicine or toys, is often complicated. The obstacles encountered included the actual journey of the goods themselves, which is hampered by bureaucratic hurdles (such as restrictive border controls and legal import restrictions) and the passive attitude of "aid consumption" by locals, or the misuse of sent goods. A frequently mentioned example in this regard was that clothes, books, and toys were resold by villagers for their own financial benefit. For these reasons, some research participants preferred to carry out object and project-bound development practices according to the principle of help for self-help. Sandra (factory worker, 55, Munich) explained her conception of "helping people help themselves":

> I am bored of pure idealism—of the idea of just giving. People should be helped, yes. But they should also do something in return, like they do in our micro-credit projects. You know, with so many aid institutions working in the country and many relatives abroad, I somehow see a risk that people start to think that they don't need to do anything anymore. This also has to do with our migrant associations, who just dump their second-hand clothes and toys in Moldova, assuming that they make children happy like this!

To round off this last section, besides discussions about cultural activities, the migrants' debate surrounding professionally run activities is another concise example of struggles within the transnational migrant space over a shared understanding of the "right transnational aid-giving practices." Moreover, the results discussed in this section reflect the importance of the fact that migrants' collective space of development practices toward Moldova is socially constituted by the relational positions of all actors involved, namely migrants, non-migrants, and development players (Bourdieu 1985). This calls for a more nuanced approach to migrants' understandings of aid-oriented contributions and their propensity to team up with development actors that also entails social-relational dynamics.

Conclusion

Drawing on a set of empirical examples of Moldovan migrant collective remittance patterns, this chapter provided an insight into the various ways in which migrants experience loyalties and affiliations with place, nation, or the local or de-territorialized transnational migrant community. I stressed how remittance practices are embedded in migrants' everyday lives and how they are a complex of understandings, commitments, and competences with different purposes, functions, and social positions. This finding confirms that collective remittance practices can account for aspects of everyday life and the conduct of a full range of temporally unfolding and spatially dispersed activities.

The findings discussed in this chapter, I argue, refine the idea of migrants' engagement in collective remittance practices in several ways. First, viewing migrants' attachments from the perspective of the places they create—the migrant space of collective development engagement—allows for an understanding of remittance patterns as processes with their own dynamics, rather than reducing them to purely complementary, contradictory, or simultaneous aspects of the migrants' integration process in their host society. Second, I showed that migrants' collective aid-giving is interwoven with their multi-sited social lives as well as their personal migration experiences, based on various socioeconomic and cultural indicators, but also on Moldova's socialist past and the country's new post-socialist realities—such as the country's marginal place within Europe. This means that migrants' remitting is governed by different logics and behaviors, embedded in a *complex array of cultural and social determinants and personal motives operating across different spatial and temporal scales.* As Nowicka (2020) argued, this focus on the entanglements of national and personal histories of migrants is precisely one of the merits of transnationalism. Third, the core-periphery dynamics as determinants for cross-border activities call for a more nuanced approach to temporal dynamics of migrants' engagements beyond the limited conceptual prism of looking at the country of origin as a pure continuity of socialist legacy as adopted by traditional studies on migrant formations in the Eastern European context. Finally, the study found significant differences between migrants and mainstream development agencies on the nature, forms, and visions of cross-border aid activities. Notable here are migrants' suspicion toward top-down approaches and professional charity practices performed by aid agencies. The migrants' definition of their practices as "bottom-up solidarity" makes them generally rather reluctant about professional development efforts. Subsequently, not all migrants want to be associated with mainstream aid practices, nor do they aspire to integrate their development efforts into the aid establishment. However, migrants' understanding of their volunteer-run development practices based on the value of "solidarity" does not easily fit into the formal professional field of "charity," as is commonly postulated in numerous policy documents on the involvement of migration associations in Moldova's development transition (IOM and MPI 2012, p. 132).

Concerning avenues for further research on this topic, I suggest to better account for the temporal dynamics implicated in the circulation of norms and ideas in general, and in migrants' understanding of transnational commitments in particular (Vari-Lavoisier 2020). The ways in which migrants' changing aspirations over time, interwoven with their past and present life trajectories, frame and change their motivations for collective engagement, for instance, have hardly been analyzed in depth.

Undoubtedly, a more time-sensitive approach to migrants' motivations in taking up collective cross-border remitting practices would be fruitful for the broader discussion surrounding collective remittances.

Moreover, there is still a lack of research accounting for the impact of aid remittance practices on destination nations (see Grabowska and Garapich 2016 for an exception). Here, it would not only be interesting to follow up on how the small-scale projects studied here have been sustained over time, but also explore whether and how they "scale out" to other domains, or whether they "scale up" from the local level to a national level (see for instance White and Grabowska 2019 with regard to Poland). Additionally, research efforts are needed to refine the analytical tools suitable to understand how dynamics of economic, social, and political remittance practices interrelate. Parallels and interactions between financial transfers and social remittances in the context of Moldova are certainly ripe for further investigation (see for instance Meseguer et al. 2016 with regard to Latin America).

Ultimately, the findings point to intra-European specificities of the migration-transformation nexus, namely the migrants' motivation to engage in transnational practices to connect their marginalized country with Europe. In this context, the impact of Moldova's territorial factors upon migrants' cross-border engagements calls for an analytical approach that goes beyond the Moldovan national space as an "integral spatio-temporal isolate" (Marcus 1998, p. 178), separated from surrounding Europe, as commonly conceptualized in formal migration-development policies (CIM/GIZ 2012). To advance this line of inquiry, I suggest re-embedding the remittance literature into the broader research agenda of migration and social change (Meeus 2016; Van Hear 2010) and to look at Moldova's transformation and migrants' transnational ties as a part of European migration and intra-European social inequalities. However, besides all these considerations, we should not forget that we are living in a time of hostile migration policies involving measures of increased surveillance of borders, mass deportations, and denials of long-standing legal rights of asylum. On a global scale, these measures are threatening financial remittance flows and migrants' ability to engage in other forms of solidarity practices toward their home countries which global financial institutions and development agencies have proclaimed as stable over a long period of time (Glick Schiller 2020).

References

Amelina, A. & Faist, T. (2012). De-Naturalizing the National in Research Methodologies: Key Concepts of Transnational Studies in Migration. *Ethnic and Racial Studies*, *35* (10), 1707–1724.

Ammassari, P. (2001). La Repubblica di Moldova: Partiti e movimenti nell'attuale contesto economico e sociale. In A. G. Pirzio, M. D'Amato & A. Montanari (Eds.), *Nazionalismo e identità collettive: I percorsi della transizione in Romania e nella Repubblica di Moldova* (pp. 75–119). Liguori.

Boccagni, P., Lafleur, J.-M., & Levitt, P. (2016). Transnational Politics as Cultural Circulation: Towards a Conceptual Understanding of Migrant Political Participation on the Move. *Mobilities*, 11(3), 444–463.

Boccagni, P. (2017). Aspirations and the Subjective Future of Migration: Comparing Views and Desires of the "Time Ahead" through the Narratives of Immigrant Domestic Workers. *Comparative Migration Studies*, 5(4), 1–18.

Bourdieu, P. (1985). The Social Space and the Genesis of Groups. *Theory and Society*, 14(6), 723–744.

Castles, S. (2016). Understanding Global Migration: A Social Transformation Perspective. In A. Amelina, K. Horvath, & B. Meeus (Eds.), *An Anthology of Migration and Social Transformation: European Perspectives* (pp. 16–41), Springer Open.

Cheianu-Andrei, D. (2013). *Mapping of the Moldovan Diaspora in Italy, Portugal, France and the United Kingdom.* Moldovan Diaspora Mapping Series II. Chisinau: IOM Chisinau.

Centre for International Migration and Development (CIM/GIZ). (2012). *Migranten als Unternehmer.* CIM and Centre for Start-Up Kompass. CIM.

Erdal, M. B. & Borchgrevink, K. (2016). Transnational Islamic Charity as Everyday Rituals. *Global Networks*, 17(1), 130–146.

Faist, T. (2000). *The Volume and Dynamics of International Migration and Transnational Social Spaces.* Oxford University Press.

Faist, T. (2010). Diaspora and Transnationalism: What Kind of Dance Partners? In R. Bauböck, & T. Faist, T. (Eds.), *Diaspora and Transnationalism: Concepts, Theories and Methods* (pp. 9–34). Amsterdam University Press.

Fortier, A. M. (2000). *Migrant Belongings: Memory, Space, Identity.* Berg.

Glick Schiller, N., Basch, L. & Szanton Blanc, C. (1999). From Immigrant to Transmigrant: Theorizing Transnational Migration. In L. Pries (Ed.), *Migration and Transnational Social Spaces* (pp. 73–105). Ashgate.

Glick Schiller, N. (2005). Transnational Social Fields and Imperialism: Bringing a Theory of Power to Transnational Studies. *Anthropological Theory*, 5(4), 439–461.

Glick Schiller, N. (2020). Migration and Development: Theorising Changing Conditions and Ongoing Silences. In T. Bastia & R. Skeldon (Eds.), *Routledge Handbook of Migration and Development* (pp. 32–41). Routledge.

Grabowska, I. & Garapich, M. (2016). Social Remittances and Intra-EU Mobility: Non-Financial Transfers between U.K. and Poland. *Journal of Ethnic and Migration Studies*, 42(13), 2146–2162.

International Monetary Fund (IMF). (2015). *Country Report Moldova*, No. 13/270, Washington, DC: IMF.

International Organisation for Migration (IOM) & Migration Policy Institute (MPI). (2012). *Developing a Road Map for Engaging Diasporas in Development: A Handbook for Policymakers and Practitioners in Home and Host Countries*. IOM.

Isaakyan, I. & Triandafyllidou, A. (2016). "Sending so Much More than Money": Exploring Social Remittances and Transnational Mobility. *Ethnic and Racial Studies*, 40(15), 2787–2805.

Lacroix, T. (2011). *Indian and Polish Migrant Organisations in the UK*. Final report of the Transnational Migration Organisations (TRAMO) project. International Migration Institute, University of Oxford.

Lacroix, T. (2014). Conceptualizing Transnational Engagements: A Structure and Agency Perspective on (Hometown) Transnationalism. *International Migration Review*, 48(3), 643–679.

Lacroix, T., Levitt, P. & Vari-Lavoisier, I. (2016). Social Remittances and the Changing Transnational Political Landscape. *Comparative Migration Studies*, 4(16), 1–5.

Levitt, P. (1998). Social Remittances: Migration Driven Local-Level Forms of Cultural Diffusion. *International Migration Review*, 34, 926–948.

Levitt, P. & Lamba-Nieves, D. (2011). Social Remittances Revisited. *Journal of Ethnic and Migration Studies*, *37*(1), 1–22.

Marcus, G.E. (1995). Ethnography in/of the World System: The Emergence of Multi-Sited Ethnography. *Annual Review of Anthropology*, 24, 95–117.

Marcus, G.E. (1998). *Ethnography through Thick and Thin*. Princeton University Press.

Mavroudi, E. (2007). Diaspora as Process: (De)Constructing Boundaries. *Geography Compass*, 1(3), 467–479.

Mazzucato, V. (2009). Bridging Boundaries with a Transnational Research Approach: A Simultaneous Matched Sample Methodology. In M.-A. Falzon (Ed.), *Multi-Sited Ethnography: Theory, Praxis and Locality in Contemporary Research* (pp. 215–233). Ashgate.

Meeus, B. (2016). Migration and Social Transformation: Interdisciplinary Insights and European Perspectives. In A. Amelina, K. Horvath, & B. Meeus (Eds.), *An Anthology of Migration and Social Transformation* (pp. 1–15). Springer Open.

Meseguer, C. Lavezzolo, S. & Aparicio, J. (2016). Financial Remittances, Trans-Border Conversations, and the State. *Comparative Migration Studies*, 4 (13), 1–13.

Montanari, A. (2001). *Romanian National Identity in the Republic of Moldova*. ECPR Workshop paper, Grenoble. https://ecpr.eu/Events/Event/PaperDetails/5247.

Mullings, B. (2012). Governmentality, Diaspora Assemblages and the Ongoing Challenge of Development. *Antipode*, 44(2), 406–427.

Nowicka, M. (2020). (Dis)Connecting Migration: Transnationalism and Nationalism beyond Connectivity. *Comparative Migration Studies*, 8(20), 1–13.

Odermatt, E. (2017). *Migrants in Development: A Multi-Perspective Analysis of the Participation of Moldovan Migrant Associations in Development Initiatives* Doctoral dissertation, University of Sussex.

Page, B. & Mercer, C. (2012). "Why Do People Do Stuff?" Reconceptualizing Remittance Behaviour in Diaspora-Development Research and Policy. *Progress in Development Studies*, 12(1), 1–18.

Piper, N. (2009). The Complex Interconnections of the Migration-Development Nexus: A Social Perspective. *Population, Space and Place*, 15 (2), 93–101.

Schatzki, T. (2001). Introduction: Practice Theory. In T. Schatzki, C. Knorr & E. Savigny (Eds.), *The Practice Turn in Contemporary Theory* (pp. 1–15). Routledge.

Sinatti, G. & Horst, C. (2015). Migrants as Agents of Development: Diaspora Engagement Discourse and Practice in Europe, *Ethnicities*, 15(1), 134–152.

Slavoka, L. (2017). The Generation of Transition in Eastern Europe: A Generation of Uncertainty, a Generation of Distrust. In L. Slavoka (Ed.), *Mapping Transition in Eastern Europe: Experience of Change after the End of Communism* (pp. 20–33). Transition Dialogue Network.

United Nations Development Programme (UNDP). (2019). *Moldovan Human Development Report: Good Corporate Citizens – Public and Private Goals Aligned for Human Development*. UNDP Moldova.

Van Hear, N. (2010). Theories of Migration and Social Change. *Journal of Ethnic and Migration Studies*, 36(10), 1531–1536.

Vari-Lavoisier, I. (2020). Social Remittances. In T. Bastia & R. Skeldon (Eds.), *Routledge Handbook of Migration and Development* (pp. 125–136). Routledge.

Verdery, K. (2005). What is Socialism, and Why Did it Fall? In M. Edelman & A. Haugerud A. (Eds.), *The Anthropology of Development and Globalisation: From Classical Political Economy to Contemporary Neoliberalism* (pp. 373–382). Blackwell Publishing.

White, A. & Grabowska, I. (2019). Social Remittances and Social Change in Central and Eastern Europe: Embedding Migration in the Study of Society. *Central and Eastern European Migration Review*, 8(1), 33–50.

CHAPTER 10

Transformative Effects of Remittances on Health Behavior, Community Resilience, and Gender Dynamics in Burkina Faso

Eric Bayala

Introduction

The health sector in Burkina Faso faces a number of problems: unequal access to health services, a lack of social safety nets to protect the poor, inefficiency in using existing resources, and weak mechanisms for coordinating partnerships (Rudasingwa et al. 2020). Only seven percent of Burkinabè feel that they benefit from social security, which increases the need of rural and poor households, especially women and children, to look for alternative sources of provision. Many rely on sources of support from family networks abroad (Ilboudo 2011; Ridde 2006). Within these transnational dynamics, the diaspora community in Italy formed a hometown association called "Association des Ressortissants de Niaogho en Italie" (ARNI), which manages projects for the Niaogho community. ARNI has a local partner called "Association pour le Developpement de Niaogho" (ADN). ARNI includes a women's section that focuses on

E. Bayala (✉)
University of Innsbruck, Innsbruck, Austria
e-mail: eric.bayala@student.uibk.ac.at

S. Meyer, C. Ströhle (eds.), *Remittances as Social Practices and Agents of Change*,
https://doi.org/10.1007/978-3-030-81504-2_10

female issues such as mother-child health, pregnancy, and economic autonomy in Niaogho. One of ARNI's main projects was to build a health center in Niaogho using financial remittances.

This chapter evaluates the transformative effects of collective remittances on the health sector and social resilience in Niaogho. Money transfers were also accompanied by social and cultural forms of remittances, such as knowledge, norms, and values, leading in sum to social change and a transformation of health practices. Regarding the transformative effects, my analysis focuses on gender dynamics. Furthermore, it explores how diaspora networks contribute to, complement, or disrupt the physical, economic, political, social, and sanitary assets of the local community. Two hypotheses structure my argument. First, I agree with the findings of Sikder et al. (2017, pp. 56–57) that diaspora networks function as a "critical 'buffer' to withstanding shocks and stresses" as well as social insurance for potential future crises through a diversification of social capital. Second, I argue that the increase in resilience of women with connections to the diaspora indirectly enhances resilience of other community members (especially in non-migrant households) because of a positive spillover effect of diaspora support and solidarity.

I understand diaspora as "any people or ethnic population that leave their traditional ethnic homelands, being dispersed throughout other parts of the world" (IOM 2004, p. 19). Transnationalism is conceptualized as "the processes by which immigrants build social fields that link together their country of origin and their country of settlement" (Glick Schiller et al. 1992, p. 1). Immigrant actors are understood as transmigrants who "develop and maintain multiple relations—familial, economic, social, organizational, religious, and political that span borders. Transmigrants take actions, make decisions, feel concerns, and develop identities within social networks that connect them to two or more societies simultaneously" (Glick Schiller et al. 1992, pp. 1–2).

Based on field research conducted between April 2018 and July 2020, I assessed the impact of two health centers called "Centre de Santé et de Promotion Sociale" (CSPS): CSPS 1 and CSPS 2 in the community of Niaogho in the Centre-Est region of Burkina Faso. CSPS 1 was established in the 1950s, while CSPS 2 was funded in 2015 by the diaspora community in Italy, including the provision of ambulances, a drugstore, and a dispensary in the rural municipality of Niaogho. This second health center now belongs to and is run by the Burkinabè government. Especially this diaspora-funded health center fundamentally changed access to healthcare services, health knowledge, and community resilience.

This chapter is organized as follows: First, I will summarize the history of migration from Niaogho to Italy to explain how a strong diaspora community developed there. I will then introduce my research questions and the methods I used to collect data during the field research before outlining my theoretical perspective. Finally, I will highlight the various forms of remittances received by community members in Niaogho and examine their effects on households and social resilience in the region.

Migration from Niaogho to Italy

Between 1967 and 1970, an agreement facilitated work migration of people from Burkina Faso to Italy (Sawadogo 2010; Zongo 2009, 2011). The agreement enabled the migrant workers to work in Italy for 90 days in the summer (Blion 1996), but the Italian administration also tolerated permanent migration to the industrial centers in the north. In the spring and summer, the migrants from Burkina Faso worked in the agriculture sector in the south of Italy, and during the autumn and winter in the factories in the region of Lombardy in the north. This migration was organized in a network of families, clans, villages, and friendships. Most of the time, men went abroad first and left behind women and children.

A seminal report of the IOM (2016) argued that after the sociopolitical crisis that occurred in the Ivory Coast in the 1990s, the emigration of Burkinabè from the Ivory Coast to Italy increased considerably. In 2015, 60,810 Burkinabè lived in Italy, more than 35,000 of whom were from the east of Burkina Faso, especially the district of Garango that comprises Béguédo, Niaogho, Boussouma, Lenga, and Bittou (IOM 2016). According to the former executive director of ARNI, about 4000 persons from Niaogho live in Italy today, more than 2000 of whom reside in the region of Lombardy—most of whom are members of ARNI.

Research Questions, Methods of Data Collection, and Theoretical Framework

Vulnerability is a reality in Burkina Faso: People suffer from poverty and a lack of infrastructure and economic perspectives. I define vulnerability as a cause of risk and a source of hazard that encompasses biophysical and social aspects (Cutter and Finch 2008; Heyman et al. 1991). Diverse forms of vulnerability may expose household or community members to health problems while at the same time preventing them from getting access to health services.

Research Questions

The objective of this study is to assess the transformative effects of financial and social remittances between the Italian diaspora and women in Niaogho and to understand their impact on vulnerability and health resilience. Thus, two research questions were formulated: First, what are the effects of remittances on health infrastructure and health behavior at a community level, especially toward women? Second, in what way did remittances strengthen or weaken community resilience? I argue that household members with a relationship to the diaspora are less vulnerable to healthcare problems because diaspora communities, transmigrants, and return migrants provide them with economic, social, and environmental capital that affects their health and increases their resilience. As Morse and McNamara (2013) showed, economic and social capital further the availability of and access to health resources, while environmental capital like housing, sleeping spaces, and places for food preparation helps to improve living conditions and to prevent some types of diseases such as respiratory illnesses and injuries.

Methods of Data Collection

To answer these research questions, I examined the influence of health infrastructure and knowledge transfer regarding mother and child health, pregnancy, health promotion, disease prevention, and curing diseases on community and household resilience. Of special interest here is women's access to healthcare resources, information, and advice.

This research was designed as a cross-sectional study that includes both quantitative and qualitative methods. The process of data collection through interviews and focus group discussions (FGDs) was interactive and flexible, responding to the needs of the field (Al-Busaidi 2008; Legard et al. 2003). I mainly dealt with interview partners who did not finish primary or secondary school, especially in FDGs and interviews with return migrants. Many of them did not speak French, so field researchers translated the questions and conversations into Bissa. The primary data was complemented by secondary data such as written documents from NGO projects, national governments, the National Institute of Statistics and Demography (NISD), local administrations, and health centers.

Forty-seven interviews with experts were conducted in Burkina Faso (35) and Italy (12). These focused on the economic situation of the region of Central East of Burkina Faso, access to healthcare services, and reasons for outmigration. Ten individual in-depth interviews were carried out in Niaogho, Tenkodogo, Garango, and Ouagadougou with eight returnees from Italy, one from Gabon, and one from Equatorial Guinea. The interviewees were aged between 26 and 65. The interviews provided a collection of life histories on migration from household and family members. Their analysis helps to identify innovations brought by returned migrants, their social networks, their contributions to improve social justice, health-seeking behavior, and the norms and rules for the transmission of knowledge regarding health resilience (Murray 1998).

In addition, a household survey in Niaogho enabled us to understand which households use health facilities, and how and why they use them. Household members were randomly selected. The following determinants of health-seeking behavior were investigated according to socio-demographic, economic, and physical factors, namely financial accessibility, women's autonomy, health service, and healthcare infrastructure (Shaikh 2012). The following variables were assessed in the questionnaire: age, gender, education, religion, ethnicity, family members, land and livestock possession, occupation, economic activities, assets and savings, income, health expenditure, food production and expenses, knowledge acquired, satisfaction with the health service, exchange with the diaspora, advice, mother and child health, family planning, participation in community activities, trust, and solidarity.

The survey included 224 heads of households in 8 villages (28 quartiers) within the rural municipality of Niaogho. Niaogho has around 23,000 inhabitants and around 3300 households (INSD 2017). Altogether 82.59 percent of the respondents were women (N = 185) and 17.41 percent men (N = 39). This is because migrants from the rural municipality of Niaogho are mainly male. However, there were also seasonal reasons: The survey took place during the rainy season when most of the remaining men were engaged in fieldwork and designated their spouses to answer the questions. Furthermore, the questionnaire, which addressed many points relating to health (especially reproductive health: prevention, prenatal and postnatal care, contraception, malaria, etc.) was quickly considered by men as a 'women's affair.' In Burkina Faso, reproductive health issues are very often considered the responsibility of women, and the involvement of men in family planning is very low.

The three FGDs in Italy included a women's group of ARNI and two youth groups with Burkinabè migration background. The FGDs in Burkina Faso were conducted with a women's group in Niaogho, with health and social workers of Niaogho, with community members, and with youth. For the FGDs, households were randomly selected with the intention of placing the findings in a more general context. The sample size for the focus groups in both countries was between 9 and 12 persons per FGD. The different FGDs helped to comprehend the interaction between ARNI and the community members of Niaogho. Moreover, I assessed the differences in health behavior in households *with* and *without* a connection to the diaspora as well as the relation between collective remittances, social capital, and transformations in community resilience.

Vignettes further explain healthcare-seeking behavior of households, the expenditures made, the corresponding attitudes, and the knowledge acquired. The vignette method enables an analysis of personalized short stories on sensitive topics (Gourlay et al. 2014; Hughes 1998) and offers a chance to compare the causal effects of individual experiences among household or community members during the FDG (Barter and Renold 2000; Guillermina 2006). The results of the vignettes are based on exchanges with the following focus groups: The first consisted of 12 women in Brescia and Prevalle aged 20 to 50. All the women were married and had children. Three had been born in Italy, the others in Burkina Faso, Ivory Coast, and Ghana. The second group comprised 9 women in Niaogho aged 18 to 65. All the women were married, five of whose husbands were in the diaspora, including three in Italy.

The results of the household survey were analyzed with SPSS 2015, while the qualitative data was manually coded and operationalized with ATLAS.ti.

Theoretical Framework: Remittances and Capital Theory

Peggy Levitt's concept of social remittances describes how experiences and knowledge are shared and remitted between diaspora groups and members of their home community (Levitt 1996, 1998). On a community level, social remittances may result in a network of relationships intended to mobilize resources for collective actions and to reduce vulnerability (Bettin et al. 2014; Vari-Lavoisier 2020). On a household level, they influence norms, attitudes, and social practices of seeking health (Levitt 2001). Household members are thus the end users of the health infrastructure and healthcare services financed by the diaspora.

Social remittances are valorized in forms of social capital. Social capital is defined as "the sum of the resources, actual or virtual, that accrue to an individual or a group by virtue of possessing a durable network of more or less institutionalized relationships of mutual acquaintance and recognition" (Bourdieu and Wacquant 1992, p. 119). Receivers of social remittances enhance their standing within the community through their diaspora relations.

Wilson (2012) combined Bourdieu's concept of capital theory with the model of community resilience and added environmental capital as a decisive factor in determining community resilience. Following his analysis, community resilience is generally defined as the capacity of a community to absorb disturbances and reorganize while undergoing change, but simultaneously retaining essentially the same function, structure, identity, and feedback (Wilson 2010). This concept helps to explore community connectedness, social system interactions, community solidarity, and the community's connection to other geographical spaces (Cutter and Finch 2008). Community resilience can be understood as a "conceptual space at the intersection between economic, social and environmental capital" (Wilson 2012, p. 1220). Nevertheless, globalization can stimulate community stakeholders' networks and therefore provide various resources to maximize community resilience (Chaskin 2008).

Remittances and Health at the Community Level

Remittances are the motor of social change and the transformation of health practices in Niaogho. They comprise money transfers, health infrastructure, advice, and knowledge exchange with the diaspora, resulting in individual changes in health behavior. Furthermore, the attitudes and lifestyles of return migrants, transmigrants, and the diaspora promote social innovation that may produce changes in beliefs, attitudes, and meanings.

The results of the household survey show that 85 households (38 percent) have at least one family member abroad while 139 households (62 percent) have no family members abroad. Furthermore, 10.3 percent of households ($N = 23$) have one family member in Italy. Around 27.7 percent of households ($N = 62$) have at least one family member in the diaspora, but not in Italy, including migrants from Niaogho who live in Ivory Coast, Ghana, Gabon, Equatorial Guinea, Algeria, Libya, and France.

However, kinship is not the only relationship of exchange: Although only 38 percent of the households queried have family members in the diaspora, 59 percent of the respondents noted that they exchange ideas and knowledge with their relatives, friends, and neighbors in the diaspora. Some household members also stated that they receive information and advice on how to cure diseases; between 61.3 percent and 88.3 percent of respondents affirmed that they are satisfied with the advice received from the diaspora. As communication means have developed and fees are being reduced, this exchange has become easier, cheaper, and broader.

During their visits to Niaogho, diaspora members give advice regarding nutrition and health to their household members. Advice is also received from husbands and other family members such as sisters, aunts, and cousins, although advice regarding dietary preferences and healthy nutrition is sometimes difficult to apply as they are part of cultural habits and require financial resources. This is why the women's section of ARNI finances dietary training activities and teaches—along with local midwives—how to cook dishes for babies.

Development of Health Infrastructure in Niaogho

The first health center in Niaogho, CSPS 1, was built in the 1950s during the colonial period and is today run by the government. In 2015, ARNI and its Italian partners in Forlì-Cesena built a second health center, CSPS 2, with a drugstore and a dispensary. This new health center enabled the district health authorities to reorganize their health services and to divide Niaogho into two sanitary areas. Today, the two sanitary areas of the rural municipality of Niaogho serve more than 30,000 inhabitants. The diaspora project greatly changed the health provision structure in Niaogho, providing more health workers, infirmaries for the treatment and cure of diseases, and delivery rooms. Furthermore, the diaspora established a network between health workers in Niaogho, Italian nurses, and NGOs who work in the two health centers for two weeks or one month. Besides health facilities, ARNI supports local institutions such as the forestry department and schools.

Both health centers are frequented by the community members of Niaogho. CSPS 2 receives some patients from other villages because it is closer to them. Since the recruitment of community-based health workers in 2017, the workload of nurses and midwives has been reduced. Furthermore, health behaviors have changed: Tables 10.1 and 10.2

show that health centers provide more prenatal and postnatal consultations, more assisted births, and less deliveries at home, thus reducing the rate of mother-child mortality. For the time period from 2014 to 2018, it is significant that no woman gave birth without assistance. The number of infants in regular consultation increased and the number of malnourished children was reduced.

The tables show the importance of visiting health centers and the role of midwives in prenatal and postnatal care. Their awareness-raising messages have a positive impact on the behavior of women in Niaogho, as shown by their frequent recourse to health facilities in the event of illness or pregnancy and childbirth. Health centers are also places where women discuss their issues with health workers and acquire health knowledge.

Trust, Health Practices, and Knowledge Transfer in Households With and Without a Connection to the Diaspora

A significant transformative effect can be found with regard to changing practices in the context of contraception and prenatal and postnatal advice. Regarding decisions to use contraception, around 10.27 percent ($N = 23$)

Table 10.1 Number of prenatal consultations in CSPS 1

Indicators in CSPS 1	*Periods*				
Number of prenatal consultations (PC)	*2014*	*2015*	*2016*	*2017*	*2018*
1st PC	922	922	470	428	398
2nd PC	855	990	508	475	429
3rd PC	666	637	405	354	295
4th PC	377	265	219	115	82
5th PC	25	78	89	18	11
Number of assisted births	690	634	415	403	322
Number of non-assisted births	0	0	0	0	0
Number of infants from 0–59 months of age in regular consultation	3712	1842	3543	3290	5492
Total number of acutely malnourished children	410	194	231	101	132
Vitamin A supplementation coverage	100.35	101.63	100.58	111.71	109.99

Source: Health district of Garango in the Centre-East region of Burkina Faso, 2019

Table 10.2 Number of prenatal consultations in CSPS 2

Indicators in CSPS 2	*Periods*				
Number of prenatal consultations (PC)	*2014*	*2015*	*2016*	*2017*	*2018*
1st PC	NA	172	457	462	433
2nd PC	NA	25	369	403	403
3rd PC	NA	8	264	308	322
4th PC	NA	5	114	118	136
5th PC	NA	3	28	21	25
Number of assisted births	NA	92	328	410	394
Number of non-assisted births	NA	NA	NA	NA	NA
Number of infants from 0–59 months of age in regular consultation	NA	37	2139	2855	3605
Total number of acutely malnourished children	NA	0	36	19	65
Vitamin A supplementation coverage	NA	ND	103.60	116.55	108.47

Source: Health district of Garango in the Centre-East region of Burkina Faso, 2019. NA: Data not available

of respondents stated that the husbands living in Italy had made this decision, while about 87.05 percent ($N = 195$) of respondents stated that the decision to use contraception was a joint decision. The FGDs revealed a new influence of men in family planning. Traditionally, these topics were regarded as a women's issue, but nowadays numerous interventions and awareness programs in the health sector in Burkina Faso are trying to integrate men in the mother and child healthcare programs. Even men living abroad now take an interest in family planning practices and the attitudes of their wives in Niaogho. This can lead to conflict in religious and traditional families, where parents and in-laws are of different opinions.

It takes *trust* to confide in health workers, not only for the people of Niaogho. Trust is an important component of health-seeking behavior, and trust and health outcomes mutually affect each other in the wellbeing of patients. Without trust in health workers, patients would not visit any health center on a regular basis. In the context of trust, the results concerning CSPS 1 and CSPS 2 and household members with or without a connection to the diaspora are striking. The findings show that respondents with a connection to the diaspora trust the government-run CSPS 1 health center slightly less (47.05 percent) than respondents without a connection to the diaspora (56.83 percent) (Table 10.3).

Table 10.3 Trust in the health workers at CSPS 1

Trust in CSPS 1	*No connection to the diaspora*		*Connection to the diaspora*	
	n	%	*n*	%
Not at all	10	7.19	9	10.58
A bit	10	7.19	14	16.47
Somewhat	40	28.78	22	25.88
Yes	79	56.83	40	47.05

Table 10.4 Trust in the health workers at CSPS 2

Trust in CSPS 2	*No connection to the diaspora*		*Connection to the diaspora*	
	n	%	*n*	%
Not at all	23	16.54	24	28.23
A bit	1	0.72	5	5.88
Somewhat	11	7.91	9	10.59
Yes	104	74.82	44	51.76

Overall, both groups have more trust in CSPS 2, probably due to the better services it provides. Interestingly, with regard to the variable connection to the diaspora, the households without a connection to the diaspora trust CSPS 2 more (74.82 percent) than households with a connection to the diaspora (51.76 percent) (Table 10.4).

The findings further show that household members without a connection to the diaspora complain less about the quality of services provided. Moreover, they do not use private health centers because of a lack of financial means and they frequently use traditional medicines. By contrast, most households with connections to the diaspora are critical of health workers and complain more. Due to financial remittances, they are able to more often use private healthcare services, which are more expensive, have reduced waiting times, and provide better quality. Furthermore, money from abroad enables them to buy medicines and to pay fees for ambulances, surgery, and X-rays.

For both groups, the development of health infrastructures reinforces knowledge about and practices concerning malaria, infectious diseases, mother-child health, and hygiene. The circulation and acceptance of health knowledge requires trust in the health services, which is given for both CSPS 1 and CSPS 2. Knowledge regarding the prevention of malaria and mother-child healthcare were highly valued by the women who participated in this study. Due to increased access, district health authorities observed changes in the use of health services in Niaogho since the opening of CSPS 2. For example, some women reported having acquired important knowledge on hygiene, the prevention of malaria, infectious diseases, the treatment of diarrhea, and mother-child healthcare. Health workers mentioned that knowledge regarding the prevention of malaria, prenatal care, and waterborne diseases is more easily accepted and incorporated into daily life than other topics (see also McKenzie and Rapoport 2005).

In Niaogho, this knowledge transfer works at an interpersonal level (individual household members with a connection to the diaspora), an organizational level (ARNI), and an institutional level (health centers). Other levels may include interaction between community members during cultural and social activities such as weddings, baptisms, and village celebrations, where information and experiences are exchanged. The level of knowledge transfer may arouse different perceptions and provoke different types of outcomes.

The findings suggest that households with a connection to the diaspora have more health-promoting attitudes and behaviors than households without a connection to the diaspora. Undoubtedly, relatives abroad give practical advices. However, a health worker at CSPS 2 rated the influence of awareness-raising activities so high that they leveled the difference between households with and without a connection to the diaspora: "as far as knowledge is concerned, I think there is no difference between households with a relative abroad and those without, because of the awareness-raising activities" (Health Worker CSPS 2, Niaogho 2019). This shows the transformative effects of awareness-raising campaigns, yet the question whether these effects are based on collective remittances remains unanswered.

It is important to note that not all health knowledge comes from having a connection to the diaspora, be it on a personal or organizational level like ARNI. Some nurses even argue that the positive results of health indicators toward mother and child health is due to two local health insurance funds, which were established by the Burkinabè government in 2015 to promote universal health coverage (Rudasingwa et al. 2020). These funds aim at improving the equity and access to healthcare services for prenatal care and mother-child care, especially free healthcare for pregnant women and children aged 0 to 5. We can see that the forms and origins of health knowledge are contested.

Health knowledge is disseminated through personal interactions. Transmigrants, the diaspora, and return migrants have a high impact on the transformation of health practices, because they are multipliers, especially when back home (Van Houte 2016). Migrants obtain social standing through their economic and biographical success abroad as well as through education, new skills, and contacts in the host country (Levitt and Lamba-Nieves 2011). However, international migration has also led to conflicts between those who left and those who stayed: Transmigrants are frequently ostracized as "white men" in Niaogho, for example, when they talk about hygiene to their household members and friends. Some people in Niaogho feel insulted and stigmatized as uncivilized and backward by the diaspora community's awareness campaigns. The local respondents often stated that they feel patronized and instrumentalized when enlightened with messages on hygiene, and some are suspicious that the health advice also contains political messages. Van Houte (2016) defined remittances as inherently controversial, ambivalent, and disruptive. In the case of Niaogho, the social remittances from Italy are also embedded in neocolonial structures, affecting the appropriation or rejection of remittances and consequently reducing resilience.

Transformative Effects of Remittances on Community Resilience

International migration enables a transfer of social capital and fosters changes in traditional communities, in daily practices of health behavior, and in attitudes and perceptions of health (Buch and Kuckulenz 2010; De Haas 2007). In the projects initiated by ARNI, transmigrants and return migrants remit social as well as economic and environmental capital. Social capital is derived from receiving financial as well as social remittances and increases community resilience. The effects of social capital for resilience can be examined according to the categories of bonding, bridging, and linking (Putnam 2000; Woolcock 2001). In the case of Niaogho, the bonding and bridging effects are dominant.

Bonding effects can be seen in the increase of health-seeking awareness on a household level in term of advice, material and financial assistance, and emotional support. Financial support reduces economic vulnerabilities. For example, remittances enable pregnant women to visit gynecologists and obstetricians in the city in case of medical emergency. These services do not exist in Niaogho. Furthermore, diaspora women during their stay in Niaogho provide local women with prenatal and postnatal alimentations, healthy eating plans, and nutritious foods.

The emotional support provided by sisters, cousins, sisters-in-law, and aunts to their female relatives encompasses advice and sharing experiences and feelings and may lessen the stress of pregnant women. Information on nutrition, health, and safety practices during pregnancy and on baby hygiene foster knowledge about prenatal and postnatal care among family members, friends, and neighbors who belong to the same network.

At the household level, the bonding social capital is strong because migrants from Niaogho first help their family members there through individual projects. Women with a connection to the diaspora privilege people who belong to their family network (cousins, sisters, and aunts). Thus, the social capital they generate may create exclusion and could be negative for community cohesion because it is monopolized by in-group members with a connection to the diaspora.

Bridging effects can be found when the women's section of ARNI encourages the participation of other women's associations in Niaogho to join in their activities on health awareness. They thus go beyond their own families and bridge their remittance transfers to all community members in Niaogho.

Other bridging effects include the cooperation between ARNI's women's section and the health and social workers at both health centers. Health centers have become places where different women's organizations meet, share activities, and exchange advice. The presence of some diaspora women during the information campaigns of the health and social workers in Niaogho may heighten trust in health workers and therefore improve health-seeking behavior like accepting advice on nutrition, mother-child care, and hygiene (including breastfeeding, control of the weight of newborns, child malnutrition, and complementary foods).

These collective social remittances increase access to health services and knowledge. They generate positive effects on collective learning through exchange and communication and lead to changes in health practices. Additionally, social remittances cause bridging effects by co-empowering rural communities and enhancing their resilience.

Positive Effects of Remittances at the Household and Community Level

The positive and negative effects of remittances have been noted at both the household and community levels (Cumming et al. 2005). Beyond doubt, remittances have increased the use of healthcare services in Niaogho, and findings show that the diaspora shapes and prepares community members to accept changes and integrate new behavior into their everyday routines. Households with connections to the diaspora are more open to health treatments because they are better informed. However, they are less trusting and respectful toward health and social workers. Additionally, they use private health services or go to higher levels of healthcare in the city to look for cures—even without referrals from nurses in Niaogho.

Financial and social remittances influence the health-seeking behavior of household members with a connection to the diaspora: They care more about their health than household members without a connection to the diaspora and consume health services more often. During the FDGs in Niaogho, they stated unambiguously that they felt freer to talk about health in health centers and were more aware of their health and wellbeing. Furthermore, they indicated a self-rated health gradient.

The positive effects on health behavior are often generated by social interactions with return migrants and transmigrants, enabling the introduction of hygiene knowledge such as washing hands and waste management as well as improved housing conditions and sanitary devices like latrines. This effect is enhanced by the high esteem transmigrants and return migrants hold in their communities of origin, although—as mentioned—their social standing is not undisputed in the Niaogho community.

At the community level, key informants and health workers stated that the most visible positive impact of diaspora projects has been the improvement of prenatal and antenatal care, as well as malaria prevention. The social remittance practices of diaspora women foster the establishment of social capital, consisting of high-quality networks and social relationships. Thus, diaspora women can generate resources for collective actions intended to engender positive outcomes (Baum et al. 2000; Levitt 1998). Moreover, some diaspora women stated that they had learned about herbal medicine from women in Niaogho. Although the remittance transfer between Italy and Niaogho is predominantly one-way, there are a few exceptional cases of mutuality, like the exchange of traditional knowledge (see also Levitt and Lamba-Nieves 2011).

Negative Effects of Remittances at the Household and Community Level

ARNI health projects have induced a dependency on financial remittances similar to international development assistance projects. This dependency is negative for self-determined initiatives for resilience and especially affects the women left behind.

Niaogho women regret that the cooperation with the women from ARNI is short-term and takes place only during the holidays. This indicates that the diaspora engagement is perceived rather as a short-term effect than a long-term commitment. Moreover, Niaogho women who do not belong to this network complain that they are left out and not informed about activities of ARNI's women's association. The diaspora support leaves out household members who are socially distant (Piché 2013). In order to reduce negative social cohesion due to the implementation of its projects, ARNI fosters interactions to generate participation among community, government, local institutional, and external stakeholders.

As regards gender dynamics, it is important to highlight that 87 percent ($N = 77$) of household heads with a connection to the diaspora are women, who live in Niaogho with their children and without their husbands. Most of these women live with their in-laws, where they face certain restrictions. For example, they feel reduced to the role of reproduction, which makes it problematic for them to use contraception. The head nurse of CSPS 2 stated:

> [I]t is because of the practices of the diaspora that our indicators on family planning are falling down. Women [whose husbands are abroad] refuse to join us because their husbands are not in Niaogho. This means that migrants do not want their wives to do family planning. When we [health and social workers] go out for family sensitization, women do not even listen to us. Here, if you do family planning it is perceived as if you want to go out [with another man]. The parents of migrants do not accept that the wives of their children or brothers who are abroad adhere to family planning. Often, it is at night that some women come to the CSPS to adhere to this practice. (Head of Health Worker CSPS 2).

Obviously, the women who are left behind suffer because of rigid family hierarchies, the absence of their husbands, and the reduction of their social contacts. The diaspora seems to be powerless in promoting autonomy, self-esteem, and social justice for the women left behind (O'Neil et al. 2017). Rather, as the statement above indicates, the opposite is the case. The results further suggest a decreasing dependency upon the community in favor of institutional support through the health centers and private healthcare. If help from outside is fast and efficient, there is no need to turn to other community members.

Conclusion

The transformative effects of remittances in health-seeking behavior have become evident in various aspects. The diaspora association ARNI funded the second health clinic, CSPS 2, which has made a significant contribution especially to the health and wellbeing of women in Niaogho, as we can see from the rising number of prenatal and antenatal consultations and assisted births as well as in a growing awareness of contraception. Further effects include health prevention, the provision of medication, and incentives to visit health centers in general. In both health centers, the people of Niaogho have a positive and trusting relationship with the healthcare services and seek treatment and advice.

We can furthermore see differences in health behavior in households with and without a connection to the diaspora. People without a connection to the diaspora accept both health centers, trust them, and make use of their services. People with a connection to the diaspora are more open to health treatment and are better informed, but they use the health centers less and seek private health services instead because they can afford to do so due to financial remittances. With regard to gender, the health centers enable women, especially, to use contraception, sometimes against the will of their (in-law) families.

Remittances function as transformative drivers of community resilience in Niaogho, as was analyzed here through the concept of bonding and bridging effects of social capital (Putnam 2000; Woolcock 2001). Bonding social capital based on transnational ties contributed to the circulation of experience, information, and best practices regarding mother and child health, and not just between close family members and neighbors. The activities of ARNI in health centers established relationships between women's associations and health social workers. These activities enhanced bridging social capital amongst different women's groups in Niaogho, producing positive outcomes for attitudes to health. Overall, with its projects, ARNI has reduced the bonding social capital at the community level, whereas the bridging capital at the individual level has increased because of the transfer of social capital by diaspora members, affecting especially the position of the women left behind.

Overall, individual (household level) and collective (community level) remittances have increased resilience in Niaogho through greater equality in access to health centers, better healthcare services, and a transfer of knowledge and social capital with bonding and bridging effects. However, these processes have also led to dependencies on financial remittances from abroad, reducing self-determined initiatives for resilience and especially affecting the women left behind.

References

Al-Busaidi, Z. Q. (2008). Qualitative Research and its Uses in Health Care. *Sultan Qaboos University Medical Journal*, 8(1), 11–19. PMCID: PMC3087733

Barter, C. & Renold, E. (2000). 'I Wanna Tell You a Story': Exploring the Application of Vignettes in Qualitative Research with Children and Young People. *International Journal of Social Research Methodology*, 3(4), 307–323.

Baum, F. et al. (2000). Families, Social Capital and Health. In I. Winter (Ed.) *Social Capital and Public Policy in Australia* (pp. 250–275). Australian Institute of Family Studies.

Bettin, G. et al. (2014). Remittances and Vulnerability in Developing Countries. International Monetary Fund. IMF WP/14/13.

Blion, R. (1996). De La Côte d'Ivoire en Italie: Pratiques migratoires des Burkinabè et logiques d'Etats. *Studi Emigrazione – Etudes Migrations*, 33(121), 47–69.

Bourdieu, P. & Wacquant, L. J. D. (1992). *An Invitation to Reflexive Sociology*. University of Chicago Press.

Buch, C.M. & Kuckulenz, A. (2010). Worker Remittances and Capital Flows to Developing Countries. *International Migration*, 48, 89–117. https://doi.org/10.1111/j.1468-2435.2009.00543.x.

Chaskin, R. J. (2008). Resilience, Community, and Resilient Communities: Conditioning Contexts and Collective Action. *Child Care in Practice*, 14(1), 65–74.

Cumming, G. S. et al. (2005). An Exploratory Framework for the Empirical Measurement of Resilience. *Ecosystems*, 8, 975–987.

Cutter, S. L. & Finch, C. (2008). Temporal and Spatial Changes in Social Vulnerability to Natural Hazards. *Proceedings of the National Academy of Sciences*, 105(7), 2301–2306. https://doi.org/10.1073/pnas.0710375105.

De Haas, H. (2007). *Remittances, Migration and Social Development: A Conceptual Review of the Literature*. Social Policy and Development Programme Paper Number 34, United Nations Research Institute for Social Development.

Glick Schiller, N., Basch, L. & Blanc-Szanton, C. (1992). Transnationalism: A New Analytic Framework for Understanding Migration. *Annals of the New York Academy of Sciences*, 645(1), 1–24.

Gourlay, A. et al. (2014). Using Vignettes in Qualitative Research to Explore Barriers and Facilitating Factors to the Uptake of Prevention of Mother-to-Child Transmission Services in Rural Tanzania: A Critical Analysis, *BMC Medical Research Methodologies*, 14(21), 1–11.

Guillermina, J. (2006). Factorial Survey Methods for Studying Beliefs and Judgments. *Sociological Methods & Research*, 34(3), 334–423.

Heyman, B. N. et al. (1991). An Assessment of Worldwide Disaster Vulnerability. *Disaster Management*, 4, 3–14.

Hughes, R. (1998). Considering the Vignette Technique and its Application to a Study of Drug Injecting and HIV Risk and Safer Behaviour. *Sociology of Health and Illness*, 20, 381–400.

International Organization for Migration (IOM). (2004). Return Migration: Policies and Practices in Europe. International Organization for Migration.

Ilboudo, L. (2011). Protection sociale au Burkina Faso. Quelle réponse face à la restructuration des solidaritésfamiliales ? Actes du Colloque international de Meknès 17-19 mars 2011, vieillissement de la population dans lespays du sud, Atelier 8 : Relations intergénérationnelles et solidarités, pp. 469–483.

International Organization for Migration (IOM). (2016). Migration au Burkina Faso-Profil Migratoire 2016. https://publications.iom.int/system/files/pdf/mp_burkina_faso_fr.pdf.

Institut National de la Statistique et de la Démographie (INSD) (2017). Online Information : Access on the 25th of december 2021 and Available at: http://cns.bf/IMG/pdf/annuaire_statis_2017.pdf.

Legard, R., Keegan, J. & Ward, K. (2003). In-Depth Interviews. In J. Ritchie & J. Lewis (Eds.), *Qualitative Research Practice: A Guide for Social Science Students and Researchers* (pp. 139–168). SAGE.

Levitt, P. (1996). Social Remittances: A Conceptual Tool for Understanding Migration and Development. Working Paper Series Number 96/04.

Levitt, P. (1998). Social Remittances: Migration Driven Local-Level Forms of Cultural Diffusion. *International Migration Review*, 32(4), 926–48.

Levitt, P. (2001). *The Transnational Villagers*. University of California Press.

Levitt, P. & Lamba-Nieves, D. (2011). Social Remittances Revisited. *Journal of Ethnic and Migration Studies* 37(1), 1–22.

McKenzie, D. & Rapoport, H. (2005). *Migration Networks, Migration Incentives, and Education Inequality in Rural Mexico*. Conference Presentation, Inter-American Development Bank's Conference "Economic Integration, Remittances and Development Conference". Washington, DC.

Morse, S. & McNamara, N. (2013). *Sustainable Livelihood Approach: A Critique of Theory and Practice*. Springer.

Murray, M. (1998, June 4–6). *Stories all the Way Down: The Narrative Construction of Health and Illness.* Conference Presentation, Annual Congress of the Canadian Psychological Association, Edmonton, Canada.

Piché, V. (2013). *Les théories de la migration*. Ined.

O'Neil, T. et. al. (2017). Women on the Move: Migration, Care Work, and Health.

Putnam, R. D. (2000). *Bowling Alone: The Collapse and Revival of American Community*. Simon & Schuster.

Ridde, V. (2006). L'accès des indigents aux services de santé au Burkina Faso : un problème public ? *Lien social et Politiques*, 55, 149–163.

Rudasingwa et al. (2020). Research Paper: Estimating the distributional incidence of healthcare spending oncurative health services in Sub-Saharan Africa: Benefit Incidence Analysis in Burkina Faso, Malawi and Zambia.AFD editions , Nr. 140, August 2020/ AFD Research Papers.

Sawadogo, R. C. (2010). La création et la suppression de la colonie de Haute Volta à la lumière de sa fonction de réservoir important de main d'œuvre. *Cahiers du Centre de recherche en lettres sciences humaines et sociales (CERLESHS)*, 25(35), 297–336.

Shaikh, B. T. (2012). *Health Seeking Behaviours and Health Service Utilization: Implications for Health System in Remote Areas of Pakistan*. Lap Lambert Academic Publishing.

Sikder, M. J. U., Higgins, V. & Ballis, P. H. (2017). *Remittance Income and Social Resilience among Migrant Households in Rural Bangladesh*. Springer.

Van Houte, M. (2016). Transnational Transformations Coupling Migration and Change. International Migration Institute, Oxford University Working Papers, N. 130.

Vari-Lavoisier, I. (2020). Social Remittances. In T. Bastia & R. Skeldon (Eds.), Routledge Handbook of Migration and Development (pp. 125–135). Routledge.

Wilson, G. (2010). Multifunctional 'Quality' and Rural Community Resilience. *Transactions of the Institute of British Geographers* 35(3), 364–381.

Wilson, G. (2012). *Community Resilience and Environmental Transitions*. Routledge

Woolcock, M. (2001). Le rôle du capital social dans la compréhension des résultats sociaux et économiques. *ISUMA, Revue canadienne de recherche sur les politiques*, 2(1), 11–17

Zongo, M. (2009). L'italian dream: coté cours. L'impact des transferts financiers des émigrés bissa en Italie sur les villages dans la province Boulgou, (Burkina Faso). *Les Annales de l'Université de Ouagadougou*, 8, 397–419.

Zongo, M. (2011). *Les enjeux autour de la diaspora burkinabè: Burkinabè à l'étranger, étrangers au Burkina Faso*. L'Harmattan.

PART III

Theorizing Materiality in Remittance Research: Exchange, Embodiment, and Transformative Effects

Remittances most often have a material side and occur in the form of transferred bank bills, food packages, medicines, schoolbooks, furniture, tools, and technological equipment. Moreover, different forms of remittances transform into materials after being transmitted; financial remittances end up in houses, consumer goods, water depots, solar power devices, and tractors. Social remittances materialize in water filters, sustainable energy, plans of cross-border business concepts, and new ambulances for the local rescue. Political remittances appear in the form of voting envelopes, political magazines, and weapons for resistance fighters. In short: remittances are "mutable mobiles," namely "objects that transform while being transferred" (Nowicka and Šerbedžija 2016, p. 14). This section comprises four chapters that reveal the transformative effects of material remittances on actors and the built environment. Altogether, they address crucial questions on the nature of remittances: In which form and with what function do remittances show up? How do objects take on different meanings when sent and received? In what way do they initiate and incorporate social change? And how are remittances embodied? These chapters follow material remittances like everyday objects, commercial objects, tools, houses, and solar panels and their means of transmission, appropriation, and further usage.

To date, two major strands can be detected in explorations of the materiality of remittance and transnational migration: First, migration and material studies scholars as well as historians have analyzed cross-border objects and their impacts on identity formations. By looking at mainly biographical objects like photos, souvenirs, letters, and gifts that were transferred from the countries of origin to the new homes, these findings have shown how objects operate as acts of communication (Thomas and Znaniecki 1918) and connectors between here and there (Frykman 2019), how they display diasporic taste, lifestyle, and status (Savaş 2014), mirror social relations (Appadurai 2010), and foster transnational belonging (Hahn and Friedemann 2019). Second, transnational migration materializes not just through a circulation of objects, but goes hand in hand with a transformation of spaces. Remittances are spatial and material agents of change. Sara Lynn Lopez coined the concept of remittance landscapes, in the form of "distinct elements of the built environment constructed and altered with migrant dollars," in order to capture the political, social, economic, and historical aspects of cross-border engagement (Lopez 2015, p. 1). The houses migrants have built in their places of origin have received the most scholarly attention. Remittance houses (Boccagni and Erdal 2020) are cross-temporal and cross-spatial manifestations of migrant's trajectories, statuses, and dreams, thus revealing the multifacetedness of remittance transactions and their effects on the actors, on belonging, and on the built environment.

In her visual essay, Stefanie Bürkle illustrates how mobility and capital ignited social and spatial change. In three interdisciplinary projects on the transformation of space through migration and tourism, Bürkle followed remittance transactions made by migrants in Germany to the built environment of their places of origin in Turkey, South Korea, and Vietnam. By combining cultural analysis, architectural theory, and spatial aesthetics, she links art and academic research through photographs, video stills, graphic methods, and qualitative interviews in order to reveal socio-spatial relations. Bürkle's visual essay arranges the photographs into a continuous band of images evoking the temporality of remittances and social change. Thus, the series recaptures the process of how remittances are engraved into landscapes and biographies. Ultimately, the continuity of images raises pressing questions regarding the future usage and heritage of these remittance houses.

Gökhan Mura examines the effects of labor migration between Europe and Turkey through the biographical stories of gifts. From a design point of view, a material remittance is a mass-produced commercial object and thus a medium which allows for an exploration of shifts in value as well as the objects' role in communicating migrant narratives. Mura introduces the theory of the "industrial exotic," explaining how non-migrant relatives in Turkey appreciate or reject rare and expensive Western consumer goods. By focusing on the appropriation and afterlife of remitted goods, Mura reveals how the mobile objects have led to social and cultural change in emigration countries.

Drawing on a multi-sited ethnography of a translocal migration corridor within Austria and Turkey, Claudius Ströhle follows the spatial and temporal trajectories of a crucial type of material remittance, namely knives and tools manufactured in Austria and remitted as gifts to relatives and villagers in Turkey. In order to understand the factors that lead to accepting and using remittances in the way intended by the sender, he introduces the theory of remittance affordances: The materiality and biography of the transmitted objects, the relations between sender and recipient, and the embodied practices of usage are decisive in whether the gifts from abroad offer the locals an additional practical and meaningful value.

Rochelle Bailey's contribution also reveals the connective as well as disruptive power of remittances, which is particularly visible when focusing on the materiality of cross-border transactions. By exploring seasonal workers' material remittances from Australia and New Zealand to the island state of Vanuatu, Bailey demonstrates their contribution to the improvement of living conditions in families, households, and broader communities, as seen most notably in the built environment, resources for education, and community projects. However, the material objects from abroad are perceived ambivalently in Vanuatu, for example, when new solar panels on houses cause a sometimes-unwanted distraction for youngsters like watching television or when material remittances and wrappings end up as waste and lead to pollution.

By presenting fresh empirical data and theorizing material remittances with the concepts of the industrial exotic, remittance affordances, and migrating spaces, this section paves the way for establishing material remittances as a worthwhile approach to understanding the transformative effects of transnational migration in the twenty-first century.

References

Appadurai, A. (Ed.). (2010). *The Social Life of Things: Commodities in Cultural Perspective* (8th printing). Cambridge University Press.

Boccagni, P., & Bivand Erdal, M. (2020). On the Theoretical Potential of 'Remittance Houses': Toward a Research Agenda across Emigration Contexts. *Journal of Ethnic and Migration Studies*, 1–18. https://doi.org/10.1080/1369183X.2020.1804340

Frykman, M. P. (2019). Transnational Dwelling and Objects of Connection: An Ethnological Contribution to Critical Studies of Migration. In J. Moser, N. Škrbic Alempijevic, A. Färber, I. Götz, I. Merkel, & F. Schmoll (Eds.), *Ways of Dwelling: Crisis—Craft—Creativity* (pp. 28–45). Waxmann.

Hahn, H. P., & Neumann, F. (Eds.). (2019). Das neue Zuhause: Haushalt und Alltag nach der Migration. Campus.

Lopez, S. L. (2015). The Remittance Landscape: Spaces of Migration in Rural Mexico and Urban USA. University of Chicago Press.

Nowicka, M., & Šerbedžija, V. (2016). Migration and Remittances in a Global Europe. In M. Nowicka & V. Šerbedžija (Eds.), *Europe in a Global Context: Migration and Social Remittances in a Global Europe* (pp. 1–20). Palgrave Macmillan UK.

Savaş, Ö. (2014). Taste Diaspora: The Aesthetic and Material Practice of Belonging. *Journal of Material Culture, 19*(2), 185–208. https://doi.org/10.1177/1359183514521922

Thomas, W. I., & Znaniecki, F. (1918). The Polish Peasant in Europe and America. Monograph of an Immigrant Group. G. Badger.

CHAPTER 11

The Afterlife of Migrant Gifts

Gökhan Mura

Thinking Through Things in Motion

"The car is full of gifts
A stereo and a pair of jeans
Creams of all sorts, and many other things
Who will they give all these gifts to
And who will eat all that food?"

These verses from the 1996 song Kapıkule'ye Kadar (Until Kapıkule, the border checkpoint between Bulgaria and Turkey) by the hip-hop duo Karakan is a portrayal of the typical homeward journeys of Turkish migrant families that started in the 1960s and continue today. A migrant family who travels to Turkey from a Western European country for their summer holiday by car or van with a trunk full of various objects and goods is a common memory in Turkey. Both members of the duo Karakan are children of first-generation Turkish migrant families in Germany, and their song paints a detailed picture of a once very familiar trip to Turkey based

G. Mura (✉)
Department of Visual Communication Design, Izmir University of Economics, Izmir, Turkey
e-mail: gokhan.mura@ieu.edu.tr

S. Meyer, C. Ströhle (eds.), *Remittances as Social Practices and Agents of Change*,
https://doi.org/10.1007/978-3-030-81504-2_11

on their own experiences. The holiday is short, the motherland is far, the trip is long, and the car is always packed with things. The image of Turkish migrants who work in different European countries and bring material things to Turkey for their own future residences or as gifts for families and friends (Zaptçıoğlu 2005) is a vivid memory in the history of Turkish labor migration. The gifts brought by the migrants tell the story of migration not only from the migrants' point of view, but also from that of those who remained, for the history of those on the move is also a history of those who stay behind. (Levitt 2006).

I suggest taking these remitted objects seriously. The personal histories of the entanglements between migrants and non-migrants and these objects provide us with an array of individual perspectives through which to study migration. The literature on remittances provides detailed and extensive economic and ethnographic studies on what is remitted, how it is remitted, and how remittances construct, affect, and manipulate relations between the transactors in a transnational network. This chapter outlines an approach to the study of the social effects of material remittances (Nowicka and Šerbedžija 2016) that places the migrant gift as a transnational object and a remitted commodity in the focus of the study. Thus, it explores migration and remittances by thinking about and thinking through objects (Candlin and Guins 2009).

This chapter discusses the reception and adoption of migrant gifts by non-migrants in Turkey. My main questions concern what happens to the migrant gift after it is relocated from its country of purchase and is received by a non-migrant in Turkey, and what this tells us about remittances, migration, and Turkish society. I here embrace the conceptual framework of the cultural biographies of things, and the changing value regimes that transnational things in motion undergo in the course of their biographies (Appadurai 1986; Hoskins 2006; Kopytoff 1986; Tilley 2006). I will apply this conceptual framework here to explore and interpret the mutable nature of the value of material gifts brought from Western European countries to Turkey from the 1960s until today.

The Biographies of Migrant Gifts

The history of Turkish labor migration to Western Europe in the second half of twentieth century can be told through things. An analysis of remittances based on the biographies of things in motion has the potential to reveal previously neglected nuances of the social history of this migration:

"biographies can make salient what might otherwise remain obscure" (Kopytoff 1986, p. 67). Mauer argued that looking at things through a biographical perspective "introduce[s] a temporal dimension to the study of material objects," through which the object's underlying value is redefined as it "gets into and out of relations of exchange" in its lifespan (Maurer 2006, p. 21). However, our view would be further sharpened by exploring the social effects of material remittances through the lens of the biography of things, taking into account the process of objectification (Tilley 2006) that occurs in a transnational migrant gift's life, and expanding our perspective on the fluidity of the value of the things in motion (Appadurai 1986). Tilley's broad definition of objectification as "a concept that provides a particular way of understanding the relationship between subjects and objects" (Tilley 2006, p. 61) was further crystalized by Giorgio de Michelis, who defined objectification as "the process through which human beings appropriate and domesticate things" (De Michelis 2014, p. 198). Throughout the lifespan of a migrant gift turned into remittance, the object constructs, reinforces, and redefines the social relations between people. Non-migrant remittance receivers re-appropriate the gifts given, attributing new roles to them in their material world, and defining new chapters in the biography of the thing.

Through the course of its life, an object witnesses several chapters as it is subject to material, functional, and social changes. In the case of migrant gifts, the impact of the spatial dimension on an object's biography is as important as the temporal dimension previously underlined. The mutable meaning and value of an object relocated across transnational borders and over the course of time is affected by the social and economic changes taking place in both the localities it originated from and where it is remitted. The biographies of things and the people who possess, use, exchange, or discard them are moreover intertwined (Hoskins 2006; Tilley 2006). Social and economic changes in the lives of the objects' owners therefore open up new chapters in the biographies of things.

I use the conceptualization "afterlife of the gift" to point to the opening of a new chapter in an object's biography. The afterlife concerns the new chapters of the biographies of transnational things after they have been displaced from their intended environment into a new material environment in the migrants' country of origin. I do not use afterlife as a metaphor to connote the death of an object, and what happens to it after it is discarded, but to emphasize the leap in the biography of a transnational migrant gift after it experiences a sharp material climate change. An exploration and creative interpretation of the various stories of this critical turn in the biographies of migrant gifts in different decades of migration history enables us to develop a comparative framework for the study of migration and remittances from the point of view of the value regimes and material cultures of the countries involved.

In an effort to explore the transformative effect of remittances, I will look at the change of the meaning, value, and reception of migrant gifts in Turkey throughout the planned labor migration to Europe. I will discuss the changing roles of migrant gifts through the interpretation of auto-ethnographic examples and according to three concepts: the narrative value of the gift, the subjective shift in the perceived value of the gift, and the intersubjective processes of adopting the gifts in Turkish society. My aim in this chapter is twofold: First, I will expound a theory of material remittances from an object-biographical point of view, and second, I will attempt to tell the history of Turkish migration through objects. In doing so, I will employ the essential "imaginative interpretation and appropriation" necessary in "any history told through things" (MacGregor 2012, p. xviii). To this end, I will introduce the concept of the 'industrial exotic' to explore the shift in the value of gifts and remittances.

Theorizing the Gift as a Medium of Migrant Narratives

The objects that people possess, interact with, and exchange can help to compose and transmit narratives. Objects also help people to communicate their self-histories (Hoskins 1998). How an object comes to be in a person's possession may reflect that person's needs, habits, wealth, or lifestyle choices. If it is an inherited object or a gift, meanwhile, it may transmit information about that person's history. How the object is utilized throughout that person's biography tells a great deal about that person's life, physical abilities, cognitive capabilities, as well as the social, economic, and material conditions that person lives through. Modern consumer society advocates the idea that what we buy, possess, or give is an expression of our preferred identity, a way of distinguishing ourselves, and thereby a reflection of what we think of the lives and identities of others. Therefore, objects can translate and transmit these personal narratives from us to others and vice versa. Besides, objects may also become an active part in people's stories, or they may be instrumental in narrating stories, with the object triggering, storing, transferring, or accompanying the narration of memories in self-histories. An object can be a prop helping to set the material scene of a narrative, or it can be used as a metaphor to impart the desired messages. Along its life cycle, the gifted object can assist in narrating the story of those actors in the migration network who participated in the gift exchange. The choice and acquisition of the mass-produced commercial object by the migrants in their country of residence defines what they think a good gift should be—a good gift for their relatives or friends back home, and a good gift for their own social role as the migrant visiting home and carrying out their ascribed role in the gift-giving practice. The purchase reflects the available material choice in the country of residence and the migrants' budget as well as the migrants' idea of the receiver's status and gift-worthiness. It represents both the status of the object in the country of purchase and the migrants' assessment of its potential value and status in the country of origin. When the gifted object is displaced from the country of residence to be given as a gift in the country of origin, the gift establishes an object-centered communication between the migrant and the remaining party through which the migrant's assessments of the appropriateness of the gift and the migrant's story can be narrated. The same object's reception and placement in a new material environment and its afterlife beyond this exchange defines yet another relation between the object and the new owners. The integration of the object into this new life exhibits the assessment of the utility, value, and meaning of the same material gift by the receiver. The change in the ascribed meaning or value to similar migrant gifts through time and the changes in the country of origin also offer new interpretations and translations in the perceived migration narrative. Different groups of people, their social relations, and the dynamics of these groups and their society can be addressed through an interpretative analysis of the many different forms in which exchange manifests itself (Carrier 2006). In the case of transnational gift exchange, the people involved in the gift exchange network constitute a web of interactions, and the dynamics of their relations are determined by their positions in the social, economic, and material circles through which they move as well as the material and non-material qualities of the gift itself. Each individual in this network is entangled in social relations in which the gift occupies a central position. Besides being a vehicle of economic and social exchange, the gift constitutes a material medium through which the transactors communicate.

Today, various channels of communication allow for a continuous audio and visual communication between the migrants and their families and friends back home. Global movement of commodities, as well as ideas, images, and mediated representations of different lifestyles in different societies, provide ever-expanding exposure to the life of other people in other places. However, in the early years of Turkish labor migration, information about the new lives of the migrants working in Western European countries was scarce. The life of the migrant was a subject of curiosity for the ones staying behind, but most of the information about the daily life of the migrant was based on personal testimonials. The migrant gift could thus be interpreted as a material manifestation, a visible account of the personal narrative of the migrant's new life.

I use the term 'migrant gifts' to signify industrially produced commercial goods and objects purchased in the migrants' country of residence with the intention of being brought to their country of origin as gifts for family and friends. These commercial and material gifts include objects like kitchen utensils, electronic consumer products, toys, and fast-moving consumer goods, such as packaged food (e.g. chocolate, instant coffee, and wafers), cosmetic products, clothing, and accessories. These commodities "provide material vehicles for narrating economic change" (Foster 2006, p. 285). The gift becomes the vehicle through which "individuals and groups identify themselves" (Tilley 2006, p. 71). When migrants transport objects to Turkey, either for their own use or as gifts, the objects become a part of a migration narrative contributing to the transmission of the personal histories of migrants. Alongside the widely discussed major concerns and grand narratives of migration, I argue that the possession and exchange of transnational objects can be considered a material manifestation and an alternative narrative of the migrants' cultural displacement. These transnational objects can translate experiences from the migrant's new life into comprehensible—and palpable—narratives to an audience lacking visual or material clues about the life of the migrant in a foreign country.

The transnational migrant objects, as material manifestations of their lived experience, provide a migration narrative for the migrants while also becoming the symbolic medium through which migrant stories are narrated. The migrant gift becomes both a medium of narrative through which the story of the life in the migrated country can be told and the materialized message itself. The medium through which the message is communicated thus becomes the message itself (McLuhan 2001).

Transnational objects can assist migrants in devising an alternative narrative about their life and experiences in their new countries of residence. The object, as a sign, a representational image of another material environment, has the potential to animate and amplify the migrants' narratives about their new lives by materializing their lives through previously inaccessible things that the non-migrant may nevertheless already have been aware of through mediated depictions in magazines or on TV. This narrative agency, that is, the foreign object's ability to enrich the story about the lives of others, is also part of the value of the migrant gift beyond its commercial or material value. From its early life to its afterlife, the narrative value of a migrant gift as the object's agency is preserved. Additionally, even after the material climates of the countries in the migration networks relatively converge, and even though the messages that were received and their interpretations might change over time, a migrant gift still retains its inherit ability to translate and transmit stories of migration from the past and provide reflections on the current remittance scene.

Experiencing the Other Land

The changes in the biography of a thing do not change its narrative agency. The object, as a part of the migrant's many narratives, becomes the medium and subject of the gift receiver's narratives after the exchange. When the gift is given to the non-migrant, this exchange causes a turn in how the narrative agency of the gift is employed. This leap from the object's previous life to its new life transforms whom the object serves and assists in composing and narrating the story of the effects of migration and social and material remittances from a non-migrant's point of view.

The recontextualization of the purchased gift in the non-migrant's life may also have impacts beyond facilitating a narrative. Levitt (2006) observed that non-migrants develop a covetous interest in migrants' lives, and they imagine their own lives elsewhere due to their continuous exposure to migrant stories, photographs, and home videos. The material narrative medium afforded by the gift, I argue, similarly becomes a material medium of experience. The gift is not only a visual representation of life in another country; it also affords opportunities for mimicking experiences of that life abroad through using the same objects and consuming the same products or cosmetics, food, or drinks. Using or consuming the gift provides the gift receiver access to a hands-on 'authentic' experience, reanimating the experiences of life of the object in the country where it was purchased. This experience, carrying out a task like the people in the country where the object come from in their own country, or consuming whatever they consume in other countries, can be viewed as a cameo role for the non-migrant in the previous biography of the object. We can thus speculate further that, by using and consuming transnational gifts, the non-migrant can, to some extent, experience life far away. The gift, which translates and transmits separate stories of the migrant and the remaining party, respectively, further becomes a mediator between the migrant and the non-migrant, allowing the latter to interactively participate in the migration story she has been listening to.

Value Shift: The History of Turkish Labor Migration Through Things

When a gift changes hands, a new chapter begins in its biography. The meaning of a thing shifts for different individuals, depending on the way it is utilized by its owner in different social situations (Foster 2006). The gift receiver redefines the meaning and value of the migrant gift; however, the revaluation of the gift by the non-migrant is not solely dependent on personal attributions, but also determined by the different value regimes (Appadurai 1986) that the commodity travels between. Furthermore, exploring the displacement of an object between different value regimes, and exploring these things in motion, "illuminate[s] their human and social context" (Appadurai 1986, p. 5). The shift in the perceived value of the gift when it arrives in Turkey and its change throughout the years of migration thus provides us a glimpse into social and economic changes in Turkey over time.

Turkey signed its first bilateral agreement with Germany concerning labor migration in 1961, which allowed skilled workers from Turkey to work in different industries and jobs in Germany. Following Germany, bilateral agreements were struck with Austria, Belgium, and the Netherlands in 1964, with France in 1965, and with Sweden in 1967. Although these bilateral labor migration agreements ceased in 1974, migration from Turkey continued in different forms, such as through family reunifications. Turkish worker families settled in their countries of employment but embarked on yearly holiday visits to their country of origin. Turkish migrant workers' remittances constituted an important boost to the Turkish economy and a major source of foreign exchange in the 1970s (Çeçen et al. 1994; Ertüzün 1976; Pamuk 1981), and the migrants' yearly holiday visits were a source of material remittances. While Turkish people migrated to Western European countries in the pursuit of a better life and were introduced to a new life in a new material environment, an import substitution policy was implemented in Turkey between 1960 and 1980 that significantly restricted the entry of imported goods into the country (Barkey 1984; Öniş 2010). This policy created a narrow market for foreign durables, as few people could afford the prices of the limited amount of available merchandise (Pamuk 1981). Even after the abolition of this import substitution policy, the import tax laws in effect until 1986 affected the import of Western goods and objects. Imported goods were thus scarce, and practically inaccessible to the masses with limited purchasing power. The few imported goods available were expensive by comparison to their local equivalents. Another result of the import substitution policy was the use of older and inferior technologies to produce local substitutes (Ertüzün 1976), which made the technologically advanced, higher quality foreign goods more desirable.

Introducing the Industrial Exotic

Kopytoff suggested that the value of a commodity, beyond the exchange worth determined by the social relations of its production, is attributed to it after it is produced "by way of an autonomous cognitive and cultural process of singularization" (Kopytoff 1986, p. 83). In the case of the gift brought from abroad, this is a particular process of singularization. The migrant gift brought to Turkey during the first decades of labor migration was a material manifestation of life in another country. It was distinguishable from other similar products, and, in most cases, it could not be found on the market. In some cases, products from abroad provided new services and introduced new ways of doing things, all of which enhanced the process of the singularization of the migrant gift. The discrepancy between the utility, accessibility, and affordability of the migrant gift and the objects available in the local market determined its status and its value for the non-migrant.

The value of the material object in its culture of origin shifts when it becomes a gift and is taken to a different country, not only because it inherits the exchange value as a gift, but also because it is singularized and inherits a different exotic quality because it is brought from abroad. I propose labeling transnational material remittances such as migrant gifts as 'industrial exotic' to highlight the cultural significance of the mass-produced goods and objects, which gain an increased value due to their culturally Western origin and their displacement from an industrially and economically developed country to a less developed one. The 'industrial exotic' is a mass-produced and mundane object that goes through a value shift and is thus perceived as more valuable compared to the place where it is produced. The 'industrial exotic' is neither rare nor hard to find in its place of origin. These are everyday consumer goods, available in developed industrial countries with free market economies. However, they become exotic in the countries where the economy or politics do not allow them to be circulated in the market, making them rare. The singularization of the 'industrial exotic' stems from its rarity, its utility, and what it represents in a developing country. Unlike the exotic as defined by geographical and natural conditions, 'industrial exotic' is not defined by natural resources, but it is a token of an economic and industrial achievement. 'Industrial exotic' is defined by the differences between the material climates of the countries the thing moves in between.

To substantiate the definition of the 'industrial exotic' and to show how its value shifts, I will provide auto-ethnographic testimonials from my own family as examples of how gifts from abroad were received back in Turkey. During my childhood in the 1980s, my dad's cousin, not a migrant, but a truck driver traveling back and forth between Europe and Turkey, used to bring various gifts from different European countries to my family. For example, he brought die-cast toy cars for me and my elder brother. Our first *Matchbox* and *Majorette* toy cars were elegantly different from their local equivalents in Turkey in the early 1980s. Besides the joyous utility they afforded through the experience of playing with them, their scarcity in the Turkish market made them even more special to us: They were objects of distinction. My dad, on the other hand, used to receive different decks of playing cards, which he kept in a special cabinet. Some of these decks were even kept in their plastic-wrapped packages, waiting for a special occasion to be used. These simple, everyday industrial products, cheaply available and accessible in Austria and Germany, were rare and exotic objects in Turkey. Playing cards are made to be used more than once, as long as their durability allows, but my dad's attitude toward these commodities changed their biographies and increased their perceived value to more than it was intended where they were produced, thus definitely extending the objects' life [Fig. 11.1].

Fig. 11.1 A deck of playing cards made in Austria. My dad still keeps this gift

One of the gifts my mum got repeatedly was a bar of soap from the German brand Fa. With its packaging, its shape, and its distinctive smell, the Fa soap was immediately perceived as different from the available soap brands in daily use in Turkey. Although it was perhaps an ordinary part of everyday life, and very accessible in Germany, Fa was not available at ordinary shops in Turkey. For us, it could only be brought from abroad. It was considered a luxury consumer product in our home, or at least a product that should be delicately consumed. Our relationship with our Fa soap, which was intended to have a short life span, artificially extended the life of this consumer good. There was a significant difference between the value and meaning of this single bar of soap in Turkey with the meaning it held in the country in which it was produced. It was not just the physical properties or the affordance of the soap that created this difference; it was where the bar of soap came from, what it represented, and not knowing when we would receive another.

At the DDR Museum in Berlin, life in the German Democratic Republic is exhibited vividly through images, videos, and the display of interiors and objects. One display drawer consists of a collection of objects that were smuggled into the GDR from Federal Republic of Germany during the Cold War. The display includes consumer goods that were abundant in West Germany, such as food products, packaged coffee, packs of nylon stockings, and basic cosmetic products like hand creams and different brands of soaps, including Fa soap [Fig. 11.2].

Apparently, Fa soap was a sought-after object, and worth the risk of smuggling. The glorified status of Fa soap both in the GDR and in Turkey during the same period, but for different people from arguably very different societies and geographies, unveils the essence of the 'industrial exotic.'

Fig. 11.2 Fa soap

It is not the distance or the difference of climate between countries, but the difference between the material climates that shapes the exotic quality of an object. The material climate of a country is shaped by the political, social, cultural, and economic climates in that country. The 'industrial exotic' reflects the prosperity and the industrial and technological achievements of the society from which it comes. In other words, its exoticness arises from the differences in the industrial capacity and the economic policy across national borders, rather than the distance the object travels. The lack of choice in the local national market and the visible distinction of quality between the existing alternatives and the objects brought from more developed industrial and consumerist societies enhance the allure of the 'industrial exotic.'

Adoption of the Gift

The economic conditions and the material climate of Turkey define the value regime in which the migrant gift becomes 'industrial exotic.' The gift's value is redefined by the gift receivers when they recontextualize it in their lives. The adoption of the transnational object is a cultural redefinition of the object in its new environment. And, as Kopytoff elegantly argued, "what is significant about the adoption of alien objects is they are culturally redefined and put to use" (Kopytoff 1986, p. 67). The gift's adoption by its new user into a new material environment, or its rejection, determine the afterlife of the migrant gift. The received gift, appropriated as an 'industrial exotic,' experiences a value shift and can have an extended life span, used infrequently, enjoying its privileged status as a valuable item at home. Even fast-moving consumer goods that are made to be sold and consumed immediately have an alternative life story as gifts. Fast-moving consumer goods were a popular choice of gift among migrants, as most contemporary fast-moving consumer goods were scarce in Turkey due to the import substitution policy. Even edible gifts like chocolate, a very common and popular small gift from abroad, experienced this shift. Cheap chocolates from budget supermarkets received an esteemed treatment in Turkey, sometimes as delicacies saved for special occasions. Sometimes, they grew stale as they waited in glass cabinets for the perfect occasion.

Aside from the symbolic meaning of the exotic, the adoption of a gift is also based on its utility and how well it satisfies a practical need in the non-migrant's life. The transnational objects accepted and used by their new owners become a part of the household and are integrated into their new material environment. However, although they may maintain their symbolic value and narrative agency, in time, the gift that becomes commonly used and adjusted in its new context loses its exotic quality and the 'industrial exotic' becomes ordinary. This ordinary object then becomes obsolete, because it not only gets worn out or broken, but its functional and cultural substitutes emerge in the market due to larger-scale changes in economic policies.

However, not all transnational objects brought from Western Europe were enthusiastically accepted or adopted in Turkey. The rejected, or perhaps better to say unadopted, remittances lived a short life as a gift or material remittance and ended up in places more suitable for the definition of afterlife. To continue with my auto-ethnographic approach, further testimonials from my family as a gift receiver help clarify what I mean by the acceptance and adoption of the gift. In the 1980s, my aunt and uncle remigrated to Turkey from Germany. Their home was always an interesting display of objects from Germany, an exhibition of the 'industrial exotic' in context. In 1988, they were visited by their neighbors from Germany, another Turkish migrant couple. The couple brought some small gifts for my parents, as was customary for migrant workers visiting Turkey. My mum got some cosmetics and a vegetable peeler. While the object fascinated me as a child on account of both its utility and the novel solution it provided to peeling vegetables, my mum was not impressed, and did not adopt it in her daily kitchen routine. The vegetable peeler experienced a not so valuable life in our kitchen drawer and was later tossed away as a useless object. Years later, while living in Sweden as a designer, I brought my mum a gift, a cheese slicer, not only as a reference to the previous family story but also because, again, I was fascinated by its form and function as an object. As in the case of the vegetable peeler, she did not adopt the ways of doing things made possible by the cheese slicer; of course, most of the cheese consumed in Turkey is not suitable to be sliced with this instrument. An alien object from abroad that cannot perform its function in a new environment and that cannot challenge user habits remains unadopted, and eventually becomes obsolete. In this particular case, the object was not discarded, but still lives an abandoned life in my mum's kitchen drawer because, as an object brought by her son, its symbolic value remains intact. During my research, I heard testimonials similar to my personal stories from different non-migrant families in Turkey, who spoke about the disdain created by some technical objects brought from abroad as gifts. Some of these misfit alien objects still live in limbo, not used, but not thrown away, lingering in cabinets and drawers [Fig. 11.3].

A further step in the rejection of migrant gifts is when they are discarded or sold to new owners. A speculative interpretation of the

Fig. 11.3 The abandoned cheese slicer from Sweden. My mum still keeps it

biography of these unadopted remittances can be compiled by tracking their afterlife in secondhand shops and flea markets. A yogurt maker found in a secondhand shop in Turkey, alongside several other electrical appliances in the same shop, were all objects alien to Turkish kitchens until recently. The ability to automatically make yogurt in 100 ml portions was technologically advanced for its time, but in a country where making large amounts of yogurt directly in a pot without mechanical assistance is a proud display of culinary talent, the technical ability of the object did not provide a happy biography. Similarly, coffee bean grinders and moka pots, in a context where espresso and filter coffee were not familiar or popular, were both doomed afterlives as items in secondhand shops [Figs. 11.4 and 11.5].

The rejection of remittances due to cultural and material differences can thus be said to prepare the way for an unanticipated afterlife for the remittances in question. While some transnational objects end up in landfill or in secondhand shops, as they from the outset did not suit the habitus of Turkey, others lost their place over time with the social and economic transformations that took place in Turkey after the 1980s. A flea market

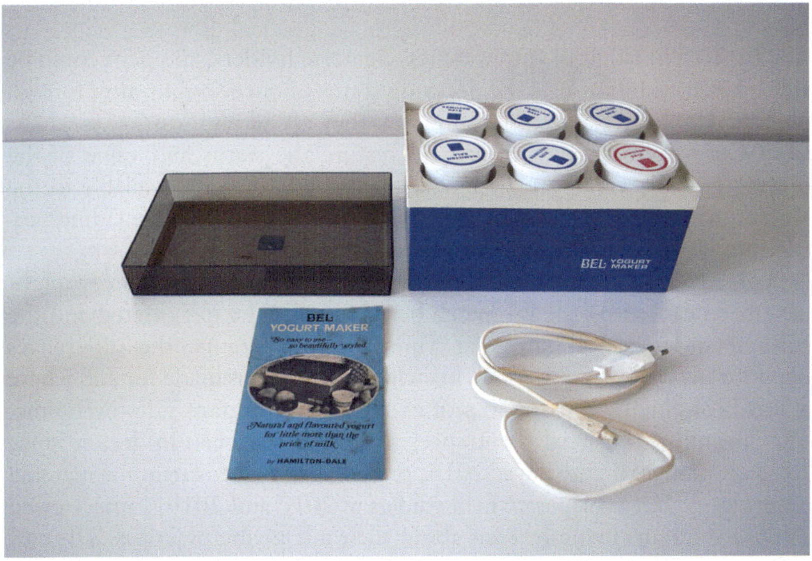

Fig. 11.4 A yogurt maker found in a secondhand shop in Turkey

Fig. 11.5 A coffee bean grinder and a moka pot for sale in a secondhand shop in Turkey

stall I visited in Istanbul with watches, cigarette holders, and pens could be viewed as an exhibition of the decaying status of once sought-after foreign objects. The handmade sign stating that they are all high-quality products from Germany no longer helped to restore the status and value of the object, as many variations of similar products have been available in the market in Turkey for decades now. This gives us an idea of the fading perception of high-quality remittances from Germany [Fig. 11.6].

A decrease in interest in migrant gifts as material remittances might have been caused by the mismatch between what the gift offered and the cultural and practical needs of Turkish non-migrants, the differences between the material environments where the gift was made for and where it was brought to, and the loss of exoticness of migrant gifts over time. The amount of financial remittances to Turkey has been in decline since 1998 (Karamelikli and Bayar 2015, p. 33). The same is true for material remittances. In two separate field studies in 2017 and 2019, I interviewed Turkish migrants living in Paris about their gift-giving practices. The participants in both studies reported that they were bringing fewer material

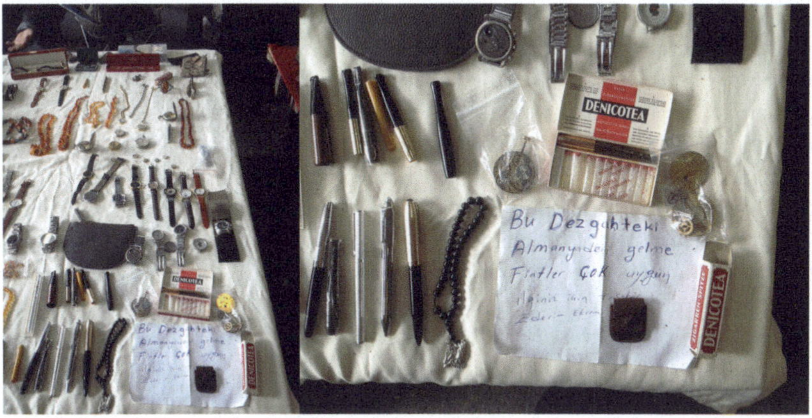

Fig. 11.6 A stall in a flea market in Istanbul for goods that are declared to come from Germany. The sign reads, in broken Turkish: "The things in this stall came from Germany. The prices are very affordable. Thank you for your interest"

gifts to Turkey than before. Aside from a reduced need for material remittances in Turkey, the decrease in the remitted commodities points to two major changes in the remittance scene in Turkey. The Turkish migrants in Paris underlined that whatever they decided to bring was accessible in the Turkish market as well. Furthermore, they reported that their families and friends back home were not always very happy with the quality of the gifts they brought, as was sometimes openly expressed to the migrants. The disdain toward migrant gifts in twenty-first century Turkey is not because of a change in the quality of the gifts, but due to the abundance of substitute goods and objects in the Turkish market and a changed perception of quality among the gift receivers in Turkey. This change in the value regime determined the attitude of the transactors at both ends toward material remittances. The change in the economic policies of Turkey, which opened its partially state-controlled economy to a free market economy, allowing more imports and a developing economy with manufacturing capabilities, provided much easier access to an extended material world. Formerly exotic and valuable objects brought into Turkey later became available and thus ordinary in the new open market, which is saturated with commodities produced in Turkey or imported from all around the world. The non-migrant, flooded with access to a much wider choice of material things, thus becomes pickier and more vocal about the indifference of the material quality of the received gift. The disdain expressed toward some of the gifts discouraged the migrants from making the effort of transporting material remittances, especially when taking into consideration luggage capacity. One reason the migrants expressed for bringing fewer material remittances than before is that they preferred air travel over cars to reach Turkey. The limited baggage allowance naturally had a direct effect on their cargo. Alongside the evolution of the perceived value and meaning of material remittances, a change in the technologies of remittance and in the means and channels to transfer remittances throughout the history of labor migration from Turkey to Western European countries is a topic deserving of further research. This topic offers a rich potential for the further exploration of the material and immaterial flow of remittances and the evolution of remittance technologies in physical and digital migration networks.

Conclusion

Turkish migrants used to bring gifts which money could not buy. These consisted of mass-produced commercial goods and objects that were difficult to find in the Turkish consumer market and were unaffordable for most people. Therefore, they were exotic. These migrant gifts were samples from the daily life of countries with a different designed material environment, affording utilities that may or may not have been accepted and adopted by Turkish people. The gradual change in the gift recipients' attitudes toward the gifts through the history of Turkish labor migration provides us an overview of the larger changes occurring at the same time in Turkey, through the lens of the objects in question. The change in the recognition of the material remittance, from 'industrial exotic' to ordinary, is a consequence of the economic and social transformations in Turkey that were also reshaping its material climate.

Carrier stated that in the UK and the US, everyday items and impersonal, purchased commodities constitute "risky gifts" that lack the personal touch and consideration one might expect from the social relation that prompted the gift exchange (Carrier 2006, p. 380). However, in the case of Turkish migrant gifts, the non-migrants welcomed the mass-produced and purchased commodities in the first decades of Turkish labor migration. The novelty and exotic quality of these foreign everyday commodities, as well as the gift's financial contribution to the non-migrant's budget, made the purchased commodities valuable and meaningful.

However, the warm welcome faded in time for those gifts that were not aligned with the Turkish way of doing things, as these did not present acceptable personal or social affordances (see Ströhle in this volume).

The various scenarios of afterlives of migrant gifts in Turkey, either their early retirement as alien objects, their disposal, or their revaluation in secondhand markets, alongside the intertwined personal life stories of the gift receivers, provide us a unique opportunity to focus on the evolution of the social impacts of material remittances. Migrant gifts are not only embodied economic transactions, but also materialized ambassadors, transmitting migration narratives from the perspectives of the migrants and non-migrants alike involved in the remittance practice. Alongside this evolution in Turkey and in other countries involved in the migration network, the value regimes changed. Consequently, the gifts' perceived value and ascribed meaning, and thus its acceptance and adoption, also evolved, reshaping the gift-giving habits of Turkish migrants. I believe we can further use this conceptual framework to develop a comparative study of the impact of remittances in different countries. A cross-cultural comparative analysis of the adoption and revaluation of transnational migrant gifts in different remittance-receiving countries would allow for an alternative object-oriented reading of the social impact of migration and remittances in countries with similar development patterns and economic and social conditions.

The biographical approach I have embraced in looking at the life and afterlife of objects, addressing the intertwined relations between people and things in order to explore the changing meaning and social impact of migrant gifts, can also illuminate the current transnational flux in which things and people are constantly on the move and interact with each other through complex networks. In this dynamic environment, the value and meaning of objects and their role in people's lives change continuously, in accordance with each actor's unfolding biographies. The global movement of commodities as well as ideas, images, and mediated representations of different lifestyles in different societies provide ever-expanding exposure to narratives of the lives of the other and challenge the object's agency as a narrative medium in the migrant story. With the abundance and accessibility of globalized commodities, the exoticness and representativeness of the 'foreign object' becomes demystified. This change in the narrative ability, meaning, and value of the transnational gift for the migrant and the non-migrant in a globalized, consumerist, post-migrant society begs further analysis. I believe the object biography approach provides us with new opportunities for further research on the social impact of material remittances in a context where migration is constantly evolving.

References

Appadurai, A. (1986). Introduction: Commodities and the Politics of Value. In A. Appadurai (Ed.), *The Social Life of Things: Commodities in Cultural Perspective* (pp. 3–63). Cambridge University Press.

Barkey, H. (1984). Crises of the Turkish Political Economy: 1960 – 1980. In A. Evin (Ed.), *Modern Turkey: Continuity and Change* (pp. 47–63). Leske und Buldrich.

Carrier, J. (2006). Exchange. In C. Tilley, W. Keane, S. Küchler, M. Rowlands & P. Spyer (Eds.), *Handbook of Material Culture* (pp. 373–383). SAGE Publications Ltd.

Candlin, F. & Guins, R. (2009). Introducing Objects. In F. Candlin & R. Guins (Eds.) *The Object Reader* (pp. 1–18). Routledge.

Çeçen, A., Doğruel, A. & Doğruel, F. (1994) Economic Growth and Structural Change in Turkey 1960–88. *International Journal of Middle East Studies,* 26(1), 37–56.

De Michelis, G. (2014). What Design Tells Us about Objects and Things. *Design and Culture,* 6(2), 187–202.

Ertüzün, T. (1976). İthal İkamesi ve Sınırları. *İstanbul Üniversitesi İktisat Fakültesi Mecmuası,* 36(1-4), 153–181.

Foster, R. (2006). Tracking Globalization: Commodities and Value in Motion. In C. Tilley, W. Keane, S. Küchler, S., M. Rowlands, & P. Spyer (Eds.), *Handbook of Material Culture* (pp. 285–302). SAGE Publications Ltd.

Hoskins, J. (1998). *Biographical Objects: How Things Tell the Stories of People's Lives.* Routledge.

Hoskins, J. (2006). Agency, Biography and Objects. In C. Tilley, W. Keane, S. Küchler, S., M. Rowlands, & P. Spyer (Eds.), *Handbook of Material Culture* (pp. 74–84). SAGE Publications Ltd.

Karamelikli, H. & Bayar, Y. (2015) Remittances and Economic Growth in Turkey. *Ecoforum Journal* 4(2), 33–40.

Kopytoff, I. (1986). *The Cultural Biography of Things: Commoditization as Process.* In A. Appadurai (Ed.), *The Social Life of Things: Commodities in Cultural Perspective* (pp. 64-91). Cambridge University Press.

Levitt, P. (2006). God Needs No Passport: Trying to Define the New Boundaries of Belonging. *Harvard Divinity Bulletin* 34(3), https://bulletin-archive.hds.harvard.edu/articles/autumn2006/god-needs-no-passport

MacGregor, N. (2012). *A History of the World in 100 Objects.* Penguin.

Maurer, B. (2006). In the Matter of Marxism. In C. Tilley, W. Keane, S. Küchler, M. Rowlands & P. Spyer, (Eds.), *Handbook of Material Culture* (pp. 13-28). SAGE Publications Ltd.

McLuhan, M. (2001). *Understanding Media: The Extensions of Man*. Routledge.

Nowicka, M. & Šerbedžija, V. (2016). Migration and Social Remittances in a Global Europe. In M. Nowicka & V. Šerbedžija (Eds.), *Migration and Social Remittances in a Global Europe* (pp. 1-20), Palgrave Macmillan UK.

Öniş, Z. (2010). Crises and Transformations in Turkish Political Economy. *Turkish Policy Quarterly* 9(3), 45-61.

Pamuk, S. (1981). Political Economy of Industrialization in Turkey. *MERIP Reports, No. 93, Turkey: The Generals Take Over* (January 1981), pp. 26-30+32.

Tilley, C. (2006). Objectification. In C. Tilley, W. Keane, S. Küchler, M. Rowlands & P. Spyer, (Eds.), *Handbook of Material Culture* (pp. 60-73). SAGE Publications Ltd.

Zaptçıoğlu, D. (2005). Önsöz. In Michael Richter, *Geldiler ve kaldılar*. İstanbul Bilgi Üniversitesi Yayınları.

CHAPTER 12

Conceptualizing Remittance Affordances: Transformations of a Knife Across Borders

Claudius Ströhle

At the Kitchen Table

The kitchen table is covered with plates, coffee cups, a birthday cake, bowls filled with fresh fruit, and a weekly pill organizer, listing the days of the week in German. As we are celebrating my birthday, Birnur[1] passes me the knife with which to cut the cake. Once again, she mentions proudly that she herself made this knife—in one of the small-scale iron factories in the Stubai Valley, a rural area in the West of Austria.

We are sitting in the apartment belonging to Birnur and her husband Eyüp, in the city of Uşak in Western Turkey. They built the four-floor apartment building in 1978, seven years after they left their home village Yaşamışlar in the province of Uşak to work and live in Austria. Now, the

[1] All names have been synonymized.

C. Ströhle (✉)
Department of History and European Ethnology, University of Innsbruck, Innsbruck, Austria
e-mail: stroehle@ifk.ac.at

S. Meyer, C. Ströhle (eds.), *Remittances as Social Practices and Agents of Change*,
https://doi.org/10.1007/978-3-030-81504-2_12

couple spend their retirement commuting between the Stubai Valley and Uşak throughout the year. While they have always been tenants in Austria, in Uşak they are landlords: the basement is rented out to a local teacher couple. The top floors stand empty, except for occasional visits from their sons who live in Austria. In the summer of 2018, I lodged in the apartment on the fourth floor during my second ethnographic field trip to Uşak.

This scene illustrates the epistemological interest underlying my ethnographic research on remittances in the history of labor migration between the Stubai Valley and Uşak from the early 1970s until today. In the course of the data collection, knives and tools of the Stubai brand appeared in multiple settings of production, transmission, and usage. The iron devices materialize stories of migration, of the hardship of labor in the iron processing factories, and of everyday life in retirement. As remitted objects, they evoke memories and emotions, maintain cross-border social relations, and afford new ways of usage or even rejection.

Introduction

Research on remittances is in vogue: the number of journal articles on the topic increased tenfold from the late 1990s to 2012, maintaining a focus on the nexus of migration and development (Carling 2020). However, fueled by Peggy Levitt's enhancement of the social and cultural forms and effects of remittances (Levitt 1998), a growing body of scholarship has emphasized that remittances constitute much more than money, taking the form of "material or non-material objects of transactions" (Nowicka and Šerbedžija 2016, p. 3). In the field of migration research, the importance of material objects to examining migrants' lives, identities, and cross-border connections has been firmly established (Pechurina 2020, p. 670). Mostly from the perspective of things brought from migrants' countries of origin to their new homes, the findings show how they function as "objects of connection" (Frykman 2019), scrutinize bi-national dichotomies (Suhr 2019), refer to a collective diasporic taste (Savaş 2014), and contribute to processes of transnational belonging and homemaking (Rosales 2010). Through a focus on biographical objects like photos, souvenirs, and gifts, everyday life objects remain underexplored, as Frykman stated. However, I disagree that the ways in which they "are used habitually are rather obvious" (Frykman 2019, 31–36). On the contrary, the aim of this chapter is to show how a relational analysis of the objects, humans, and everyday practices in transnational settings can contribute to a deeper understanding of the transformative effects of remittances on the involved actors and the built environment. To do so, I here introduce affordance theory into qualitative remittance research. In a nutshell, affordances are the possibilities that objects offer for action (Hutchby 2001), like a chair, for example, which affords a human the possibility to take a seat. I enquired which ways of appropriation, usage, or rejection of remitted objects *afford* their recipients. What do we learn through the perspective of affordance theory about the power relations between senders and receivers? Which factors must exist for a remittance to be accepted and used in the intended way? And how can the objects *afford* social change in their new environment?

To answer these questions, the remitted objects must be tracked in their various ways of transmission, appropriation, and usage, which in turn extends affordance theory with a cross-border lens. Thus, the empirical data analyzed here follows a multi-sited ethnography (Falzon 2016; Marcus 1995, 2016) which was conducted in Austria and Turkey between 2016 and 2020. Whereas most transnational multi-sited research is based on qualitative interviews (Mazzucato 2016, pp. 215–216), the long stay in the research field allowed me to observe the usage of the Stubai knives in everyday life routines, like in the scene at the kitchen table sketched above.

The next section provides a historical perspective that follows the trajectories of knife production in the Stubai Valley and the transnational migration from the region of Usak initiated therein. Based on the historical backbone of the transnational exchange of knives, the subsequent section provides the theoretical and methodological framework. The last section analyzes the empirical data concerning the sending, receiving, and using of the objects by introducing the concept of remittance affordances.

Iron Manufacturing in the Stubai Valley: A History of Cross-Border Migration

Since the early fifteenth century, the Stubai region, a 35-kilometer-long Alpine valley in the Western part of Austria, has been known for its iron manufacturing. Even though only small amounts of ore were found, over the centuries, the iron processing industry came to characterize the region. High-quality iron and steel products like weapons, tools, and knives were exported and led to vivid forms of exchange (see Figs. 12.1 and 12.2). In the eighteenth century, traveling vendors could not master the growing

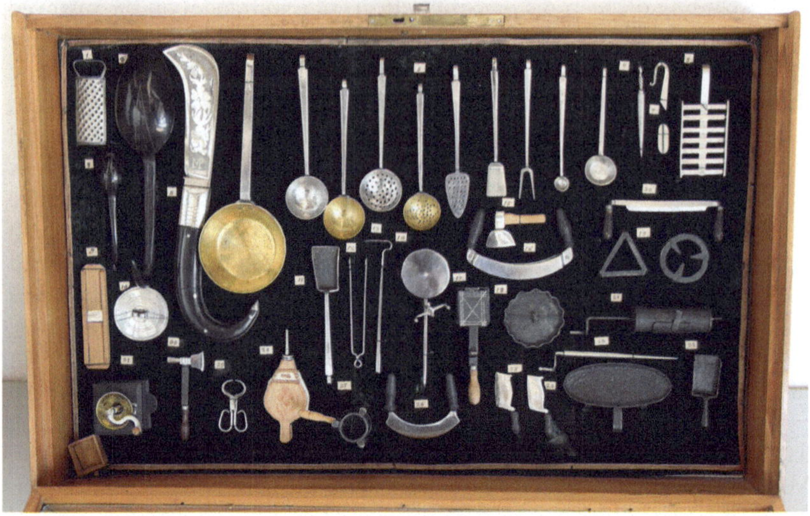

Fig. 12.1 Miniatures of iron tools, manufactured in the iron-processing industry in Fulpmes, Stubai Valley, in 1824. Tyrolian State Museum Ferdinandeum, Historical Collections, Technik/6/2

supply and so branch offices were opened all over the Alps. A contemporary witness cited in the chronicle of the village of Fulpmes in the Stubai Valley described the practice of remitting to Stubai: "The managers of the branch offices were people from Stubai who came back home at least once a year to give advice, buy houses, properties, restaurants, and smithies in order to care for their children and in order to prepare for their retirement in their beloved homeland" (Leutelt 1987, p. 255, my translation). This depiction of the eighteenth-century Stubai Valley reflects the broad understanding of remittances as applied in this article: as an exchange not only of money but also of ideas, norms, objects, and symbolic capital. Driven by familial obligations rooted in the past, the remitted money and advice from the branch managers can be also interpreted as social and economic preparations for the future.

Fig. 12.2 Iron laborers in Fulpmes, Stubai Valley, 1930s. Fulpmes Village Chronicle

The Guest Worker Regime from the Perspectives of Austria and Turkey

Iron manufacturing in Stubai Valley thrived throughout the nineteenth century, but came to an abrupt halt with the outbreak of World War One. As in many other Central European countries, the economy of the Stubai Valley began growing gradually again in the late 1950s, causing an extensive labor bottleneck in industry, tourism, and construction. After protracted political negotiations about the employment of foreigners in the Austrian labor market, the Raab-Olah Agreement was concluded in 1961 between the Austrian Trade Union Federation and the Austrian Federal Economic Chamber (Bakondy 2017, p. 117). Based on this compromise, which stipulated annual contingents for the foreign workforce and a principle of rotation, the state signed agreements on labor recruitment with Spain (1961), Turkey (1964), and Yugoslavia (1966). Whereas Austria anticipated the migration regime to meet its actual demand for labor and to keep the economy growing, the other signing states were in the opposite position. In Turkey, the mechanization of the agricultural sector had led to a massive rural-urban migration process and increasing unemployment. After the military under Colonel Alparslan Türkeş staged a coup d'état against the ruling government of Adnan Menderes, the new decision-makers banked on emigration as a key factor in reducing unemployment and offsetting the negative trade balance. Based on an analysis of historical sources of the key state institutions, Ahmet Akgündüz summarized Turkey's view that "unskilled and/or rural migrants would return from Europe with newly-acquired skills, an experience of modern life, self-confidence, and their remittances to Turkey. They therefore would make up for the skilled manpower shortages in the Turkish economy, particularly in the manufacturing industry and contribute considerably to hard currency revenues. As a result, the economic and social development processes of the country would accelerate" (Akgündüz 2016, p. 53). Both the Austrian and the Turkish states viewed the migrants as economic gaming pieces, whom they could move according to their own interests. However, the Turkish state vision was much more elaborate, linking the incoming remittances with social and cultural effects like a transfer of skills and lifestyles. Ultimately, many migrants opposed the restrictive migration regime and decided to stay in Austria. Today, approximately 270,000 migrants from Turkey and their descendants live in Austria.

In terms of remittances from the European diaspora to Turkey, the evaluations are ambivalent: researchers state the positive impacts on household welfare, even though the money was mostly used to satisfy basic consumption needs (Koç and Onan 2004, p. 108). The foreign currency mitigated the negative trade balance, but also due to the failure of the state's remittance channeling programs, the effects were lower than expected (Içduygu 2012, pp. 31–32). Abadan-Unat called attention to the often-neglected boomerang effect of remittance for receiving communities: for the Turkish state, remittance also led to inflationary pressure, increased imports, and skill needs (Abadan-Unat 1976, pp. 24–25).

Participating Simultaneously Here and There: The Cross-Border Space in the Stubai Valley and Uşak

In the Stubai Valley, the first migrants of the labor recruitment agreement arrived in the late 1960s and came from Yugoslavia. However, in the early 1970s, a net migration from the region of Uşak in Western Turkey set in, which was to characterize the region throughout the next decades. Today, approximately 800 of the 4000 inhabitants of Fulpmes have family ties to Turkey, ninety percent of them to the region of Uşak. Since the 1970s, migrants have worked in iron manufacturing, hotels, ski lifts, and construction sites, advancing the expansion of industry and winter tourism. In interviews, the research partners stressed the hardship of labor and criticized the disgracefully poor housing conditions. This corresponds with the research outcomes in other areas in Austria (Hahn and Stöger 2014), yet the case of the Stubai Valley illustrates the specific conditions of migration in rural areas: whereas cities are used to accommodating large numbers of newcomers, the remote Stubai Valley lacked rental apartments and plenty of locals made money by housing migrants in empty stables and sheds. On the other hand, the short distances and numerous face-to-face interactions within the rural community facilitated settling processes. Moreover, the pioneering migrants shaped their new environment, by introducing new products like tomatoes, olives, and melons to the Alpine valley and by teaching their neighbors and colleagues how to plant them. In 1978, a first Muslim prayer room was established, followed by the religious and cultural hometown association in Fulpmes in 1982. Alongside these collective investments, the migrants established shops, supermarkets, cafés, and hairdressers, thus becoming a crucial part of the village's material and social environment.

Aside from these multifaceted networks and practices in the Stubai Valley, the migrants and their descendants maintained and fostered ties with their relatives and friends in the region of Uşak. The bulk of our research partners purchased land and built houses and apartments in both the city of Uşak and the adjacent villages of origin. Some opened shops and restaurants or established transnational companies, for example an EU-Turkey cattle dealer. The summer turns out to be the crucial time for remitting, as most of the migrants visit their places of origin then: in this intensive phase, gifts are exchanged, apartments renovated, and further investments discussed and arranged. The presence of the cross-border families at weddings, celebrations, graveyard visits, and trips bolsters economic and emotional relations and simultaneously paves the way for a potential return. Additionally, official visits by municipal delegations strengthen the transnational ties between the two regions. Thereby, the connections are reciprocated through an exchange of gifts, most notably with regional products like hand-woven carpets from Uşak and knives from the Stubai Valley.

Theoretical and Methodological Framework: Following Affordances in Remittance Landscapes

The historically developed and migrant-driven processes of cross-border remittance practices opened up a transnational space between Uşak and the Stubai Valley, in which both migrants and non-migrants think, act, and participate. Sarah Lynn Lopez stressed in her research on transnational migration between Mexico and the USA how spatial and material implications of remittances shape everyday life environments. She argued that remitted and incorporated materials form a remittance landscape, meaning "distinct elements of the built environment constructed and altered with migrant dollars" and expanded upon this as an "amalgam of migrants' life stories and the macro political, social, economic, and historical forces that shape migration" (Lopez 2015, 1; 8). By focusing on migrants' construction practices and narratives, Lopez revealed how the transferred desires, dreams, and fears drive both personal and social change. However, it is not just the built environment but also remitted objects that matter. Qualitative research on material culture has shown how objects can be read as a concentration of social circumstances when their material, function, and meaning are analyzed within the specific contexts and situations in which they are used, exchanged, ignored, or appropriated (Hahn 2015; Miller 1998). International migration scholars have described the crucial role of biographical objects in the cross-border processes of homemaking and self-positioning (Frykman 2019, p. 31). Remitted objects do comprise multi-placed memories, reflect social relationships, and represent cross-border lifestyles. Moreover, they yield new forms of appropriation and usage. In order to grasp the specific relations between objects, actors, and practices from a transnational point of view, I want to introduce affordance theory approaches into qualitative remittance research.

Donald Norman provided a vivid access to the concept: "The term affordance refers to the relationship between a physical object and a person [...]. An affordance is a relationship between the properties of an object and the capabilities of the agent that determine just how the object could possibly be used. A chair affords ('is for') support and, therefore, affords sitting" (Norman 2013, p. 11). Webb Keane highlighted the issue of potentiality, as a chair invites, but does not determine sitting. One could also use a chair as a stepladder or as a desk—or simply ignore it. Also, affordances create meaning through constituting an in-group who respond to the particular affordances in a particular way: a chair does not invite a person to sit who is most comfortable squatting on the floor. In other words, objects enable or constrain certain practices for certain groups. Keane elaborated: "if the characteristics of the 'we' summons up the affordance, their interaction may transform the 'we' in turn—a world of chairs, let's say, produces chair-sitters" (Keane 2018, p. 31). This makes the concept particularly applicable to cross-border, practice-oriented ethnographic research and contours a new approach to remittance research: material remittances are "mutable mobiles," namely "objects that transform while being transferred" (Nowicka and Šerbedžija 2016, p. 14). Simultaneously, they transform the individuals exchanging, using, or rejecting the objects and therefore constitute certain cross-border social groups. In order to gain a deeper understanding of remittance objects by focusing on the various contexts they are used in, a multi-sited ethnography needs to be applied.

Multi-Sited Ethnography as a Spatial and Temporal Research Strategy

Remittance practices are entangled in various localities and temporalities. Thus, current research draws on George E. Marcus's "multi-sited ethnography," following the remittance actors, narratives, and objects by taking "unexpected trajectories in tracing a cultural formation across and within multiple sites of activity" (Marcus 1995, p. 96). There have been numerous justifiable critiques of Marcus's postulated adjustment of ethnographic methodology focusing on an increasingly glocalized, dispersed, and fluid lifeworld: Hage stated that a focus on mobility and movement suggests that people and things were always on the move and therefore ignores that not every crossing of a border constitutes a significant experience for people (Hage 2005, p. 469). Others have claimed that the core of ethnography—namely to reach a deep understanding—is threatened by this approach as ethnographers move from one site to another and thereby trade thick descriptions and deep vertical understandings for horizontal ones, leading to thin, diluted depictions (Falzon 2016, p. 7).

In order to tackle the main blind spots, the current research strategy is based on a long-term presence in the research field, embedding the empirical data in its spatial and temporal contexts and co-constructing the research sites collaboratively with the research partners (Marcus 2016). Thereby, my position in the field as a white scholar from Austria reflects global inequality. During the research process I discussed and challenged these hierarchies recurrently with my interlocutors (Alonso Bejarano et al 2019). The participant observation (2016-2020) included countless visits to the Stubai Valley and nearby towns and villages and three long-term field trips to the region of Uşak. The ethnographic data comprise field notes documented in settings like homes, cafes, mosques, post offices, duty-free shops, jewelers' shops, and cultural associations, at events like weddings, breaking the fast, birthdays, and Kermes Festivals or during work, travel, and vacations. Accompanying actors in different and unexpected settings generates trust and mutual recognition, which is indispensable for ethnographic research, especially in cross-border spaces. Additionally, I recorded ten semi-structured narrative interviews with pioneer migrants and their descendants, transnational entrepreneurs, local authorities, and returnees. Tracking remittance objects like the Stubai knives in unexpected places and situations over time produced satiated data on their transmission, usage, meanings, and narrative frames. The juxtaposition of multi-placed and -timed material, practices, archival sources, and photographs seek to gain a deep understanding of remitting as transformative, connective, and disruptive practices of positioning in cross-border spaces (see Meyer in this volume), forming the built landscape and constituting transnational society and belonging.

Stubai Knives and Tools as Remitted Objects

The region of Uşak has been shaped by the various materializations of the Schillings, Deutschmarks, Francs, and Euros sent back by migrants since the mid-1960s. In the city's districts Elmalıdere and Sarayaltı, which are on the way to becoming the villages most affected by emigration, one can find streets containing houses of the diaspora, with parked cars displaying European number plates (see also Bürkle 2016). Many of the adjacent villages experienced a huge emigration both to Turkish cities like Uşak, Izmir, and Istanbul and to West European countries. Whereas in the first years of emigration, remittances spurred investments in agricultural machines and housing renovations, the villages are today characterized by desolation and a rupture of earlier transnational connectedness.[2]

In the region of Uşak, the remittance landscape is not just formed by the migrant-financed houses, shops, streets, and water depots, but also by

[2] Remittance inflows to Turkey decreased exorbitantly from a peak of USD5.4 billion in 1998 to USD0.8 billion in 2019 (Karamelikli and Bayar 2015; World Bank 2020).

the countless objects that shape everyday life. During my ethnographic fieldwork, I observed knives and other tools of the Stubai brand in almost every migrant household, but also in the homes of their relatives, neighbors, and friends. The high-quality iron products, imprinted with the distinctive logo of the Serles (Fulpmes's backyard mountain), are produced in the iron manufactories in Fulpmes. The iron products found their way to Uşak not via commercial flows of commodities in terms of globalization, but through the hands and in the luggage of the migrants and their transnational networks. Thus, the objects occurred in two different settings: first as everyday objects of the returnees, and second as remitted to relatives, neighbors, and friends.

Knives and Tools in the Everyday Life of Returnees

Stubai knives and tools are crucial and meaningful objects for returnees in Uşak. The following extract from my field notes brings us back to the kitchen table, to the retired migrant couple Birnur and Eyüp in the city of Uşak:

> After a long day of fruit and herb picking in the hills, I returned home with my landlords. It was already late, but we decided to wash and cut the fresh herbs, which would later be dried on the terrace for a couple of days. Eyüp and I sat at the kitchen table, which was covered in delicious-smelling thyme. Birnur handed us knives: "I made them," she proudly said. She picked one up herself and, while cutting the thyme, both Birnur and Eyüp told me about their experiences in the iron manufactories in Fulpmes, about the details of making a good knife, about their early living conditions in Fulpmes, and the difficulties of life abroad. Even though Birnur hardly speaks German, she all of a sudden used very specific German terms like "Stemmeisen" (crowbar), a tool she used to produce in her factory. She had incorporated this term during her work in Fulpmes and never forgot it over the years. After some time, Birnur left, and Eyüp and I kept sitting face to face at the small kitchen table; the smell of the fresh thyme, the mechanical work with the materials, hardly any eye contact and the use of the Stubai knife as a trigger created a specific atmosphere in which Eyüp told me his life story. He told me about a man who returned to his village after a year in Fulpmes, telling about the abundance of work there; he told me about the adventure of migration, his experience working as a dishwasher and smith, his first experiences skiing, the house-building process in Uşak, and his present retirement in two different places.
> Field notes, Uşak, June 29, 2018

In this scene, the knife functioned as meaningful trigger of memories and emotions, evoked through the interaction between things and people. Analyzed from an affordance-theoretical approach, the properties of the object and the capabilities of the agents determine its usage: here, this meant chopping the herbs into small pieces. As transferred objects with a historical dimension, the knives afforded an additional practice, namely narrating specific stories of migration and work. As the European ethnologist Christoph Bareither applies affordance theory, the relations between material, medium, and everyday practice need to be carved out (Bareither 2020). In our context, the high-quality knives brought back successfully fulfilled their duty; simultaneously, the work in the iron manufactories and the migration project, in general, were recounted as success stories by both Birnur and Eyüp. The sharp knives cut through and worked well; the result was obvious. Thus, the presence of the former factory workers and a researcher from Austria in the four-floor apartment in Uşak, satisfyingly using these everyday objects, mediated multi-placed memories and revealed the achievement of upward social mobility.

The embodiment of memories can also be tracked by looking at the situational code-switching performed by Birnur. Her use of an iron tool while recollecting the time she worked in the manufactories of the Stubai Valley evoked the term "Stemmeisen." Moreover, the depicted scene brings the surplus value of multi-sited, material-focused, and practice-based ethnographic fieldwork to light: in a setting spatially and temporally distanced from Austria and its pejorative integration discourse, differentiating perspectives emerged, such as migration as success, cross-border belonging, and learned skills. Meanwhile, the mechanical manual activity of cutting alleviated a steady eye contact and created an atmosphere of trust and levity, which classic interview situations often lack.

As observed in multiple other settings, a great number of the returnees trust their knives brought along from the Stubai Valley. Similarly, I documented toolboxes filled with tools of the Stubai brand in most of the households I entered. They are frequently used in the endless handicraft activities carried out in and around the house, like repairing kitchenware or furniture, restoring the apartment, refining the façade of the house, or gardening. When Ferit, a return migrant in his sixties, invited me to his newly built family house in the village of Dağyenice, I helped him to repair the garden hose. I was impressed by the dexterity with which Ferit used various tools to solve the problem. It was an immediate physical connection of tool and human, which together built a functional action unit, a "handiness," as Fél and Hofer described it in their ethnological research in the Hungarian village Átány (Fél and Hofer 1974, p. 291). I observed this handiness in many sites during my ethnographic research, which consistently led back to the iron manufactories in Fulpmes, where the young laborers produced the tools and knives they now use for their own purposes. They manufactured the iron products, which now conversely provide multiple ways of usage that characterize the migrants' retirement lifestyles, namely performing construction and gardening projects. Following Keane (2018), the specific ways in which the returnees respond to the Stubai tools summon up the cross-border affordances, which in turn transform them into a group: a group of prosperously retired laborers. This also points to a transformation of class: whereas the bulk of the migrants grew up in peasant families, they now use the tools in their garden and fieldwork not to assure their livelihoods, but for leisure.

Tools also contain distinctive elements. As Fél and Hofer stated: "The uniformity of the stock of tools is not just an expression of one and the same technological standard, but at the same time an expression (and on the other hand also a source) of social and cultural unity in a rural village" (Fél and Hofer 1974, p. 47, my translation). As the Stubai knives and tools were brought via transnational networks, they mark a distinctive line within the population in Uşak. The following example shows how these mechanisms are performed and negotiated: when I left the apartment one morning, I found Eyüp with a craftsman working on the automatic garage door, which was obviously broken. "Alles Pfusch" (everything botched), "türkisches Patent" (a Turkish patent), Eyüp shouted furiously in German. By complaining about the local building standards, he referred to the hegemonic discourse that Western products are of a higher quality than the ones of other countries. By doing so in German, he additionally marked a line between the two of us and the Turkish-speaking craftsman. The situation gained momentum when the three of us desperately tried to fix the halting garage door. Eyüp dismissed the handyman's tools as Chinese junk. When the handyman objected that they were "yerli" (local), Eyüp murmured that this would not make it any better. He left and shortly afterward returned with his neatly sorted Stubai toolbox. Having first declared that he would rather work with his own tools, the handyman eventually grabbed one of Eyüp's hammers. Afterward, when Eyüp and I drank a cup of coffee in the kitchen, he said: "Nothing works without good material!"

However, *good* tools are the tools someone is used to work with and therefore trusts in. The depicted scene at the automatic garage door revealed not only that Eyüp and the local craftsman appropriated different equipment in their life trajectories, but also how this led to specific practices of distinction. Eyüp, who had grown up in one of the adjacent villages and migrated to the Stubai Valley as a young man, appraised the garage door and tools of the craftsman as Turkish, and thus of low quality. In doing so, he expressed what Özlem Savaş called "taste diaspora," a form of belonging to Austria as someone from Turkey, "which is achieved through a collective taste shaped within specific processes and paths of displacement and dwelling of both people and objects" (Savaş 2014, p. 203). Savaş detected a collective reference to a specific transnational belonging in the migrants' objects. On the contrary, the example above shows that taste can rather function as a differentiation from a certain kind of belonging to Turkey in the (re)migration context. When Eyüp offered the craftsman his own tools, he positioned himself as superior and at the same time marked a division between the non-migrant Uşakers and the (seasonal) returnees. Thus, the social space of a city, shaped to a remarkable degree by remittances, exhibits its layers of power and distinction regarding the interactions of people and objects maintaining the built landscape.

Between Connection and Disruption: Remitted Knives as Ambivalent Cross-Border "Tie-Signs"

The knives and tools brought along from the Stubai Valley evoke multi-placed memories and emotions, afford construction projects in and around the house, mediate social upward mobility, and display distinctive aspects of possessing and using certain objects in cross-border contexts. Another dimension is added when the objects are remitted to kin, friends, or neighbors.

Actually, knives and tools are awkward remittances: they are sharp and dangerous objects. Yet the steel form has a soft core: they are personal objects, as the makers invested hard work and sweat to produce them. As expensive, high-quality products from abroad, they increase the symbolic capital of the donor. With the Stubai logo imprinted on the blade, they are meaningful souvenirs from abroad. That is why the knives and tools are popular gifts for friends, kin, and neighbors in both the home villages and the city of Uşak. They form part of an extensive exchange of material remittances, in large part performed during the summer months. Although the bulk of my field partners claimed that everything is now available in Turkey, and that there is thus no need to bring back any goods, in practice, they still do so in abundance. This narrative positioning, which conflicts with the practice, contains a political message: Turkey used to be a poor country in the 1960s, but now it is economically strong and no longer in need of support from Europe (nor of its products). This narrative gained further momentum in the context of the political dispute between the Turkish government and the EU countries in the aftermath of the failed coup d'état in July 2016.

However, the practice of transmitting material remittances still occurs and sustains social ties. Approached from a perspective of gift exchange, remittances can be read as "tie-signs" (Adloff and Mau 2005, p. 13), which are based on trust and subsequently foster social relations. Lisa Cliggett demonstrated in her research on remittances in Zambia that migrants sent rather small amounts of money, but all the more presents, goods, and food. She called these practices of exchange "gift-remitting": "In particular, 'gift-remitting' can express affection and remembrance of families and communities 'at home', and thus establish a process of mutual recognition between migrants and their relatives and friends. This mutual recognition, created over time through a combination of social and material investments, can translate into options for migrants to return to sending communities sometime in the future" (Cliggett 2005, p. 37). Whether material or intangible, remittances are a remarkably sticky form sociocultural glue. However, when we look closely at the act of transmission, the "transactors' relations" (Åkesson 2011, p. 327), and the "afterlife of migrants' gifts" (see Mura in this volume), we also find disruptive tendencies and practices of embracement as well as rejection. This aspect is central in the last ethnographic vignette that I wish to present here:

> I was sitting on the balcony in Uşak in the district Elmalıdere with one of the third-generation youngsters. He had just spent a couple of weeks in Turkey on vacation visiting his grandparents, who had returned to Uşak. The young man works in a small-scale iron factory in Fulpmes, which is part of the Stubai Cooperation. They produce knives. He told me that he frequently brings these to his uncles Halil and Kemal as gifts. Both of his uncles are butchers. When their fathers got in a fight, they went their separate ways, and each tried his own luck. The two shops are a stone's throw away from each other, in the center of Uşak. The young man on the balcony continued to elaborate on the production of a good knife and the importance of its

maintenance. In doing so, he got upset. In his view, his uncles don't know how to grind the knives properly. Therefore, they become dull very fast and he receives complaints.
Field notes, Uşak, July 24, 2018

* * *

In Kemal's butcher shop, I didn't see any Stubai knives. Therefore, I brought the topic up in the evening when I was invited for dinner. Both the senior partner and the son told me that they have Stubai knives, but don't use them. The knives were too hard and stiff, they explained to me. They prefer the local knives, which are more flexible and bend more easily. Apparently, the knife they received from their Austrian nephew isn't flexible enough for their cutting technique. It is an unused gift, which the donor most likely doesn't know.
Field notes, Uşak, August 1, 2018

* * *

I entered Halil's butcher shop. He and his employee were just chopping liver. After some chatting and without me mentioning knives, he proudly showed me the Stubai knife he had just used and pulled various other examples out of the drawer. While his employee continued working, he lit a cigarette and struck up a conversation: "I was born in Fulpmes," he started excitedly. His father, a shepherd back then, migrated to Fulpmes after his military service, wishing to spend a year there before returning with enough money to build a farm in the village where he was born. The one intended year became four and, in the meantime, he was joined by his wife. One year after the birth of their son, they returned with money and transformed dreams. A butcher shop in the city, rather than a farm in the village, that was the new plan. A couple of years ago, the senior partner retired, and Halil expanded the shop to a modern butchery right on the main street. Since he left the Stubai Valley as a baby, he hasn't returned. But he will do so right after retiring, he told me with sparkling eyes. After that, Halil again joined his employee. With the Stubai knives in their hands, they posed for a picture.

* * *

Right afterwards, his father turned up in the shop. Halil immediately took a portrait off the wall. It showed his father just before the adventure to Stubai Valley. I took another photo.
Field notes, Uşak, August 2, 2018 (see Figs. 12.3 and 12.4)

Fig. 12.3 Fulpmes-born Halil with his employee posing with Stubai knives in his butcher shop in the city of Uşak, summer 2018. Picture taken by the author

Fig. 12.4 The senior partner of the butcher shop with a portrait of himself in his hand, depicting him before his migration to Fulpmes as a young man, summer 2018. Picture taken by the author

The act of remitting knives from a third-generation man to his uncles reveals the double relation of the exchange. As a young man in his early twenties, the nephew would not have been in a position to gift. However, the fact that he worked at the very factory that produced the knives earmarked the gift with a personal story and also as a bargain because he did not have to pay full price for them. Now and then, he brings knives to his uncles and can thereby partake while physically being absent. Maurice Godelier called attention to the dual relation that gifts create between the transactors, namely proximity and distance: “A relation of solidarity, as the one who gives shares what he has, even what he is, with the one to whom he gives; and a relation of superiority, as the one who receives the gift and accepts it is indebted to the one who has given it to him” (Godelier 1999, p. 22, my translation). In the example above, the transaction of the remitted object points toward both vectors: horizontally, the knives frequently brought along sustain the social relationship between the nephew and his uncles. However, the vertical vector of social positioning also becomes evident on both sides: whereas the nephew claimed that neither of his uncles knows how to properly grind the knives, his uncle Kemal eventually rejected its usage altogether. The remitted knives derive from the same factory and are identical in form, yet they afford opposite ways of appropriation. Halil embraced the knives and appreciated them as part of the transnational migration project his father initiated and advanced throughout his life. Himself born in the village where the knives are made, it is also the historical and personal context that frames the interaction of individual and object. Thus, it affords usage, recounting family stories, and posing for a picture on the one hand and ending up in the drawer on the other. Following Keane, who proposed that “the characteristics of the ‘we’ summons up the affordance” (Keane 2018, p. 31), the example of Halil shows how the in-group can transgress borders of nation states and open up new contexts. His butcher shop forms a remittance landscape in the heart of Uşak and is a central meeting point for the local townspeople as well as for the Austrian diaspora.

Another approach which can contribute to a deeper understanding of the depicted context is Bourdieu’s concept of capital conversion (Bourdieu 1983). Halil inherited the economic capital his father earned during his labor migration to Fulpmes and by establishing the butcher shop after his return. What is more, he inherited the transnationally based social capital (Eckstein 2010) that made him a receiver of the personally and materially meaningful knives and provided him with regular diasporic customers.

Halil converted the cross-border economic and social capital into symbolic capital. This is what Silke Meyer called "transnational capital," that is, an established cross-border form of capital "which enables individuals to draw on their (family's) past mobility and to weigh in transnational experiences and knowledge to their benefit" (Meyer 2020, p. 276). This is visualized in the pictures above: the knife held firmly in Halil's clutch refers to the devotion with which he expedites the family business. The picture of his father right before he left for the Stubai Valley hangs on the wall behind him. He later passes the picture over to his father, thereby setting the narrative frame for the second picture: the act of migration marking the beginning of the family's success story mirrored in the gentle and pleased gaze of the senior partner with his portrait in hand.

The cross-border conversion of cultural capital, however, has reached its limit: the grinding techniques used by the uncles in Uşak no longer appear appropriate for the remitted object, nor does the functionality of the knife meet the cutting techniques used by the butcher Kemal and the retired senior partner. The local knives they still prefer are the ones they grew up with; they are used to these objects, which flexibly bend in their hands. Fél and Hofer described such elementary everyday objects as objects that "give their users signs," like a good spade, which stops when touching a hard item, and neither bends nor breaks; that solely indicates that it has fallen into a wrong place. (Fél and Hofer 1974, p. 295). People are unlikely to exchange tools that they are used to and trust in. Fél and Hofer showed in their research that even if the villagers of Átány returned with new tools that promised a technological surplus value after working in Budapest or the USA, they were often not used. The authors explained this ambivalent practice by emphasizing the cultural and social meaning of tools and their usages for constituting community (Fél and Hofer 1974, p. 45). However, in the case of the remitted Stubai knives, it becomes evident how the relations between objects, humans, and practices need to be analyzed more thoroughly and expanded with a cross-border perspective: in Halil's case, the knives enable acceptance and lead to connection, while in Kemal's case, they constrain usage and lead to disruption. The relational and habitual aspects of affordances (Hutchby 2001) lead to different forms of usage of the remitted objects. It is the finely woven, historically accumulated, and hierarchically constituted frame of the transactors' relations, the material and biography of the transmitted object, and the bodily incorporated practices of usage that mark what remittances either enable or constrain. This I call remittance affordances.

Conclusion: Conceptualizing Remittance Affordances

Drawing on a multi-sited ethnography in the Stubai Valley (Austria) and Uşak (Turkey), this chapter followed the spatial and temporal trajectories of a crucial type of material remittances in the encountered research field, namely knives and tools of the Stubai brand, in order to examine their acts of production, transmission, and embodiment. By introducing affordance theory into remittance research, the analysis revealed the multifaceted forms of transformation that the exchanged objects and practices exerted on the remittance actors as well as on the built landscape.

The chronicle of the Stubai Valley provided a historical research site, demonstrating how the iron processing industry was an economic as well as cultural driver in the valley, leading to vivid forms of exchange and transnational networks. In this context, young villagers from rural Uşak migrated to the Stubai Valley in the 1970s and 1980s, working in small-scale iron factories producing knives and tools for the Stubai cooperation. Thereafter, the iron devices were remitted to Uşak, where they constituted a crucial part of the built landscape and the everyday life of the returnees as well non-migrant family members. In everyday life in retirement, when processing food, renovating the house, or gardening, the objects evoked cross-border memories, emotions, and the recollection of migrant narratives that form homemaking on the other side of migration. The handiness with which the returnees used the iron devices moreover demonstrates how the objects transform the group of users into a group of prosperously retired laborers. Thereby, the remittance objects' affordances comprise accumulated and objectified history, incorporated into the bodies as a form of transnational habitus (Schmidt 2012, p. 66). This also reveals a transformation of class: whereas the bulk of the migrants grew up in peasant families, they now use the tools in their fieldwork not to assure their livelihoods, but for leisure.

As remitted objects, the Stubai knives and tools evoke multi-placed memories and emotions, afford construction projects in and around the house, and mediate social upward mobility. Thereby, they mark a distinctive boundary within the population in rural and urban Uşak. Remittances are agents of social change, however with the potential to polarize the social structure in the place of origin.

Seen from gift-theoretical approaches, the objects remitted to family and neighbors appear as "tie-signs" (Adloff and Mau 2005, p. 13), thus sustaining, fostering, and controlling social relations in order to maintain a place while being physically absent. As high-quality products, the gifted Stubai knives and tools increased the symbolic capital of the donors. The factory-made iron devices are also personal objects, as the migrants once worked in the company that produced them. However, as the analysis of ethnographic material above revealed, the remitted knives enabled acceptance and led to connection in some cases, while constraining usage and leading to disruption in others. Even if the remitted object is accepted by the recipient, this does not say anything about its further appropriation and usage. This corresponds to the relational and habitual affordances that remittances comprise: the material and biography of the object, the bodily incorporated practices of usage, and the personal as well as macro-transnational hierarchical relations between sender and receiver. Thus, by focusing on the practices of using transmitted objects, the concept of remittance affordances can make a rewarding contribution to analyzing the transformative effects of transnational migration on the involved actors as well as on the built landscape.

References

Abadan-Unat, N. (1976). Turkish Migration to Europe (1960-1975): A Balance Sheet of Achievements and Failures. In N. Abadan-Unat (Ed.), *Turkish Workers in Europe 1960-1975: A Socio-Economic Reappraisal* (pp. 1–44). Brill.

Adloff, F., & Mau, S. (2005). Zur Theorie der Gabe und Reziprozität. In F. Adloff & S. Mau (Eds.), *Vom Geben und Nehmen: Zur Soziologie der Reziprozität* (pp. 9–57). Campus.

Åkesson, L. (2011). Remittances and Relationships: Exchange in Cape Verdean Transnational Families. *Ethnos, 76*(3), 326–347. https://doi.org/https://doi.org/10.1080/00141844.2011.577229

Akgündüz, A. (2016). *Labour Migration from Turkey to Western Europe, 1960–1974: A Multidisciplinary Analysis.* Routledge.

Alonso Bejarano, C., López Juárez, L., Mijangos García, M. A., & Goldstein D. M. (2019). *Decolonizing Ethnography. Undocumented Immigrants and New Directions in Social Science.* Durham.

Bakondy, V. (2017). "Austria Attractive for Guest Workers?": Recruitment of Immigrant Labor in Austria in the 1960s and 1970s. In G. Bischof & D. Rupnow (Eds.), *Migration in Austria* (pp. 113–137). innsbruck university press; uno press.

Bareither, C. (2020). Affordanz. In T. Heimerdinger & M. Tauschek (Eds.), *Kulturtheoretisch argumentieren: Ein Arbeitsbuch* (pp. 32–55). Waxmann.

Bourdieu, P. (1983). Ökonomisches Kapital, kulturelles Kapital, soziales Kapital. In R. Kreckel (Ed.), *Soziale Welt* (pp. 183–198). Otto Schwartz Verlag.

Bürkle, S. (Ed.). (2016). *Migration von Räumen: Architektur und Identität im Kontext türkischer Remigration*. Vice Versa Verlag.

Carling, J. (2020). Remittances: Eight Analytical Perspectives. In T. Bastia & R. Skeldon (Eds.), *Routledge International Handbook. Routledge Handbook of Migration and Development* (pp. 114–124). Routledge.

Cliggett, L. (2005). Remitting the Gift: Zambian Mobility and Anthropological Insights for Migration Studies. *Population, Space and Place*, *11*(1), 35–48. https://doi.org/https://doi.org/10.1002/psp.355

Eckstein, S. (2010). Immigration, Remittances, and Transnational Social Capital Formation: A Cuban Case Study. *Ethnic and Racial Studies*, *33*(9), 1648–1667. https://doi.org/https://doi.org/10.1080/01419871003725410

Falzon, M.-A. (2016). Multi-sited Ethnography: Theory, Praxis and Locality in Contemporary Research. In M.-A. Falzon (Ed.), *Multi-Sited Ethnography: Theory, Praxis and Locality in Contemporary Research* (pp. 1–23). Routledge.

Fél, E., & Hofer, T. (1974). *Geräte der Átányer Bauern*. Akadémiai Kiado.

Frykman, M. P. (2019). Transnational Dwelling and Objects of Connection: An Ethnological Contribution to Critical Studies of Migration. In J. Moser, N. Škrbic Alempijevic, A. Färber, I. Götz, I. Merkel, & F. Schmoll (Eds.), *Ways of Dwelling: Crisis - Craft - Creativity* (pp. 28–45). Waxmann.

Godelier, M. (1999). *Das Rätsel der Gabe: Geld, Geschenke, heilige Objekte. C. H. Beck.*

Hage, G. (2005). A Not So Multi-Sited Ethnography of a Not So Imagined Community. *Anthropological Theory*, *5*(4), 463–475. https://doi.org/https://doi.org/10.1177/1463499605059232

Hahn, H. P. (2015). *Vom Eigensinn der Dinge: Für eine neue Perspektive auf die Welt des Materiellen*. Neofelis.

Hahn, S., & Stöger, G. (2014). *50 Jahre österreichisch-türkisches Anwerbeabkommen*. Studie im Auftrag des Bundesministeriums für Europa, Integration und Äußeres. Salzburg. Universität Salzburg. https://www.uni-salzburg.at/fileadmin/multimedia/Geschichte/documents/Studie_Anwerbeabkommen_-_Uni_Salzburg.pdf

Hutchby, I. (2001). Technologies, Texts and Affordances. *Sociology*, *35*(2), 441–456. https://doi.org/https://doi.org/10.1177/S0038038501000219

Içduygu, A. (2012). 50 Years After the Labour Recruitment Agreement with Germany: The Consequences of Emigration for Turkey. *Perceptions*, *17*(2), 11–36.

Karamelikli, H., & Bayar, Y. (2015). Remittances and Economic Growth in Turkey. *Ecoforum*, *4*(2), 33–40.

Keane, W. (2018). Perspectives on Affordances, or the Anthropologically Real: The 2018 Daryll Forde Lecture. *HAU: Journal of Ethnographic Theory*, *8*(1-2), 27–38. https://doi.org/https://doi.org/10.1086/698357

Koç, I., & Onan, I. (2004). International Migrants' Remittances and Welfare Status of the Left-Behin Families in Turkey. *International Migration Review*, *38*(1), 78–112.

Leutelt, H. (1987). Die Eisenindustrie: Vom Handelshaus Pfurtscheller bis heute. In Kontaktverlag Fulpmes (Ed.), *Fulpmes* (pp. 255–260). Kontaktverlag.

Levitt, P. (1998). Social Remittances: Migration Driven Local-Level Forms of Cultural Diffusion. *International Migration Review*, *32*(4), 926–948.

Lopez, S. L. (2015). *The Remittance Landscape: Spaces of Migration in Rural Mexico and Urban USA*. University of Chicago Press.

Marcus, G. E. (1995). Ethnography in/of the World System: The Emergence of Multi-Sited Ethnography. *Annual Review of Anthropology*, *24*, 95–117.

Marcus, G. E. (2016). Multi-Sited Ethnography: Notes and Queries. In M.-A. Falzon (Ed.), *Multi-Sited Ethnography: Theory, Praxis and Locality in Contemporary Research* (pp. 181–196). Routledge.

Mazzucato, V. (2016). Bridging Boundaries with a Transnational Research Approach: A Simultaneous Matched Sample Methodology. In M.-A. Falzon (Ed.), *Multi-Sited Ethnography: Theory, Praxis and Locality in Contemporary Research* (pp. 215–231). Routledge.

Meyer, S. (2020). "Home Is Where I Spend My Money": Testing the Remittance Decay Hypothesis with Ethnographic Data from an Austrian-Turkish Community. *Social Inclusion*, *8*(1), 275–284. https://doi.org/10.17645/si.v8i1.2435

Miller, D. (Ed.). (1998). *Material Cultures: Why Some Things Matter*. University of Chicago Press.

Norman, D. A. (2013). *The Design of Everyday Things*. Revised and Expanded Edition. Basic Books.

Nowicka, M., & Šerbedžija, V. (2016). Migration and Remittances in a Global Europe. In M. Nowicka & V. Šerbedžija (Eds.), *Europe in a Global Context. Migration and Social Remittances in a Global Europe* (pp. 1–20). Palgrave Macmillan UK.

Pechurina, A. (2020). Researching Identities through Material Possessions: The Case of Diasporic Objects. *Current Sociology*, *68*(5), 669–683. https://doi.org/https://doi.org/10.1177/0011392120927746

Rosales, M. V. (2010). The Domestic Work of Consumption: Materiality, Migration and Home-Making. *Etnografica*, *14*(3), 507–525. https://doi.org/https://doi.org/10.4000/etnografica.191

Savaş, Ö. (2014). Taste Diaspora: The Aesthetic and Material Practice of Belonging. *Journal of Material Culture*, *19*(2), 185–208. https://doi.org/https://doi.org/10.1177/1359183514521922

Schmidt, R. (2012). *Soziologie der Praktiken: Konzeptionelle Studien und empirische Analysen*. Suhrkamp.

Suhr, M. (2019). Bewegte Dinge: Materielle Kultur und transnationale Mobilität zwischen der Türkei und Deutschland. In H. P. Hahn & F. Neumann (Eds.), *Das neue Zuhause: Haushalt und Alltag nach der Migration* (pp. 289–305). Campus.

World Bank. (2020). *COVID-19 Crisis through a Migration Lens* (Migration and Development Brief No. 32). http://documents1.worldbank.org/curated/en/989721587512418006/pdf/COVID-19-Crisis-Through-a-Migration-Lens.pdf

CHAPTER 13

Remittances and Migrating Spaces in the Context of Turkish, Vietnamese, and Korean Remigration

Stefanie Bürkle

The following visual essay explores the social dynamics of remittances through photographs of transnational houses, interiors, and objects in Turkey (Aksary, Kicilca), South Korea (Dogil Maeul, Namhae), and Vietnam (suburban area of Hanoi). The common thread is that all three countries share a history of migration with Germany. Furthermore, all cases show that remittances shape urban space in multiple ways.

Migration has long been a part of our globalized world. It is manifest in dramatically growing global movements of refugees on the one hand and the increasing demand for extremely mobile, flexible, and internationally trained highly skilled employees along with tourism as a global economic factor on the other. The global movement is expedited by the disappearance of national differences in the Western metropolises and by delocalization through the worldwide availability of internet services and social media. It is precisely for this reason that physical spaces are more

S. Bürkle (✉)
Technische Universität Berlin, Berlin, Germany
e-mail: stefanie.buerkle@tu-berlin.de

S. Meyer, C. Ströhle (eds.), *Remittances as Social Practices and Agents of Change*,
https://doi.org/10.1007/978-3-030-81504-2_13

important than ever for negotiations on belonging and formation of identity.

Migration can be interpreted as a window through which locals can view the world (Flusser 2007). Migrants are pioneers in comparing and combining localities: they know the frictions and contradictions of the experience of migration and have not only integrated these into their biographies, but also into their spatial sense of being-in-the-world (Heidegger 2001, p. 104). When people move and remit, spaces, images, cultural practices, and lifestyles become mobile, too and ignite social and spatial change.

In my interdisciplinary art and research projects I focus on the transformation through migration. Thus, I have been able to open up new perspectives on the "familiar," the "typically German" by taking a foreigner's view on my own culture and surroundings.

The Spatiality of Remittances

The project "Migrating Spaces—Identity through Architecture in the Context of Turkish Remigration" (2013–2016) investigated the apartments and houses of returned migrants from Germany, which were built by former "guest workers" themselves, without an architect. The own house is a main remittances agent: saving money and bearing a modest working life in Germany allows to build a house back in Turkey. Similarly, Vietnamese migrants send back money from Germany to Vietnam not only to support their relatives, but also to commission them with the construction of a house after German architectural models. My projects "Loi chao tu Hanoi" (Bürkle 2006) and "Placemaking" (Bürkle 2009) analyze the translocal or even transnational dynamic between the country of origin or destination—and in the case of remigration—vice versa. The photographs show that the inter- and transcultural realities in migrants' lives and the question of identity through architecture are very closely linked. These transnational relationships change the image and structure of urban spaces. In the housing projects, physical spaces, financial investment, and construction of identity convene.

In "Migratourispace" (Bürkle 2021) one of the case studies is named *Dogil Maeul*, which means "German Village." It appears to be made up of German single-family houses from towns in Central Germany. What is translated and taken along are ideas and concepts from the migrants' own experience: the presence of the labor migration and experiences from working lives in Germany. These are "diasporic homescapes" (Tschoepe 2016, pp. 418–425), because here they are linked to the migration and remigration biographies of Korean nurses and their husbands, who are often German. Added to this is the role of the village as a tourist attraction in Namhae County, which has meanwhile led to the establishment of tourist infrastructure such as restaurants for day trippers, souvenir shops, and bus car parks on the periphery of the village.

This visual essay illustrates and investigates the aesthetic links between migration, space, and culture. It might also evoke thoughts about the economic aspects of homes. Further questions address the future use of these houses, their inhabitants, and possible renovations: How will these first-generation houses be used once they are inherited by children usually living in Germany? Will the houses be sold to local villagers? Will the houses be renovated or left as they are to be used by family members as holiday homes? In any case, we can assume that issue of space use will remain important for the next generation of users and that the often disproportionately large rooms, sometimes the equivalent or several floors and guest rooms will have to be adapted and updated to suit contemporary requirements.

Using visual field research made it possible to develop a typology of remigrant housing. Furthermore, interviews with the owners gave more insights and information about the design process and the meaning of built space. By intersecting scientific results and spatial aesthetics, the projects are connecting art and academic research through photographs, video stills, and graphic methods of analyzing, uncovering the socio-spatial relations. The pictures do not just illustrate a text, but they are autonomous sources of scientific knowledge. In the following photographs, I have arranged the single images into a series, a continuous band of images. The absence of captions frees the viewers from a purely content-based classification of the images, transforming them into travelers between the spaces. Isolated motifs reappear in the preceding or following image, thus creating new compositional and content-related connections beyond the images. Objects and perspectives link the pictures and form a new visual texture. Connections and transitions are the focus of the observation. Single images become interrupted, only to be continued when flipping to the next page. Hence, this series of images sheds light on the complex spatial overlapping of migration and remittances and their multi-contextuality.

BISTRO 36
30

Next & NextStar
Next & NextStar

NHÀ VƯỜN TÙNG SƠN
BON SAI-CÂY THẾ

2013
Tarin

19세 미만 청소년에게
술·담배 판매금지

References

Flusser, V. (2007) *Von der Freiheit des Migranten. Einsprüche gegen den Nationalismus*. Bollmann.
Heidegger, M. (1927): Sein und Zeit, Tübingen 2001.
Tschoepe Yildirim, Aylin (2016): "Diasporic Homescapes". In: Stefanie Bürkle: Migrating Spaces, Architecture and Identity in the Context of Turkish Remigration. Berlin, p. 418–425.
Mentioned Projects by Stefanie Bürkle (www.stefanie-buerkle.de).
Bürkle, Stefanie: Loi chao tu Hanoi, Exhibition: babette, Berlin 2006.
Bürkle, Stefanie (ed.): Placemaking. Die Migration von Räumen. Berlin 2009. Exhibitions: Haus der Kulturen der Welt, Berlin; Berlinische Galerie, Berlin; HAU II, Berlin; Kunstraum Scheringstiftung, Berlin.
Bürkle, Stefanie (ed.): Migrating Spaces – Identity through Architecture in the Context of Turkish Remigration. Berlin 2016. Exhibitions: Haus der Kulturen der Welt, Berlin; SALT, Istanbul.
Bürkle, Stefanie (ed.): MigraTouriSpace. Berlin 2021. Exhibition: Collaboratorium CLB Berlin.

Photographs taken in South Korea, Turkey and Vietnam by Stefanie Bürkle © VG Bild-Kunst Bonn

CHAPTER 14

Material Remittances in the Context of Seasonal Work: Social and Economic Change in Vanuatu

Rochelle Bailey

Introduction

"Remittances reflect and build the social status of the sender as funds flow to support not just family, but also community, local government, development and traditional practices as well as celebrations" (Cohen 2011, p. 106). This quote from anthropologist Jeffrey Cohen reflects my observations drawn from over a decade of research on ni-Vanuatu temporary migrant workers in Australia and New Zealand's seasonal worker programs.[1] With the money earned through temporary work abroad, senders have provided both financial and material remittances and thus improved the living standards of thousands of families in the Pacific region. The migrants and their families have thereby become agents of change (Bedford

[1] Ni-Vanuatu is the term is for people from the island Republic of Vanuatu.

R. Bailey (✉)
Australian National University, Canberra, ACT, Australia
e-mail: Rochelle.bailey@anu.edu.au

S. Meyer, C. Ströhle (eds.), *Remittances as Social Practices and Agents of Change*,
https://doi.org/10.1007/978-3-030-81504-2_14

et al. 2009). While financial remittances receive much attention in research, material remittances tend to be overlooked. However, they greatly contribute to social transformation and are, in some cases, of higher value than financial remittances, for example in the form of boats, cars, and objects used in ceremonial celebrations. Moreover, material remittances which are called gifts-in-kind or informal remittances in Pacific literature (Connell and Brown 2005) are essential in achieving or fulfilling societal obligations. The argument here is not that material remittances are superior to financial ones, but unlike other global studies and reports on material remittances, they are largely absent in literature on these seasonal worker programs.

As a new naïve researcher embarking on this academic journey 13 years ago, I aimed to examine how seasonal worker programs contributed to development. However, I soon realized that the meaning of local developments in communities in Vanuatu varied and thus readjusted my research to reflect localized forms of household and individual development. Workers viewed income from seasonal overseas work as an opportunity to improve their lifestyle and address their specific needs, as opposed to aid-sponsored programs that do not always take into consideration local contexts. Therefore, the term transformative in this chapter will reflect the local character of ni-Vanuatu ideas and concepts of change. In order to grasp the locality of social change, I use an ethnographic approach in a longitudinal study of the same communities over several years.

This chapter firstly discusses seasonal labor mobility schemes available to ni-Vanuatu citizens and the uptake in these programs, followed by a brief introduction of Vanuatu and the applied methodology. The next sections are divided into various areas of transformation: the home, education, community, customary practices, the built environment, and transportation. I will then discuss the impact of remittances on inequality. Lastly, I will link remittance practices with ways of (be)longing.

Australia's and New Zealand's Seasonal Worker Schemes

In Australia, there are two labor schemes for Pacific Island nations and those from Timor-Leste, the Seasonal Worker Programme (SWP) and the Pacific Labour Scheme (PLS), which began in July 2018.[2] The SWP was

[2] Due to the PLS being new, data from that scheme is still limited and this scheme is therefore not examined in this chapter.

introduced in 2012 after a four-year pilot, the Pacific Seasonal Worker Pilot Scheme (PSWPS 2008–2012). The SWP allows workers from the Pacific and Timor-Leste to work up to nine months in a twelve-month period in sectors such as hospitality, agriculture, aquaculture, the cane sector, horticulture, and tourism. The PLS meanwhile offers visas to work for up to three years in rural and regional Australia in aged care, agriculture, and hospitality. However, it has been most successful in the meat processing industries.

New Zealand's Recognised Employer Scheme (RSE) was established in April 2007 to address labor shortages in the horticulture and viticulture industries. It allows workers from Pacific Island countries to stay for up to seven months in a twelve-month period, except for workers from Kiribati and Tuvalu, who can remain for nine months due to the higher travel costs associated with getting to New Zealand. New Zealand extended its labor mobility opportunities with the recent introduction of the Pacific Trades Partnership (PTP). The PTP includes two new skilled sectors, construction and fisheries, which are still in their pilot phases. The focus here is on the short-term temporary seasonal labor schemes RSE and SWP, with the objective of encouraging economic development for sending nations.

The participating countries are Fiji, Kiribati, Nauru, Papua New Guinea, Samoa, Solomon Islands, Tonga, Tuvalu, and Vanuatu. All eligible Pacific Island nations for these programs are members of the Pacific Islands Forum[3] (except for Timor-Leste, which is the only non-Pacific country in Australia's programs). Labor from the Pacific has positively transformed New Zealand's horticulture and viticulture sectors (Bedford et al. 2020, p. 16). Before the COVID-19 lockdowns in March 2020, Australia and New Zealand were projected to have at least 12,000 workers in each of their seasonal worker programs (see Fig. 14.1).

Material and Financial Remittances in the Context of the RSE and the SWP

Based on information from interviews with RSE migrants, we can estimate that they spent between NZD500 and NZD2000 annually on material remittances from New Zealand. This does not include remittances

[3] The Pacific Islands Forum consists of 18 Pacific Island member nations: Australia, Cook Islands, the Federated States of Micronesia, Fiji, French Polynesia, Kiribati, Nauru, New Zealand, Niue, New Caledonia, Palau, Papua New Guinea, the Republic of the Marshall Islands, Samoa, Solomon Islands, Tonga, Tuvalu, and Vanuatu.

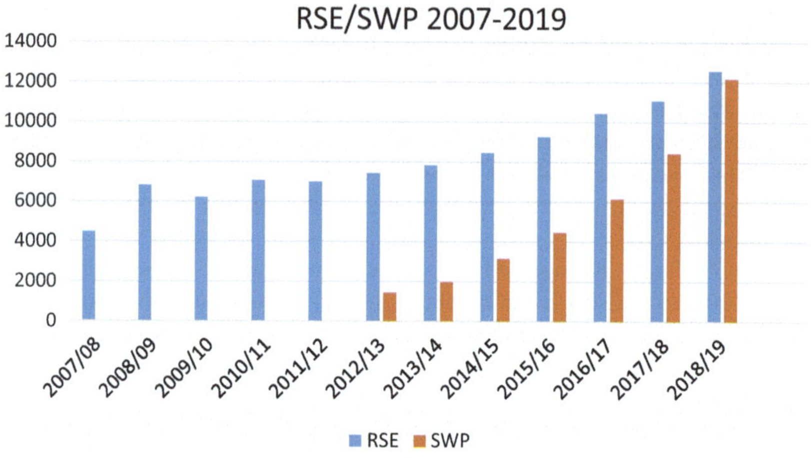

Fig. 14.1 Participation rates of RSE and SWP. (Source: Author)

purchased in Vanuatu. When using lower estimates of the 24,000 migrants in both the RSE and SWP spending NZD500 in material remittances, the total is NDZ12 million—an impressive sum.

Yet these material remittances remain under-researched. The limited definitions of what material remittances encompass mean that large portions of remittances remain misunderstood. Workers that send money home for their families to spend on consumable items is recognized as a remittance, the purchase of food and other goods, typically bags of rice or household items, with overseas earnings that returned migrants distribute to various family and community members is not formally recognized as a remittance. Whether material goods are purchased in New Zealand, Australia, or the respective home countries, these items are purchased with income from seasonal worker programs. Migrants return home with these goods to provide for their families and maintain social relationships within their communities, the same way they do with cash. In this case, however, the migrant has more control over how the remittances are distributed. Nonetheless, migrants often convert their income into material remittances while in their host countries due to the perceived lack of quality and cost of goods back home.

In contrast to the gap in the literature on material remittances, financial remittances are mainstream and sit center-stage in labor mobility research.

There are various projections of how much migrants remit from these schemes. The figure used here reflects costs taken out from participating in the programs, reducing it to a lower estimate that economists use in relation to the RSE of NZD5500, totaling NZD132 million for 24,000 workers. This is a significant cash injection into the Pacific region that did not exist before the RSE and SWP. The Pacific has one of the highest remittance fees in the world and migrants from this study, therefore, preferred to return with their money in their pocket, only remitting when requested.

Another interesting outcome of the prospect of financial remitting is the fact that migrants have access to loan systems that were previously not accessible for those in informal sector employment or seasonal worker schemes, forcing potential migrants to obtain high-interest loans upwards of 24 percent interest from local lenders. Today, once migrants secure a placement and have evidence from the Vanuatu Department of Labour that they are eligible for bank loans with lower interest rates, they finance not only their upcoming trips but also leave money behind for their families. These schemes have not only transformed bank institution approaches to loans for potential migrants but also banking systems for migrants, many of whom never held a bank account prior to their participation in these schemes.

Introducing the Research Field: Vanuatu

Vanuatu is located approximately 2000 kilometers from New Zealand. In 2020, the estimated population was just under 300,000. It is an archipelago comprising 83 islands and has a colonial legacy linked to both the United Kingdom and France via condominium rule (1906–1980). The historical condominium still influences many social structures and cultural and linguistic environments within Vanuatu. Since obtaining independence on July 31, 1980, Vanuatu has heavily relied on its subsistence sector, with 76 percent of the population living in rural areas. Vanuatu has a dual economy: both cash and non-cash activities shape social and economic relationships. There are limited formal sector employment opportunities in Vanuatu, making labor mobility opportunities attractive for many.

Since joining the RSE, Vanuatu has transformed into a labor-sending country, starting with 1698 workers in the RSE for the 2007/2008 season and growing to approximately 8000 workers in Australia and New Zealand in the 2019/2020 season. Before this, there were limited opportunities for ni-Vanuatu to migrate to these countries, whereas Vanuatu is currently the largest Pacific-sending country to the RSE and SWP.

In Vanuatu, exchanges are essential for building and maintaining relationships, as these form a central part of social interactions. Transactions between ni-Vanuatu have consequences for broader economic and social relationships. Reciprocal exchanges, especially those that are obligatory, secure a sense of belonging, a social position, and an identity within communities. Within this context of reciprocity, the role of remittances is highlighted: seasonal migrants are expected to contribute to their families and communities, while failing to do so has repercussions.

Methodology

Since 2007, I have conducted ethnographical research on the RSE and SWP seasonal worker programs. I have worked and lived with communities in New Zealand and Vanuatu, while Pacific seasonal workers in Australia's SWP have also become a large part of my research since 2014. Over the years, I have participated in hundreds of interviews, spent time working in vineyards, living in Vanuatu, and documenting the lives of workers, their families, and communities and the cultural, economic, political, and social outcomes of participating in these Pacific labor mobility programs. The longitudinal research presented here started with 22 ni-Vanuatu RSE migrants in 2007 and has since expanded to hundreds more in both programs. Thus, I have been able to document changes for workers and their families and communities, whether they remained in labor mobility or exited.

During my research, I followed workers' movements in multi-sited ethnographical research (Marcus 1995). Following the flows of people also included observing the goods and money they obtained as a result of participating in the labor mobility schemes. There have been advantages and limitations to this research. I have been able to access information on people's personal choices in their finances and their decisions on employment opportunities, and I have observed how remittances from these overseas seasonal employment schemes have transformed the lives of not only households but also, in many cases, whole communities. Some of the limitations arose due to my gender and how this impacted my acceptance into particular families. Like migrants themselves, I have had to negotiate what information I can have access to and collaborate with research participants on the information that they want to share or to be kept private. Although I have never discussed exact dollar figures on their overall earnings, which vary from season to season, workers have always shared this information with me and shown me material remittances they sent home or the results of what they produced with their earnings. I have also observed migrants purchasing goods and transporting them home, and witnessed the results of their overseas incomes, which mostly mirror the information obtained in interviews.

Remitting Material Goods

From 2007 to 2009, RSE workers returned material remittances in their suitcases. Many bought bigger suitcases for this purpose because the small bags and backpacks they arrived with would not hold the newly purchased goods. Two years later, workers had the opportunity to remit material goods home in containers. This opportunity dramatically changed what products migrants could purchase. There was a shift from purchasing small personal use items to larger merchandise, in greater quantities, which were collected by migrants when they returned home to Vanuatu. In some cases, the containers would arrive up to one month after their return, meaning that migrants often spent that extra month in the capital city before returning to their home island.

Exporting material goods via shipping containers was challenging in the initial years. The financial or material costs associated with remittances to the Pacific are high and can be a barrier. Migrants factored in the costs of transportation to Vanuatu, but were unprepared for the processes of offloading the items from containers, dealing with customs authorities, and the associated costs and taxes. Furthermore, there was no systematic monitoring of remitted goods, and migrants complained that belongings disappeared. Fortunately, service and protocols have improved, possibly prompted by additional prerequisite security documentation due to attempts to import illegal goods, such as guns.

Eventually, workers had the opportunity to purchase shipping containers. The cost of these containers was approximately NZD10,000 to NZD15,000. Large groups of 15 to 30 workers collectively contributed to the purchase and sold space to others. In 2012, purchasing containers became problematic. Too many were being transported, meaning fewer opportunities to sell them upon return. Migrants did not know what to do with the containers they could not sell. After observing the Christchurch earthquake in 2011, workers had the new idea of transforming unsold containers into tourism bungalows. However, only very few took this opportunity due to limited land ownership and costs to transport and renovate.

Not all seasonal workers have access to shipping containers. Groups of SWP workers interviewed in Australia are actively discouraged to do so because it is perceived as a waste of money. Without access to this shipping method, migrants are reliant on putting goods in suitcases, which often also results in excess baggage costs. However, these workers do return to Vanuatu and purchase larger items in the main centers, which support the regional economy.[4] The export of material remittances has expanded from suitcases to shipping freights, which has in turn enabled larger goods and higher quantities remitted to Vanuatu, thus providing various opportunities to transform different sectors of social systems.

In interviews with migrants, the emotional and social quality of remitting became evident. Material remittances are not only gifts in return for the maintenance of workers' properties or care for their family members, but compensate for absence and express guilt, especially in transnational families. Many migrants admitted to buying children gifts such as laptops, DVDs, phones, and clothing out of guilt—coined by one migrant as "a gift of forgiveness" (Gloria, Ambrym Island 2019).

Transforming the Village: Homes, Households, Everyday Life, and Schools

"Look at my house—mi glad tumas my sister. I have many nice things now" (Sonia, Ambrym Island 2012). Many stories of transformation begin with such statements about home, whether building or renovating a house and altering the décor. These transformations are related to changing family and community dynamics. In this section, I will discuss the impact of material remittances on the built environment, households, daily lives, and schools in Vanuatu.

[4] See Durand et al. (1996) for Mexican examples. However, the Vanuatu context does vary from Durand's work in Mexico, where nationalized production rates are higher. Ni-Vanuatu migrant remittances flow, directly and indirectly, throughout households, communities, and business operators in the islands.

From Thatched to Permanent Homes: The Transformation of the Built Environment

Transformational processes are most evident in the built environment. Many villages with seasonal migrants have transformed from traditional thatched huts to permanent homes. Purchasing land and building homes was an objective for 85 percent of participants spoken to from both the RSE and SWP. In 2009, one permanent material home belonging to an RSE worker stood out among the traditional thatched houses in Fanto village. Due to an increase of residents entering the RSE or SWP, this village now, in 2020, has multiple permanent homes and few traditional housing structures. Similar transformations have been observed in all larger migrant-sending villages.

The increase in houses and cash has also contributed to a change in community labor. Initially, when questioning the costs of building homes, most people spoke of labor costs equating to the price of boarding and meals while assisting in the construction. Two years later, migrants commented on a change in this traditional reciprocity approach. Community members now ask for cash or material payments for their labor. As one participant said, "things are changing now the village asks to be paid to help build houses. It's because we have money" (Simon, Ambrym Island 2016; for similar findings, see Zotova and Cohen 2016, p. 11). However, this has not lessened the production of new homes by migrants, who not only build homes for themselves but also for their extended families. In some cases, the houses for extended family are built beside the migrant's houses to provide more space for growing families, while in other cases, migrants have built larger homes to accommodate extended families.

These transformations in housing production and styles have been influenced by remittances from those living abroad, with many houses on the island now being modeled on housing observed overseas. How houses are designed and built is also influenced by building courses undertaken by migrants in New Zealand (see Bailey 2019a). In addition to these changes, the materials used and the social organization have altered from previous conventional practices noted by Durand (2016) as migrants are acquiring new knowledge and skills, and their kin are demanding cash payments for what were once seen as traditional roles and obligations. Kitchen houses (those built outside the main house for cooking and storage) have remained the same, using the same customary materials (Durand 2016, p. 258). However, they are now filled with material items such as freezers, ovens, and other kitchen goods that were previously not accessible.

In a household survey of seasonal workers on Epi Island, Vanuatu, Smith found that "traditional plant materials for walls and roofs was halved" (2016, p. 46). The transformation of houses from thatched to permanent was also discussed in interviews I conducted in 2011. The migrants and their families stated that the new homes can withstand cyclones and were moreover seen as a symbol of their achievement. However, the research participants also noted that permanent houses were not always practical because of the heat (see also Smith 2016, p. 51).

Within the Household

This section examines remittances generally located within the household. Except for solar panels and appliances, the remittances discussed in this section are usually considered trivial and are rarely documented. What is seldom reflected is that these resources are targeted commodities for migrants and their respective households. Family and community members provide migrants with lists of material goods to purchase, ranging from schoolbooks, laptops, solar panels, household goods, recipe books, and in one season an organ for the church.

Second-hand clothing is the most popular material remittance and is easily transferred in suitcases. Studies have shown that migrants return with second-hand clothing not only for personal use but for trade and commercial purposes (Bailey 2019a; Hansen 2000). The migrants and their families set up stalls or have home shops selling clothing purchased in New Zealand, with high profits. In one interview, a migrant's wife told me that she made NZD1000 in less than an hour with such a stall. Many migrants also purchase or are given second-hand clothing, which they redistribute among their families and communities, replacing torn clothing articles.

The introduction of shipping containers enabled the remittance of furniture such as beds, mattresses, sofa, chairs, tables, and drawers. Prior to participation, most household members slept on mats or thin foam mattresses. Remitted furniture and interior design goods also transformed households to resemble the "Western" homes that migrants had become accustomed to abroad. Furniture is also a status symbol reflecting the material success of their employment overseas. Observations in several households revealed that beds, sofas, and chairs are held in special esteem and are not used every day, but are kept for special occasions and guests. Often, the transformation of the household involves a combination of wanted goods and a reflection of achievable outcomes. For some, it is seen to fit into a modernization category, even if those material goods are impractical or not used.

Everyday Life and Solar Power

Since 2009, and following access to shipping containers, workers purchased solar panels and accessories. Increased power generation via solar systems remitted by migrants is notable in many parts of Vanuatu and has transformed many rural households. Prior to this, most power was produced using petroleum generators, which few homes owned as they are expensive to fuel and thus used on special occasions only. Changing to solar energy has brought many advancements like permanently available electricity in the households Villages are now lit up at night, prolonging daytime activities like working and studying. However, changes through solar energy have also been viewed critically. Bedford et al. (2020, p. 172) described the view that although solar power has greatly changed electricity provision, it comes with negative effects like children spending too much time on electronic devices.

Village chiefs have reiterated this observation not only with regard to children but also with returning migrants. One chief told me in an interview that out of frustration he had confiscated material goods such as DVD players from younger RSE workers in order for them to conform to village expectations: "When it is time for the men to be working in the garden, many are not to be found. They were gone watching movies on their portable DVD players that they had purchased while in New Zealand" (Chief Saksak, Ambrym Island, 2011). After the men finished their obligations to the village, the chief returned their goods. These incidents occurred in the early years of the RSE and, although chiefs in Ambrym argued that they had control over these new behaviors, there was concern that these new material goods would become timewasting habits in the community that would negatively impact on traditional societal practices.

With the addition of solar energy, appliances such as ovens, freezers, microwaves, kettles, and washing machines have increased. Freezers are popular not only as storage for family and community foods, but also because they generate income from selling freezer space or using the appliance as a shop selling frozen goods, such as frozen chicken or ice cream. However, there is also skepticism toward new appliances: one migrant's wife was given a microwave and told me that she was too scared to use it, as she traditionally cooked on an open fire and occasionally used the electric oven at her workplace. The first year, she only used the microwave to store food until she observed her husband use it and became confident. Nonetheless, these material goods have allowed migrant families to reduce cooking labor time and provide an additional source of income for many families.

In addition to these new goods, photos of household members working in Australia and New Zealand adorn the walls of living spaces. Cameras and cell phones were popular items to purchase in the first few seasons (2007–2009), though developing photos was costly. Many saved photos on their mobile phones. In the first few seasons, images of their life in New Zealand were not on display in their Vanuatu homes until costs reduced. Now migrants often develop these photos to show their journey to family and community members back home. Family members have noted that the photos help them to cope with the physical absence of their partners, and these photo displays often reflect the achievements and transformations that migrants and their families have accomplished in participating in overseas seasonal work.

Schools

Paying school fees is a priority. Like material remittances, studies have rarely focused on human capital outcomes of the RSE and SWP. Other than housing, I argue that the most significant transformation occurs in the sector of education. The opportunity to attend school, to finish high school, and, for some children, to finish tertiary studies would not have occurred without the RSE and SWP (Bailey 2019a). Furthermore, migrants are also financing extended family members' education, some even up to university degrees. Many migrants hope that these new educational opportunities may in future create new transformations for their children and communities. Additionally, a good student in Vanuatu is considered a good citizen, a motto that is written on many educational facilities.

In addition to school fees, supplies such as stationery, electronics, educational resource books, and other related resources are remitted in bulk. As will be discussed further below, migrants also remit desks, chairs, and school uniforms. In interviews, several teachers and principals mentioned the generosity of migrants returning with goods for the students and supplies for their schools like solar panels and generators, enabling students to return to school at night and continue their homework and thereby transforming the learning opportunities for ni-Vanuatu pupils (see also Bedford et al. 2020, p. 72).

New modes of transportation have also assisted with access to education. For some children, school is a long distance from their villages, up to two hours walking in some areas. Migrants and teachers commented that remittances such as bicycles, trucks, and buses have assisted in improved attendance rates.

Collective Community Projects

The Lolihor Development Council (LDC) in North Ambrym was involved in the selection process of my original research group of 22 men for the RSE in 2007. The expectation of those selected was that they would financially contribute to community-led projects with their earnings from New Zealand. The aim was strategic recruitment for development. The LDC was established in 1993 with the aid of the United Nations Development Programme (UNDP) to encourage cooperation between villages in North Ambrym. Several studies have noted the expectations of RSE migrants to contribute to local development projects (for a range of RSE community projects in Tonga, Samoa, and Vanuatu, see Bailey 2009; Bailey 2014; Bedford et al. 2020; Cameron 2011; MacLellan and Mares 2008).

In the case of the LDC, contributions were a prerequisite. Initially, there were successful projects that workers' incomes contributed to, such as a market house, the purchase of an engine for the LDC boat, scholarships, and a microcredit scheme. The market house provided a space where women from the 12 villages in the region could come together and sell their produce, and also became a local meeting place. The microcredit scheme transformed banking for local community members.

However, after a while workers ceased providing financial and material remittances due to tensions and misappropriations of funds. When interviewing families of workers in 2011 about the LDC, many stated that although their husbands' overseas incomes contributed to projects, they were not directly involved. This disconnection, a change in recruitment practices, and mistrust over the financial management of migrants' incomes for community projects contributed to the decline of money given to the LDC over time.

Contributions from migrant workers to the LDC ceased during negotiations for funds to relocate a new health center to the Lolihor region. Migrants had initially provided a portion of their overseas incomes in order to purchase building materials for the new clinic. Those building materials lay waiting for over 18 months before the community gave up on the clinic project and repurposed the materials to extend the local church. However, there are also positive examples in Vanuatu of new health clinics and material supplies from migrant and employer remittances.

Although remittances to the LDC ceased, contributions to other community groups such as the church remain constant. This is in part due to membership and obligations. Migrants contribute significantly to community needs like paying for the construction of wells, community halls, churches, and schools. Vanuatu is prone to natural disasters, cyclones, acid rain, and ash from volcanoes. Overseas incomes often support repairs and maintenance of community infrastructure. Such projects often go undocumented (Bailey 2015; Goldring 2004), yet they bring to light the reasons for participation and provide a window into remittance spending. Migrants also refer to advancements in their social status through participation, or the improvements they have made in their housing and the generosity of gifts given to their communities (Bailey and Wells 2016).

Host Country Community Contributions

What has often been neglected in studies to date are the numerous donations from workers' host communities and employers. An example is a fundraiser by a New Zealand community to complement migrant workers' fundraising and purchasing school desks, chairs, as well as school uniforms and other school materials (see Fig. 14.2).

Two months after these goods arrived in Vanuatu, a New Zealand government delegation visited the school. Not only was the school, like many others in Vanuatu, transformed through material remittances, but also became a model for other communities with RSE migrants.

New relationships are produced through the exchanges between Pacific seasonal workers and their employers and host communities. As a result of these new connections, both in New Zealand and in Pacific Island nations, employers have contributed to the workers' social, material, and financial remittances through donations such as water pumps, hospital beds, and contributions to medical infrastructure projects. Employers stated at a meeting with Ambrym communities in 2011 that they saw the RSE as mutually beneficial and as a partnership. Employers are proud of assisting migrant communities in reaching their goals through donations and providing upskilling courses, reiterating that they value the work that ni-Vanuatu have done for them in New Zealand and that in return they wish to assist the communities that sent the workers.

Since Cyclone Pam devastated Vanuatu in 2016, New Zealand government initiatives and employers have offered courses on strengthening housing structures for RSE migrants. The New Zealand government provides a suite of free educational courses for RSE migrants through the Vakameasina training program. Interviewees stated that these courses changed the way they managed money or conducted business. These small

Fig. 14.2 Remitted goods for Mele School, Vanuatu. (Credit Alex George)

yet subtle changes are powerful agents of change in the everyday life in Vanuatu.

Workers also receive gifts from local communities in Central Otago. These donations increase in size when workers have access to shipping containers. Donations have ranged from clothing and sewing machines to mattresses and televisions. For example, between 2011 and 2012, New Zealand replaced analog TV with digital TV. Communities offered migrants their redundant analog televisions to remit without considering whether they had power in their homes—at the time, the majority did not. Nonetheless, returning with televisions was seen as a status symbol.

Kastom[5] Ceremonies

Cultural traditions such as rites of passages, grade-taking ceremonies, and other localized practices can decrease or increase through the process of migration. For Vanuatu, we find that local customs and rituals have been revived and reinforced through financial remittances from short-term seasonal workers. There is an expectation of sharing remittances for rituals and ceremonies. These new sources of income and material goods are enabling ni-Vanuatu to participate in *kastom* ceremonies in new ways, for

[5] *Kastom* is the Bislama term for custom or tradition (Crowley 2003).

example in wedding ceremonies where received gifts are displayed. Gifts from families of migrant workers are often more extravagant and costly, money may be exchanged in the bride-wealth ceremony, and wealth is shown through the gifting of livestock or contributions to food in prestation piles. These piles are central to what Rio (2007, p. 186) called the "relational economy." He argued: "[T]he heaping of food and money is the vehicle that drives all social transformations on Ambrym, creating a motion that is crucial to Ambrym *kastom* and social reproduction." Money is also remitted as a sign of symbolic participation in ceremonies where migrants are absent. By spending money earned abroad on ritual and life-cycle events as well as by participating in relations of reciprocity, the migrants secure a sense of belonging and identity within their communities.

Transformations in the Business Sector, Agriculture, and Transportation

Many businesses require cash injections. However, migrants taking material goods home have enabled opportunities for microbusinesses as well as additional resources for current agricultural ventures. In the longevity study, I showed that 71 percent of workers purchased material goods to start a business (Bailey 2019a, p. 43). These ranged from agricultural tools, second-hand clothing, and kitchenware for the establishment of bakeries and restaurants, groceries to set up shop, and vehicles (mainly vans used as buses) and boats for transportation. Moreover, in that study 32 percent reported providing funds or material goods for a spouse or a family member to initiate a business.

In another study of 174 combined RSE and SWP workers (Bailey 2019b), transportation was the largest investment, followed by agriculture. While overseas, workers explore various crops and gain experience from using multiple agricultural tools. Many of these items were then remitted. These vary from small pruning cutters and chainsaws to tractors, often transforming labor practices. Many migrants form relationships in their host communities and with their employers, who offer advice on different business ideas. In New Zealand, the RSE Worker Training Program Vakameasina also assists migrants with business skills training programs.

A transformational change in workers' approaches to agriculture results from the tools they acquire and the diversification of production and work practices. Initially, migrants took home portable agricultural tools in their suitcases. Later, containers allowed for larger tools such as chainsaws, ploughs, and in one case materials to construct a sawmill—all expensive tools that are difficult to acquire in Vanuatu. Remitted tools serve different purposes and have multiple meanings and ways of contributing: For example, grass cutters are not only for personal use; workers rent them and use them to fulfill village obligations by cutting grass on church grounds or community roads. Therefore, although seen as an item for personal use, they achieve much more: earning income, meeting obligations, and establishing various interactions between individuals and the community.

Migrants credited remitted tools for easier and quicker practices on their farms. Some of the new skill sets such as varieties in pruning methods have assisted in changes. After working with various crops in Australia and New Zealand, migrants have attempted to replicate them in Vanuatu (some legally and some not). Education in biodiversity when transplanting goods internationally has been reinforced for migrants. Many transplanted crops failed, what did not fail, though, were attitudes toward diversification. Migrants still actively seek new crops and methods, many with ideas of future food security and transformation of income opportunities in mind. They also experiment with new crops that are less laborious to plant and harvest that could possibly survive localized climatic impacts. Vanuatu has been driving agricultural diversity for many years. However, consuming and working on various crops in seasonal worker schemes has encouraged migrants to diversify not only in agriculture but in other business ventures since 2007.

Rejection of Remittances, Perceived Negative Impacts, and Inequality

There is an encouragement of a "culture of saving" among seasonal workers. Home communities, employers, and government officials enforce this by either controlling savings or discouraging workers from spending money on goods seen as wasteful. Not all remittances are accepted. As mentioned before, a community leader in West Ambrym did not like "timewasters" such as televisions and DVD players brought home, and insisted that the men should invest their earnings more wisely toward agricultural resources.

It is also crucial to approach the question whether remitted material items create new demands in consumption or change the social fabric of Vanuatu societies. In the interviews with RSE migrants, migrants denied this and stated that the needs already existed before the scheme (Bailey 2009). Nonetheless, migrants purchased household items and tools that they thought would enhance their home and work lives in Vanuatu and thus made these items popular. Remittances have an impact on consumer patterns, creating new desires and causing new expenses, as Zotova and Cohen observed in their research on remittances in the context of Tajikistan. At the same time, remittance receivers and the wider community members also influence the decisions of migrant senders by placing judgment values of what is and what "should be" remitted. These judgments have been placed on RSE and SWP migrants by governments, employers, communities, and households since day one, often limiting migrants' purchases or creating deceptive remittance practices to hide material goods.

A perceived negative impact of remitted material goods is waste: "RSE workers return with goods and packaging that cannot be easily disposed of, and local communities lack the facilities to deal with the waste. Rubbish is left to accumulate within the village" (Bedford et al. 2020: pp. 107–8). This observation is especially important in rural settings, where there is no set infrastructure to deal with large quantities of waste. Waste from goods and food packaging from the capital city to rural areas was evident in my early observations in Ambrym (2011–2012). Bedford's study (2020) highlights that additional waste from material remittances is a pressing issue in the transformation of rural environments.

Remittances can also create inequalities and dependency (Bailey 2019a; Bedford et al. 2020; Brettell 2007; Cohen 2004; Massey et al. 1993; Reichert 1981). Although not always vocalized in public domains, community members raised concerns with migrant workers' long-term participation in labor mobility. There have been references to jealousies over opportunities to migrate and the remittances returned. This is often observed in the built environment and the material objects carried or worn. As migrants accumulate material goods, household security increases. Bedford et al. (2020, p. 108) mentioned with regard to Lamen Bay on the island of Epi that households with locks on doors now dominate the dwellings. On Ambrym, very few migrants used to lock the rooms in their homes, but migrants now understand the tensions and jealousies that are associated with newly acquired goods and have also increased locking their properties. This transformation is not only seen in providing additional security but contributes to a relationship of mistrust. Participation and the attainment of financial and material wealth have exacerbated these tensions.

Inequality and transformations have also included gendered aspects. Initially, females were excluded from the schemes by the LDC council in North Ambrym. However, in 2012, the council approved a woman to go to Australia with her brother and since then many have followed. With the participation of women in the scheme, village dynamics including gender roles are being transformed. However, this change is not always depicted positively within communities.

Youth are now looking at the RSE and SWP when they finish school, whereas prior to this there were limited formal employment opportunities. Over half of my original 22 research participants now see the RSE as a career for seven months of the year, as opposed to limited cash work in copra, kava, or other local agricultural ventures. The seasonal worker programs have transformed ideas of work, with overseas labor being seen as valuable due to the outcomes from remittances and local employment practices being seen as lower in status because of limited cash resources and the time needed to gain income.

Material Remittances as Practices of Belonging

Remittances are interwoven with ideas of belonging. Often, the remitted objects stand for the host country and, when moved to a new locality, represent a specific form of prestige, status, and nostalgia for workers (see also Mura and Ströhle in this volume). Evidence of working in the seasonal programs is displayed in the landscapes of Vanuatu, through symbolic motifs on houses and vehicles, architecture, and the naming of businesses. When I first visited Vanuatu in 2009, I spotted mostly symbols of Australia in Port Vila, like Australian rugby jerseys and flags in stores. Two years on, this had changed fundamentally, with the inclusion of New Zealand symbolism from returned migrants. Connections to Australia and New Zealand are displayed proudly, like the New Zealand flag or All Blacks merchandise, which are popular with those participating in the RSE. When one sees a picture of a Kangaroo or the Australian flag on a bus or taxi, it is clear that this person participated in the SWP.

This plays out in many different areas, even in sports. In 2007, RSE migrants were football fans and had limited knowledge of or interest in rugby. Today, when New Zealand and Australia compete against each other, seasonal workers show their support for their work location on social media sites and in celebratory parades, for example in Port Vila. Parades for these rugby teams did not occur before the RSE and SWP. Participation in these schemes has provided new forms of demonstrating social ties with the host countries. Identity in Vanuatu is strongly localized and "being of place" (Hess 2009) will always remain dominant in Vanuatu societies. Nonetheless, migrants that have returned to Australia or New Zealand over several seasons also feel a strong connection to their host communities, adding this new strand to their sense of identity.

Conclusion

Material remittances play an important role in transformative processes. In some cases, the financial, social, and cultural values of material remittances are significantly higher than monetary transfers. Most remitted incomes are allocated to essential items such as daily consumption, living costs, school fees, building homes, buying land, or contributing to customary and community obligations. The establishment of businesses is further down the list, depending on the migrant's positionality. Rethinking negative notions around consumable and productive remittances leads to a better understanding of remittance societies.

Remitted material goods can contribute to new income-generating opportunities and provide positive transformations in migrant households and community domains. This is obvious in the built environment through infrastructure projects and within household dwellings. Goods that add to décor are highly valued, referred to as transformative in the developmental sense of the term "modern," and contribute to comfort in everyday life. Shipping provides migrants with the opportunities to remit larger goods. Solar equipment has been most notable in the transformative processes. The increase in solar equipment has provided electricity in rural areas, assisting with the creation of new businesses, light for homework, and household use. Migrants also ship a range of goods such as furniture and trucks and boats for transportation. Access to transportation has improved mobility and provided income opportunities.

The benefits from remittances are widespread, though not all remittances are welcomed, and there are tensions in regard to migrant participation and their remittance choices. Although there are negative outcomes from remittances, like dealing with waste, these are largely outweighed by the positive consequences of remittances and participation in labor mobility more broadly. If given both a dollar and social value, material remittances might become of more interest in the future.

References

Bailey, R. (2009). *Unfree Labour: Ni-Vanuatu Workers in New Zealand's Recognised Seasonal Employer Scheme.* Master thesis, University of Canterbury, Christchurch.

Bailey, R. (2014). *Working the Vines: Seasonal Migration, Money and Development in New Zealand and Ambrym, Vanuatu.* Doctoral dissertation, University of Otago.

Bailey, R. (2015). Using Material Remittances from Labour Schemes for Social and Economic Development: Case Study Vanuatu. *SSGM In Brief* 2015/15. ANU Press.

Bailey, R. & Wells, S. (2016). Temporary Labour Schemes, the New Avenue of Social Mobility: Case Study Vanuatu. *SSGM In Brief* 21. ANU Press.

Bailey, R. (2019a). *New Zealand's Recognised Employer Scheme (RSE): 10 Year Longitudinal Case Study.* ANU Press.

Bailey, R. (2019b). Ni-Vanuatu 'Making Business' through Seasonal Worker Programs. DPA *In Brief 13.* ANU Press.

Bedford, C., Bedford, R. & Ho, E. (2009). *The Social Impacts of Short-Term Migration for Employment: A Review of Recent Literature.* Research Report for NZAID.

Bedford, C., Bedford, R. & Nunns, H. (2020). RSE Impact Study: *Pacific Stream Report.* https://www.immigration.govt.nz/documents/statistics/rse-impact-study-pacific-stream-report.pdf.

Brettell, C. (2007). Adjustment of Status, Remittances, and Return: Some Observations on 21st Century Migration Processes. *City and Society, 19*(1), 47–59.

Cameron, E. (2011). *Social Development Outcomes of Participation in the New Zealand Recognised Seasonal Employer (RSE) Scheme for Ni-Vanuatu Seasonal Migrant Workers.* Master's thesis, Massey University, NZ.

Cohen, J. (2004). *The Culture of Migration in Southern Mexico.* University of Texas Press.

Cohen, J. (2011). Migration, Remittances and Household Strategies. *Annual Review of Anthropology, 40*, 103–114.

Connell, J. & Brown, R. (2005). *Remittances in the Pacific: An Overview.* Asian Development Bank.

Crowley, T. (2003). *A New Bislama Dictionary.* Bluebird Printery.

Durand, J., Parrado, E. A., & Massey, D. S. (1996). Migradollars and Development: A Reconsideration of the Mexican Case. *International Migration Review, 30*(2), 423–444.

Durand, M. (2016). Thinking through Houses: The Materiality of Kitchen Houses and History on Mere Lava, Vanuatu. *Journal of Material Culture, 21*(2), 253–273.

Goldring, L. (2004). Family and Collective Remittances to Mexico: A Multi-dimensional Typology. *Development and Change, 34*(4), 799–840.

Hansen, K. (2000). *Salaula: The World of Secondhand Clothing and Zambia.* University of Chicago Press.

Hess, S. (2009). *Person and Place: Ideas, Ideals and the Practice of Sociality on Vanua Lava, Vanuatu.* Berghahn Books.

MacLellan, N. & Mares, P. (2008). *Workers for all Seasons: Issues from New Zealand's Seasonal Employer (RSE) Program.* Swinburne, Australia, Institute for Social Research.

Marcus, G. E. (1995). Ethnography in/of the World System: The Emergence of Multi-Sited Ethnography. *Annual Review of Anthropology, 24*, 95–117.

Massey, D., Hugo, G., Kouaouci, A., Pellegrino, A. & Taylor, J. (1993). Theories of International Migration: A Review and Appraisal. *Population and Development Review, 19*(3), 431–466.

Reichert, J. (1981). The Migrant Syndrome: Seasonal US Wage Labor and Rural Development in Central Mexico. *Human Organization, 40*(1), 56–66.

Rio, K. (2007). *The Power of Perspective: Social Ontology and Agency on Ambrym Island, Vanuatu.* Berghahn Books.

Smith, R. (2016). *"The Goal of the Good House": Seasonal Work and Seeking a Good Life in Lamen and Lamen Bay, Epi, Vanuatu.* Doctoral dissertation, University of Manchester.

Zotova, N. & Cohen, J. (2016). Remittances and the Social Meaning in Tajikistan. *Remittances Review, 1*(1), 5–16.

PART IV

Remittances in the Light of Conflict, Climate Change, and the Postcolonial: Contemporary Issues and Upcoming Challenges

Remittances transform biographies, landscapes, and social groups. It is therefore no surprise to encounter them in the center of pressing issues in global migration society like civil wars, climate change, and neocolonial backdrops. In order to analyze current and future challenges, we have to follow remittance transactions along these pathways.

Remittances originate from the differing qualities of life and power constellations across the globe, and in their very essence, they reproduce this global imbalance along the path of the coloniality of power, exploitation, imperialism, and climate inequality (Fagen 2006; Mignolo 2011; Van Praag and Timmerman 2019). At the same time, they are an effective remedy to improve the living conditions of those who have been affected by structural inequity worldwide (Bastia and Skeldon 2020; Carling 2014). This predicament is discussed in the chapters on remittances and climate change by Lore van Praag and Justice Issah Musah-Surugu and Samuel Weniga Anuga. Environmental and climate transformation is one of the most pressing issues in the present and will be even more so in the future of transnational society. Remittances can be part of the solution to these problems, but how can we conceptualize green remittances in terms of motivations, effects, and responsibilities? Lore Van Praag stresses that the mitigation of and adaptation to environmental change should not rely on individual sending of financial remittances. Instead, policymakers need to govern transnational practices like sending money as well as improving infrastructure, raising awareness, and sharing knowledge. In an example from Ghana, Justice Issah Musah-Surugu and Samuel Weniga Anuga show how smallholder farmers adapt to climate change by engaging in off-farm jobs, irrigation farming, and cultivating new crops. Remittances are vital in their endeavors to accommodate changing environments.

Structures of inequality are often manifest in conflict, and remittances can be part and parcel of transnational conflict as well as its resolution. Informal money transfers like *hawala* improve economic resilience and, at the same time, transform the social and political order (Güran 2020). Through the example of the Sri Lankan civil war, Rina Alluri shows how remittances from Switzerland to Sri Lanka were used as a way to sustain and perpetuate conflict and were thus highly politicized. When the civil war ended, remitting decreased and also changed from political support and activism to financial transfers. The first generation of the Tamil Swiss diaspora felt the need to support their homeland in times of conflict more than in times of peace. The second generation felt a need to distance themselves from the conflict and reduced remittances.

While social change in terms of conflict resolution, promoting sustainability, preventing climate change, and fostering academic exchange, is generally considered a positive development by migrant senders as well as non-migrant recipients, we cannot neglect the fact that these are mostly Western concepts that are sent along with technology, knowledge, and conflict solution. However, they also further transnational dependencies and foster neocolonial relations. Brigitte Bönisch-Brednich reflects on the role of universities in this context. While it is obvious that financial remittances are preferred in Western currencies, we need to open our eyes to the history of knowledge production and distribution in the academic world. When we interpret global knowledge transfers as remittance practices, we can reveal the neocolonial structures of the academic market. This shows how remittances follow an economic, social, and political script that determines legitimacy, value, and the currency of knowledge in a world of economic and social inequalities. In sum, remittances are paid in Western currency.

References

Bastia, T., & Skeldon, R. (Eds.). (2020). Routledge Handbook of Migration and Development. Routledge.

Carling, J. (2014). Scripting Remittances: Making Sense of Money Transfers in Transnational Relationships. *International Migration Review*, 48(4), 218–262. https://doi.org/10.1111/imre.12143

Fagen, P. W. (2006). *Remittances in Conflict and Crises: How Remittances Sustain Livelihoods in War, Crises and Transitions to Peace* (No. 38957, pp. 1–3). The World Bank.

Güran, G. (2020): *Brokers of Order: How Money Moves in Wartime Syria*. [Doctoral dissertation, Princeton University].

Mignolo, W. (2011). *The Darker Side of Western Modernity: Global Futures, Decolonial Options (Latin America Otherwise)*. Duke University Press

Van Praag, L. & Timmerman, C. (2019). Environmental Migration and Displacement: A New Theoretical Framework for the Study of Migration Aspirations in Response to Environmental Changes, *Environmental Sociology*, 5(4), 352–361. https://doi.org/10.1080/23251042.2019.161303

CHAPTER 15

Remittances as a Game Changer for Climate Change Adaptation Financing for the Most Vulnerable: Empirical Evidence from Northern Ghana

Justice Issah Musah-Surugu and Samuel Weniga Anuga

Introduction

The earlier choruses of conflict, dictatorship, and poverty as the main obstacles to Africa's development are gradually waning. Perhaps, progress in consolidating the rule of law and good governance, albeit with some hitches, accounts for this changing perspective on Africa (Henri 2019; Kalabamu 2019). However, at the center stage of the continent's struggle today are the destructive effects of climate chang (Makuvaro et al. 2018; IPCC 2014; Tsegaye et al. 2013). The region has experienced a significant increase in the intensity and frequency of extreme climate events such as floods, storms, and droughts, with the number of events surging from 85 in

J. I. Musah-Surugu (✉)
United Nations University, Bonn, Germany

S. W. Anuga
University of Ghana, Accra, Ghana

S. Meyer, C. Ströhle (eds.), *Remittances as Social Practices and Agents of Change*,
https://doi.org/10.1007/978-3-030-81504-2_15

the 1970s to over 540 between 2010 and 2019 with attendant high socio-economic cost (Kamer 2022). While the exact the total cost associated with these extreme events on the continent remains inconclusive, there is a broad consensus that there exists a substantial "adaptation finance gap" (Bahadir et al. 2018; Randazzo and Piracha 2019). Studies have consistently shown that public adaptation finance flows to the continent are considerably below the estimated needs and this gap continues to widen (OECD 2023; UNEP 2022).

The adaptation finance gap refers to the gap between the costs of meeting a given adaptation target and the amount of finance available (UNEP 2015). Amidst poor commitment from developed countries and massive resource rent coupled with poor gross domestic product (GDP) in some African countries, the adaptation finance gap is expected to grow exponentially (Watkiss et al. 2010; Stern 2008). Traditional public financing sources projected under the United Nations Framework Convention on Climate Change (UNFCCC) financial mechanism have arguably performed abysmally in their efforts to support Africa's adaptation needs. Indeed, the seemingly poor commitment of developed countries to fulfil their pledges makes many scholars and practitioners doubt the USD100 billion climate finance pledge made in Paris in 2015 (Musah-Surugu et al. 2018; Bendandi and Pauw 2016). Describing the failure of international public finance for climate change, Buchner and Wilkinson (2015) stated: "since its emergence, the USD 100 billion goal has been both a touchstone of good faith and a hallmark of mistrust."

Identifying new and additional private sources of finance to complement the ailing public sources is therefore topical in the climate finance discourse (Fridahl and Linnér 2016; Bodansky 2010). Climate finance scholars contend that private sector finance would be more sustainable, predictable, and stable to complement public finance (Pauw 2015). Emerging studies that focus on private sources of financing adaptation have identified remittances as showing prominence in this subset (Musah-Surugu et al. 2018; Pauw 2015). They indicate that remittances reach the core of the poor and could be a significant source in closing the adaptation financing gap, specifically at the household level. For instance, using propensity score matching and multinomial treatment methods, Randazzo and Piracha (2019) found an overall productive use of remittances at the household level in Senegal. Also, Bui et al. (2015) established that rural households in Vietnam increased investment in education and productive businesses, which augmented their human capital and financial gains for livelihood improvement.

Given the volume of remittance flows into developing countries and their potential to reach the poorest of the poor, many recent climate change financing studies have underscored their significance to support climate change adaptation (Kissinger et al. 2019; Marke and Sylvester 2018). Since 2007, remittance flows to developing countries have increasingly outstripped Official Development Assistance (ODA), net export, portfolio equity, tourism receipt, as well as foreign direct investment (FDI) (World Bank 2019). As a result of their predictability, lower volatility, counter-cyclical nature, and ability to bypass aid bureaucracies in reaching the poor, remittances have been tipped as a significant complementary source of financing adaptation (OECD 2016; Pauw 2015).

Previous studies in economics and development show that remittances have been a shock absorber for many vulnerable households in poorer countries (Couharde and Generoso 2015). Remittances contribute to financing adaptation-related investments ranging from short-term priorities, such as irrigation equipment, to longer term goals related to health and education (see Bayala in this volume; Couharde and Generoso 2015). Remittances are a form of self-insurance in developing countries. The insurance function is reflected in the tendency of migrants to send more remittances to their countries of origin following downturns in economic crises, natural disasters, and/or political/civil conflicts (Ratha 2007).

In spite of the evidence presented for the case of remittance flows as a strong complementary source of adaptation financing, the existing literature in the emerging field of climate change focused mainly on sources such as central governments, donors, FDIs, solidarity and philanthropic with only cursory attention given to the role of remittance flows (Musah-Surugu et al. 2018). Thus, this chapter seeks to fill the gap by examining the role of remittances as a finance adaptation tool among smallholder farmers in Ghana. This is done by answering the questions of the extent of influence remittances has on climate change adaptation and the share of income spent on adaptation. The findings of the chapter provide an informed basis for designing strategies that support existing private adaptation measures of local farmers through appropriate public policy, investment, and collective actions so as to reduce the adverse impact of climate change. Therefore, the findings are useful to public policy makers, NGOs, the private sector, and philanthropists with an interest in climate governance.

Materials and Methods

This chapter employs both quantitative and qualitative approaches to data-gathering and analysis. Data was sourced from smallholder farmers in the Bole-Bamboi and Sawla-Tuna-Kalba districts of the Northern Region of Ghana (Fig. 15.1). The specific communities involved were Gbogdaa, Nahari, Bali, Mankuma, Bole, Nyanoa, Belma, Jilinkon, Sawla, and Kalba. These communities were selected due to their perceived climate change vulnerability (MoFA 2014). Maize, millet, and yam farmers were selected due to the large production of these food crops in the communities. For this study, the Food and Agriculture Organization of the United Nations (FAO 2010) definition of smallholder farmers was adopted: Thus, smallholder farmers are farmers who farm plots of two hectares or less and rely exclusively on family labor. The data collection was done by the researchers and assisted by two carefully chosen and well-trained field assistants. A convenience sampling technique was used in selecting 400 farmers, comprising 40 farmers from each community. The convenience sampling approach was appropriate because no lists of farmers (sample frame) in the communities existed and hence did not offer an opportunity for probability sampling.

A disproportionate allocation was made to the districts to ensure representativeness. A semi-structured questionnaire was used in soliciting quantitative information. Section A of the questionnaire collected information on farmers' perceptions and knowledge of climate change, with Section B focusing on adaptation strategies. While Section C looked at the flow of remittances, Section D focused on remittances and climate change adaptation. Section E collected socio-demographic information. Twenty Focus Group Discussions (FGDs) were conducted, two per community. These included male and female farmers with an average of nine participants per group. In-depth interviews were also conducted with the district assemblies and representatives from the MoFA (Ministry of Food and Agriculture).

Adaptation Strategy Index (ASI) was used to rank the adaptation practices in order of importance on the farm. Questions in that section of the questionnaire provided response options placed on a continuum (Likert scale): high, medium, low, and not at all. The scores assigned to the responses were 3, 2, 1, and 0 respectively. Farmers were asked to assess the different strategies by using the four-point rating scale and subsequent ranking was done using the weighted means. This approach has been established as efficient in ranking elements (Uddin et al. 2014; Devkota 2014; Ndamani and Watanabe 2016).

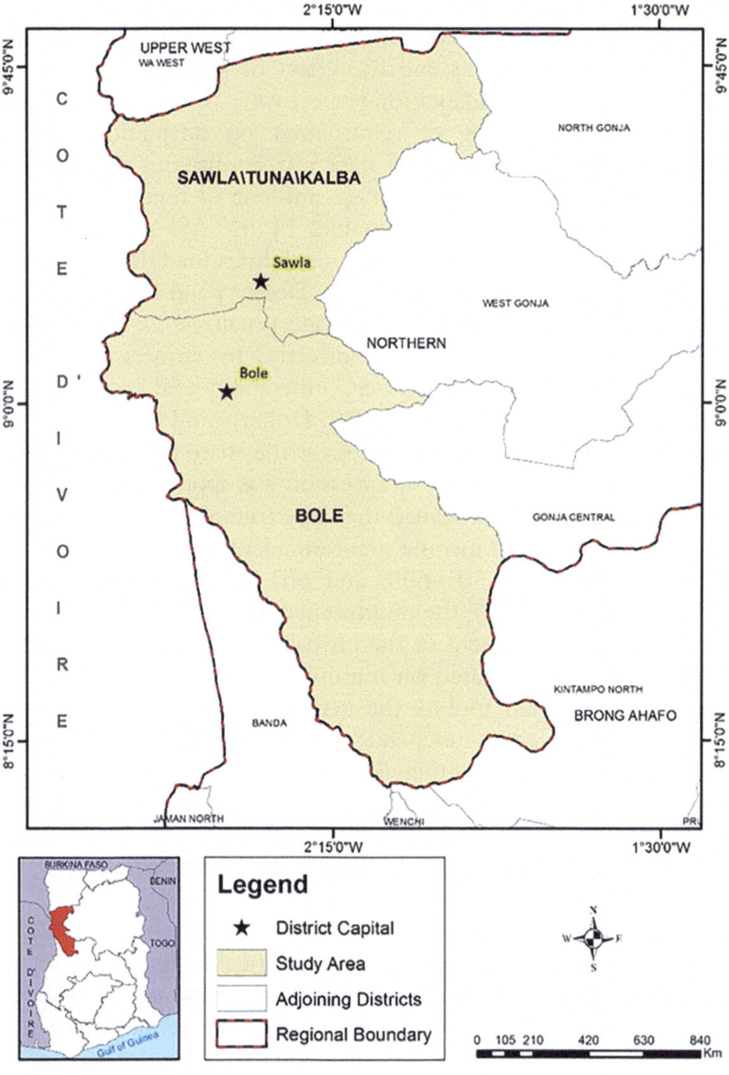

Fig. 15.1 Map of the study area (Bole-Bambio and Sawla-Tuna-Kalba districts). (Source: University of Ghana Geographic Information Systems Lab (UGGIS), 2017)

The Order Rank Logit (ORL) and multinomial logit structural decomposition models were used to examine the effect of remittances on climate change adaptation strategies and the effect of remittances on farmers' share of income spent on adaptation respectively. The ORL was employed to examine the influence of remittances on adaptation strategies. Remittance (explanatory variable) data was continuous as respondents were allowed to indicate their average amount of remittance per year. Adaptation strategies (outcome variable) by the ASI provided ranking options (Likert scale), offering ample possibilities for ORL analysis (Hill and Jones 2014; Stock and Watson 2012; Doherty and Clayton 2011). In this study, adaptation strategies are conceptualized as the responsive mechanism adopted (directly and indirectly) by farmers to offset the effects of climate change and reduce vulnerability (Huang et al. 2018; Descheemaeker et al. 2017; IPCC 2015; Doherty and Clayton 2011). In testing for the influence of remittances on the share of income spent on adaptation, the multinomial logit regression was appropriate. In this case, the independent variable remained the same (remittances as a continuous variable) and the share of income spent on adaptation was categorized in sums of USD100–300, 301–600, and 601–900. According to Hilbe (2011) and Allison (2014), the multinomial logistic regression is used to predict categorical placement or the probability of category membership in a dependent variable based on multiple independent variables, hence making it an appropriate tool for the analysis.

The models enabled an independent testing of the direct paths of the variables involved. The resulting R^2s for both models indicate that the exogenous variables are significant and fitted predictors of variance in adaptation and share of income. These were further confirmed by all post-estimations tests (such as margins) carried out. All estimations were made using STATA 15.

The major limitation of the study is that it did not disaggregate farmers who received national (internal) and international (external) remittances. This was because the number of recipients of international remittances was insignificant for statistical analysis. The authors propose that future studies with enough financial capacity expand the geographical dispensation in order to attract more international remittance recipients for a disaggregate analysis.

Results of the Study

Information on Sampled Farmers

The mean age of respondents was 46 years and more than half (59 percent) were males. Fifty percent had no formal education and 89.5 percent were married. The average household size was seven people, the average farm consisted of four acres, and the average number of years spent farming was 35 (Table 15.1). Eighty-five percent owned a bicycle and 82 percent a mobile phone. Many had a radio and motor bicycle (78.8 percent and 65 percent respectively). Water pumps (28 percent), televisions (33 percent), and motor kings/tricycles (35 percent) were not owned by many (Table 15.2). Eighty-two percent held the view that the climate has changed over the past fifteen years (Fig. 15.2). According to the distribution of perception on climate change, all respondents (100 percent)

Table 15.1 Socio-demographic characteristics of respondents ($n = 400$)

Socio-demographic characteristics	*Frequency (n)*	*Marginal (%)*	*Average*	*SD*
Sex				
Male	236	59.0		
Female	164	41.0		
Age			46.0	7.9
21–30	3	0.8		
31–40	132	33.0		
41–50	137	34.3		
51–60	70	17.5		
>60	58	14.5		
Religion				
Christianity	181	45.3		
Islam	157	39.3		
Traditional	62	15.5		
Marital status				
Married	358	89.5		
Unmarried	42	10.5		
Educational status				
No formal education	203	50.8		
Basic/primary	169	42.3		
Tertiary	28	7.0		
Household size	–	–	7.0	2.7
Farm size	–	–	4.0	0.7
Farm experience	–	–	35.0	7.7

thought rainfall had decreased while 98 percent perceived temperatures as having increased. There was also a perceived increase in the occurrence of storm surges (74 percent) and a 100 percent increase in the occurrence of prolonged drought (Table 15.3). Exactly half (50 percent) of respondents thought the change in climatic conditions in the area is caused by human activities, 20 percent saw it is a punishment from ancestors, 15 percent saw it as a punishment from a natural God, and 15 percent thought it is a natural cycle (Fig. 15.3). Figure 15.4 shows that the major effect of climate change as stated by respondents is low productivity (97 percent).

Farmers' Perception and Knowledge of Climate Change

Table 15.2 Property ownership

Farm properties	*Yes (%)*	*No (%)*
Mobile phone	82.0	18.0
Bicycle	85.0	15.0
Car/tractor	0.0	100.0
Motor king/tricycle	35.0	75.0
Motor bicycle	65.0	35.0
Radio	78.0	22.0
Water pump	28.0	72.0
Television	33.0	67.0

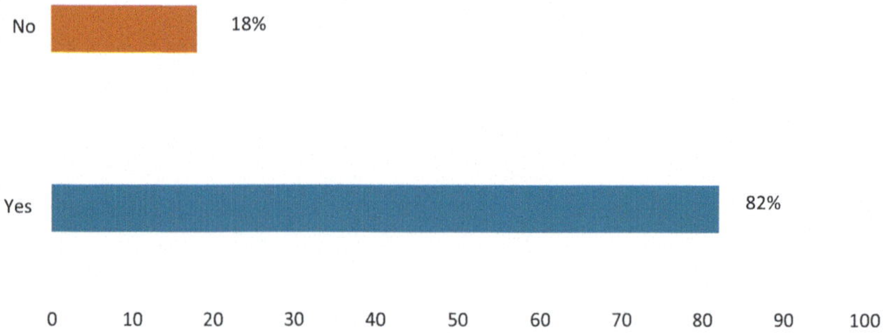

Fig. 15.2 The climate has changed over the past fifteen years

Table 15.3 Distribution of responses to perceived changes in specific climatic events (n = 400)

% of respondents indicating the level of change in climatic events over the past fifteen years				
Climatic events	*Increased*	*No change*	*Decreased*	*Don't know*
Precipitation			100	
Temperature	98.0			2.0
Occurrence of storm surges	74.0	20.0		6.0
Occurrence of drought	100			
Occurrence of floods	40.0	55.0		5.0

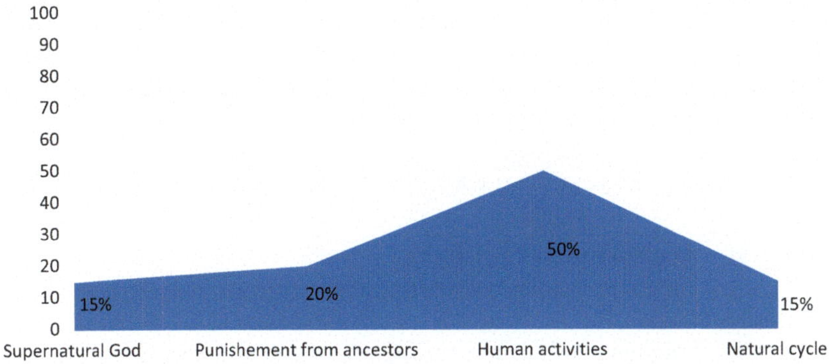

Fig. 15.3 Perceived causes of climate change

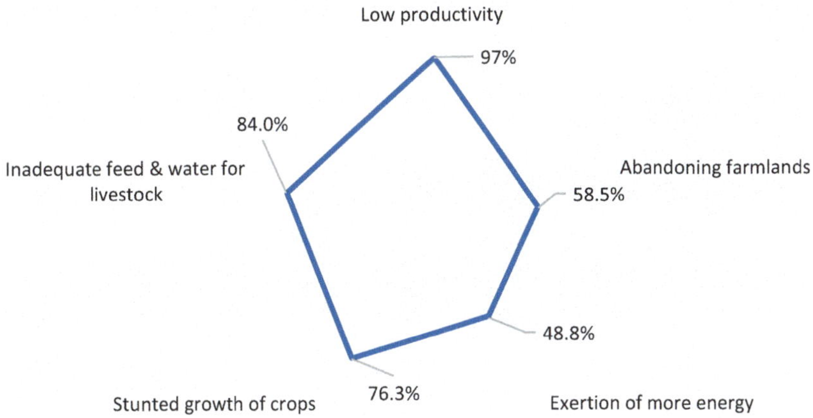

Fig. 15.4 Perceived effects of climate change

Climate Impacts and Adaptation

Due to the rising effects of climate change, many (85.5 percent) of the farmers were implementing various types of adaptation strategies as responsive mechanisms (Fig. 15.5). For strategic policy toward remittance-based adaptation, the study identified the adaptation strategies employed by farmers. The response options were placed on a continuum (Likert scale): "high, medium, low, and not at all," and as above were assigned scores of 3, 2, 1, and 0 respectively. Backyard gardening was the foremost activity implemented by farners as an adaptation strategy (ASI, 318.5), with cultivation of drought-tolerant crops (ASI, 300.0) ranking second and mixed cropping ranking third (ASI, 282.5). Off-farm jobs, residue management, and alternating planting dates were ranked fourth, fifth, and sixth respectively. Index-Based Insurance (ASI, 174.9), use of compost/animal manure (ASI, 198.3), and land fallowing (ASI, 192.4) were all given lower ranks of importance (Table 15.4).

$$ASI = AS_n \times 0 + AS_l \times 1 + AS_m \times 2 + AS_h \times 3$$

- ASI = Adaptation Strategy Index
- AS_n = Frequency of farmers rating adaptation strategy as having no importance
- AS_l = Frequency of farmers rating adaptation strategy as having low importance

Fig. 15.5 Implemented adaptation practices

Table 15.4 Ranked order of adaptation strategies to climate change

Order of importance on the farm						
Adaptation practices	*High*	*Medium*	*Low*	*No*	*ASI*	*Rank*
Backyard gardening	90.3	9.8	–	–	318.5	1
Cultivation of drought-tolerant crops	100	–	–	–	300.0	2
Mixed cropping	82.5	17.5	–	–	282.5	3
Off-farm jobs	80.0	20.0	–	–	280.0	4
Residue management	55.5	44.5	–	–	255.5	5
Alternating planting dates	49.3	9.8	41.0	–	252.4	6
Crop rotation	40.0	27.5	32.5	–	207.5	7
Afforestation	25.8	41.3	33.0	–	200.5	8
Irrigation farming	57.8	19.0	23.3	–	199.4	9
Use of compost/animal manure	22.5	54.3	23.3	–	198.3	10
Land fallowing	44.5	17.8	23.3	14.5	192.4	11
Index-Based Insurance (IBI)	25.5	23.8	50.8	–	174.9	12

- AS_m = Frequency of farmers rating adaptation strategy as having moderate importance
- AS_h = Frequency of farmers rating adaptation strategy as having high importance

Flow of Remittances and Use of Remittances for Adaptation

On average, our respondents receive USD369.00 of remittances annually. Half (50 percent) receive USD100–500 per year, 31.8 percent USD501–1000, and only 18.2 percent receive above USD1000. The main medium of receiving remittance was through friends or relatives (72.8 percent) (Table 15.5). Only 27 percent received wage-based income. Table 15.6 indicates that remittances enabled respondents to engage in some practices that could potentially become adaptation strategies. Buying chemicals or fertilizer (21.6 percent), acquiring extra food to supplement family needs (17.8 percent), and buying drought-tolerant maize seeds (14 percent) were indicated as activities remittances are used for. Other practices outlined were investing in children's education (13.4 percent), buying irrigation equipment (10.3 percent), and putting up a storage facility (7.2 percent) (Table 15.6). Major challenges associated with receiving remittances were mobile network problems (29.2 percent), traveling longer distances to redraw remittances (22.5 percent), and remitters being too busy to send money (20 percent).

Table 15.5 Amount of remittances received by respondents per year (USD)

Amount of remittances	*Frequency (n)*	*Percentage (%)*	*Average*
100–500	200	50.0	
501–1000	127	31.8	369.0
>1000	73	18.2	
Number of times remittance is received in a year			2.0
Medium of receiving remittance			
Sent through a friend/relative	291	72.8	
Mobile money transfer	109	27.2	
Other sources of income	Yes (%)	No (%)	
Farm crop-based income	100.0	–	
Livestock-based income	65.0	35.0	
Wage-based income	27.0	73.0	

Table 15.6 Practices smallholder farmers use remittances for that can potentially become adaptation practices

	Responses (n)	*Percentage (%)*
Practices		
Buy chemicals/fertilizer	382	21.6
Acquire extra food to supplement family needs	320	17.8
Buy drought-tolerant maize seeds	247	14.0
Invest in children's education	236	13.4
Buy irrigation equipment	180	10.3
Put up a storage facility	127	7.2
Sponsor relative travel outside the community	98	5.5
Hire labor	94	5.4
Expansion of farmland	85	4.8
Total	1,769	100.0
Challenges of receiving remittances		
Mobile network problems	259	29.2
Traveling longer distances to redraw remittance	200	22.5
Remitters being too busy to send money	179	20.2
Limited financial institutions in the area	178	20.1
Poor communications from intermediaries	54	6.1
High transaction costs (for both senders and receivers)	17	1.9
Total	887	100.0

Multiple responses

Influence of Remittances on Adaptation

For Table 15.4, respondents were asked to indicate in order of importance the adaptation strategies implemented on their farms. Consequently, provided a general overview of the adaptation strategies respondents deemed important without remittance. The study also examined the influence of remittance on adaptation. A Rank Order Logit (ORL) regression was employed in examining the influence remittance on adaptation. The ORL model was developed based on the adaptation practices ranked by the ASI. The ASI offered an opportunity for respondents to rank their most preferred adaptation practices in the order of importance. Adequate information can be obtained if respondents are asked to rank the set of alternatives (Doherty and Clayton 2011; Stock and Watson 2012). In statistical terms, the preferences can then be estimated more efficiently. In a situation where respondents are asked to select their preferred option out of a set of presented alternatives, appropriate estimation choice would have been a standard discrete model, like the multinomial logit model. However, it is empirically established that more information can be obtained from a respondent when asked to give a complete ranking of all presented alternatives. Moreover, Hill and Jones (2014) indicate that when a dependent variable has more than two categories and the values have a meaningful sequential order where a value is indeed "higher" than the previous one, then an ORL model is the most appropriate.

The model predicted a 64 percent variation of the explanatory variable (remittance) on the outcome variable (adaptation practices). This implies that holding all other things constant, the probability of farmers engaging in climate change adaptation given remittance is 64 percent. More specifically, remittance positively predicted off-farm jobs ($0.19 = \rho$), implying that respondents are 19 percent likely to engage in off-farm jobs with an increase in remittance. Remittance also positively correlated irrigation farming ($0.18 = \rho$), cultivation of improved crop varieties ($0.17 = \rho$), and use of compost/animal manure ($0.14 = \rho$). An inverse relationship was established for Indexed-Based Insurance ($-0.12 = \rho$) and no association observed for alternating planting dates and mixed cropping (Table 15.7).

As shown on Table 15.8, using multinomial logit regression, the Nagelkerke R^2, Cox, Snell, and McFadden R-square values show that the multinomial logit model was fitted and remittance significantly predicted respondents' share of income spent on adaptation. Multinomial logistic regression is used to predict categorical placement in or the probability of

Table 15.7 Influence of remittance on adaptation practices

	Predictor variable (remittance)		
Adaptation practices (outcome)	*Coefficient (ק)*	*P value*	*S.E*
Off-farm jobs	0.19	0.00**	0.02
Irrigation farming	0.18	0.00**	0.03
Cultivation of improved crop varieties	0.17	0.00**	0.05
Use of compost/animal manure	0.14	0.00**	0.02
Crop rotation	0.10	0.02*	0.03
Index-Based Insurance (IBI)	-0.12	0.00*	0.07
Backyard gardening	0.90	0.05*	0.04
Afforestation	0.13	0.04*	0.05
Residue management	0.09	0.04*	0.03
Alternating planting dates	0.16	0.90	0.09
Mixed cropping	-0.16	0.90	0.08
Base category	Land fallowing		
Chi square, degree of freedom, *p*-value	chi square = 374.89, df = 2, p = 0.00,		
Log-Likelihood	R^2 = 0.64		
	5867.30		

$**p < 0.01$, $*p < 0.05$

Table 15.8 Amount of remittance received influences the share of income spent on adaptation

	Share of income spent on adaptation (USD)								
Explanatory variable	*100–300*			*301–600*			*601–900*		
Remittance	Exp (β)	Wald	P	Exp (β)	Wald	P	Exp (β)	Wald	P
	2.85	20.84	0.04*	2.65	18.50	0.03*	1.92	14.4	0.05*
Base category	>901								

*Significant at 5 percent level; Nagelkerke's R-squared = 0.321; Cox and Snell's R-squared = 0.311 and McFadden's R-squared = 0.224

category membership on a dependent variable based on multiple independent variables (Allison 2014; Hilbe 2011). The independent variables can either be dichotomous (i.e., binary) or continuous (i.e., interval or ratio in scale). Multinomial logistic regression is a simple extension of binary logistic regression that allows for more than two categories of the dependent or outcome variable. Unlike binary logistic regression, multinomial logistic regression uses maximum likelihood estimation to evaluate the probability of categorical membership (Al-Mudhafer 2014). In testing for the influence of remittance on the share of income spent on adaptation, the multinomial logit was appropriate as the independent variable (remittance) was continuous whereas share of income spent on adaptation was categorized (USD100–300, 301–600, and 601–900). The basic assumption developed indicates that receiving remittances would be a determining factor in the amount of money farmers are willing to spend on adaptation. The model showed that respondents are 28 percent likely to spend USD100–300 of their share of income on adaptation given that there is an increase in remittance ($\beta = 2.85$). Similarly, the model predicted a 26 percent and a 19 percent likelihood of spending between USD301–600 and USD601–900 respectively of the share of income on adaptation given an increase in remittance.

Discussion

Climate change risks are profound and evidential rather than perceptual (Luís et al. 2018; Hu et al. 2017; IPCC 2015). Literature shows that climate change is associated with negative impacts on the natural environment, society, and the physical and psychological health of individuals (Huang et al. 2018; Descheemaeker et al. 2017; IPCC 2015; Doherty and Clayton 2011). The majority of respondents in this study ascribed a change in the climate as manifested in decreased precipitation, increased temperatures, and prolonged drought. This climate cognition is not out of the ordinary because the mercurial nature of the Sudan Savanna and the Guinea Savanna zones have made farmers conversant and knowledgeable about the vagaries of weather conditions in the area (Antwi-Agyei et al. 2012). The finding does not depart substantially from Ndamani and Watanabe (2016), who found that 87 percent of respondents perceived a decrease in rainfall, with 82 percent perceiving an increase in temperature in parts of the study area. Climate change is undoubtedly affecting agriculture and the entire agricultural value chain. Smallholder farmers in developing countries are at the serious core of this extreme change due to their weak adaptive capacity (Liu et al. 2016; Mulatu Debalke 2011). The concomitant effect is low productivity and impoverishment of more households. Empirical studies (Descheemaeker et al. 2017; IPCC 2015; Laube et al. 2012) further show that higher temperatures and less rainfall have resulted in reduced yield in Ghana and other African countries. The findings of this study point to a similar direction as it was established that the major effect of climate change was low productivity. Smallholder farmers were further devastated by inadequate feed and water for livestock and in critical situations abandoned their farms. Indeed, climate-induced water stress has caught up with many farmers due to the drying up of rivers, streams, and underground aquifers (Kundzewicz et al. 2018; Smerdon 2017). Consequently, livestock, which is a valuable household livelihood asset and supplements the needs of many, is at a crossroads as farmers can no longer engage in this lucrative venture with ardent interest (Descheemaeker et al. 2017).

The introduction and integration of sound adaptive strategies has been identified as a necessary pathway to mitigating climate change effects (Ndamani and Watanabe 2016). Even though Mulatu Debalke (2011) is of the view that a minority of smallholder farmers are vehement implementers of adaptation strategies, the dividend of these strategies cannot be underestimated. Using ASI to assess the order of importance of adaptation practices implemented by farmers knowingly or unknowingly (autonomous and planned), backyard gardening, cultivation of drought-tolerant crops, and mixed cropping were ranked as the top three most important. Traditionally, backyard gardening has long been a practice associated with the people of the area (Yiridoe and Anchirinah 2005). Having larger and flourishing farmlands elsewhere did not discourage farmers from backyard gardening (Danso et al. 2004). Accordingly, this was used to usher farmers into the harvesting season as they start consuming the produce from their backyard gardens before venturing into their main farmlands (Yiridoe and Anchirinah 2005). In recent happennings, backyard gardening is used more as a risk management strategy as farmers who proclaimed they are confronted with climate change see the need for backyard gardening to support their main farmlands as confirmed in the FGDs. The study also found that vulnerable groups including women and migrants build their livelihood mostly from backyard gardening due to limited access to land. Mixed cropping was also perceived as a risk management strategy as farmers felt that having multiple crops on a piece of land could save them from disappointment. "When one crop fail the other will not." Hence, farmers are unwilling to engage in only a single crop for a farming season. Simply, farmers adopted mixed cropping to reduce overall risk while expanding opportunities for farm profit, thus boosting their average income (Ndamani and Watanabe 2016; Uddin et al. 2014; Mulatu Debalke 2011). An interviewee stated:

> It is not advisable to keep one farmland. Farmers engage in backyard gardening to get more yield to feed their families. Farmers get less produce due to the harsh weather conditions, so it is better not to waste time and walk longer distances to bring home nothing. Mixed cropping helps to give alternative produce if other crops fail.

Justifiably, the pervasive decline in precipitation, prolonged drought, and increased temperature could be reasons for farmers engaging in the cultivation of drought-tolerant crops, as is corroborated by the significant rating of the practice (Uddin et al. 2014). Weather Index-Based Insurance (WIBI) was ranked the least important adaptation strategy, most likely due to the significant lack of good management of financial institutions in the country underwriting agriculture and offering farm-based insurance products. Also, poor deployment of technical assistance and low levels of farmer awareness about the use of agricultural insurance explain its low adoption (Ndamani and Watanabe 2016; Uddin et al. 2014).

Studies have indicated a certain unanimity regarding the medium-to long-term impact of climate change (Fosu-Mensah et al. 2012; Apata 2011; Mertz et al. 2009), which has driven a plethora of adaptation strategies to militate against climate-induced effects (Nhemachena and Hassan 2007). The novelty and nuance related to this study is the integral role of remittance in adaptation. The twenty-first century has seen remittance represent one of the key issues in economic development (Inoue 2018; Acosta et al. 2007; Adams Jr 2004) by reducing the level, depth, and severity of poverty in most developing countries (Vacaflores 2017; Akobeng 2016), increasing incomes (Oduro and Boakye-Yiadom 2014; Adams and Cuecuecha 2013), and smoothening household consumption (Schiantarelli 2005). A study by Adams and Cuecuecha (2013) using a two-stage multinomial logit model revealed that increased remittance provides available working capital for small-scale entrepreneurs. Similarly, Bang et al. (2016) established that a rise in remittances increased self-employment and private sector investment in Kenya. The increase in remittance positively predicting engagement in off-farm jobs as found in this study relates to findings of (Inoue 2018; Bang et al. 2016; Akobeng 2016; Oduro and Boakye-Yiadom 2014; Adams and Cuecuecha 2013). It can be inferred that smallholder farmers are beginning to look beyond farming, which is seen as mundane, due to the extreme effects of climate change. Therefore, given available remittances, they are more likely to delve into other income-generating activities outside of the farm, which is contrary to what most of the farmers currently use remittances for (such as buying chemicals or fertilizer) as seen in Table 15.6. This could insinuate that their current state of remittance is low (USD369 on average per annum) as shown in Table 15.5, thereby committing some of it to agricultural output with the aim of sustaining their farms. The objective nonetheless is to divert into other economic sectors and/or activities should there be an increase in remittances. An interviewee stated:

> If I (interviewee) get more money from my family outside [(remittance)], I want to buy a motor-king (tricycle) that will be used to fetch water, carry goods and passengers at a fee. I also want to open a provision shop where I will sell provisions to make more money. Investing money on the farm is useless these days because the rains will not come and everything will be destroyed.

Apart from the harsh weather conditions under which farmers work, the respondents acknowledged limited access to land, the unattractiveness of farming as a trade, the seasonality of farming, and poor farm income as the reasons why they would divert their remittance into other economic activities they consider attractive and economically rewarding and that can be operated all year round. One interviewee said:

> Unlike the past, farmers currently engaged in farming have less resources. Those doing other businesses are better off economically and are able to complete their houses. However, those into only farming are seasonal workers, and unable to catch up with basic responsibilities required of every responsible person.

Remittances highly influenced irrigation farming and the cultivation of improved crop varieties. Farming cannot be alienated from the livelihood and culture of rural folks. Some hold it in high esteem and as a valuable inheritance passed on by generations which needs to be protected and enhanced (Al-Hassan and Poulton 2009; Braimoh 2009). Despite being challenged by current trends in weather events, which is motivating farmers to wanting to engage in off-farm jobs, this might be done concurrently as respondents are more likely to buy irrigation equipment and drought-tolerant seeds to augment their farms given increased remittances (Tables 15.6 and 15.7). An increase in remittances, however, inversely predicted Indexed-Based Insurance (IBI). IBI is an innovative approach to insurance provision that pays out benefits or compensates clients on the basis of a predetermined index (e.g., rainfall level or temperature variation) for the loss of assets and investments resulting from weather and catastrophic events (Conradt et al. 2015).

The expectation is that when farmers' income increases, they will exhibit a higher potential to take up IBI (Carter et al. 2016; Conradt et al. 2015). However, the inverse was found, which could be attributed to the fact that remittance itself is a form of insurance against shocks. For instance, Adams and Cuecuecha (2013) stated that remittance is a strong insurance policy for rural and poorer households to mitigate weather-related risks. Remittances may lessen credit constraints because a stable stream of remittance income may make households more creditworthy in the eyes of formal sector financial institutions (Adams and Cuecuecha 2013; Schiantarelli 2005). Lucas and Stark (1985) found that remittances to Botswana increased with the extent of drought in the remitters' place of origin and that the responsiveness of remittance levels to drought was greater for households with more drought-sensitive assets. As found in this study, remittance also significantly predicted respondents' share of income spent on adaptation. Respondents were more likely to spend between USD100–300 of their income on adaptation, which arguably might be insufficient to enhance a farmer's adaptive capacity considering the frequency and magnitude of current climatic events.

Conclusions

Several studies have pointed to the potentially valuable complement of remittances to broad-based development and economic growth. In a disaggregate milieu, this study examined the potential of remittances in financing climate change adaptation at the local level. Using ASI analysis to assess general adaptation strategies of smallholder farmers, it was discovered that farmers rated backyard gardening, cultivation of drought-tolerant crops, mixed cropping, off-farm jobs, and residue management as the most important adaptation strategies. On average, a farmer receives USD369 of remittance per annum, which is channeled into buying chemicals or fertilizer to use on farms, acquiring extra food to supplement family needs, buying drought-tolerant maize seeds, and investing in children's education. Receiving remittances was cropped with challenges including mobile network problems, traveling longer distances to redraw remittance money, limited financial institutions, and poor communication from intermediaries. The ORL model predicted that an increase in remittances is significantly associated with off-farm jobs, irrigation farming, cultivation of improved crop varieties, use of compost/animal manure, and crop rotation. However, it inversely predicted IBI. Similarly, a multinomial logit model showed that farmers are highly likely to invest USD100–300 of their income in adaptation with increased remittances.

References

Acosta, P., Fajnzylber, P., & Lopez, J. H. (2007). The Impact of Remittances on Poverty and Human Capital: Evidence from Latin American Household Surveys (Vol. 4247). World Bank Publications.

Adams Jr, R. H. (2004). Remittances and Poverty in Guatemala. Policy Research Working Papers. The World Bank.

Adams, R. H., & Cuecuecha, A. (2013). The Impact of Remittances on Investment and Poverty in Ghana. *World Development*, *50*, 24–40.

Adu, K. K. (2018). The Paradox of the Right to Information Law in Africa. *Government Information Quarterly*, *35*(4), 669–674.

African Development Bank (AFDB) (2011) The Cost of Adaptation to Climate Change in Africa, https://www.afdb.org/fileadmin/uploads/afdb/Documents/Project-and-Operations/Cost%20of%20Adaptation%20in%20Africa.pdf

Akobeng, E. (2016). Out of Inequality and Poverty: Evidence for the Effectiveness of Remittances in Sub-Saharan Africa. *The Quarterly Review of Economics and Finance*, *60*, 207–223.

Al-Hassan, R., & Poulton, C. (2009). Agriculture and Social Protection in Ghana. FAC Working Paper 09. Future Agricultures Consortium.

Allison, P. D. (2014, March). Measures of fit for logistic regression [Conference Presentation]: Proceedings of the SAS global forum 2014 conference, 1–13.

Al-Mudhafer, W. J. (2014, March). Multinomial logistic regression for Bayesian estimation of vertical facies modeling in heterogeneous sandstone reservoirs [Conference Presentation]. Offshore Technology Conference-Asia:

Antwi-Agyei, P., Fraser, E. D., Dougill, A. J., Stringer, L. C., & Simelton, E. (2012). Mapping the Vulnerability of Crop Production to Drought in Ghana Using Rainfall, Yield and Socioeconomic Data. *Applied Geography*, *32*(2), 324–334.

Apata, T. (2011). Factors Influencing the Perception and Choice of Adaptation Measures to Climate Change among Farmers in Nigeria.

Bahadir, B., Chatterjee, S., & Lebesmuehlbacher, T. (2018). The Macroeconomic Consequences of Remittances. *Journal of International Economics*, *111*, 214–232.

Bang, J. T., Mitra, A., & Wunnava, P. V. (2016). Do Remittances Improve Income Inequality? An Instrumental Variable Quantile Analysis of the Kenyan Case. *Economic Modelling, 58*, 394–402.

Bendandi, B., & Pauw, P. (2016). Remittances for Adaptation: An 'Alternative Source' of International Climate finance? In A. Milan, B. Schraven, K. Warner & N. Cascone (Eds.), Migration, *Risk Management and Climate Change: Evidence and Policy Responses* (pp. 195–211). Springer.

Bloomberg (2013). Africa Faces 350 Billion a Year Adaptation Cost as Planet Warms, https://www.bloomberg.com/news/articles/2013-11-19/africa-faces-350-billion-a-year-adaptation-cost-as-planet-warms.

Bodansky, D. (2010). The Copenhagen Climate Change Conference: A Postmortem. *American Journal of International Law, 104*(2), 230–240.

Boone, C. (2017). Sons of the Soil Conflict in Africa: Institutional Determinants of Ethnic Conflict over Land. *World Development, 96*, 276–293.

Braimoh, A. K. (2009). Agricultural Land-Use Change during Economic Reforms in Ghana. *Land Use Policy, 26*(3), 763–771.

Buchner, B., & Wilkinson, J. (2015). 33 Pros and Cons of Alternative Sources of Climate Change Financing and Prospects for 'Unconventional Finance'. In S. Barrett, C. Carraro & J. de Melo (Eds.), *Towards a Workable and Effective Climate Regime* (pp. 483–496). CEPR Press.

Bui, T. T. N., Le, T. T. N., & Daly, K. J. (2015). Microlevel Impacts of Remittances on Household Behavior: Viet Nam Case Study. *Emerging Markets Review, 25*, 176–190.

Carter, M. R., Cheng, L., & Sarris, A. (2016). Where and How Index Insurance Can Boost the Adoption of Improved Agricultural Technologies. *Journal of Development Economics, 118*, 59–71.

Conradt, S., Finger, R., & Spörri, M. (2015). Flexible Weather Index-Based Insurance Design. *Climate Risk Management, 10*, 106–117.

Couharde, C., & Generoso, R. (2015). The Ambiguous Role of Remittances in West African Countries Facing Climate Variability. *Environment and Development Economics, 20*(4), 493–515.

Danso, G., Cofie, O., Annang, L., Obuobie, E., & Keraita, B. (2004). *Gender and Urban Agriculture: The Case of Accra, Ghana*. Resource Centre on Urban Agriculture and Forestry (RUAF).

Descheemaeker, K., Zijlstra, M., Masikati, P., Crespo, O., & Tui, S. H. K. (2017). Effects of Climate Change and Adaptation on the Livestock Component of Mixed Farming Systems: A Modelling Study from Semi-Arid Zimbabwe. *Agricultural Systems*, 159, 282–295.

Devkota, J. (2014). Impact of migrants' remittances on poverty and inequality in Nepal. *Forum of International Development Studies, 44*, 36–53.

Doherty, T. J., & Clayton, S. (2011). The Psychological Impacts of Global Climate Change. *American Psychologist, 66*(4), 265–276.

Food and Agriculture Organisation (FAO) (2010). The state of food insecurity in the world 2010. www.fao.org/docrep

Fosu-Mensah, B. Y., Vlek, P. L., & MacCarthy, D. S. (2012). Farmers' Perception and Adaptation to Climate Change: A Case Study of Sekyedumase District in Ghana. *Environment, Development and Sustainability, 14*(4), 495–505.

Fridahl, M., & Linnér, B. O. (2016). Perspectives on the Green Climate Fund: Possible Compromises on Capitalization and Balanced Allocation. *Climate and Development, 8*(2), 105–109.

Hilbe, J. M. (2011). Logistic Regression. *International encyclopedia of statistical science, 1*, 15–32.

Hill, D. W., & Jones, Z. M. (2014). An empirical evaluation of explanations for state repression. *American Political Science Review, 108*(3), 661–687.

Henri, P. A. O. (2019). Natural Resources Curse: A Reality in Africa. *Resources Policy, 63*, 101406.

Hove, M., & Gweme, T. (2018). Women's Food Security and Conservation Farming in Zaka District-Zimbabwe. *Journal of Arid Environments, 149*, 18–29.

Hu, S., Jia, X., Zhang, X., Zheng, X., & Zhu, J. (2017). How Political Ideology Affects Climate Perception: Moderation Effects of Time Orientation and Knowledge. *Resources, Conservation and Recycling*, 127, 124–131.

Huang, S., Lv, L., Zhu, J., Li, Y., Tao, H., & Wang, P. (2018). Extending Growing Period is Limited to Offsetting Negative Effects of Climate Changes on Maize Yield in the North China Plain. *Field Crops Research, 215*, 66–73.

Inoue, T. (2018). Financial Development, Remittances, and Poverty Reduction: Empirical Evidence from a Macroeconomic Viewpoint. *Journal of Economics and Business, 96*, 59–68.

International Development Finance Club (IDFC) (2014). "Mapping Of Green Finance Delivered by IDFC Members In 2013." IDFC supported by Ecofys.

International Energy Agency (IEA). (2013). "RD & D Budget." IEA. http://wds.iea.org/

Intergovernmental Panel on Climate Change (IPCC) (2007). Summary for Policy Makers. *Climate Change: Synthesis Report.* https://www.ipcc.ch/pdf/assessment-report/ar4/wg1/ar4-wg1-spm.pdf.

Intergovernmental Panel on Climate Change (IPCC) (2014). Summary for Policy Makers. *Climate Change: Synthesis Report.* https://www.ipcc.ch/pdf/assessment-report/ar5/wg3/ipcc_wg3_ar5_summary-for-policymakers.pdf.

Intergovernmental Panel on Climate Change (IPCC) (2015). Summary Report for Policy Makers. Final Report. https://www.ipcc.ch/site/assets/uploads/2018/02/ar4_syr_spm.pdf

Kalabamu, F. T. (2019). Land Tenure Reforms and Persistence of Land Conflicts in Sub-Saharan Africa: The Case of Botswana. *Land Use Policy, 81*, 337–345.

Kamer, L. (2022). Number of reported weather, climate, and water related disasters in Africa from 1970 to 2019. Accessed on 25/06/2023 at https://www.statista.com/statistics/1307332/number-of-climate-disasters-in-africa/

Keshavarz, M., & Karami, E. (2014). Farmers' Decision-Making Process under Drought. *Journal of Arid Environments, 108*, 43–56.

Kissinger, G., Gupta, A., Mulder, I., & Unterstell, N. (2019). Climate Financing Needs in the Land Sector under the Paris Agreement: An Assessment of Developing Country Perspectives. *Land Use Policy, 83*, 256–269.

Kundzewicz, Z. W., Krysanova, V., Benestad, R. E., Hov, Ø., Piniewski, M., & Otto, I. M. (2018). Uncertainty in Climate Change Impacts on Water Resources. *Environmental Science & Policy, 79*, 1–8.

Laube, W., Schraven, B., & Awo, M. (2012). Smallholder Adaptation to Climate Change: Dynamics and Limits in Northern Ghana. *Climatic Change, 111*(3-4), 753–774.

Liu, T., Ma, Z., Huffman, T., Ma, L., Jiang, H., & Xie, H. (2016). Gaps in Provincial Decision-Maker's Perception and Knowledge of Climate Change Adaptation in China. *Environmental Science & Policy, 58*, 41–51.

Lucas, R. E., & Stark, O. (1985). Motivations to Remit: Evidence from Botswana. *Journal of Political Economy, 93*(5), 901–918.

Luís, S., Vauclair, C. M., & Lima, M. L. (2018). Raising Awareness of Climate Change Causes? Cross-National Evidence for the Normalization of Societal Risk Perception of Climate Change. *Environmental Science & Policy, 80*, 74–81.

Makuvaro, V., Walker, S., Masere, T. P., & Dimes, J. (2018). Smallholder Farmer Perceived Effects of Climate Change on Agricultural Productivity and Adaptation Strategies. *Journal of Arid Environments, 152*, 75–82.

Marke, A., & Sylvester, B. (2018). Decoding the Current Global Climate finance Architecture. In *Transforming Climate Finance and Green Investment with Blockchains* (pp. 35–59). Academic Press.

Mertz, O., Mbow, C., Reenberg, A., & Diouf, A. (2009). Farmers' Perceptions of Climate Change and Agricultural Adaptation Strategies in Rural Sahel. *Environmental Management, 43*(5), 804–816.

Ministry of Food and Agriculture (MoFa) (2014). Agriculture in Northern Ghana. http://www.ghanadistricts.com/districts

Mulatu Debalke, N. (2011). *Determinants of Farmers' Preference for Adaptation Strategies to Climate Change: Evidence from North Shoa Zone of Amhara Region Ethiopia*. Munich Personal RePEc Archive. https://mpra.ub.uni-muenchen.de/48753/1/MPRA_paper_48753.pdf

Musah-Surugu, I. J., Ahenkan, A., Bawole, J. N., & Darkwah, S. A. (2018). Migrants' remittances: A complementary source of financing adaptation to climate change at the local level in Ghana. *International Journal of Climate Change Strategies and Management, 10*(1), 179–196.

Ndamani, F., & Watanabe, T. (2016). Determinants of Farmers' Adaptation to Climate Change: A Micro Level Analysis in Ghana. Scientia Agricola, 73(3), 201–208.

Nhemachena, C., & Hassan, R. (2007). *Micro-Level Analysis of Farmers' Adaption to Climate Change in Southern Africa*. International Food Policy Research Institute.

Oduro, A. D., & Boakye-Yiadom, L. (2014). Gender, Migrant Remittances and Asset Acquisition in Ghana. *Ghana Social Science Journal, 11*(1), 1–25.

Organization for Economic Cooperation and Development (OECD) (2016). Project-Level Data for Every Climate-Related Development Finance Project in 2013–14. www.oecd.org/dac/stats/climate-change.htm

Pauw, W. P. (2015). Not a Panacea: Private-Sector Engagement in Adaptation and Adaptation Finance in Developing Countries. *Climate Policy, 15*(5), 583–603.

Randazzo, T., & Piracha, M. (2019). Remittances and Household Expenditure Behaviour: Evidence from Senegal. *Economic Modelling, 79*, 141–153.

Ratha, D. (2007). Leveraging remittances for development. *Policy Brief, 3*(11), 1–16.

Schiantarelli, F. (2005). *Global Economic Prospects 2006: Economic Implications of Remittances and Migration*. The World Bank.

Smerdon, B. D. (2017). A Synopsis of Climate Change Effects on Groundwater Recharge. *Journal of Hydrology, 555*. https://doi.org/10.1016/j.jhydrol.2017.09.047

Stern, N. (2008). The Economics of Climate Change. *American Economic Review, 98*(2), 1–37.

Stock, J. H., & Watson, M. W. (2012). Generalized shrinkage methods for forecasting using many predictors. *Journal of Business & Economic Statistics, 30*(4), 481–493.

Tsegaye, D., Vedeld, P., & Moe, S. R. (2013). Pastoralists and Livelihoods: A Case Study from Northern Afar, Ethiopia. *Journal of Arid Environments, 91*, 138–146.

Uddin, M. N., Bokelmann, W., & Entsminger, J. S. (2014). Factors Affecting Farmers' Adaptation Strategies to Environmental Degradation and Climate Change Effects: A Farm Level Study in Bangladesh. *Climate, 2*(4), 223–241.

United Nations Environment Programme (UNEP) (2015). Adaptation Finance Gap. http://web.unep.org/sites/default/files/gapreport

United Nations Environment Programme (2022). Adaptation Gap Report 2022: Too Little, Too Slow – Climate adaptation failure puts world at risk. Nairobi. Accesses on 25/06/2023 at https://www.unep.org/adaptation-gap-report-2022

Vacaflores, D. E. (2017). Are Remittances Helping Lower Poverty and Inequality Levels in Latin America? *The Quarterly Review of Economics and Finance*, 68. https://doi.org/10.1016/j.qref.2017.09.001

Watkiss, P., Downing, T. E., & Dyszynski, J. (2010). *Adapt Cost Project: Analysis of the Economic Costs of Climate Change Adaptation in Africa*. UNEP.

World Bank (2019). Money Sent Home by Workers Now Largest Source of External Financing in Low- and Middle-Income Countries (excluding China). https://blogs.worldbank.org/opendata/money-sent-home-workers-now-largest-source-external-financing-low-and-middle-income

Yiridoe, E. K., & Anchirinah, V. M. (2005). Garden Production Systems and Food Security in Ghana: Characteristics of Traditional Knowledge and Management Systems. *Renewable Agriculture and Food Systems*, *20*(3), 168–180.

CHAPTER 16

Transnational Society in Light of Environmental Change

Lore Van Praag

Introduction

Migrants have always sent money, ideas, and goods to their countries and regions of origin. However, the extent of these flows and the impact of such transnational practices have only come to the attention of policy makers in recent decades. These practices are mainly used to sustain people's livelihoods and investments and have a significant potential to reduce poverty in the receiving countries (De Haas 2005; Carling 2020). This growing interest in remittances is partly derived from innovations that have allowed statisticians to more precisely calculate and document remittance flows and demonstrate their large contribution to national economies (Fagen 2006). This has led to a form of remittance euphoria (De Haas 2005) or a remittance mantra on the part of policy makers (Kapur 2004), who have used remittance policies to their own advantage or to assist international agents, directing their attention to the governance of remittances (e.g. Horst and

L. Van Praag (✉)
Erasmus School of Social and Behavioral Sciences, Erasmus Universiteit Rotterdam, Rotterdam, The Netherlands
e-mail: vanpraag@essb.eur.nl

S. Meyer, C. Ströhle (eds.), *Remittances as Social Practices and Agents of Change*,
https://doi.org/10.1007/978-3-030-81504-2_16

Van Hear 2002; Regan and Frank 2014). For example, despite the previous contribution of remittances to the rapid growth of the private sector in Somalia (Ahmed 2000), during the war on terror, remittance agencies were shut down, assets were confiscated, and telecommunication lines were cut for specific listed people or organizations that were suspected to have links with Osama Bin Laden (Horst and Van Hear 2002). This clearly shows how remittances and other transnational practices are subject to governance and are seen as potential resources to manage crises, wars, and transitioning environments. This is particularly relevant in countries currently in transitioning phases (e.g. from war to peace or in the process of decolonization) or still experiencing war, conflict, and crisis. Under such circumstances, migrants continue to send remittances to support, build up, and invest in their countries of origin long after other types of support and investment have ceased (Fagen 2006).

The idea that remittances might be used for development purposes has also entered the body of literature focusing on environmental change adaptation (Black et al. 2011a; IPCC 2014; McLeman and Gemenne 2018). To increase societal impact, scholars often borrow terminology and concepts, such as climate change adaptation, from general climate change policies in this field of research (e.g. IPCC 2014). Therefore, studies of transnational practices related to environmental change often lack the aspect of remittances, with the importance of other transnational practices for adapting to and mitigating environmental changes emphasized. In most cases, migration is framed as an adaptation strategy to deal with environmental change and is then seen as one solution for dealing with the changing natural environment.

In the following, I will first provide an overview of this migration as adaptation discourse, with the aim of giving remittances a prominent place in the development of adaptation strategies dealing with environmental change. Second, I will discuss how remittances relate to environmental change, and how this adds to the development of a transnational society that facilitates adaptation to environmental change, increases knowledge-sharing on environmental change, and alters perceptions of environmental change. Special attention will be given to how transnational practices contribute to the circulation of ideas, knowledge, and an increasing awareness of environmental change, which is a necessary condition for the development of adaptation strategies for dealing with such change. Finally, I will reflect on the potential and the pitfalls of transnational practices when dealing with environmental change.

First, however, some notes on terminology are needed. In this chapter, the concept of environmental change encompasses all types of environmental change, including that linked to climate change and disasters. This avoids confusion about whether environmental change is attributable to climate change or not. I will only refer to climate change when explicit references are made by other authors or in the prevailing discourses. Additionally, the term remittances here not only includes money flows but also the circulation of ideas and knowledge, political views, norms, and values (Carling 2014; Faist 2007). To avoid conceptual confusion, I will explicitly refer to the distribution of human capital with regard to knowledge-sharing when discussing topics such as climate change discourses and adaptation strategies, and to social capital when referring to the establishment, expansion, or maintenance of particular social networks and ties (Eckstein 2006).

Migration as an Adaptation Strategy for Dealing with Environmental Change

In the 1980s, scholars and policy makers became increasingly aware that the effects of environmental change were irreversible, arguing that these effects would inevitably force people to migrate or be displaced. Although environmental change has always been a driver of migration, scholars, and policy makers now expect increasing mass displacement and voluntary migration in the coming years (IPCC 2014; McLeman and Gemenne 2018). However, according to a migration as adaptation discourse, migration might also be seen as a solution for dealing with such environmental change. More specifically, migration might reduce the demographic pressures on the affected region and diminish the vulnerabilities of social and/or biological systems to environmental change. For instance, as many large cities are located by the seaside and are therefore vulnerable to coastal flooding due to rising sea levels (Hanson et al. 2011; Huong and Pathirana 2013), reducing the number of inhabitants living there could facilitate the reorganization of the given city in light of these changes. Furthermore, it may limit inequalities in the exposure to risk through the development of adaptation strategies. The latter might be done by considering local organization structures, cultures, environmental hazards, and impacts combined to define a specific adaptive capacity.

Proponents of the migration as adaptation discourse place much importance on the role of remittances in the development of adaptation strategies other than ongoing migration from the region in order to deal with environmental change and its adverse impact on people's lives. Diaspora communities and migrants already living abroad are especially suited to develop and support alternative adaptation strategies, given their familiarity with local organization structures, cultures, and environmental changes, as well as the hazards in their regions of origin. Consequently, remittances that could help deal with environmental change might be increasingly shared (knowledge), sent (money), and discussed (ideas). In turn, these remittances might influence the need to migrate, have an impact on the adaptation strategies used to deal with environmental change, and affect how people categorize the drivers of their migration trajectories. In doing so, such transnational practices might entirely transform the relationship between environmental change and migration, and the migrant diaspora might become a real transformative agent in the region of origin (Black et al. 2011a, 2011b; Gemenne 2010; Gemenne and Blocher 2016, 2017).

In this regard, it makes sense to apply a transnational perspective to the study of the relationship between environmental change and migration. The migration as adaptation discourse offers an interesting line of thought, as remittances sent through migrant networks are expected to increase the resilience of local communities and people's agency with respect to environmental change (Methmann and Oels 2015). Transnational practices and migration could contribute to innovative approaches to the development of countries/regions in response to environmental change—especially through the sending/receiving of remittances.

A conceptual framework developed by Adger et al. (2002) proposes that both emigration and immigration make communities more socially resilient and enable them to deal with external shocks, such as sudden weather events and slow-onset environmental changes (see also Bayala in this volume). Emigration, immigration, and the environment all impact each other. This relationship is characterized by constant feedback loops in which the social resilience of communities plays a mediating role. On the one hand, emigration reduces direct consumption and pressures on the local environment, which may reduce unsustainable resource use. Emigration also results in higher incomes and linkages through remittances, allowing more space for investments. On the other hand, immigration may lead to more consumption, which may jeopardize the sustainable use of resources. Nonetheless, despite increasing pressure on the local environment, immigration could introduce a new knowledge base and increase the human capital of a community, expanding its available networks. This may lead to more innovation, technological development, and a widening of the social capital of a community. This feedback loop between migration, immigration, and the environment has consequences for poverty, health, inequality, risk-spreading, and the livelihood options of communities.

Remittances as such reduce dependency on the environment by encouraging the search for and investment in alternative ways to sustain one's livelihood (such as through education, training, or investment in alternative businesses). For example, remittances might lead to the sharing of and investment in more human capital through greater levels of enrollment in education. These investments in human capital diversify household incomes, reducing reliance on sectors sensitive to environmental change and increasing household savings and investments. Moreover, human capital might not only reorient people's careers and diversify household incomes, but also increase human capital and knowledge-sharing concerning environmental issues and adaptation strategies.

Such knowledge transfers may occur through both emigration and immigration, and could directly increase the awareness of environmental change discourses and knowledge of adaptation strategies for dealing with environmental change (Adger et al. 2002). Recipients of remittances might request specific kinds of remittances (Carling 2014) to deal with an environmental issue they are confronting (such as investment in solar panels, water pumps, local projects dealing with climate change mitigation, housing, etc.). This could also further knowledge-sharing about and awareness of local environmental issues and potential solutions. Furthermore, the expansion of social networks through migration might increase access to information and technological knowhow (Adger et al. 2002), with remittances leading to more investments in agriculture or aquaculture, for example, and other sectors that are susceptible to the adverse impacts of environmental change (see also De Haas 2005; Taylor et al. 1996). An example of such practice was found in fieldwork conducted in Morocco (Van Praag et al. 2021). During this study, a bottom-up project in Tinghir offered an interesting example of what this knowledge transfer could look like. In this newly set up project, an emigrant currently living and working in Spain stayed in contact with his former school colleague still living in Tinghir. Their interactions inspired them to set up a project in a neighborhood in Tinghir the design of which includes ongoing societal trends and issues. The project aims to tackle youth unemployment and emigration, changing standards of living, working with obsolete and polluting materials and hereditary rights, as well as with growing desertification. This knowledge transfer is accompanied by financial remittances to put its ideas into practice. The project aims to mitigate climate change by installing solar panels and a greenhouse to grow specific crops and to make the community more socially resilient to ongoing climate changes. The knowledge on climate change was adapted by members of the community to the local climatic, social, and economic context. For instance, alternatives were sought to prevent young people from migrating elsewhere and to circumvent current land rules and policies. This exchange inspired the project members to add additional social objectives to the project and to expand the project's objectives. This example demonstrates how knowledge transfers work in both directions and inspire mitigation and adaptation strategies for dealing with environmental changes (see Van Praag et al. 2021). Finally, immigration could introduce context-specific factors and nuances in ongoing scientific debates on climate change in the reception society, debates which are often too generic, and which consequently complicate the development of local and differentiated climate change knowledge and solutions. The actual impact of climate change on a certain region may vary depending on local geography, system flexibility, resources, and so on. These context-specific climate changes and impacts need to be considered together with the adaptive capacity of the region by consulting local stakeholders and sector-specific experts (Bierbaum and Stults 2013). Apart from these context-specific climatic factors, cultural and religious factors also need to be taken into account, as they matter in how people adapt to climate change. For example, in a study by Mertz et al. (2010) conducted in the Sudano-Sahelian zone of West Africa, 'prayer' was indicated as one of the most important ways of dealing with environmental change, aside from migration.

The model proposed by Adger et al. (2002) discusses how migration could generally contribute to the development of adaptation strategies for dealing with environmental change. The following discusses two points that need further consideration to better understand the potential and also the pitfalls of using transnational practices to adapt to environmental change. The first concerns the understanding, awareness, and circulation of ideas on environmental issues. The second concerns the importance and structures of migration histories, practices, and cultures. These points of attention are relevant when studying the potential of transnational practices, as there is a large variation in such practices in relation to the conditions in which remittances are sent and received, to specific remittance sending patterns, and to the frequency and quantity of remittances sent (Faist 2007; Carling 2008a, 2014; Isaakyan and Triandafyllidou 2017).

Understanding, Awareness, and Circulation of Ideas on Environmental Issues

Remittances occupy a central place in the growing body of research on transnational societies. Sometimes, distinct forms of remittances are distinguished (such as financial and social remittances), which may be conceptually useful to understanding the importance of remittances in dealing with environmental change. The concept of social remittances (Levitt 1998; Levitt and Nyberg-Sørensen 2004; Boccagni and Decimo 2013, Vari-Lavoisier 2020) was introduced to describe the ways migration has contributed to the diffusion of knowledge, ideas, norms, and values. Social remittances should not be seen as entirely separate from financial remittances, with this distinction mainly used to emphasize that remittances are more than just money flows (Carling 2014). In this section, I will delve deeper into these social remittances by focusing on the circulation of ideas and knowledge that often accompanies money flows. This is especially important in the context of environmental change, because such flows are crucial in the development of policies and strategies for adapting to environmental change.

In Adger et al.'s model (2002), awareness of environmental change and adaptation strategies derives from knowledge-sharing between migrant networks and is thus a part of remittance transfers. In migrant networks, people can more readily discuss their understanding of environmental change and make each other aware of particular environmental/climate changes and the surrounding discourses. In this context, such information and dialogue could be especially enlightening, as not all parties may necessarily be aware of climate change and/or environmental issues, or refer to them using similar terms. By gradually becoming more familiar with environmental issues or distinct discourses on these matters, people can more easily and successfully develop adaptation strategies (De Longueville et al. 2020; Van Praag and Timmerman 2019; Van Praag et al. 2021). Developing an awareness of environmental/climate change and how this applies to the local context could thus be the first step toward a discussion of scientific and other discourses on this topic.

Too frequently, ongoing debates and adaptation/mitigation policies on environmental change assume that everyone perceives environmental change in a similar fashion (IPCC 2014; Van Praag and Timmerman 2019; Van Praag et al. 2021). This leads to a lack of inclusion of the views and agency of the people involved (Stern 2000; McLeman and Gemenne 2018; Khare and Khare 2006; Rigby 2016). At the same time, to develop inclusive local adaptation plans, to encourage people to implement and invest in innovative strategies, it is necessary that they are aware of ongoing climate change in particular, as it is important to understand how this accelerates all kinds of environmental change, leading to social tipping points, often jeopardizing sustainable livelihoods.

Thus, it is important that all the parties involved understand that environmental change and the associated risks are perceived differently across and even within cultures (Vedwan 2006; Mertz et al. 2009, 2010; Leclerc et al. 2013). These differences are further reinforced by perception biases concerning different types of environmental change, in which some changes are easier to acknowledge than others are (Howe et al. 2014; Few et al. 2017; De Longueville et al. 2020; Bele et al. 2014). For example, environmental change is especially acknowledged when it affects people's own livelihood activities (Bele et al. 2014; Howe et al. 2014; Wodon and Liverani 2014; De Longueville et al. 2020). In many cases, this means that especially people working in agricultural production are aware of climate changes. For transnational communities, this often means that, if migrants have relatives conducting agricultural activities and/or living in rural areas, they are themselves also more familiar with climate changes in their regions of origin. However, this is not necessarily the case for all migrants. As for instance shown by Hut and Zickgraf (in Van Praag et al. 2021), migrants from the Democratic Republic of the Congo living in Belgium often come from more advantaged families and urban areas. Despite the large impact of climate changes in DR Congo, the livelihood activities of their migrant networks are not necessarily confronted with climate change, which reduces their awareness of climate change in their region of origin as well.

Therefore, to better conceptualize and prevent the disadvantageous effects of environmental change, additional sources of information are required that allow for a more comprehensive understanding of local and changing needs related to accelerating environmental change (Vedwan 2006; Mertz et al. 2009, 2010; Leclerc et al. 2013; Van Praag et al. 2021). Failing to include local people's views on and thoughts about their immediate natural environment impacts the way people respond to change and whether they actively develop adaptation strategies. As knowledge-sharing is a mutual process, both the senders and the receivers of remittances can play an active role in knowledge construction on environmental issues and the development of adaptation strategies (Carling 2014). For example, in my Moroccan fieldwork in Tinghir, I discovered that large migration flows occurred after World War Two, which also shaped remittance flows. People with migrant networks still receive remittances, but mainly for special occasions, religious festivities, or for a particular cause (such as training enrollment, surgery, house renovation, diesel pumps, etc.). Only when inhabitants of Tinghir and/or migrants themselves had set up a specific non-governmental association dealing with poverty, pollution, renovation of the sewer system, and so on, were remittances also spent on adaptation to climate change (such as solar panels for water pumps, trees, etc.).

In this regard, it could be argued that migrants could contribute and become transformative agents in their regions of origin and in the design and development of environmental policies, and they could do so in multiple ways. First, as noted by Isaakyan and Triandafyllidou (2017), transnationally mobile migrants in particular could serve as such transformative agents. These migrants are those "who travel frequently (more than once a year or more than three times in two years) between their place of origin (in North Africa, Asia, and Eastern and Central Europe) and their place of destination in the EU because they are involved in economic or civic activities in both places" (Isaakyan and Triandafyllidou 2017, pp. 2787–2788). Thus, being physically present and spending time in their regions of origin enable them to design, follow up, and implement projects and, more specifically, to circulate ideas, knowledge, and awareness of environmental issues. These migrants can learn more about local specificities, translate boundaries and cultural structures, and support policies that are better adjusted to the local needs and structures of their communities of origin.

Second, migrants could serve as translators and cultural mediators for both regions and the various discourses and debates involved. This is important, as the acquisition of knowledge relies on various learning methods, which can themselves shape people's perceptions of environmental change. Two main learning methods can be distinguished: the first involves direct, personal experience and the second relies on statistical evidence description (Weber 2010; Spence et al. 2011). This distinction might also include a differentiation between skills and tacit knowledge on the one hand and knowledge of the official discourses and statistics on environmental change and environmental migration on the other (Bremer et al. 2017). The outcomes of these learning methods are also affected by distinct cultural interpretations, religious beliefs, and local specificities (Van Praag et al. 2021). Given the specific local focus of the transmission of such remittances, including the circulation and sharing of ideas and knowledge, this entails a lengthy process that demands a lot of effort that is also tailored to the specific context.

Migration Histories, Practices, and Cultures

The second point of attention when considering the model of Adger et al. (2002) is that migration patterns, migration histories, the relationships between senders and receivers, the characteristics of both sending households/individuals and migrant networks, as well as the environments in which they all live need to be taken into account to develop an understanding of the role of remittances (Carling 2008a) in a changing natural environment. Environmental change has a different impact on different segments of a population living in an affected region. For example, people in wealthier groups, who are often affected by environmental change to a lesser extent, are often the first to migrate. This could lead to brain drain at both the national and regional levels in the country of origin (Stilwell et al. 2004). By contrast, the groups most vulnerable to environmental change often do not have the option to migrate or are only able to migrate to nearby villages or cities. Thus, people whose everyday livelihoods are most impacted by environmental change are more likely to migrate internally (Gemenne 2010; Black and Collyer 2014).

These differences in migration trajectories and possibilities are also reflected in people's abilities to send financial remittances to those left behind. The nature of knowledge-sharing and the circulation of divergent ideas concerning environmental change are also affected. Thus, the differential impact of environmental change on populations affects their ability to migrate or not. This has resulted in very specific migration trajectories and/or immobile groups who want to migrate but are unable to do so (McLeman and Gemenne 2018), which affect the potential of migrants to become transformative agents in dealing with environmental change and/or in developing adaptation strategies. Based on these differences in the ability to migrate, a distinction should also be made between internal and transnational migrants, and consequently internal and international remittances (Carling 2008b). Thus, the distance of the migration trajectory, and especially moving to regions in which distinct discourses on environmental change prevail, determines the significance of knowledge transfers (Van Praag et al. 2021). Hence, the combination of sending financial remittances and knowledge transfer are decisive factors in determining the extent to which remittances actually lead to climate adaptation in the region of origin.

Keeping this in mind, if migrants are more aware of the local context and specific environmental change, they may be more conscious of the need to send remittances to deal with environmental change and undertake action. In line with the premises of the new economics of labor migration (Stark and Bloom 1985; Taylor 1999; Stark 2005), being able to remit might even be seen as an important motivation for migration. These remittances may also increase migrants' capital in their regions of origin. They can be used to ensure the maintenance of their assets in their communities of origin and to prepare for a potential return to this community (Carling 2008a). In this case, sending remittances to deal with environmental change not only enhances the subsistence of non-migrant members of the immigrants' household and social networks, but also prevents devaluation and degradation of their property, inheritance, and assets.

However, in other cases, concerns about environmental change mitigation and adaptation may only arise after migration and after being exposed to climate change discourses in the immigrant country. Finally, behind the need to send and receive remittances, it could also be argued that environmental change itself is a significant driver of migration. This would also make the link between environmental change and migration more straightforward (Gemenne 2010), but as we have seen above, the role of environmental change in the decision to migrate remains complex.

Migrants as Transformative Agents in Transnational Societies: Potentials and Pitfalls

As Carling pointed out (2014, p. 2019): "Remittances can transform receiving communities, and they weigh heavily in the assessment of the benefits and vulnerabilities that migration brings." This is no different when investigating the transformative potential of remittances in rapidly changing natural environments of communities/regions of origin. More specifically, in the context of environmental change, the sending and receiving of remittances could have far-reaching transformative effects. Due to the specificity of environmental change discourses, remittances in which knowledge about environmental change and how to deal with this is exchanged can especially contribute to transnational societies. In such societies, changes can be discussed and innovative solutions sought to deal with such complex matters at the local level. The mutual impact of such knowledge transfers is strengthened by money flows that ensure this knowledge is implemented in such way as to improve the social resilience of communities.

In addition, there should also be some kind of sustainability in the sending of remittances. This could, for example, be ensured through the visits and cooperation of transnationally mobile migrants (Isaakyan and Triandafyllidou 2017). Such agents contribute more actively to the sharing of human capital, as they spend more time in their regions of origin, facilitating the circulation of ideas. This exchange is important in taking into consideration local realities, difficulties, and structures, and in order to correctly interpret the 'new' kinds of information shared by migrants. Another way in which the sustainability of remittances might be enhanced is by structurally embedding them in community building, for example by targeting them at community projects. Overall, what is important is that there is mutual understanding and alignment between receivers and senders concerning how remittances will be used, leading to the development of better adaptation strategies.

Dealing with environmental change in terms of mitigation and adaptation is often approached from a local/international policy perspective. However, it remains important to bear in mind that although remittances are appealing to policy makers, remittance flows mainly comprise the sum of many individual transfers (Carling 2008a). Thus, one should be aware that remittances are generally not shared by entire communities or implemented at the community level. As migrants usually communicate with their immediate social network—consisting of family members and friends—at the community level, remittances may be fragmented, widespread, and not necessarily shared with those implementing adaptation strategies dealing with environmental change. Thus, if policy makers wish to rely on remittances as part of their environmental strategy, policy initiatives should stimulate and coordinate the use of remittances for community-wide development projects. They could be done, for example, by promoting the channeling of remittances, through the stimulation of direct and indirect investment of remittances, or through the sound management of remittances (Carling 2008b).

Moreover, in addition to the increased control and management of money transfers, there is also a need for better coordination of knowledge transfers and human capital, which may also not be equally distributed across all community members and/or migrants. This could lead to fragmented information and knowledge-sharing that is not necessarily applied to the local context. In the case of environmental/climate change discourses, for example, this could result in the sharing of discourses and theories on issues such as the ozone layer, the melting of the ice caps, or the general need for a reduction in CO_2 emissions. Insofar as such discourses and information remain abstracted from local specificities and lack insight into practical adaptation strategies, they may jeopardize the development of local environmental change strategies (Van Praag et al. 2021).

Conclusion

This chapter gave an overview of the linkages between migration trajectories, transnational practices, and environmental change to foster an understanding of how migrants and their transnational practices could potentially serve as agents of change. It considered how these factors might contribute to a growing awareness of and adaptation to environmental change through financial remittances accompanied by knowledge exchange, thereby enhancing the social resilience of their communities. Thus, the chapter reflected on how transnational practices might reduce future vulnerabilities to environmental change in a sustainable way.

The potential and actual impacts of remittances on the receiving countries have already been largely debated within and outside academia. It has been argued that remittances do function as transformative agents in the context of increasing and disruptive environmental changes. Simultaneously, however, remittances are often sent to regions that are relatively unattractive for investments and/or are hindered by restrictive immigration policies, jeopardizing the full potential of remittances (De Haas 2005; Fagen 2006). Thus, both senders and receivers should be actively involved in any transformative process aiming to develop transnational societies (Carling 2014). At the same time, we should heed Kapur's (2004) warning against the remittance mantra, as remittances should not be considered a holy grail in solving all developmental issues or in coping with environmental issues.

While other scholars have already taken up this line of thought, I would like to emphasize some specific differences when applying it to environmental issues. In general, the use of remittances—in the form of money flows, knowledge, political ideas, norms, and values—has largely been seen to complement existing initiatives and policies of the state, market, and international organizations, turning migrants into development agents (Faist 2007). An adapted version of this approach can be found in policy documents and in academic literature on environmental migration. Analogous to the main premises of the 'migration as development' discourse, migration has also been conceptualized as an adaptation strategy for dealing with environmental change. Migration is here seen as a way to reduce demographic pressure, change the demographic composition of the communities of origin, and facilitate the development of adaptation strategies through remittances (Adger et al. 2002; Black et al. 2011b; Gemenne and Blocher 2016, 2017).

Despite the potential of such a 'migration as adaptation' approach, the research remains inconclusive on its actual effects. It appears that contextual and organizational factors play a determining role in whether migration can actually serve as a means to adapt to environmental change (Hillman et al. 2015; Wiegel et al. 2019). Furthermore, the extent to which migration is an adaptation strategy itself remains conceptually unclear, as does the question of whether it might be used when other adaptation strategies fail (Gemenne 2010) or whether it should even be considered a form of maladaptation (Juhola et al. 2016).

Building on the insights presented in this chapter, the premises of the migration as adaptation discourse and/or migration as development discourse need to be reconsidered, as they jeopardize the development of sustainable policies dealing with environmental change. First, migrants have to meet demands that are hard to accomplish. More specifically, many migrants feel a pressure from their country/region of origin to be loyal and care for their families, their region, and their natural environment. Moreover, the remittances they send should be spent on development purposes and to support their entire region of origin when dealing with climate change. These demands are reflected in the fact that many diaspora policies are seen as supplementary to actions undertaken by the state, the market, and international organizations (Kapur 2004; Faist 2007). At the same time, in the receiving country, migrants are also expected to work, integrate, and spend their money there. Both perspectives seem to overlook or ignore the fact that this is a lot to ask from a specific group in society, namely migrants, who also migrate for specific purposes, interests, and ambitions. Additionally, both perspectives tend to forget the fact that they are discussing private money, approaching it rather as a policy solution.

Thus, due to the specific position that migrants occupy both in their regions of origin and in their immigration countries, alternative structural solutions and policies are needed to deal with the mitigation of and adaptation to environmental change, without relying on individual money transfers sent by migrants. In this regard, policy makers could provide more structural support for and facilitate the sending of remittances and specific types of investment. However, this still mainly refers to money flows. The sharing of knowledge, raising awareness, and brainstorming on adaptive solutions to deal with environmental change are far more difficult to monitor and manage than the provision of funds or the sending of money. In this respect, transnationally mobile agents could play an active role in the creation and transformation of transnational societies in which knowledge, in particular, is shared (Isaakyan and Triandafyllidou 2017).

Nevertheless, it should be kept in mind that the presence of such transnationally mobile agents will vary across migrant networks, communities, and cultures, as will their interest in environmental issues. Moreover, due to the unequal distribution of remittances within and across communities and countries, this solution clearly would not benefit all those who are confronted with environmental change. Remittances could even strengthen existing inequalities within and across communities and countries. As we saw, migrants do not necessarily originate from the regions most affected by environmental change, nor are they always the most affected by or most vulnerable to the effects of environmental change on their daily livelihoods (McLeman and Gemenne 2018). Consequently, there remains a need to develop innovative policies and actions that do not rely solely on such transnational practices.

References

Adger, W. N. et al. (2002). Migration, Remittances, Livelihood Trajectories, and Social Resilience. *AMBIO: A Journal of the Human Environment, 31*(4), 358–366.

Ahmed, I. I. (2000). Remittances and Their Economic Impact in Post-War Somaliland. *Disasters, 24*(4), 380–389.

Bele, M. Y., Sonwa, D. J., & Tiani, A. M. (2014). Local Communities' Vulnerability to Climate Change and Adaptation Strategies in Bukavu in DR Congo. *The Journal of Environment & Development, 23*(3), 331–357.

Bierbaum, R. & Stults, M. (2013). Adaptation to Climate Change: Context Matters. *Michigan Journal of Sustainability,* 1, 15–30.

Black, R., et al. (2011a). The Effect of Environmental Change on Human Migration. *Global Environmental Change, 21*(1), 3–11. https://doi.org/10.1016/j.gloenvcha.2011.10.001

Black, R. et al. (2011b). Climate Change: Migration as Adaptation. *Nature, 478*(7370), 447.

Black, R. & Collyer, M. (2014). Populations 'Trapped' at Times of Crisis. *Forced Migration Review, 45*, 52–56.

Boccagni, P. & Decimo, F. (2013). Mapping Social Remittances. *Migration Letters, 10*(1): 1–10.

Bremer, S., Blanchard, A., Mamnun, N., Stiller-Reeve, M., Haque, M. M., & Tvinnereim, E. (2017). Narrative as a Method for Eliciting Tacit Knowledge of Climate Variability in Bangladesh. *Weather, Climate, and Society, 9*(4), 669–686.

Carling, J. (2008a). The Determinants of Migrant Remittances. *Oxford Review of Economic Policy*, 24(3), 581–598.

Carling, J. (2008b). *Interrogating Remittances: Core Questions for Deeper Insight and Better Policies. Migration and Development: Perspectives from the South.* Geneva: International Organization for Migration, 43–64.

Carling, J. (2014). Scripting Remittances: Making Sense of Money Transfers in Transnational Relationships. *International Migration Review, 48*, 218–262.

Carling, J. (2020). Remittances: Eight Analytical Perspectives. In: T. Bastia & R. Skeldon (Eds.) *Routledge Handbook of Migration and Development* (pp. 114–124). Routledge.

De Haas, H. (2005). International Migration, Remittances and Development: Myths and Facts, *Third World Quarterly*, 26(8), 1269–1284, https://doi.org/10.1080/01436590500336757

De Longueville, F. et al. (2020). Comparing Climate Change Perceptions and Meteorological Data in Rural West Africa to Improve the Understanding of Household Decisions to Migrate. *Climatic Change*, 160, 1–19.

Eckstein, S. (2006). Transnational Family Based Social Capital: Remittances and the Transformation of Cuba. *International Journal of Sociology of the Family, 32*(2), 141–171.

Fagen, P. W. (2006). *Remittances in Conflict and Crises: How Remittances Sustain Livelihoods in War, Crises and Transitions to Peace* (No. 38957, pp. 1–3). The World Bank.

Faist, T. (2007). Migrants as Transnational Development Agents: An Inquiry into the Newest Round of the Migration-Development Nexus. *Population, Space and Place, 14*(1), 21–42. https://doi.org/10.1002/psp.471

Few, R., Martin, A. & Gross-Camp, N. (2017). Trade-Offs in Linking Adaptation and Mitigation in the Forests of the Congo Basin. *Regional Environmental Change, 17*(3), 851–863.

Gemenne, F. (2010). Migration, a Possible Adaptation Strategy? Institut du développement durable et des relations internationales, 3, 1–4.

Gemenne, F. & Blocher, J. (2016). How Can Migration Support Adaptation? Different Options to Test the Migration-Adaptation Nexus. Migration, Environment and Climate Change. Working paper IOM. https://doi.org/10.13140/RG.2.1.2010.6008

Gemenne, F. & Blocher, J. (2017). How Can Migration Serve Adaptation to Climate Change? Challenges to Fleshing Out a Policy Ideal. *The Geographical Journal, 183*(4), 336–347.

Hanson, S. et al. (2011). A Global Ranking of Port Cities with High Exposure to Climate Extremes. *Climatic Change, 104*(1), 89–111.

Hillman, F., Pahl, M., Rafflenbeul, B. & Sterly, H. (2015). Introduction: (Re-) Locating the Nexus of Migration, Environmental Change and Adaptation. In F. Hillman et al. (Eds.) *Environmental Change, Adaptation and Migration. Bringing in the Region* (pp. 1–17), Palgrave Macmillan.

Huong, H. T. L., & Pathirana, A. (2013). Urbanization and Climate Change Impacts on Future Urban Flooding in Can Tho City, Vietnam. *Hydrology and Earth System Sciences, 17*(1), 379.

Howe, P. D., Thaker, J., & Leiserowitz, A. (2014). Public Perceptions of Rainfall Change in India. *Climatic Change, 127*(2), 211–225

IPCC (2014). Summary for Policymakers. In: C. B. Field et al. (Eds.). *Climate Change 2014: Impacts, Adaptation, and Vulnerability. Part A: Global and Sectoral Aspects. Contribution of Working Group II to the Fifth Assessment Report of the Intergovernmental Panel on Climate Change* (pp. 1–32), Cambridge University Press.

Isaakyan, I. & Triandafyllidou, A. (2017). "Sending So Much More Than Money": Exploring Social Remittances and Transnational Mobility. *Ethnic and Racial Studies, 40*,15, 2787–2805, https://doi.org/10.1080/01419870.2016.1259491

Juhola, S. et al. (2016). Redefining Maladaptation. *Environmental Science and Policy*, 55, 135–140. https://doi.org/10.1016/j.envsci.2015.09.014

Horst, C. & Van Hear, N. (2002). Counting the Cost: Refugees, Remittances and the 'War against Terrorism'. Forced Migration Review.

Kapur, D. (2004). Remittances: The New Development Mantra? G-24 Discussion Paper Series, 29. https://unctad.org/system/files/official-document/gdsmdpbg2420045_en.pdf

Khare, A. & Khare, K. K. (2006). Towards a Global Environmental Ethics: A Review Discussion. *Asian Journal of Experimental Sciences, 20*(1): 101–106.

Leclerc, C. et al. (2013). Indigenous Past Climate Knowledge as Cultural Built-In Object and Its Accuracy. *Ecology and Society, 18*(4), 22. https://doi.org/10.5751/ES-05896-180422

Levitt, P. (1998). Social Remittances: Migration Driven Local-Level Forms of Cultural Diffusion. *International Migration Review, 32*(4), 926–948.

Levitt P. & Nyberg-Sørensen, N. (2004). The Transnational Turn in Migration Studies. Global Commission on International Migration (GCIM), *Global Migration Perspectives*, 6.

McLeman, R. & Gemenne, F. (2018). *Routledge Handbook of Environmental Displacement and Migration*. Routledge.

Mertz, O. et al. (2009). Farmers' Perceptions of Climate Change and Agricultural Adaptation Strategies in Rural Sahel. *Environmental Management, 43*(5), 804–816. https://doi.org/10.1007/s00267-008-9197-0

Mertz, O. et al. (2010). Climate Factors Play a Limited Role for Past Adaptation Strategies in West Africa. *Ecology and Society, 15*(4), 25.

Methmann, C., & Oels, A. (2015). From 'Fearing' to 'Empowering' Climate Refugees: Governing Climate-Induced Migration in the Name of Resilience. *Security Dialogue, 46*(1), 51–68.

Regan, P. M., & Frank, R. W. (2014). Migrant Remittances and the Onset of Civil War. *Conflict Management and Peace Science, 31*(5), 502–520.

Rigby, K. (2016). Religion and Ecology: Towards a Communion of Creatures. In S. Oppermann, & S. Iovino (Eds.), *Environmental Humanities: Voices from the Anthropocene* (pp. 273–294). Rowman and Littlefield.

Spence, A. et al. (2011). Perceptions of Climate Change and Willingness to Save Energy Related to Flood Experience. *Nature Climate Change, 1*(1), 46.

Stark, O. (2005). Comment on 'Migration and Income in Source Communities: A New Economics of Migration Perspective from China', *Economic Development and Cultural Change, 53*(4): 983–986.

Stark, O. & Bloom, D. E. (1985). The New Economics of Labour Migration. *The American Economic Review, 75*(2), 173–178.

Stern, P. (2000). Toward a Coherent Theory of Environmentally Significant Behavior, *Journal of Social Issues, 56*(3), 407–24. https://doi.org/10.1111/0022-4537.00175

Stilwell, B. et al. (2004). Migration of Health-Care Workers from Developing Countries: Strategic Approaches to its Management. *Bull World Health Organ, 82*, 595–600

Taylor, J. E. (1999). The New Economics of Labour Migration and the Role of Remittances in the Migration Process. *International Migration, 37*(1), 63–88.

Taylor, J. E., Arango, J., Hugo, G., Kouaouci, A., Massey, D. S., & Pellegrino, A. (1996). International Migration and Community Development. *Population index*, 397–418.

Van Praag, L. & Timmerman, C. (2019). Environmental Migration and Displacement: A New Theoretical Framework for the Study of Migration Aspirations in Response to Environmental Changes, *Environmental sociology, 5*(4), 352–361. https://doi.org/10.1080/23251042.2019.161303

Van Praag, L., Ou-Salah, L., Hut, E. & Zickgraf, C. (2021). Migration and Environmental Change in Morocco: In *Search for Linkages between Migration Aspirations and (Perceived) Environmental Changes*. Springer.

Vari-Lavoisier, I. (2020): Social Remittances. In T. Bastia, & R. Skeldon (Eds.): *Routledge Handbook of Migration and Development* (pp. 125–135). Routledge

Vedwan, N. (2006). Culture, Climate and the Environment: Local Knowledge and Perception of Climate Change among Apple Growers in Northwestern India. *Journal of Ecological Anthropology, 10*(1), 4–18.

Weber, E. U. (2010). What Shapes Perceptions of Climate Change? *Wiley Interdisciplinary Reviews: Climate Change, 1*(3), 332–342.

Wiegel, H., Boas, I., & Warner, J. (2019). A Mobilities Perspective on Migration in the Context of Environmental Change. *WIREs Climate Change*, https://doi.org/10.1002/wcc.610

Wodon, Q. & Liverani, A. (2014). Climate Change, Migration, Adaptation in the MENA Region. In Q. Wodon, A. Liverani, G. Joseph, & N. Bougnoux (Eds.), *Climate Change and Migration: Evidence from the Middle-East and North Africa* (pp. 3–36). A World Bank Study.

CHAPTER 17

Political Remittances: The Post-war Transformation of the Tamil Swiss Diaspora

Rina Malagayo Alluri

Introduction

This paper aims to explore how practices of remittances have been used as a form of political activism by the transnational Sri Lankan Tamil diaspora broadly, and the Sri Lankan Tamil diaspora in Switzerland (henceforth referred to as 'the Tamil Swiss diaspora') specifically. It explores these practices within the context of the Sri Lankan civil war (1983–2009) and post-war period (2010 to present) to analyse how remittance practices change with the second-generation Tamil Swiss diaspora. It aims to answer the following research questions: In what ways have the Tamil Swiss diaspora used political remittances? And what intergenerational changes, from the first to the second generation, can we observe?

The paper is structured as follows. Firstly, it will provide an overview of the method and framework and introduce key concepts to the reader. Then, it will introduce the transnational Sri Lankan Tamil diaspora and the politicization of remittances, to be followed with an outline of the

R. M. Alluri (✉)
University of Innsbruck, Innsbruck, Austria
e-mail: rina.alluri@uibk.ac.at

S. Meyer, C. Ströhle (eds.), *Remittances as Social Practices and Agents of Change*,
https://doi.org/10.1007/978-3-030-81504-2_17

Tamil Swiss diaspora. Further, it will provide some empirical reflection on the second-generation Tamil Swiss diaspora and on how they are engaging in post-war political activism. Finally, it will share some concluding remarks.

Methodology

This chapter is predominantly based on data collected as part of a post-doctoral research project on the role of the transnational Sri Lankan Tamil Diaspora in Peacebuilding and Development with the University of Zurich and, to a lesser extent, on data collected during PhD research on the role of local economic actors in peacebuilding in Sri Lanka with the University of Basel (Alluri 2014). The research approach is qualitative and relied on analysing and interpreting academic, policy and organizational documents, social media sources and interview material.

The bulk of the empirical data is based on qualitative semi-structured interviews that were carried out face-to-face in Switzerland from April 2017 to January 2019 as part of my post-doctoral research. A small number of interviews were carried out via Skype and telephone with persons based in Germany, India, Italy, Sri Lanka and the UK. Interviews were also conducted with representatives from the Tamil Swiss diaspora and abroad, Tamil diaspora organizations, Swiss and international governmental and non-governmental organizations working on Sri Lanka, diaspora and migration issues. Twelve (five male and seven female) interview partners between 27 and 38 years old belong to the second-generation Tamil Swiss diaspora. For the purpose of this chapter, second-generation Tamil diaspora are understood as comprising of youth who were either born in Switzerland or came to Switzerland in the 1990s when they were under the age of 13. All of the second-generation interviewees were predominantly raised in the Swiss German-speaking part of Switzerland, where the majority of Tamils reside.

Theoretical Concepts

Transnationalism

Transnationalism can be conceptualized as the interconnected linkages between home and host land that reflect the alternating relations of migrants (Glick-Schiller, et al. 1992). Transnationalism includes the ways in which migrants establish bonds and durable ties that span across countries to capture ideas of community, social formations such as cross-border active networks, groups and organizations (Faist 2008). It further includes the movement and practices of migrants, the migratory flows of commodities, capital and resources, questions related to nation-states, physical borders as well as spaces of transnational citizenship and belonging (Leitner and Ehrkamp 2006).

When looking at transnational diaspora, there are "the multiple ties and interactions linking people or institutions across the borders of nation states" (Vertovec 1999b, p. 447). However, while it appears that "politics has been unlinked from territory", locality remains important: "much of the new transnational politics is intensely focused on specific locations, identities and issues. Politics remains fundamentally about local, parochial issues even while political processes are increasingly transnational" (Lyons 2007, p. 530). Transnationalism may include formal forms of engagement such as electoral politics or also other forms of collective action such as cross-border political organizations (Chaudhary and Moss 2016). It may include non-institutional activities such as political protest, demonstrations or social media campaigns or activities that aim to sustain linkages to the politics of the homeland (Lyons 2007). Transnational processes are also very much centred in the home environment and used to connote everyday practices and life experiences of migrants engaged within various activities (Bloch and Hirsch 2018).

Conflict-generated Diaspora and Translocal Communities

Diaspora communities are more than just 'war mongers' or 'peacemakers' (Smith and Stares 2007). They manifest their politics of belonging through international networks and events, political action and online spaces that comprise social relationships, a tension of political orientations and economic strategies. The diaspora engages in these domains via "a 'triadic relationship' between a) globally dispersed yet collectively self-identified ethnic groups *[the transnational]*, (b) the territorial states and contexts where such groups reside *[hostland]*, and (c) the homeland states and contexts whence they or their forebears came *[homeland]*" (Vertovec 1999a, p. 5, insertion and emphasis by Alluri).

In particular, 'conflict-generated diasporas' that have been forcibly displaced and detached from their homeland territory as a result of violent conflict tend to have an amplified symbolic attachment and thus shared identity that is linked to the politics of belonging to their homeland (Lyons 2007). Here, conflict-generated diaspora are composed of "networks of those forced across borders by conflict or repression [who] commonly have a specific set of traumatic memories and hence retain symbolic ties to the homeland" (Adamson 2005). In order to maintain these ties and establish a politics of belonging, conflict-affected diaspora create 'translocal' networks of social relations they sustain across locations networks in their host land (Lyons 2007). The diaspora creates symbolic and imagined communities through forming local households, kin networks, elite fractions, religious communities, language schools, cultural centres and other social clubs and associations to celebrate ethno-religious holidays or to mark other important dates (Smith and Guarnizo 1998, p. 7). These are seen as common processes of identity formation, community formation and integration support (Lyons 2007, pp. 532–533). The creation of de-territorialized 'translocal' communities (Appadurai 1996) helps to ensure an ongoing relationship with (an often mythical) homeland, hostland and transnational spaces. These communities become sites not only of refuge or collective engagement within the group, but also as sites of political mobilization, activism and the creation of organizations that contribute to social change and political transformation. Through translocal place making and identity formation, the diasporas are "holding together both de-territorialization and re-territorialization" (Carter 2005, p. 61) as they are in constant motion, evolution and fluidity.

Political Remittances

Conflict-generated diaspora engage in different forms of transnational practices in order to maintain ties to their homeland. Diaspora engagement can include individual and collective aspects, through both financial and human capital and through voluntary or for-profit activities (Erdal and Horst 2010). This chapter focuses on how remittances have become a transnational practice that is bound with an intrinsic desire to maintain not only economic and social but also political ties to the homeland. Diaspora may send remittances in the form of money, goods, services and knowledge contributions but they also contribute by political mobilization such as political rallies, voting practices, social organizations or fund-raising events that are closely linked with an orientation and identification that motivates them (Vélez-Torres and Agergaard 2014). Political remittances can encompass both political mobilization and supporting religious organizations and sites (Baumann 2010; Hollenbach et al. 2020). They are an "act of transferring political principles, vocabulary and practices between two or more places, which migrants and their descendants share a connection with. Political remittances [...] influence political behaviour, mobilization, organization and narratives of belonging in places of destination and origin" (Krawatzek and Müller-Funk 2019, p. 1004).

Second-generation Diaspora

The second generation of the conflict-generated diaspora establishes multiple 'ways of belonging' (Levitt and Glick-Schiller 2004) through different forms of transnational and translocal engagement. They create an 'interculturality' of identities (Burgio 2016) that are connected to the political and cultural aspirations of the homeland, the symbolic and material ties in their hostland as well as to the globally dispersed yet collectively self-identified transnational communities (Burgio 2016. pp. 107–113; Vertovec 1999a, p. 5). Some studies on second-generation diaspora show that they tend to have weaker ties to the homeland and tend to remit less than the first generation (Bloch and Hirsch 2018). Rather, they engage in translocal activities that may include fundraising, donations to religious or local organizations, or to the family pool of remittances (Hammond 2013; see also Erdal in this volume). Class and region-based inequalities amongst diaspora groups impact not only the way in which they can engage in transnational activities such as remittances but also impact their ability to travel back to the homeland (Viruell-Fuentes 2006). Further, the ability of the second generation to travel back to the homeland plays an important role in influencing the way in which they construct their linguistic, cultural and ethnic identities and their sense of belonging in the homeland (Viruell-Fuentes 2006). However, Barber (2017) argues that homeland visits can also have the opposite effect on the second generation, as they may feel alienated should there be stark differences in wealth, culture and linguistic connections. This could have a direct effect on their motivation to send remittances to family members who they feel close or distant to. Finally, the connection to homeland politics also has an impact on how the second generation approach political remittances and whether they direct these engagements to the homeland, hostland or transnational communities.

The Civil War, Transnational Sri Lankan Tamil Diaspora and Political Remittances

The Sri Lankan civil war (1983–2009) between the Government of Sri Lanka and the Liberation Tigers of Tamil Eelam (LTTE) was a violent, protracted and multi-faceted conflict that lasted 26 years. Following anti-Tamil pogroms in 1983 and numerous clashes between different Tamil militant groups in the 1980s, the LTTE emerged as the dominant protagonist or the self-proclaimed 'sole representative' of the Tamil nation in 1987, demanding self-governance for the country's Tamils in a separate state in the North and East (Nadarajah and Vimalarajah 2008, pp. 7–9). The civil war is understood as a "grievance-driven ethnopolitical conflict" (Palmer 2005, p. 3) that relied on an organized system of external financing, particularly through diaspora remittances, taxations and illicit activities to maintain its military undertakings (Alluri 2014). After numerous failed attempts of mediated peace processes, the Sri Lankan civil war ended militarily when the Government of Sri Lanka defeated the LTTE in April 2009.

The Sri Lankan civil war led to the large emigration of (predominantly) Tamils particularly to Europe, North America and Australia. The transnational Sri Lankan Tamil diaspora is highly diverse, sometimes fragmented and conflictive, then collaborative and community-oriented and other times still, passive, apolitical or indifferent. In this vein, different parts of the diaspora community have played pivotal roles in Sri Lanka's political life. An estimation of the size of the Tamil diaspora is over one million, or about one quarter of the entire Sri Lankan Tamil population (International Crisis Group 2010, pp. 1–4). The Tamil diaspora are as heterogeneous as the society within the country and can often be categorized based on their date of arrival, length of stay and legal status in their host countries, gender, caste, region, socio-economic standing and political orientation. However, there is still an important element of collective identity or 'global Tamilness' that is "linked to a de-territorialized diaspora that is cemented and constantly recreated through artefacts, popular culture, and a shared imagery" (Cohen 2008, pp. 6–8).

While there are many factions within the Tamil diaspora which were avidly against the war and highly critical of the LTTE (Vimalarajah and Cheran 2010), there were other influential groups that have been categorized through their strong economic, political and social support of the LTTE throughout the war as "'externally situated internal actors' [...]

who acted as an extension of the Tamil aspiration for self-determination within the country, provided a financial support base, facilitated critique of the Government of Sri Lanka and impacted foreign policy towards Sri Lanka from within their 'host countries'" (Hettiarachchi 2011, p. 4). This came predominantly in the forms of: global communication and information exchange; awareness raising and political lobbying, and; lawful as well as illegal fundraising that directly supported the perpetuation of conflict (Amarasingham 2013; Wayland 2004). This chapter focuses on the factions of the Tamil diaspora who have actively engaged in political remittances through, for example, their financial support of the LTTE, their participation in transnational networks and organizations that fight for the cause of Tamil Eelam, through raising awareness on Tamil issues in their hostland or sending money to their families in Sri Lanka.

Significant research has been carried out on the Sri Lankan Tamil diaspora and their use of political mobilization in the hostland to engage in homeland politics in Sri Lanka. Specific research has looked at the larger diaspora communities in the UK (approximately 100,000) (Bloch and Hirsch 2018; Hettiarachchi 2011; Thangarajah and Holdaway 2011; Van Hear et al. 2004; Vimalarajah and Cheran 2010) and Canada (approximately 400,000 Tamils) (Amarasingham 2013; Thurairajah 2017). Considerably less research has been carried out in Switzerland with the exception of a few (Hess and Korf 2014; Lüthi 2005; McDowell 1996; Stürzinger 2002; Thurairajah 2015; Thurairajah et al. 2020).

Political Remittances During the Civil War (1983–2009)

The role of the Tamil diaspora amidst the Sri Lankan civil war has always been complex. From afar, they often bore witness to atrocities taking place in their homeland in Sri Lanka at the hands of the Government of Sri Lanka as well as the LTTE. This led to the harbouring of deep-seated resentment towards one or both conflict parties as they found themselves helpless at a distance (International Crisis Group 2010). During the war, the LTTE was able to appeal to Tamils as a 'victim diaspora' that had a collective sense of trauma as linked to their common territory, forced migration, persecution and exile, as well as a sense of guilt for leaving the country while others were left behind (McDowell 1996, p. 12). The common and specific set of traumas and the symbolic ties to the homeland enabled the LTTE to gain significant political, financial and social support from the diaspora.

One way in which the Tamil diaspora was able to stay engaged was through financial support such as remittances. Family and friends that were left behind shared accounts of the situation on the ground with the diaspora abroad. Much of the diaspora sent money home to Sri Lanka, either in the form of financial support for their friends and family, through payments to organizations and charities based in the country, or in some cases directly to the LTTE to support their fight for Tamil Eelam (Chalk 2008). In the absence of natural resources, the LTTE created a war economy that relied on diaspora remittances and contributions (allegedly forced), 'taxation' and illicit activities to help finance the war effort. The LTTE established overseas branches and campaigns through business networks, systematic fundraising and arms procurement, often using an informal money transfer system (International Crisis Group 2010). They also permeated diaspora organizations and institutions such as Tamil language schools, community groups, temple management committees and social and cultural organizations. In this way, the LTTE created their own informal war economy that helped ensure they were able to maintain the costs of their war effort against the state (Alluri 2014, p. 290). The LTTE used its finances for military purposes, to support the families of its supporters and to engage in income generation projects in areas under its control (Weiss Fagen and Bump 2006). This contributed to a historical politicization of remittances (International Crisis Group 2010) that was intrinsically linked to the war economy and the armed struggle for a 'Tamil homeland' (Alluri 2014, p. 292). The LTTE used the diaspora (both willingly and through coercion) as a tool to remit financial, ideological and logistical contributions for its insurgency (Chalk 2008; Wayland 2004). Thus, the diaspora has historically used political remittances to maintain political, social and personal ties to the homeland and to have an impact on political processes and activities. In this case, the Tamil diaspora's remittances had a direct effect on the continuation of the civil war. Diaspora organizations, fundraising events and front companies and organizations were set up worldwide to help facilitate remittances and fundraising for the LTTE (Amarasingham 2013, pp. 10–20; Vimalarajah et al., 2011). In 2009, the diaspora were remitting approximately USD 2.8 billion, one of the largest sources of foreign exchange (International Crisis Group 2010, p. 5).

In the aftermath of the terrorist attacks on September 11, 2001, and the subsequent naming of the LTTE as a terrorist organization, fundraising and remittances from diaspora communities in countries such as the

United States, United Kingdom, Canada and Switzerland became much more challenging as investigations and raids of LTTE front organizations persisted (Amarasingham 2013; Crinari 2019). As the diaspora became increasingly criticized as the financiers of the LTTE and thus supporters of a separatist state, a deep-rooted mistrust between the Government of Sri Lanka and the Sri Lankan Tamil diaspora was harboured that continues until today.

Transformation of Remittance Practices: The Tamil Diaspora after the Civil War

With the military defeat of the LTTE and subsequent end of the civil war in April 2009, the role and relationships of the Tamil diaspora significantly changed (Amarasingham 2013); however, the deep-seated mistrust between the Government of Sri Lanka and the Tamil diaspora persisted. While some efforts have been made to reconcile these differences by some politicians, the term 'diaspora', particularly when linked to the Tamil diaspora, has become somewhat of a pejorative term. This has led to the strategic use of a more ethnically inclusive and investment-oriented term, Overseas Sri Lankans (OSLs) when trying to support diaspora engagement in Sri Lanka (International Alert 2016).

The defeat of the 'old guard' of pro-LTTE activists and LTTE cadres working within the Tamil diaspora (Brun and Van Hear 2012) led to a new and different approach to diaspora politics (Amarasingham 2013), particularly through the creation of global diaspora initiatives to fill the political vacuum that the LTTE left in order to continue to advocate for issues related to human and cultural rights of Tamils (Guyot 2017). In particular, groups such as the Transnational Government of Tamil Eelam (TGTE) and the Global Tamil Forum (GTF) were formed with different goals to support the Tamil cause. But these organizations tend to reflect some of the ongoing cleavages and fragmentation within the diaspora itself as they pit themselves against one another instead of finding unity of purpose (ibid.). Despite their different approaches, the establishment of a separatist state of Tamil Eelam (Hess and Korf 2014; Vimalarajah and Cheran 2010) and a fight for minority rights issues in Sri Lanka (Thangarajah and Holdaway 2011) tend to be the main goals of these initiatives. While some of these initiatives raised awareness on the Tamil plight in the hostland (such as Canada, Switzerland, UK, Australia, etc.) and on a global scale, and succeeded in creating linkages to Tamil political parties in Sri Lanka, these have not been translated into more political rights of Tamils in Sri Lanka itself. The post-war context appears to have, in some ways, contributed to wider divides between the politically active within the diaspora itself. Amidst these changing political leanings, the second-generation Tamil diaspora have been perceived as a potential force for change in Tamil political activism, while still appearing as a sort of an interesting enigma to researchers (Brun and Van Hear 2012; Hess and Korf 2014; Vimalarajah and Cheran 2010).

The Tamil Swiss Diaspora

The emergence of a Tamil Swiss diaspora is based on several waves of migration, with a first wave coming with the outbreak of widespread violence in the 1980s. These were migrants predominantly from more educated and upper caste groups who were able to access economic opportunities and achieve some form of renewable residence (McDowell 1996, pp. 227). Many European countries during the 1980s allowed a large number of Sri Lankan Tamils to enter the country without obtaining a visa (Thangarajah and Holdaway 2011, p. 6). The largest wave came during the early 1990s as a reaction to the civil war and mostly comprised asylum seekers and political refugees who were less educated, less able to integrate into the Swiss economy and faced the risk of repatriation to Sri Lanka (McDowell 1996, p. 227). Moreover, these asylum seekers were identified as predominantly single young men who had been deeply affected by the war and were particularly keen to support the LTTE's campaigns and activities in Switzerland (McDowell 1996, p. 254). A third but significantly smaller wave of Sri Lankans came towards the end of the war, and after the war ended, and mostly comprised asylum seekers (swissinfo 2019).

Of the approximately 50,000 Sri Lankans in Switzerland, approximately 17,800 have gained Swiss citizenship and 28,000 have a secure legal stay based on their resident permit status (Swiss Federal Office for Statistics 2018; Baumann 2010). Of this population, about 90–95% of them are Tamil with about 35% having been born in Switzerland. The majority of the Tamil Swiss diaspora are Hindus (87%), some Christians (13%) (McDowell 2005) and a few Muslims (Lüthi 2005). Of the first generation of Tamils who came to Switzerland, 65.5% of them had primary education, while only 17.5% had a secondary education and 17% held an advanced education. This is comparable to the Swiss national education of 19.2% held an advanced and 51.3% a secondary education (Alluri 2020; Bovay 2004; Baumann 2010).

While considerable research has been carried out on the Tamil diaspora in UK and Canada, significantly less research has been conducted in Switzerland. A seminal work is that of McDowell (1996), which remains a key source of in-depth demographic information and Swiss asylum policies until today. Others have provided reflections on their migration demographics, how they are organized, their religious and caste relations and their post-war roles (Gazagne and Sánchez-Cacicedo 2015; Markus 2005; Moret et al. 2007; Stürzinger 2002). Of particular relevance to this study is Hess and Korf (2014) who provided insights into the political activism of the second-generation Tamil Swiss diaspora towards the end of the Sri Lankan civil war. Alluri (2020) has also explored the 'interculturality' of identities that exists within the second-generation Tamil Swiss diaspora.

The Tamil Swiss diaspora has been specifically referred to as an 'asylum diaspora' that holds a collective sense of persecution, uniqueness and a myth of return. In particular, this group migrated primarily through "chain migration, in which a family member, most often a younger male, makes the initial move overseas, providing the anchor attached to which is the change that pulls in later arrivals of all ages and sexes" (McDowell 1996, p. 12). There were also some who falsely claimed political asylum but who often sought out to come to Switzerland for economic opportunities as 'immigrant Tamils' rather than as a result of direct persecution.

In particular, the Tamil Swiss diaspora have been classified as a diaspora group, which were particularly supportive of the LTTE through remittances (Crinari 2019). While there are ultra-nationalists within the Tamil Swiss diaspora community who still aspire for a future independent state of Tamil Eelam, the end of the war and the defeat of the LTTE have opened up space for Tamil Swiss diaspora to redefine their motives and forms of political engagement. In an interview (April 2018), a Swiss government official stated that despite the transnational diaspora's collective demonstration and movement to create new leadership with the end of the war, apathy, disappointment and in some ways, disillusionment seems to have taken over many diaspora members. Although they used transnational political activism and had a strong financial role throughout the civil war, the diaspora failed in a way to influence global politics, the outcomes of the Sri Lankan civil war and the post-war political transformation.

The Second-generation Tamil Swiss Diaspora and Political Remittances

The first-generation Tamil Swiss diaspora's engagement in remittances has often been intrinsically linked to issues such as their socio-economic status, religious practices, political ideologies, caste, natal village identities (*ur*), family histories, historical connections to the LTTE in Sri Lanka and abroad, history of migration and so on (Lüthi 2005; Paramsothy 2018). Over time, other issues such as an aging diaspora, health, access to social services, retirement, old-age homes and so on have also influenced the first generation's remittance practices, fostering a longing to return to the 'homeland' (Gerber and Hungerbühler 2018). While many of these factors still play a role (such as political ideologies, caste, religious practices, historical connections to the LTTE in Sri Lanka and abroad, etc.), they are often manifested differently amongst the second generation.

Diasporic youth, particularly the second generation, forge new multiple identities through their primary socialization process where they have "self-consciously selected, syncretised and elaborated from more than one heritage" (Vertovec 1999b, p. 20). In this way, the second-generation Tamil Swiss diaspora establishes multiple 'ways of belonging' (Levitt and Glick-Schiller 2004) or 'hybrid identities' (Atputharajah 2016). They become straddled, not only between different identities but also between distinct discourses and practices as they navigate a complex 'balancing act' (Alluri 2020). While the second generation have not experienced the same migration scars as the first generation of conflict-generated diaspora, they inherit traumas and develop hybrid identities that may serve as motivation to engage in political issues in a way that their parents did not. This serves as impetus to use their intercultural identities to further social and political issues that not only affect them or their ethnonational identity, but broader diaspora groups (Levitt and Glick-Schiller 2004).

This section explores the politicization of remittances and their intergenerational transformation. Whereas the first generation sent financial remittances to support families and friends, the second generation concentrated on political and social remittances. Thus, for many amongst the second-generation Tamil Swiss diaspora, the sending of remittances has historically been a political act, due to the way in which it was intrinsically linked to the LTTE and the fight for a separatist state; also, it has been a social act in the way in which it linked their family to cultural and religious traditions or community groups.

Due to the way in which remittances have been historically politicized amongst the Tamil diaspora generally and the Tamil Swiss diaspora specifically, this chapter looks at three forms of political remittance practices: a political act, a social act, a personal act. Many of these acts overlap and the lines are often blurry, however, the three forms speak to how the second generation see themselves, their forms of engagement and types of contribution to their translocal and transnational 'Tamilness'.

Many interviewees expressed that while they had some knowledge of the conflict from their parents and from engagement in Tamil community events, there were several media-heavy events such as the 2004 Tsunami and the final months of the civil war that were triggers for awakening them to their Tamil identity, to the civil war in Sri Lanka and their potential role in political activism (Interview, second-generation Tamil diaspora, April 2018; Interview, second-generation Tamil diaspora, January 2019). Despite the long duration of the civil war, it was the brutality of the final months and the images of civilians bearing the weight of the violence that led to global demonstrations, the creation of transnational spaces and significant participation and political activism of the second-generation Tamil diaspora in homeland politics (Thurairajah 2017; Wayland 2004).

For one interviewee who was usually wary of events in Switzerland that support the LTTE ideology such as the annual Hero Day celebration, he did feel compelled to participate in one large demonstration in Geneva in 2009 that was aimed at raising awareness on the civilian casualties in the civil war (Interview, second-generation Tamil diaspora, April 2018). For others, the visual realization of the human casualties was a pivotal moment in kick-starting a longer engagement in supporting the Tamil cause and a realization that they had a role to play in creating awareness on Tamil rights issues in their host land. Another interviewee stated, "Until 2008, I had no contact with Tamils specifically. [...] I felt like a Swiss but I had no voice. In 2008, the past came to present. The civilian casualties in the Vanni hurt me a lot and I started joining diaspora youth and academic groups to bring the background of the struggle up. The emotions and capacity were there" (Interview, second-generation Tamil diaspora, February 2018).

Political Remittance Practices

With the end of the war and the defeat of the LTTE in April 2009, members of the second generation have engaged in political remittances as political acts. This has taken several forms. Firstly, some actively continue to support the political ideals of the LTTE through diasporic nationalism (Anderson 1983)—they call for an independent and sovereign Tamil Eelam in the North and East of the island of Sri Lanka. Their political remittance practices comprise supporting the formation of global diasporic networks and organizations that continue to aspire for the plight of Tamil Eelam (Amarasingham 2013). One nationalist group has issued Tamil Eelam national identity cards for members and use social media, small events and flash mobs to inform youth about political issues and events (Interview, second-generation Tamil diaspora, January 2019b). For these diaspora members, there remains a direct and intimate connection to the homeland of Sri Lanka and to the LTTE ideology as a central point of reference.

Secondly, some engage in political remittances by partnering directly with Sri Lankan human rights organizations and human rights defenders based in Sri Lanka to organize protests and demonstrations on particular issues such as disappearances, harassment and militarized violence. However, this direct engagement in Sri Lankan political protests is the exception, also because it is highly politically sensitive (Interview, Swiss civil society representative, November 2017).

Thirdly, there are those who claim to support Tamil rights but who do not feel connected to LTTE ideologies and are opposed to supporting organizations that continue to fight for a separatist state (Interview, second-generation Tamil diaspora, January 2019a). These rights-based activists focus less on the direct impact on political processes in Sri Lanka and more on creating translocal spaces that raise awareness on Tamil human rights issues within the context of the Swiss host land (Hess and Korf 2014, p. 428). They do this through the creation of Tamil student's organizations, community organizations, fundraisers and so on as well as by joining Swiss legal, human rights and advocacy organizations that tackle rights more broadly and see the Tamil community as one of many target groups (Interview, second-generation Tamil diaspora, July 2018). Some second-generation diasporas feel connected to human rights issues more broadly and its relevance within the Swiss host land and less connected to the political processes in the homeland of Sri Lanka and the nationalist ideologies of the LTTE. Second-generation diaspora have expressed that although they engage in raising awareness on Tamil rights in Switzerland, they are relatively unaware about the Sri Lankan party politics, and they have no desire to return to the homeland (Lüthi 2005).

Social Remittance Practices

Some second-generation diaspora engage in social acts through spreading ideas, behaviours, identities and social capital (Levitt 1998) in different forms.

Firstly, through collaborating with and fundraising for local organizations in Sri Lanka. This can be linked to different issues such as supporting access to education, building and supporting temples, supporting village associations, access to health and so on (Baumann 2010; Hollenbach et al. 2020).

Secondly, by leading communication and organizing platforms for exchange and events that are held in Switzerland with the aim of raising awareness about issues affecting Tamils in Sri Lanka. These can range from podium discussions with different representatives from government, civil society and the diaspora to photo exhibitions or projects that connect Tamil Swiss communities to counterparts in Sri Lanka (Interview, second-generation Tamil diaspora, January 2019).

Thirdly, through forging transnational co-operations such as organizing visits and trips to Sri Lanka to facilitate exchange and collaborate with local initiatives and organizations, sponsor educational opportunities and raise awareness on particular issues (Interview, second-generation Tamil diaspora, January 2019).

Fourthly, through supporting projects that are linked to issues such as arts, culture and integration within the Tamil community. This can be linked to events that promote Tamil arts and culture, that engage with refugee or state-based organizations that support integration projects or initiatives that focus on inter-cultural exchange between Tamils in Switzerland to those in Sri Lanka (Interview, second-generation Tamil diaspora, March 2018a).

Transformation in Remittances in the Second-generation Tamil Diaspora

Sending financial remittances was a deeply personal act for the first generation of migrants as a direct contribution to the sender's family's well-being in Sri Lanka. However, despite engaging in political and social acts of political remittances, with the exception of a few, second-generation interviewees did not send financial remittances back home to Sri Lanka. While the first-generation diaspora was heavily engaged in sending financial remittances to their families in Sri Lanka, the shift of the second generation away from this personal act is likely due to a number of factors.

Firstly, an absence of the close family ties that are associated with remittances (Kasinitz et al. 2008). While the first generation may be financially supportive of their immediate family (parents, siblings) for the second generation these ties are much distant as they are less likely to have had a lot of exposure or close relationships with these family members. Due to the highly volatile situation in Sri Lanka during the civil war, and the continued discrimination of Tamils in the country today, many second generation felt reluctant and unsafe to travel back to their homeland. For those who did travel back to Sri Lanka, many experienced disenchantment, disconnect to their Tamil culture and a feeling of relief when they were "going home to Switzerland" (Interview, second-generation Tamil diaspora, March 2018b). A lack of affinity to their family specifically and the country of Sri Lanka more broadly contributes to less connection and a feeling of responsibility to financially support their family members.

Secondly, the act of sending financial remittances is often linked to a desire to return to the homeland more permanently, particularly for the first generation. While there may exist a curiosity and a desire to see and experience the homeland, none of the second-generation interviewees expressed interest to return 'home' to Sri Lanka to settle down. On the contrary, despite being politically engaged within the Tamil Swiss diaspora, involved within translocal community spaces such as temples, integration projects, awareness raising of Tamil culture, the second-generation Tamil Swiss diaspora do not appear to have a desire to return to Sri Lanka. When asked whether returning to Sri Lanka would be an option, one interviewee stated, "No. Because I haven't grown up there, I don't know anything about the country" (Interview, second-generation Tamil diaspora, January 2019a).

Thirdly, the end of the civil war in 2009 and opening up of the North and the East gives a perception of an improvement in the safety and security in Tamil areas and relatively better access to the rest of the country and to economic opportunities. Despite the fact that Tamils continue to face structural inequalities and ongoing militarization, there is a perception by some in the second generation that Tamils are now better off since the end of the war and their families now have education and work opportunities that negate the need to rely financially on the diaspora (Interview, second-generation Tamil diaspora, April 2018).

Fourthly, while there are some second generation who continue to send money to their families in Sri Lanka, it is understood more as a form of 'familial support' and less like the first generation who felt a reciprocal social obligation to send remittances out of guilt because they left their family behind during the civil war (Interview, second-generation Tamil diaspora, April 2018). As a 'classic victim diaspora' (Cohen 2008), factions in the first generation are driven by guilt, nostalgia and deprivation (Vimalarajah and Cheran 2010) to continue their moral, political and social responsibility to support family in the homeland. However, with the second generation, a moral obligation to send remittances back becomes less significant.

Fifthly, despite the end of the war, there is also a historical link between the sending of remittances and the financing of the non-state armed group the LTTE. Therefore, the practice of sending financial remittances has become inherently politicized to the point where second generation may choose to explicitly remit if they feel a political affinity to a particular group or opt out should they want to refrain from being associated with any political group. In the case of Sri Lanka, there is the additional fear that any remittances sent are also indirectly supporting the current Government of Sri Lanka, an act that many in the diaspora are likely to want to avoid.

Sixthly, the act of sending financial remittances home to their extended family is still seen as a practice which is still predominantly led by the first generation. This is also likely due to the working and earning age of the second generation who do not feel that they are in the financial position to send money home. However, the aging group of first generation that are soon going into retirement is likely to affect the relationship to this personal act in the near future (Gerber and Hungerbühler 2018).

We thus see that while the second-generation Tamil diaspora may engage in political and social acts of political remittances, their connection to the personal act of sending money home to family appears to be waning.

Conclusion

The chapter concludes that there is a changing relationship between the second generation and the way in which they engage in political remittances. While the first generation engaged in financial remittances, the second generation participate more in political and social remittances through translocal and transnational political activism and by supporting education and exchange respectively. Similar to other second-generation diasporas, the Tamil Swiss diaspora are searching for ways to "combine home- and host-country values and practices in order to meet competing expectations about gender, generation and community" (Levitt 2009, p. 1227). While there may be an increased interest to engage in issues that connect them with their transnational Tamil heritage, the second-generation Tamil Swiss diaspora appear to feel less of a moral, financial and political responsibility to send financial remittances to the homeland of Sri Lanka. Instead, there is an emphasis on the transnational identity that connects them with other like-minded Sri Lankan Tamils and a translocal identity that connects them to their host land of Switzerland. Due to the way in which remittances have been politicized, and in some ways, manipulated by the LTTE during the civil war, some second generation feel a need to distance themselves from the practice altogether. It will be interesting to see how this may change with the aging of the first-generation Tamil Swiss diaspora and thus potentially a further weakening of familial ties between Sri Lanka and Switzerland. As the financial remittances are not just economic but help create social ties between diaspora and their homeland, the absence of remittances over time is likely to contribute to a gap, or even rift as there is no longer a financial tie that binds them, no longer a sense of responsibility and perhaps no longer a feeling that they are contributing to the further development of their home country.

Acknowledgements The author is grateful to the Swiss National Science Foundation for the financial support for both research projects and the University of Basel Political Science department and University of Zurich Human Geography Department for hosting this research. In particular, the author would like to thank all interviewees in Sri Lanka, Switzerland and elsewhere who agreed to share their stories and perspectives with her.

References

Adamson, F. B. (2005). Globalisation, Transnational Political Mobilisation, and Networks of Violence. *Cambridge Review of International Affairs, 18*(1), 31–49.

Alluri, R. M. (2020). "Take me as I am": Insights from the second-generation Sri Lankan Tamil diaspora in Switzerland. In P. Vethanayagamony (Ed.), *Tamil diaspora: Intersectionality of migration, religion, language and culture*. Serials Publications Pvt. Ltd.

Alluri, R. M. (2014). *Politics of peace and conflict: The role of local business actors in Sri Lanka*. [Doctoral dissertation, University of Basel].

Amarasingham, A. (2013). *A History of Tamil Diaspora Politics in Canada: Organisational Dynamics and Negotiated Order, 1978–2013*, ICES Research Papers No.

Anderson, B. (1983). Imagined Communities: Reflections on the Origin and Spread of Nationalism, Verso.

Appadurai, A. (1996). *Modernity at large: Cultural dimensions of globalization.* University of Minnesota Press.

Atputharajah A. (2016). *Hybridity and Integration: A Look at the Second Generation of the Sri Lankan Tamil Diaspora in Toronto.* [MA Thesis, Ryerson University].

Barber, T. (2017). Achieving ethnic authenticity through 'return' visits to Vietnam: paradoxes of class and gender among the British-born Vietnamese. *Journal of Ethnic and Migration Studies, 43*(6), 919–936.

Baumann, M. (2010). Civic social capital and Hindu Tamil priests and temples in Switzerland. *Finnish Journal of Ethnicity and Migration, 5*(2), 7–15.

Bloch, A. & Hirsch, S. (2018). Inter-generational transnationalism: the impact of refugee backgrounds on second generation. *CMS 6*, 30. https://doi.org/10.1186/s40878-018-0096-0

Bovay C. (2004). *Religionslandschaft in der Schweiz: Eidgenössische Volkszahlung 2000.* Bundesamt für Statistik.

Brun, C. & Van Hear, N. (2012). Between the local and the diasporic. The shifting centre of gravity in war-torn Sri Lanka's transnational politics. *Contemporary South Asia,* 20(1), 61–75.

Burgio, G. (2016). When interculturality faces a diaspora. The transnational Tamil identity. *Encyclopaedia XX,* 44, 106–128. https://doi.org/10.6092/issn.1825-8670/5992

Carter, S., 2005. The geopolitics of diaspora. *Area, 37* (1), 54–63.

Chalk P. (2008). The Tigers Abroad: How the LTTE Diaspora Supports the Conflict in Sri Lanka. *Georgetown Journal of International Affairs,* 9(2), 97–104.

Chaudhary, A.R. & Moss, D.M. (2016). *Triadic political opportunity structures: Reconceptualising immigrant transnational politics.* International Migration Institute. Working Paper 129.

Cohen, R. (2008). *Global Diasporas. An introduction.* Routledge.

Crinari, A. (2019). Tamil Tigers return to Swiss court. *Swissinfo.ch.* https://www.swissinfo.ch/eng/justice_tamil-tigers-return-to-swiss-court/44910146

Erdal, M. B. & Horst, C. (2010). *Engaging Diasporas in Development: A Review of Pilot Project Pakistan.* PRIO.

Faist, T. (2008). Migrants as transnational development agents: an inquiry into the newest round of the migration-development nexus. *Population, Space and Place, 14*(1): 21–42.

Gazagne, P. & Sánchez-Cacicedo, A. (2015). *Understanding the Politics of the Sri Lankan Tamil Diaspora in Switzerland Insights for the FDFA.* Global Migration Paper, No. 14. Global Migration Center.

Gerber, ML & Hungerbühler, H. (2018). Lebenssituation und Bedürfnisse der älteren tamilischen Migrationsbevölkerung in der Schweiz. Swiss Red Cross.

Glick-Schiller, N., Basch, L. G & Blanc-Szanton, C. (Eds.). (1992). *Toward a Transnational Perspective on Migration*. New York Academy of Sciences.

Smith, M. P. & Guarnizo, L. E. (1998). *Transnationalism from below*. Transaction Publishers.

Guyot, L. (2017). *From arms to politics: The new struggle of the Tamil diaspora*. NORIA.

Hammond, L. (2013). Somali transnational activism and integration in the UK: Mutually supporting strategies. *Journal of Ethnic and Migration Studies, 39*(6), 1001–1017.

Hess, M., & Korf, B. (2014). Tamil diaspora and the political spaces of second-generation activism in Switzerland. *Global Networks, 14*(4), 419–437. https://doi.org/10.1111/glob.12052

Hettiarachchi, R. (2011). *Engaging the diaspora for peacebuilding in Sri Lanka: Reflections from a practitioner.* International Alert.

Hollenbach, P., Thurairajah T. & Subramaniam. J. (2020). Gift of a temple: socio-economic and cultural changes around diasporic engagement in Jaffna Peninsula, Sri Lanka. *Contemporary South Asia*. https://doi.org/10.1080/09584935.2020.1819960

International Alert. (2016, October 17–18). *Engaging overseas Sri Lankans: Promoting responsible investment and technical assistance* [Conference Report]. Conference on Promoting Responsible Investment and Technical Assistance, Cinnamon Lakeside, Colombo.

International Crisis Group. (2010). *The Sri Lankan Tamil Diaspora after the LTTE*. (London: International Crisis Group: 1–4).

Kasinitz, P., Mollenkopf, J. H., Waters, M. C., & Holdaway, J. (2008). *Inheriting the City: The children of immigrants come of age*. Russell Sage Foundation

Krawatzek, F. & Müller-Funk, L. (2019). Two centuries of flows between 'here' and 'there': Political remittances and their transformative potential. *Journal of Ethnic and Migration Studies, 46*(6), 1003–1024. https://doi.org/10.1080/1369183X.2018.1554282

Leitner, H. & Ehrkamp, P. (2006) Transnationalism and migrants' imaginings of citizenship. *Environment and Planning, 38*, 1615–1632.

Levitt, P. (1998). Social remittances: Migration driven local-level forms of cultural diffusion. *International Migration Review, 32*(4), 926–948.

Levitt, P. & Glick-Schiller, N. (2004). Conceptualizing Simultaneity: A Transnational Social Field Perspective on Society. *International Migration Review, 38*, 1002–10039.

Levitt, P. (2009). Roots and routes: Understanding the lives of the Second Generation Transnationally, *Journal of Ethnic and Migration Studies*, 35(7), 1225–1242. https://doi.org/10.1080/13691830903006309.

Lüthi, D. (2005). *Soziale Beziehungen und Werte im Exil bewahren. Tamilische Flüchtlinge aus Sri Lanka im Raum Bern*. Arbeitsblatt Nr. 30, Instituts für Ethnologie, Universität Bern.

Lyons, T. (2007). Conflict-generated diasporas and transnational politics in Ethiopia, *Conflict, Security & Development, 7*(4), 529–549. https://doi.org/10.1080/14678800701692951

Markus, V. (2005). *In der Heimat ihrer Kinder. Tamilen in der Schweiz*. Offizin.

McDowell, C. (1996). *A Tamil asylum diaspora: Sri Lanka migration, settlement and politics in Switzerland*. Berghahn Books.

McDowell, C. (2005). 'An Asylum Diaspora: Tamils in Switzerland'. In C. Ember, M. Ember, and I. Skoggard, (eds.) *Encyclopedia of Diasporas Immigrant and Refugee Cultures Around the World, Part Two: Topics - Types of Diasporas*. Yale: Kluwer.

Moret, J., Efionayi, D. & Stants, F. (2007). *Die Srilankische Diaspora in der Schweiz*. Bundesamt für Migration BFM.

Nadarajah, S. & Vimalarajah, L. (2008). *The Politics of Transformation. The LTTE and the 2002–2006 peace process in Sri Lanka*. Berghof Research Centre for Constructive Conflict Management.

Palmer, N. (2005). *Defining a different war economy. The case of Sri Lanka*. Berghof Center for Constructive Conflict Management.

Paramsothy, T. (2018). Caste within the Sri Lankan Tamil Diaspora: *Ur* Associations and Territorial Belonging, *Anthropology Matters Journal, 18*(1), 52–82.

Smith, H. & Stares, P. (Eds.). (2007). *Diasporas in Conflict: Peace-Makers or Peace-Wreckers?* UNU Press.

Stürzinger, M. (2002). *Mapping der srilankischen Diaspora in der Schweiz*. Kurzstudie für Berghof Forschungszentrum für konstruktive Konfliktbearbeitung.

Swiss Federal Office of Statistics. (2018). Einwanderung der ständigen Wohnbevölkerung nach Staatsangehörigkeit 1991–2016, *Bundesamt für Statistik*, su-d-01.05.04.02.01

Thangarajah, C.Y. & Holdaway, L. (2011). *The Sri Lankan Tamil diaspora and the challenges for ethnic reconciliation*. Working Paper II. International Alert.

Thurairajah K. (2017). The case of the Sri Lankan Tamil diaspora and homeland: A shared ethnic identity? *Studies in Ethnicity and Nationalism, 7*(1), 115–132.

Thurairajah, T. (2015). *Sri Lankan Tamil Diaspora and the Ethos of Belonging: A Cartography of Relevant Theories*. [MA Thesis, University of Innsbruck].

Thurairajah, T., Hollenbach, P. & Alluri, R. (2020). Vertical Living: Transnational Urbanisation and Diasporic Returns to Wellawatte/Colombo, Sri Lanka, *South Asian Diaspora, 12*(1), 73–91. https://doi.org/10.1080/19438192.2019.1602105

Van Hear, N., Pieke, F. & Vertovec, S. (2004). *The contribution of UK-based diasporas to development and poverty reduction.* University of Oxford: ESRC Centre on Migration, Policy and Society (COMPAS).
Vélez-Torres, I. & Agergaard, J. (2014). Political remittances, connectivity, and the translocal politics of place: And alternative approach to the dominant narratives on 'displacement' in Colombia. *Geoforum, 53*, 116–125. https://doi.org/10.1016/j.geoforum.2014.03.001
Vertovec, S. (1999a). Three meanings of diaspora, exemplified among South Asian religions. *Diaspora, 7*(2), 1–37.
Vertovec, S. (1999b). Conceiving and Researching Transnationalism. *Ethnic and Racial Studies, 22*(2), 447–462.
Vimalarajah, L. & Cheran, R. (2010). *Empowering Diasporas: The Dynamics of Post-war Transnational Tamil Diaspora.* Berghof Occasional Paper No. 31.
Vimalarajah, L. et al. (2011). Berghof Peace Support. Engaging Tamil Diaspora for peace and development. Berghof Peace Support. (January 2009–March 2011).
Viruell-Fuentes, E. A. (2006). "My heart is always there": the transnational practices of first-generation Mexican immigrant and second-generation Mexican American women. *Identities, 13*(3), 335–362.
Wayland, S. (2004). Ethnonationalist networks and transnational opportunities: The Sri Lankan Tamil diaspora. *Review of International Studies, 30*(03), 405–426. https://doi.org/10.1017/S0260210504006138
Weiss Fagen, P. & Bump, M.N. (2006). Remittances in Conflict and Crises: How Remittances Sustain Livelihoods in War, Crises, and Transitions to Peace. Security-Development Nexus Program Policy Paper. New York; Washington, DC: International Peace Academy; Georgetown University.

CHAPTER 18

Receiving the Gift of the Master's Voice: How White Western Academic Paradigms Shape Knowledge and Remittance Economies: A De-Colonial Perspective

Brigitte Bönisch-Brednich

Introduction

In 2011, a group of eminent anthropologists founded the journal *HAU: Journal of Ethnographic Theory*. It is independent of any publishing house, free to download, and does not take any fees from authors wishing to publish therein. Indeed, it claims to be founded on the concept of hau, the spirit of the gift, of reciprocity, as Marcel Mauss explained this Māori concept in his famous book on the gift (1923/1924). The journal's spirit of reciprocity is clearly expressed in its open access policy. Early in 2018, a scandal broke out around *HAU,* concerning the mistreatment of young academic associates, wage theft, and bullying. What is interesting here is that, in the same year, Māori scholars and New Zealand anthropologists

B. Bönisch-Brednich (✉)
Victoria University of Wellington, Wellington, New Zealand
e-mail: brigitte.bonisch-brednich@vuw.ac.nz

S. Meyer, C. Ströhle (eds.), *Remittances as Social Practices and Agents of Change*,
https://doi.org/10.1007/978-3-030-81504-2_18

had raised serious concerns about the journal appropriating a living Māori concept without exploring or explaining its indigenous context, rather relying solely on Mauss. They argued that, as the spiritual essence of hau is reciprocity and connection, its understanding should be reconnected to its past and present meaning inside Māoridom.

Jade Gifford, a Māori anthropologist, has traced the appropriation of hau, the history of handing on this knowledge and interpretation from the eminent Māori chief Tamati Ranapiri, who first shared this knowledge with the white New Zealand ethnographer Elsdon Best, and then its appropriation following from Mauss. She called this linear form of the appropriation of indigenous knowledge "the gift that keeps on giving" (Gifford 2018; Stewart 2017). Clearly, the rules of reciprocity and knowledge exchange and the respect that such exchange requires had followed colonial rule: The ethnographer was *the* author, the Māori holder of knowledge was seen simply as *a* storyteller. The problem Jade Gifford pointed to is less the history of how hau came to be known to the Western world; the problem is that this direction of travel and the lack of respect for indigenous knowledge are still pervasive. Clearly, anthropology is still a long way away from its goal of being a decolonized and epistemically diverse discipline. Tracing social and academic remittances is one way to envisage the many possibilities through which we can contribute to this process.

The second story I will use as an introduction is quoted from a conversation I had with a colleague who joined a New Zealand university about ten years ago.[1] As a person of color—or more to the point of 'African color'—they felt very visible and often uneasy on the new campus. Speaking about there first year at her New Zealand campus, they said:

> But then I couldn't help feel different, in that, if you are looking different, you know you can't think about that you are black or white or whatever, but it was a constant question; how do these people see me? Do they accept me or, am I doing things the right way, so all of those questions kept cropping up in my mind, and so it was, it was good to have the support but at the same time I felt that there was a little bit of self-sabotaging that I was doing to myself because of these notions that I am probably not as good as others,

[1] The interview quotes and stories used in this chapter are data I collected for a long-term project on international academic mobility and migration. This project has been approved by the ethics committee of Victoria University of Wellington. All quotes are anonymized and universities are not identified.

> different from others, therefore I am not going to progress as much as others. So, yes, I am still here and that's because I'm determined to go, to get ahead and succeed. (Scholar from West Africa, New Zealand campus)

Their experience of being different, but being determined to succeed, while also harboring anxieties of not being good enough, about self-sabotaging, about having to change, to adjust to the 'master's voice,' is at the heart of what I am going to discuss here: namely, that higher education, its ideal of free-flowing knowledge exchange, and the reality of power dynamics serve to imbalance the structure that exchanges and determines the avenues and direction of this exchange. The 'master's voice' stands for the conditions and requirements to be accepted into the game of international academia, to attain the right habitus, and to enable a future career. In the following, I will analyze the intersection of the knowledge economy and power imbalances from the perspective of social remittances. As opposed to the general understanding of remittances as a path to a better life, I will take a critical look at social remittances: What does circulating knowledge mean from a decolonializing perspective? The aim is to trace how, in receiving countries, colonial structures perpetrate remittance scripts on an economic, social, and emotional level (Carling 2014). Here, I am guided by Walter Mignolo's concept of the coloniality of power, of which he states that, apart from obvious forms of colonial power (such as control of the economy, policing, nature and natural resources, gender, and sexuality), colonial power also controls and determines subjectivity and knowledge (Mignolo 2016, p. 50). Coloniality controls and still holds a monopoly over what counts as knowledge and, therefore, constantly enacts colonizing strategies of epistemological violence. Most current practices of remitting exist because the world is a place of deep inequalities that can be mapped into 'First World' or 'Third World,' developed and developing countries, regions of wealth, and regions of desperate poverty.

> Colonization was more than material exploitation. It entailed the imposition of the colonizer's form of knowing and conceiving the world [...]. This racialized social classification, which places Western-oriented forms of being and thinking at the top, still influences both material structures and intersubjective relations of power. (Arashiro et al. 2015, p. XI)

Knowledge and Remittance Economy

Despite the unbalanced direction of knowledge flows and the inherent brain drain from the academic periphery to the center (Levitt and Crul 2018), the academic world also opens up great integrative possibilities. Remittances, viewed in terms of intellectual flows, enrich and curtail simultaneously. Exchanging ideas and "trying to know better or more" is one of the leading concepts underpinning academic work. The gift of giving knowledge, sharing research, and ensuring a free flow of ideas is seen as pivotal to the functioning of academic networks and the generation of academic currency. When mapping the world in terms of where remittances come from and where they go, these maps are tightly related to a political and economic structuring of the global knowledge economy. Money flows and educational 'standards' are directed in similar streams of gifting and receiving remittances. Knowledge exchange, however, is hardly ever seen as a political and cultural system worthy of anthropological analysis.

Thinking in terms of Emmanuel Levinas's concept of gift-giving, we can see the exchange of knowledge as the basis of academic work and scholarship: "Giving is first and foremost [...] a metaphysical act that makes possible the communication between a self and an Other—as trans-ontological—as well as the sharing of a common world" (cited in Maldonado-Torres 2007, p. 258). This kind of exchange, as a true dialogue, is however only possible when the self and the Other view each other as equal partners and both view the dialogue as an act of reciprocity of knowledge exchange and the furthering of knowledge as a true trans-ontological moment. For this to happen, we need "to restore the logic of the gift through a decolonial politics of receptive generosity" (Maldonado-Torres 2007, p. 261).

We know that Elson Best received the gift of Tamati Ranapiri's knowledge about the Tūhoe; Ranapiri was considered the expert on his tribe's knowledge and history (Holman 2010). Best went on to write one of the most influential books on Māori anthropology and one could argue that he left a treasure trove for Māori to read and reclaim some of this knowledge. Best also went on to be acknowledged by European scholars such as Mauss, whereas Ranapiri's co-authorship was never acknowledged as such. The concept of hau thus miraculously became what we call a 'Maussian concept,' shedding the ties that bind it to its origin and its academic and cultural ancestry. It could therefore be used to title an open access journal that views itself as a gift to anthropologists who are interested in theory. Which theory? The direction of knowledge travel is obscured but obvious to the non-Western scholar. The knowledge economy invites selected scholars from developing nations and settler nations alike to join their circles and send back remittances to their compatriot academics. They remit money to support their families, but they also remit in the currency of knowledge, giving back to their home universities in terms of sending downloaded articles, negotiating scholarships and grants, gifting library books, and returning for the odd sabbatical to share 'up-to-date' knowledge. The gateways to an academic career appear not so much as a cycle of exchange but a gifting of knowledge that devalues other forms of knowledge (by calling them stories or data). This marks certain ontologies as valid currency and others as raw material that needs shaping.

Social remittances encompass ideas, values, norms, and different forms of knowledge (Levitt and Crul 2018; Vari-Lavoisier 2020). When remitted 'knowledge' is discussed in developmental terms, it is framed either as brain drain or as brain gain. What is largely missing from this research approach is the people owning those brains: How does it feel when scholars have to live with knowledge systems that are constraining, silencing, and devaluing? What are the effects of the moments when an academic experiences a knowledge exchange in which she/he/they is given the role of the apprentice listening to the master's voice? These situations are subtle or aggressive encounters and they almost always reflect skewed power relationships, which can be based on differences of class, gender, race, or nationality. As Meyer (in this volume) points out, these situations project global inequalities onto personal relationships. They are most often encountered when academics migrate to another country and campus. They also take place in so-called settler societies with an indigenous minority whose members struggle to participate fully in higher education and knowledge systems that remain white in color and Western in terms of accepted ontology and epistemology. In this sense, academic remittances contribute to both a condensation of institutional centers and the possibility of partial inclusion of knowledge from the peripheries and participation of its academics. In that sense, knowledge refers to Levitt's and Lamba-Nieves's (2011) argument that remittances can contribute to national and transnational shifts in power relations.

I will discuss these issues in three sections, each accompanied by an example and each with a distinctive emphasis on what working inside 'the master narrative' can mean to different academics. To this end, I am using

Carling's concept of 'remittance scripts' as a framework to detect such scripts and how they play out in the drama that is the international knowledge economy. As Carling pointed out, remittance scripts give us parameters of comparison, they make visible "segmented transfers and layered transaction" (Carling 2014, p. 252). By interrogating such scripts, we can stage academic scenarios that help us develop a decolonial lens for appreciating the social drama that is international academia.

In the first such reading of a script, I will adopt an intersectional approach to discuss the shaping and reshaping of academic habitus. If academic second-language speakers (non-English, that is) or bilingual indigenous knowledge systems are made invisible and/or are colonized, then we need to think along a stratum of colonializations that disadvantage different scholars to different degrees.

In the second scenario, I will discuss the topic of the English language. The global 'universal knowledge,' the global knowledge hegemony, has been able to utilize English not only as a tool that enables us to talk with each other but to rule the academic world with an abundance of epistemic and symbolic violence. It makes sense to link Bourdieu's analysis of 'Ce que parler veut dire' to the challenging question of "How come if an academic does not speak in English, they do not exist?" An interrogation of the economy of language, exchange, and power needs to look at the meaning of a proclaimed *lingua franca*. Not only linguistic exchange with all its enriching possibilities, but also epistemic violence and (mono)linguistic colonialism and provincialism seem to rule the academic world.

Third, I will address the powerful script of declaiming 'universal knowledge,' a concept that has served well to disguise, normalize, and empower the master's voice. To state that there is universal knowledge by upholding a paradigm of global knowledge, it is necessary to make invisible all other knowledges or at least to confine them to the realm of knowledge deficit, of lacking the 'right' kind of knowledge.

In short, we need to read these remittance scenarios as a means and practice of reproducing colonial structures. Academic remittance scripts, like most other scripts, are controlling and patronizing but simultaneously also empowering and liberating. Hence, remittances do not supply the means for a better life but they should also be framed critically as a tool of colonialism. They are a developmental tool, but within academia the concept of development is void of positionality and therefore has limited reach and limited reciprocity.

Scenario 1: Who is Speaking? Who is Listening?

Theodor Adorno, one of Germany's most influential academic migrants of the twentieth century, famously wrote that

> every intellectual in emigration is, without exception, mutilated, and does well to acknowledge it to himself. He lives in an environment that must remain incomprehensible to him [...] he is always astray. [...] His language has been expropriated, and he is cut off from the historical dimension that informed his knowledge. (Adorno 1951, pp. 32–33, my translation)

When Adorno wrote about his experience as an exile in the USA, he wrote from the position of somebody with good networks, somebody who was highly educated, male, white, and who at the time of writing enjoyed a wide intellectual reputation (Coser 1984, pp. 91–99). Still, he felt mutilated; he mourned the loss of his first language, the position from which his knowledge had evolved.

How, then, does academic mobility shape scholars who are less privileged, maybe less male and white, and do not speak a first language that might at least fit into historically formed Western categories of certified knowledge? We can view the German language and the knowledge of the first half of the twentieth century as valid and even highly influential: It was directly informed by the European Enlightenment and was based on a commonly shared and known set of canonical authors such as Hegel, Marx, and Kant. In sum, Adorno's knowledge base was thus very close to what one would expect US American scholars to be familiar with. And still he felt 'mutilated' and 'astray.' How, then, do scholars fare whose knowledge is not part of that canon of Enlightenment, whose knowledge can only partially claim a kinship connection to the Western history of ideas? And, more to the point, how is their education flipped when they try to settle into a 'Western' campus and participate in the global knowledge economy? Alexandra Macht rightly pointed out that the act of translating one's academic self into English means both entering into a process of hybridization that can be enriching and liberating and also enacting a process of emotional diminishment (Macht 2018).

Interrogating how it feels to be mutilated and astray is a first step for me—a white academic migrant—to start listening in a meaningful manner. To get how it feels to be mutilated can be a first step toward understanding the ruptured and painful realization that only one party will determine the modes of academic exchange (see also Pherali 2012; Schütz 1944, p. 499). The following short vignette, which was written in a writing workshop for mobile academics that I chaired, will help illustrate this (Bönisch-Brednich 2017, 2018). The writing exercise I had set was to try and write about a scene in which the mobile scholar was very conscious of being an academic migrant. This vignette is titled *Welcome to Scandinavia (With Conditions)* and was written by a senior British academic telling the story of how she and her partner enrolled in a compulsory language school to learn the respective Scandinavian language:[2]

> The form asked the usual personal details, our first language, employment position or status, level of education, and whether we had previously learnt a second language. I put down English, PhD, Professor, and Persian. My partner put down English, BA, retired, none. A few weeks later I received a letter asking me to come to the language school for a test. The teacher collected me from the waiting area and took me to her room and sat down behind her desk with an exasperated sigh, all without yet looking at me. (This was strange as I'd learnt it was polite to shake hands when meeting someone in Denmark and look them in the eye). Head still bowed, and still sighing, she wrote a sentence in English in big letters on a scrap of paper and handed it to me saying, 'Point out the adverb'. I asked her if it was a trick question, as there wasn't an adverb. 'Well, the adverbial phrase, then,' she said angrily. I read out the clause that modified the verb, and she said OK. The test was obviously over. As I stood up, I asked if everyone had to have such a test, as my partner had not yet been invited. She said no, there must be something on your form. She took up my form and looked at it for the first time, stabbing at the word Persian with her finger, 'You speak Persian, so we have to be sure you have enough understanding of English to learn Danish, as that's the teaching medium.' I pointed out that I had also put British, PhD, and Professor on the form, as well as saying English was my first language. She looked and saw that I had, but just repeated, we have to check because you wrote 'Persian.' (Female, white British mobile academic 2016)

This scene is written and conceptualized like a report and closes with the word 'Persian.' The writing academic avoids directly describing her feelings. Her emotions are, however, signaled by the mention of the teacher being exasperated, sighing, not looking at her, stabbing her finger at the form, and stressing the word 'Persian.' This final word marks the end of a conversation; no apology is offered, no exchange that resembles

[2] All personal and geographical details in this text have been changed to ensure anonymity.

polite behavior takes place. Her academic titles, her English ethnicity, her age are rendered invisible; she experiences disrespect and suspicion and she is made to feel like a nuisance that needs to be checked on; she is a managed Other. The relevance of this encounter for the author can be traced in these wordings, and in the fact that this is what she chose to write about when she was asked to describe a scene when she had felt like a migrant or a stranger. For her, a very senior academic with a significant international reputation, this story encapsulated feelings that serve as a powerful reminder that, even now, after fifteen years in her host country, she is made to feel foreign. I would also like to add that she was made to feel astray, despite her privilege of being white, European, and speaking with an educated English accent.

To further explore how these unbalancing conversations devalue and unsettle academics on their new campuses, I will add the voice of Rosalba Icaza, a non-white, Mexican, female academic writing about her realization of being Other:

> From Mexico to Warwickshire in the United Kingdom, then to Gothenburg in Sweden, and finally to The Hague in the Netherlands: as highly skilled female migrants, the un-rooted ones imagine ourselves as highly mobile and flexible (neoliberal) workers, ready to adjust, to learn, and in doing so, ready to continue forgetting. As the ultimate emancipated being we wanted to imagine ourselves as not genderized, and not racialized; as global placeless citizens and without a predetermined future.
>
> Until the day someone asks you who do you think you are? And reminds you not to forget what is supposed to be your role in 'their society.' That is the day when the falseness and the violence of this supposedly free-from-past-place-domesticated subjectivity is painfully experienced in our incarnated encounter with academia in the North. (Icaza 2015, p. 5)

She continues, citing a PhD student:

> The experience of being a female 'Latin American' student and then a PhD in a European university has changed me a lot. It made me much more aware of the forces of coloniality [...]. I find this obsession to classify people and ourselves very oppressive. Being a migrant and having experienced racism and discrimination has taught me so much about power and identity. (Icaza 2015, p. 5)

Icaza and, I am sure, the PhD student as well imagined themselves—at the beginning of their mobility—as not genderized, not racialized, as global citizens without a predetermined future; they moved with hope and optimism. In comparison to their English colleague in Scandinavia who experienced the shock of status loss and doubt about her hitherto unchallenged right to belong in Europe, the two 'Latin American' academics felt astray in different and, probably, even more painful ways. They were constantly made aware of their different 'bodily' appearance, they felt colonized, labeled, and oppressed. They also had to give up their language of instruction (Mexican Spanish) and to operate in English as well as the local language. In order to be able to remit, the ability to unlearn and switch was required. Again, this shows that the concept of remittances entails inequity and an incline in power (see Meyer in this volume). Before Icaza could remit, she had to adopt the subject position of the Western academic.

Their above-quoted English colleague in Scandinavia learned the local language, but she could continue to write and teach in English, her mother tongue, and continue teaching inside a Western scholarly framework. They, however had to switch, unlearn, and relearn. Scenarios of switching and of entering the English-speaking 'international' academic world are often managed by giving scholarships to postgraduates and postdocs scholars, which are designed to support knowledge transfers. These are gifts to the gifted, they are viewed as empowering, as gate openers, as bridges between worlds. To switch academic codes, to accept power imbalances and sliding hierarchies, is seen as part of the deal. Such switching is expected on several levels. The most obvious ones for the two above-quoted academics were leaving their Mexican academic framework (losing their academic history and habitus) and switching to the master's voice and tools: the English language and Anglophone scholarship and pedagogy (gaining entry by deprioritizing their language). These gives and takes are part of the academic exchange. The gains will flow back to home countries as knowledge remittances in terms of inclusions into networks, access to international grants, and an enriched curriculum vitae.

Scenario 2: The Listening Language, or the Monolingual Knowledge Economy

Let us remind ourselves of Adorno's statement about the migrant/exile scholar, whose "language has been expropriated." The script of 'learning the language' is hugely powerful and, albeit empowering and exhilarating for many, it is also an (unbalancing) experience.

What it means to have few language skills and to arrive in a new place is well-described by a New Zealand scholar who teaches Asian languages at an Australian university. Although being perfectly aware of his own privilege, he cares deeply about his students from Asia and the way they are treated on arrival:

> Yeah. You can sink or swim. In fact, there's a great deal of—Australia is a very racist place. I think there's a great deal of resentment, you know. I don't know how many times I've seen this happen. You've got this group of students mainly from China now. Often quite bright, but their English is not particularly good, and they are treated with absolute contempt by everyone here. It's really scary. Particularly if they are girls. The racist, sexist way of... I had occasions where I made a point of going on to the enrolment process and just to see how the whole thing worked, and these kids from China were lining up to get their forms signed, and this and that, and it was just ghastly. The way they were talked at. Shouted at. Kind of, 'Why are you [not speaking properly]...' You know .... (Male NZ scholar, Australian university)

It is imperative on arrival to learn English as fast as possible but learning English means so much more than simply learning a language. Academics and students alike are required to accept a monolingual way of doing academic work, of functioning in one language only, of thinking inside an Anglophone academic framework, and abandoning or shelving the academic habitus they had previously acquired in their home culture. "To many of us," wrote Zuleika Arashiro et al., "for whom English is not our first language, writing and learning how to think within it has impacted on our academic identity. In Anglo-American universities, we have learned to use well the tools of the master" (Arashiro et al. 2015, p. XIII).

It is helpful here to reread what Bourdieu had to say on the power of language conventions and the symbolic violence that is enacted around the forces that define correct language use. "Integration into a single 'linguistic community,' which is a product of the political domination that is endlessly reproduced by institutions capable of imposing universal recognition of the dominant language is the condition for the establishment of relations of linguistic domination" (Bourdieu 1991, p. 46; see also Hua and Kramsch 2016). Bourdieu was thinking about social distinctions in France when he wrote his book on language and symbolic power. However, if we read his analysis as also being relevant to power imbalances inside the knowledge economy, we can gain important insights into the forces at work that push the agenda of a monolingual academia. It is not just a question of who is allowed to speak; it is who is able to speak in English, with one of the accepted English accents, and to display an academic habitus that indicates membership in the club of international academic speech criteria. Bourdieu wrote:

> Speakers lacking the legitimate competence are de facto excluded from the social domains in which this competence is required, or are condemned to silence. What is rare, then, is not the capacity to speak, which, being part of our biological heritage, is universal and therefore essentially non-distinctive, but rather the competence necessary in order to speak the legitimate language which, depending on social inheritance, re-translates social distinctions into the specifically symbolic logic of differential deviations, or, in short, distinction. (Bourdieu 1991, p. 55)

There is, therefore, more at stake than simply the creation of a *lingua franca*. Scholars who move into Anglophone university domains experience the dominance of that language as claustrophobic, as silencing a multilingual and multicultural academia that could and should be characterized by epistemic diversity.

Thus Arashiro et al. argued that

> while English has provided a global link for scholarly communication, its dominance defines the contours of what is relevant to know and what can be ignored by academics. Much like the Eurocentric transformation of the local into an abstract universal, the hegemony of English creates the fiction of the partial as totality. As Ortiz observes, 'under the condition of global modernity, then, it is perfectly plausible and commonplace to be globally provincial.' (Arashiro et al. 2015, p. XIII)

Language, therefore, is much more than simply a mode of understanding each other (Bachmann-Medick 2018; Inghilleri 2017). English also directs the flow of knowledge, the direction of travel. The knowledge market is dominated by English scholarship, with few translations from other European languages, even fewer from the Global South. It creates a "reductionist notion of international as monolingual" (Arashiro 2015, p. 153). Similarly, Arashiro asked in her analysis of the Global South and its relationship to Western academia: "How many political scientists from the Global South can we cite who have been recognized in Western universities for their contribution to the understanding of US or European politics? Why do scholars from the Global North find it so natural to study the Global South but so hard to imagine the reverse?" (Arashiro 2015, p. 144).

What is important to notice here is not just who is allowed to speak in which language and who is required to learn that master voice. We also need to interrogate the positionality from which the terms of the knowledge exchange are imparted. When thinking in terms of remittance scripts, we can ask what it does to academia when the terms of exchange are determined in a different currency. The gifting currency is defined as giving the language, the opportunities; the receiving currency is the ability to switch, to unlearn, to accept loss, and to feel empowerment by switching.

Scenario 3: The Terms of Knowledge Exchange

For the purposes of this discussion, I would like to remind the reader of the last point in Adorno's above-quoted statement. When he wrote that every emigrant scholar is "cut off from the historical dimension that informed his knowledge," or, as Schütz termed it, a "man without history" (Schütz 1944), and that every academic is well-advised to acknowledge that to himself, he made a very important point about the positionality of knowledge. When referring to positionality, we have to think of English as the universal language and therefore English-speaking universities as the giving institutions of universal knowledge. To claim belonging, to accept the gift of the master's knowledge system, we need to think of the necessary processes of translation involved in sharing in the privileges of positionality (Bachmann-Medick 2018; Hua 2016; Macht 2018; Spieker 2021).

The task presented to a migrant scholar is to unlearn or shelve the historic dimension of their knowledge and to relearn to live with a new position of scholarly engagement. Again, I will here start with an empirical example. Although the following vignette records an auto-ethnographic experience of a South Asian scholar, it was written in the third person and therefore suggests an intersubjective experience that could and does happen to more than one person. It is set in an introductory university course in Scandinavia. The language of tuition is English and the aim of the course is to teach foreign early-career academics 'proper academic writing':

> Mette (the teacher) asked 'where are you from?'... Mette repeated the question with her strong Scandinavian accent and relatively loud voice. From the facial expression, this second question really meant 'why are you here?'...

> her ego hurt, her 'expat hormone' started to rise... She remembers being told by a colleague that 'most Scandinavian teachers on our course said that we—international students from developing countries do not know how to write an academic paper. They never questioned, in the first place, why their academic expectations are the only standards against which our performance must be measured, how much do they know about our academic traditions. We were perceived as what we lacked instead of what we were able to contribute'.... Having been an international student in four different European countries, a migrant worker, and a mobile researcher [she came] to realize that her identity is multi-layered and sometimes 'hybrid'. (South Asian scholar, Scandinavian campus, 2016)

Two important points are raised here. The first is the pain of being labeled as lacking the 'right,' that is, Western knowledge, and thus having one's education and historic dimension devalued and made invisible. The second is a clearly expressed anger about being colonized and forced into a Western knowledge system that is based on ontological intolerance and a false sense of superiority. However, this was also written from a personal position of somebody who has made it, who also lives the empowering aspects of the knowledge economy. The script is now co-written, produced and viewed as being author and reader alike.

The term global knowledge economy has propagated a universal system of knowledge. The existence of satellite campus locations, of canonized literature that influences academic disciplines on a worldwide scale, and the universal demand for English-speaking tuition promises students and academics the possibility of going 'everywhere.' They can acquire, distribute, and enlarge the world's knowledge wherever they choose to go. That, at least, is the implication of the narrative that surrounds and shapes the knowledge economy. Academic remittances in this sense are a means of controlling knowledge beyond the Western world as script. If the ubiquitous and therefore invisible positionality of knowledge is a powerful script that is handed as a gift, it can be both a wonderful enriching opening and a slow-releasing poison.

In her reflections on her own mobility, Zuleika Arashiro, a political scientist from Brazil working at an Australian university, wrote:

> Latin American thinkers can trigger in me a deep sense of familiarity, with their emphasis on history and critical thinking as foundational for the construction of knowledge and meanings. Moreover, there is something in the writing style that immediately takes me back to the kind of full communica-

> tion that I was used to before moving into English-speaking academia. The power of language to take us back to places, to carry hidden meanings available only for those who share histories, is what links me to both Portuguese and Spanish as my languages. (Arashiro 2015, p. 139)

She continues her reflection with a recollection of the silence that greeted academic migrants coming to Australia. Nobody, she remembered, asked where you came from, nobody wanted to know what you knew. For her and fellow migrant scholars, it was as though they only became alive at the moment one appeared on an Australian campus. There was a lack of curiosity or a need to silence migrants that seemed to apply especially to non-white migrants. Again, we can observe the exchange of different currencies. Participation is remitted to academics from the periphery. The expected reciprocity has to be paid by starting anew, by forgetting and unlearning, and by not insisting on the existence of other knowledges. This lack of curiosity is the first signal of a refusal to engage with other forms of knowledge outside the accepted canon. Reflecting on this, Eugenia Demuro pointed out that

> those of us speaking from de-centred positions are witness to—and worse, are expected to knowingly partake in and be an accomplice to—the exclusion of other knowledges and ways of being. I studied and taught in programs where Literature (with a capital L) meant Anglo-American and European literature, excluding almost entirely other traditions and works—although making concessions for a minor number of authors selectively curated as 'world literature'. Similarly, many of the Latin American course syllabi that I have seen in Australian universities contain extensive lists of authors writing about Latin America and exclude almost entirely authors from Latin America [...]. It is as much in these omissions that the coloniality of knowledge materializes. (Demuro 2015, p. 122)

Knowledge, however, always emanates from the place in which it is conceived. It is therefore most rich and honest when it is situated and positioned. It is indeed unsettling to watch the normalization of a so-called universal knowledge that can be voiced from nowhere, and therefore conceals its origin in a Western Anglophone worldview. Satellite campus locations and monolingual scholarship distribute and gift a master narrative of and to the world that is colonizing, homogenizing, and silencing other possible narratives. However, scholars who resist this brief and insist on consciously positioning knowledge as coming from diverse locations are gaining a stronger voice. We also see more and more academic texts written in English, but interspersed with quotes in other languages. This is not accidental; it is a conscious act of pointing to the valid existence of academic languages other than English. It is also pointing out the fact that the author is capable of functioning in more than one language, whereas the reader might not be. Epistemic disobedience, the calling for epistemic diversity, demands a different kind of gifting of knowledge. This kind of gifting unbalances white, Western, privileged ontologies; it offers a multilingual and multicultural tapestry of knowledges. It is richer and in its disobedience quite unsettling. Such positioning "is about finding the place where one has been put. It is about stating the place from where one can speak" (Arber 2000, p. 58).

Such positioning demands epistemic justice and a decentering of knowledge exchange. It asks for a surrendering of epistemic privileges on the side of Western, colonizing academia, and it is driven by a pan-global movement of scholars who are calling for a practice of epistemic disobedience; scholars who aim for a true sharing of knowledges. They basically ask to trade academic currencies that offer a valuable exchange and therefore an equitable multilingual remittance script.

Conclusion

The fascinating part of such academic disobedience is that, in order to gain a position from which to resist and change, the habitus of a Western-type of academic first needs to be acquired. The shock of leaving one's own academic world and moving to a Western country and campus will involve an initial unsettling of one's own academic habitus. To a scholar, migration, especially from the periphery into the center of paradigmatic power, will involve loss (unlearning) and intellectual reformation (colonization). It is likely to come with a deep feeling of being astray, of one's knowledge being devalued or even being made invisible, and of the silencing of one's own language if it is other than English. This will be followed by the acquisition of what decolonial scholars have come to term the master's tools and the master's voice in order to be accepted into the game, to attain the right habitus, and to enable a future career. It is also very likely to come with a heightened sense of reflexivity and self-consciousness that is required to change habitus, even more necessary if the next step is a resistance to and reshaping of the academic habitus.

If such migrants simultaneously embrace academic work and resist and try to change its hegemonic ontological insistence on Western knowledge systems, then they must also work on changing the academic habitus that is still mainly male, white, and exclusionary of alternative modes of playing the game. Walter D. Mignolo is such a migrant scholar from the Global South who set out to enlarge paradigms of knowledge construction and actively changed the way we perceive and distribute knowledge. Linda Tuhiwai-Smith is a powerful example of a Māori, female, socially mobile academic who fundamentally transformed the ways in which we look at past and present colonizing methodologies and disciplinary politics. Mignolo's book *Epistemic Disobedience* (2016) and Tuhiwai Smith's work *De-colonizing Methodologies* (2012) have had a lasting impact on such discussions. They are game-changers and goal-post shifters who have been followed by new generations of mobile and indigenous scholars who are inspired by their work. Such an academic politics of liberation needs to involve resistance to a narrow alignment of scholarship inside Western ontologies. It must also include resistance to neoliberal academic violence by auditing systems that cement such ontologies in the form of journal rankings, publishing strategies, and performance reviews that exclude, for example, activism, community engagement, and publications in non-mainstream languages.

As the exchange of social remittances in the form of knowledge is the basis of academic work and scholarship, it needs to be rethought as a true international process of reciprocity and listening. Going back to Maldonado-Torres's argument that "giving is first and foremost [...] a metaphysical act that makes possible the communication between a self and an Other—as trans-ontological—as well as the sharing of a common world" (Maldonado-Torres 2007, p. 258), academic remitting requires a new global outlook on postcoloniality and decolonial politics of reciprocity.

For scholars, migrant, indigenous, or otherwise, to experience a restored logic of the gift or in order, to quote Gifford again, for the gift to be able to keep giving, we need a new definition of sharing in the global knowledge and remittance economy. We need to challenge the master's narrative and its monolingual voiceover. We need to trace concepts such as hau to their origins and stop viewing indigenous voices as storytellers and Western voices as knowledge converters. There is a groundswell of resistance, especially from the Global South. One tiny example of how such challenges are laid down can be read in the (second) open letter to the board of trustees of the journal *HAU*. It was sent by Mahi Tahi, a group of activist scholars in Aotearoa New Zealand that aims to decolonize its ways of knowing (in anthropology):

> Finally, we encourage you, along with all anthropology journals, to think hard about how specific issues, like the claiming of an indigenous name, are symptomatic of much wider structures of inequality. We should all take a hard look at the way our 'top' journals reproduce and reinforce privilege and power for certain circles of academics (often white, often based at high prestige institutions in the US, the UK and Europe, often linked to editors through personal networks, often invited to contribute) and how this too is part of the ongoing effects of colonisation that are still writ large within anthropology. In other words, decolonising a journal doesn't just mean consulting on indigenous terms, it means challenging the hierarchies of knowledge that systematically exclude BIPOC scholars.[3]

The gifting of knowledge needs to challenge the direction of knowledge dissemination, it seems. We need to rethink the directions in which remittances flow. Making visible these avenues and, therefore, the positions of knowledge acquisition and conversion into a social remittance will initially make most Western academics uncomfortable. It is hard to acknowledge and name Western privilege and it is difficult to accept the presence of other knowledges. Trying to do this, even to start with acknowledging it, feels like losing one's academic balance along with many certainties. However, learning to be okay with being uncomfortable and being challenged would be a first step to a new reciprocity in scholarship.

Epilogue

It is worth taking a moment to think about academic remittances and the politics of recognition in the global knowledge economy when looking at the content of this book. The editors tried to gather an international group of authors, most of whom are from countries that have a national

[3] BIPOC means Black, Indigenous, and People of Color. Mahi Tahi is a collective working under the auspices of the New Zealand national anthropology association, ASAA/NZ. Mahi Tahi seeks to foster a space for exploring the relationship between Māori and anthropology and to recognize the important role that Māori scholars have played and continue to play in shaping our discipline in Aotearoa. Mahi Tahi letter to the board of trustees of *Hau* 2018, http://www.asaanz.org/blog/2018/6/21/a-response-and-second-open-letter-to-the-hau-journals-board-of-trustees

language other than English. We also see a certain Austrian positionality in terms of the recognition of Europe and specifically Eastern Europe. Yet the attempt is to map remittances on a truly international scale. This means that English is the *lingua franca* of this book, but we also see a level of reflexivity and willingness to engage with new academic politics of hospitality and perspectives from different peripheries.

Acknowledgements I would like to thank both editors for their thoughtful and constructive comments on my draft, Graeme Whimp for many discussions and readings of different versions, and Angela McCarthy and Frances L. Collins for some last-minute tweaks in my thinking.

References

Adorno, T. (1951). *Minima Moralia: Reflexionen aus einem beschädigten Leben*. Suhrkamp.

Arashiro, Z. (2015). Silence and Voice in the Other South. In Z. Arashiro & E. Demuro (Eds.), *Women in Academia Crossing North-South Borders: Gender, Race and Displacement*. (pp. 137–157). Lexington Books.

Arashiro, Z., Demuro, E. & Barahonha, M. (2015). Introduction: Thinking Through our Voices. In Z. Arashiro & E. Demuro (Eds.), *Women in Academia Crossing North-South Borders: Gender, Race and Displacement* (pp. VII–XVII). Lexington Books.

Arber, R. (2000). Defining Positioning within Politics of Difference: Negotiating Spaces 'In between'. *Race, Ethnicity and Education* 3(1), 45–63.

Bachmann-Medick, D. (2018). Migration as Translation. In D. Bachmann-Medick & J. Kugele (Eds.), Migration. Changing Concepts, Critical Approaches (pp. 273–293). De Gruyter.

Bönisch-Brednich, B. (2017). An Ethnographic Writing Workshop on Academic Mobility. In C. Balaban & S. Wright (Eds.) *Policies and Experiences of Mobility in Doctoral Education: UNIKE Notes on Doctoral Education* 5 (pp. 11–16). UNIKE.

Bönisch-Brednich, B. (2018). Reflecting on the Mobile Academic: Autoethnographic Writing in the Knowledge Economy. *LATISS: Learning and Teaching. The International Journal of Higher education in the Social Sciences*, 69–91.

Bourdieu, P. (1991). *Language and Symbolic Power*. Polity Press.

Carling, J. (2014). Scripting Remittances: Making Sense of Money Transfers in Transnational Relationships. *International Migration Review* 48(1), 218–262.

Coser, L. A. (1984). *Refugee Scholars in America: Their Impact and their Experiences*. Yale University Press.

Demuro, E. (2015). Delinking from the Zero Degree: Reflections from the Antipodes. In Z. Arashiro & E. Demuro (Eds.), *Women in Academia Crossing North-South Borders: Gender, Race and Displacement* (pp. 117–136). Lexington Books.

Gifford, J. (2018). *Ka whiti-te-rā, Ka tō te rā, Ka ahatea te rākau me tōna puawaitanga? Glimpses into the History of Māori and Anthropology in Aotearoa* [Honours dissertation, Te Herenga Waka—Victoria University of Wellington].

Holman, J. Paparoa (2010). *Best of Both Worlds: The Story of Elsdon Best and Tutakangahau.* Penguin Books.

Hua, Z. (2016). 'Where are you from?': Interculturality and Interactional Practices. In A. Komisarof & Z. Hua (Eds.), Crossing Boundaries and Weaving Intercultural Work, Life, and Scholarship in Globalizing Universities (pp. 147–159). Routledge.

Hua, Z. & Kramsch, C. (2016). Symbolic Power and Conversational Inequality in Intercultural Communication: An Introduction. *Applied Linguistics Review,* 7(4), 375–384.

Icaza, R. (2015). Testimony of a Pilgrimage: (Un)Learning and Re-Learning with the South. In Z. Arashiro & E. Demuro, *Women in Academia Crossing North-South Borders: Gender, Race and Displacement* (pp. 1–25). Lexington Books.

Inghilleri, M. (2017). *Translation and Migration.* Routledge.

Levitt, P. & Crul, M. (2018). Deconstructing and Reconstructing: Embracing Alternative Ways of Producing, Classifying and Disseminating Knowledge. *etnoloska tribina* 48(41), 3–50.

Levitt, P., & Lamba-Nieves, D. (2011). Social remittances Revisited. *Journal of Ethnic and Migration Studies* 37(1), 1–22.

Macht, A. (2018). From Romanian "Soul" to English "Heart": Dilemmas of Cultural and Gender Representation in Translating Qualitative Data. *Forum Qualitative Sozialforschung/Forum Qualitative Social Research* 19(2), 1–18.

Maldonado-Torres, N. (2007). On the Coloniality of Being: Contributions to the Development of a Concept. *Cultural Studies* 21(2–3), 240–270.

Mignolo, W. D. (2016). *Epistemischer Ungehorsam: Rhetorik der Moderne, Logik der Kolonialität und Grammatik der Dekolonialität.* Turia PLUS_SPI Kant.

Pherali, T. J. (2012). Academic Mobility, Language, and Cultural Capital: The Experience of Transnational Academics in British Higher education Institutions. *Journal of Studies in International Education* 16(4), 313–333.

Schütz, A. (1944). 'The Stranger': An Essay in Social Psychology. *American Journal of Sociology* 49, 499–507.

Spieker, Ira (2021). Übersetzung: Überlegungen zu einem kulturwissenschaftlichen Konzept. In Hinrichs, P., Röthl, M. & M. Seifert (Eds.): *Theoretische Reflexionen—Perspektiven der Europäischen Ethnologie*. Waxmann (In Press).

Stewart, G. (2017). The 'Hau' of Research: Mauss Meets Kaupapa Māori. *Journal of World Philosophies*, 2, 1–11.

Tuhiwai Smith, L. (2012). *Decolonizing Methodologies*, 2nd Ed. Otago University Press.

Vari-Lavoisier, I. (2020). Social remittances. In T. Bastia & R. Skeldon (Eds.), Routledge Handbook of Migration and Development (pp. 125–135). Routledge.

CHAPTER 19

Conclusion: A Transformative Perspective on Remittances—Towards the Future of Transnational Society

Claudius Ströhle and Silke Meyer

Remittances are often told as a success story and, in general, remittance research contributes to this exuberant representation of transnational transactions. There is, of course, another side to this story and remittance research also addresses the human costs of remitting and the challenges it poses to personal relationships (e.g. Åkesson 2011; Carling 2014; Erdal 2014; Lindley 2010; Rahman and Fee 2012). However, embedded in the field of policy making and remittances economies, the consistency and uniformity in the master narrative of successful development are not surprising. Agencies like the World Bank and Western Union do not tire in promoting the universal account of development through remittances, and like most powerful narrators, they are not wrong to stress the positive effects of the enormous amounts of money that support and advance struggling regions and neglected areas. Worldwide, the sum of private

C. Ströhle (✉) • S. Meyer
Department of History and European Ethnology, University of Innsbruck, Innsbruck, Austria
e-mail: stroehle@ifk.ac.at; silke.meyer@uibk.ac.at

S. Meyer, C. Ströhle (eds.), *Remittances as Social Practices and Agents of Change*,
https://doi.org/10.1007/978-3-030-81504-2_19

money transfers is more than three times as high as official development aid. In 2022, global financial transfers were estimated to a record high of USD794 billion, the unofficial sum even surpassing this figure considerably (World Bank 2020, 2022).

Introduction: Two Sides of the Same Remittance Coin

The significance of these transfers for migrants' families and the countries of origin is beyond question: Remittance transfers improve living conditions, provide food, clothing, housing, and transportation, and facilitate access to education and health services. On the individual level, remittance actors are bolstered through this cross-border exchange and they find ways to express multiple belongings, as the examples of Mura, Odermatt, and Ströhle have demonstrated in this volume. The financial flows can free unbanked households from credit constraints and enable the accumulation of capital, as Suri and Jack (2016) show for the money transfer service M-PESA and especially for their credit service M-Shwari. Using these mobile money services has introduced unbanked parties into the formal financial system and, as a consequence, has lifted 2 percent of households or a total of 194,000 households in Kenya out of poverty. Furthermore, political remittances can influence non-migrant communities by promoting peacebuilding processes (Alluri in this volume), political participation, democratic rights, and gender equality. Remitting as a social practice has multifaceted impacts on the involved actors and produces a specific migrant subjectivity of being a loyal provider, a patriotic investor, a keen modernizer, or an avid keeper of traditions (Meyer in this volume). On a meso-level, collective remittances enable the building of infrastructure like community centers and churches, support hometown associations, and connect communities between the diaspora and the homeland. Remittances enhance agriculture and further technologies for improving crops and water supplies, as Musah-Surugu and Anuga and Van Praag have shown in this volume. Technological advancements can contribute to the fight against climate change where it is needed the most. On a macro-level, remittances boost a country's economy, attract investments, and promote economic growth. Access to foreign currencies furthermore stabilizes the national economy.

The other side of the remittance coin encompasses financial and social dependencies between migrants and their communities of origin. Migration and remittance practices can have a profound and sometimes traumatic impact on family relations, as Bajić-Hajduković and Bernard have shown with regard to different generational and class-related expectations (see also Van Hear 2014). When the money stream runs dry, the possibilities for social change toward a better life become sparse or have to be extracted from other channels. State campaigns are not always successful in channeling foreign currency toward what state officials believe is their best use (Miletić in this volume). Remittances can also lower labor force participation because recipients may be discouraged from seeking employment. Furthermore, recipients of economic and social capital flows might show less interest in developing local infrastructure and local politics, as Eric Bayala has shown for the health sector here. Household members of migrants are privileged and, sometimes, the means of support from abroad do not trickle through to the community level, thus deepening inequality in the countries of origin and increasing economic dependency on the diaspora in "the West." Moreover, remittance-induced materialism and lifestyles in imitation of Western consumption patterns can boomerang when they lead to an increase of import rather than investing in local economies. In sum, remittances as expressions and practices of belonging need to be read with a multiscalar approach, taking into account the complexities and ambiguities related to "where things happen but also, how they are understood, which depends on the perspective of involved actors, across time, space and position" (Erdal 2020, p. 2). Only this multiscalar approach can do justice to the multitude and diversity of migration drivers: Next to economic, religious, and political factors, environmental and climate-related aspects, the sentiment of relative deprivation and being poor compared to others as well as personal aspirations and hopes for oneself and for one's family need to be taken into account when we look at the future of migration and remittances (Bijak 2016; Czaika and Reinprecht 2020).

A Transformative Perspective on Transnational Society

In this final chapter, we add a transformative perspective on remittances and shed light on the future of transnational society in two steps. The first follows the promises of digitalization and the technological development of the remittance-scape. The second links remitting to global society in crisis with regard to the COVID-19 pandemic and climate change. Before doing so, we aim to outline our concept of transnational society and transformative perspectivation.

By transnational society, we mean a post-migrant civil society in which multiple belongings, cross-border forms of capital and mobility have become a social normality. Individuals and communities have developed routines in dwelling, working, and socializing in more than one geographical location. Today, most immigration countries experience a transformation in which affiliations, collective national identities, political participation, and equality of opportunity are being renegotiated and adjusted in a post-migrant state, thus *after* migration has happened and has been recognized by governments, academia, and the public as inevitable. Hereby, the prefix "post" is not meant to signify the end of migration but rather the social negotiations in the phase after migration (Foroutan 2019; Hill and Yıldız 2018; Römhild 2017). It is important to note that, for us, this notion of transnational society does not represent a cosmopolitan utopia or a political vision. It is a social reality, constituted, contested, negotiated, and reproduced in the economic, social, cultural, and political practices and narratives of migrants and non-migrants. As such, it implicates social tension and ruptures both on the level of individuals and collectives but also ways of constituting a specific transnational belonging beyond national borders.

In transnational society, remittances are a key driver of social and economic processes. Relating money transfers and social change, the following questions about future developments arise: Do we envision the remittance market as ever growing, or do we anticipate limits and disconnections in the development of transnational society (Waldinger 2015)? What are the effects of digitalization and mobile monies? How will the COVID-19 pandemic affect the strength of remittance ties? How are climate change and remittance practices related: Will the future focus be on sustainability and green remittances or on expansion and limitless growth? Do we believe in remittances as a means for everybody to participate in global wealth? Or do we fear even more division through the structural inequality in remitting? In short: Will transnational society be a place for hope or despair?

We cannot predict the future of the remittance economy (we wish!), nor can we address the vast amount of literature on this topic here. When we think "towards the future of transnational society," we still find ourselves firmly rooted in the present, conceptualizing the future as "post-contemporary" (Avanessian and Malik 2016). The use of the future in present rhetoric, imaginaries, and regulations is the link between the status quo and envisioning society in the making. We are drawn to this future in a "teleoaffective structure" (Schatzki 2002) and through practices like anticipating, expecting, speculating, hoping, and believing (Bryant and Knight 2019). In this sense, we can read remitting itself as a future practice: Investing in transnational relations and businesses, establishing schools and community centers, building houses for return migration, securing a gravesite in family villages, or investing in one's own repatriation also constitute future-oriented cross-border transactions.

Chakkalakal and Ren remind us that, when thinking ahead, we also need to keep in mind the past relations and logics of time and space, co-constituting colonialism and inventing concepts like "development," "history," and "modernity" (Fabian 1983; Mignolo 2011). Their notion of the "fallacy of developmentalism" (Chakkalakal and Ren 2021) points to a normative streak in shaping the future, which is inserted into the production of knowledge, as Bönisch-Brednich and Rupnow have demonstrated here. Yet this fallacy is also embedded in the construction and hierarchies of differences along spatial and temporal axes, as manifested in remittance relations. It is therefore important to note that the future of transnational society is not a united global vision and that it is not the future that remittance actors in New York, Washington, London, Paris, and Berlin would prefer the world to be (Mignolo 2007, p. 498)

Jørgen Carling pointed out that remittances are prone to the fallacy of developmentalism because they project the global divide into personal relationships (Carling 2014, pp. 218–219). We therefore need to view remittances as "two-sided transactions" that must be explored from a "transactional perspective" (Carling 2014, p. 227). However, to understand the impact of remittances on social groups and the built environment in the context of global power relations, we have to capture the transactions themselves as agents of change. When embedding remittances in the transactors' relations and analyzing their cohesive as well as disruptive effects from a temporal and spatial dimension, we can generate a transformative perspective. With this focus, we aim to break with the normative underpinnings and biases of the migration-development nexus and question the modernist, Eurocentric success story of social change as progress in "Western" terms. Such a transformative perspective highlights the structural embedding of societal shifts and links them to globalized relations of power and inequality as manifested in the interplay between social, cultural, political, economic, and environmental dynamics (Amelina et al. 2016, pp. 2–3). By applying this approach to researching remittances as social practices, we aim to carve out the "complexity, interconnectedness, variability, contextuality, and multilevel mediations of global change" (Castles 2016, p. 20).

We further argue that following remittance practices is a key to analyzing the impact of transformation in its interdependence of social actors and structures. As Bivand Erdal (in this volume) demonstrated, interpreting transformation in remittance practices further allows insights into the future of transnational society. By examining the confluences of remittance money and Islamic charity as a changing remittance script with a temporal dimension and a focus on intergenerational change, she highlighted the contingency and variability of transnational transactions. Moreover, this volume shows that remittances not only mirror and reinforce social relations but also transform interior design and the material environment, houses, architecture, and landscapes (Bürkle in this volume), thereby creating new cultural practices and forms of belonging. Hence, we stress the angle of historically anchored, socially generated transformations rather than assuming change and inequality as natural and legitimate. By applying this focus, we aim to shed light on possible future developments in transnational society.

The Future of Remitting is Digital

In a first step, we will address technological development and its effects on remittance practices. We have seen that remittance practices depend upon means of communication and transfers. The temporal span from historical pocket remittances between North America and the Habsburg Empire to contemporary digital remittances worldwide is aligned with the social span and density of transnational society (Steidl in this volume). While sending letters and money across the ocean used to take time and effort, a digital transfer is now convenient and fast and thus suggests proximity and simultaneity. The social field has moved closer together, social media create a transnational sphere of communication and diaspora identity (Karner in this volume). However, it is unlikely that digitalization will result in leveling structural inequality, as we highlight in this chapter.

Financial agencies emphasize the growing influence of the customers and their demands as well as the widening of the market to include international retailers, multi-service vendors, and hub-type operators such as Amazon, Paypal, Alibaba, and Walmart, who compete with banks and money operators. Customers seek a transparent and reliable remitting experience in real time, and they want to choose their preferred payment methods and to track exchange rates in order to schedule their transactions accordingly (McKinsey and Co 2018, p. 6). However, the manner in which digitalization of remittances and biometric technologies will invade the senders' and receivers' private spheres will be a pressing question in the future (Kloppenburg and van der Ploeg 2020).

Sending agent locations will disappear as transactions are undertaken remotely and electronically, by remittance cards or smartphone applications. The receiving market will be split into a small section of cash-out and a larger section of electronic withdrawal. This has effects on remittance costs, which are predicted to be less than 3 percent of face value (Isaacs 2015). With lower costs, the average transaction size will decrease: People will send less money but will do so more often, as long as the transactions are convenient and well-embedded into daily routines (such as through one-click payments). Looking at the social effects of these transformations, we can conclude that remitting will become easier, faster, and cheaper. Money flows will become more regular, reducing the stress and risk of handling larger sums. This development might also cut out middlemen and empower individual senders and receivers. However, transactions will be difficult without an ID or passport (Isaacs 2015) and will therefore exclude undocumented actors. With transaction locations disappearing, migrants will miss a place to meet, but they will also appreciate the comfort and safety of doing remittance business from home.

The rise in digital technology will change the way remittances develop. Digital tools, especially smartphones and mobile apps, have become widespread, embedded in everyday life, making the sending and receiving of cross-border payments relatively safe and easy. The collaboration of key financial and government players in the remittance industry has made a robust compliance framework available which also aims to ensure convenient, fast, and secure digital payments worldwide. These developments meet customer demands: Digital payments have become more accepted, also because they echo the trend of demonetization in worldwide consumption (Giriyan 2020). Suri and Jack have analyzed how digital payments have boosted consumption as well as facilitated access to banking services. For example, the mobile money service of M-PESA is used by at least one person in 96 percent of all households in Kenya. Customers also have access to 110,00 agents who provide deposit and withdrawal services—in comparison: the country has only 2700 ATMs (Suri and Jack 2016, p. 1288). With the introduction of M-PESA as a secure storing place, people have started to save money and were thus able to plan larger acquisitions both privately and in their small-scale businesses. M-PESA also has a bitcoin equivalent, Bitpesa. However, the Bitcoin-based transfer systems are less accepted than mobile money, perhaps because they pose a greater challenge in infrastructure and in technical literacy, and they seem to be more prone to fraud (Metzger et al. 2019, pp. 18–22). Experts are also watching the role of cryptocurrencies in general but cannot predict any developments here other than that blockchain technology may further reduce the price of remitting. For future remittance research, the analysis of big data related to digital remitting can facilitate new perspectives on remittance cycles and global developments.

Cashless financing options, however, need transparency and trust in the money operators. Cabalquin and Wood-Bradley (2020) explored the emotive mechanisms used to promote connectivity in digital payment services. What is sent, according to their analysis of money operators' advertisements, are "happiness" and "love," delivered with "joy," which emphasizes the emotional bond between senders and receivers. At the same time, remittance actors are addressed as economic subjects and valued customers. The online platforms constitute a "platformed migrant subjectivity" and a new digital form of governance in remittance transactions. Trust in technology is built by the construction of connectivity. The remittance market of the future will operate more on an affective level appealing to clients as economic subjects and caring family members.

Drawing on the chapters about material remittances, we can further assume that digital consumption and remitting will be joint ventures when the technologies and logistics provide cheap or even free delivery of the desired goods. The tendency to order products online and have them sent to relatives and friends in their places of origin will reduce the role of remittance senders and loosen the social bonds compared to the role of objects in remittance relations, as laid out by Mura and Ströhle in this volume. However, with free and fast delivery, more goods might be sent and thus the remittance network might even be strengthened by those weaker ties.

Digitalization increases participation but also generates a new digital divide. Older people may be excluded from digital remitting. Rural areas might fall behind even further, compared to urban regions with a strong digital infrastructure. Digitalization will empower some remittance clients by taking their demands and needs into consideration. Digital remittances will thus alleviate some imbalances, but create new inequalities on the way.

Remittances are Disparate, but Stabilizing Practices in Times of Crises

In a second step, we explore the function and transformation of remittance practices in past and current crises. Overall, with lower fees, more money is sent worldwide. However, average fees for remittance transactions wordwide were over 6% in 2022, twice as much as called for in the United Nations's Sustainable Development Goal. The World Bank estimated that in 2022 a record high of USD626 billion were sent to low- and middle-income countries. In light of the COVID-19 pandemic, these flows were predicted to decrease to USD445 billion in 2020, with far-reaching effects on the globally most vulnerable regions of the Global South (World Bank 2020). This will result in a decline in the consumption of goods and services, which will strongly affect the remittance economy.

During 2020 and 2021, lockdowns, travel bans, and closed borders have shut down economic and social life around the globe. Migrants have found themselves stranded and unable to return to their places of work or origin. Even more problematically, without adequate access to housing or social safety nets, international workers have faced the risk of a COVID-19 contagion and of losing employment, wages, and health insurance coverage (World Bank 2020). The global lockdown also affected banks and money service providers, increased the costs, and decreased the possibilities of sending and receiving remittance money. Closed borders deadlocked informal channels of pocket remittances. Thus, the pandemic impaired remittances as the biggest safety net in the world, increased the pressure on migrants, and amplified the hardships for their families and communities of origin. The fear of a decrease in private money transfers led to a call to action called "Remittances in Crisis: How to Keep Them

Flowing," by multiple international organizations like the International Organization for Migration (IOM), the World Bank, and the United Nations Development Programme (UNDP) (Call to Action 2020). However, migrants' remittances turn out to be much more stable than expected and more resilient than other forms of financial flows like foreign direct investment (FDI) or portfolio debt and equity flows (see Fig. 19.1).

A nuanced analysis is needed to understand the development and roles of remittances in the pandemic situation. Recent studies on Latin American countries and the Caribbean show that remittances took a hit from March to May 2020, but then picked up through the summer, ending the year even with a growth compared to 2019. Similar trends have been noticed in Sri Lanka. One important reason for these particularly resilient figures—in a global comparison—is the increased availability of mobile money apps and services (López-Calva 2020; Welsh 2021). Contrarily to these results, Kalantaryan and Mcmahon (2020) showed that in eight of 33 researched African countries, more than half of the people who depend on remittances have no access to the internet through mobile phones. The families left behind, who are most in need of incoming money flows, cannot receive digital remittances in times of closed borders. Similarly, migrants and their families were the ones most affected by the financial crisis in 2007/08, confronted with layoffs and anti-immigrant discourses

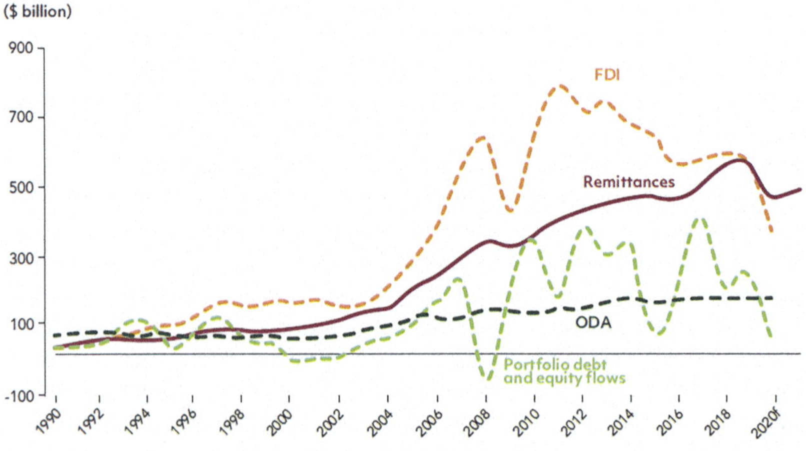

Fig. 19.1 Remittance flows to low- and middle-income countries expected to decline in 2020. (Source: World Bank 2020)

pressuring them to return to their countries of origin (Orozco 2013). Globally, remittances in 2007/08 decreased by only 6 percent, an insignificant drop compared to other external financing like FDI and portfolio debt and equity flows, which declined between 40 and 80 percent (Bisong et al. 2020; see also Fig. 19.1). Ratha and Sirkeci (2011) pointed out, as most currencies in developing countries depreciated, migrants tended to send higher amounts of remittances in order to invest or even to return, and start businesses using the remainder of their savings carried with them.

Global crises have thus had multifaceted effects on the remittance economy, both unveiling and fueling global inequality. Facing one of the most pressing questions of our generation, the incoming Biden administration released an executive order on February 4, 2021, instructing the assistant to the president for National Security Affairs (APNSA) to prepare a report on climate change and its impact on migration (The White House 2021). The choice of institution commissioned to compile the report suggests that the movement of people is increasingly viewed in terms of a "securitization of migration" (Bourbeau 2013). Furthermore, simplistic future scenarios suggesting that the effects of climate change like rising sea levels will lead to a massive out-migration have been questioned by migration scholars, who have pointed out that people's decisions to move are shaped by multiple factors, while adaptation strategies like flood defenses, changes in livelihood patterns, and short-distance mobility are often overseen. However, migration can be a transformational adaptation to environmental change and may be an effective way to build resilience (Castles et al. 2014, pp. 209–213).

It will be a striking issue for future research to carve out the multilayered functions and effects of green remittances in the context of transformation. For example, Musah-Surugu and Anuga (in this volume) point out how remittances finance climate change adaptation among smallholder farmers in Northern Ghana on the local level. While remittance money is used for technological innovations to adapt to the effects and reduce the threats of climate change, the smallholder farmers also invest remittances in chemicals and fertilizers that might contribute to global warming. Furthermore, some remittance recipients increasingly look for jobs and future livelihoods beyond farming. We need such detailed analyses of transformative effects in order to oppose populist debates and visions of migrating masses. On the other end of the argumentative spectrum, such analyses help to avoid establishing the position of the "resilient migrant who engages in successful adaptation to climate change" (Faist

2018, p. 202), thereby fueling the neoliberal agenda of migrants who anticipatorily take responsibility and thereby relieve states and industries from the duty to clean up their own mess.

Conclusion and Outlook: The Social Question and the Future of Transnational Society

Migration is a global phenomenon and shows many forms: internal, cross-border, and transcontinental mobility is structured in different ways, regular and legal migration obviously differ from flight and human trafficking. Almost all forms of migration, however, are accompanied by remittance transfers. These transfers aim to alleviate and compensate economic and social inequality, but they can also create new inequalities. This is particularly true for remittance exchange between the Global South and the Global North. Here, the private transfer of money, objects, knowledge, and symbolic capital appears in a "Western" currency (Bönisch-Brednich in this volume) and follows the historical tracks of global inequality and colonial imperialism.

Milanovic (2012) reminded us that in order to understand inequality in the twenty-first century, we need an empirical and mental shift from questions of class to questions of location—that is a shift from proletarians to migrants. While in the nineteenth and twentieth centuries, the class/capital divide determined inequality, Milanovic used today's global Gini coefficient to show that 85 percent of inequality is attributed to differences in mean country incomes, and only 15 percent to class (Milanovic 2012, p. 127). Against this backdrop, transnationality—conceptualized as migration-driven cross-border belonging, social relationships, and networks—has to be seen as an axis of inequality, enabling or disabling access to resources and intersecting with categories like ethnicity, class, gender, age, and citizenship. The unequal cross-border access to resources can lead to divisions into a small capital-intensive and highly skilled transnational elite and a larger transnational precariat (Schäfer 2021).

Location-based privileges and discrimination are produced and reinforced through migration regimes, spawning new social and cultural heterogeneities. Thus, the social question has to be transnationalized, as cross-border migration can become an issue of inclusion and exclusion in every existential field like education, work, health, and housing (Faist 2019). Remittances can here act as cross-border social protection strategies that improve the livelihoods of individuals and families when invested in education, healthcare, and consumer goods. However, inequalities between the regions of origin and settlement tend to persist, as institutionally embedded forms of public social protection in the regions of origin are often exposed to additional pressures (e.g. brain drain). Remittances can moreover induce new inequalities between households who do or do not have family abroad, or in terms of a gendered inequality in the remittance-sending countries, where the emancipation of women results in women from peripheral countries taking over the vacant positions for care work in the household (Faist 2014, pp. 218–219).

Dependencies created along remittance pathways are certainly fragile, and threatened by global economic, environmental, and health crises, as shown above. Moreover, remittances are dependent on border regimes and thus decline when migrants acquire permanent residence in their countries of settlement (Mahmud in this volume). Thus, powerful global actors like the World Bank, development agencies, nation states, and multinational companies enforce a restrictive temporary migration management that keeps people and money on the move (see Bailey in this volume with specific regard to seasonal worker programs). Against this backdrop, the response of the nineteenth and twentieth centuries to growing inequality, namely the welfare state, is not seen as responsible for temporary migrants, who are mostly not represented by trade unions, either (Faist 2019). Hence, voices demanding a broader system of "transnational social protection" of labor, education, health, and senior care (Levitt et al. 2017) or a "European citizenship" (Bauböck 2019) are growing louder.

When we aim to conceptualize the future of transnational society, we have to keep in mind that migration between the Global South and the Global North is a result of European colonialism and imperialism and constitutes "a post-colonial counter flow" (Faist 2019, p. 8). Remittances mirror this asymmetrical relationship: They can be seen as postcolonial money flows. At the same time, migration can serve to mitigate social and economic inequalities. However, border regimes and migration management obstruct these forms of global reallocation of income and produce new inequalities: Without the legal right of residence and of work, a social and cultural right to belong is rendered impossible. Migration is still class-specific and selective, and it is not the same as mobility in the utopia of a cosmopolitan and borderless world.

By looking at the transformative effects of the most striking cross-border transactions made by migrants, namely remittances, we can generate a lens for inequality and a spotlight for the previously marginalized and unseen contributions of migrants to transnational society. Given the development of digitalization, crises like the COVID-19 pandemic, and the new transnational social question, we can conclude that we will witness several simultaneous trends: Digitalization will enhance and upvalue the position of remittance actors, while a new focus on their demands will result in cheaper and faster transactions. This will, on the one hand, broaden access to remittance transactions but, on the other hand, will exclude people without the means, knowledge, and infrastructure from participating in digital remitting. In the course of the COVID-19 pandemic, remittance flows are estimated to have declined by 20 percent in 2020—varying significantly in different remittance corridors, as the comparison of African and Latin American countries have shown. Globally, the numbers have probably plummeted considerably, compared to other crises, when remittances acted as shock absorbers (e.g. during the financial crisis in the Sub-Saharan region, Singh 2014). At the same time, studies from Latin-American countries and Sri Lanka indicate that remittances tended to be also countercyclical during the COVID-19 pandemic, that is remittances increased when the situation in the countries of origin deteriorated (López-Calva 2020). Remittance research will need to open a new chapter in exploring the transformations and limitations of remitting in the aftermath of the pandemic.

Finally, remittances will play a decisive role in cross-border inequality. Along with financial remittances, transnational social, cultural, and symbolic capital will continue to shape migrant economies and identity politics. A growing transnational entrepreneurship will go hand in hand with migrants' social upward mobility based on transnational capital like language skills, comparative knowledge, and networks. Remittances, though originating from asymmetric global power relations, could thus function as multifaceted practices of cross-border social redistribution. At the same time, remittances tend to privilege individuals with diaspora connections. At the extreme end, it does not matter anymore who you are or what you do, but only whether you have family abroad. Apart from this inner-societal divide, remittances can fuel a global divide into a transnational elite and a transnational precariat. On which side the pendulum is more likely to fall depends on global politics: Will we observe policies of renationalization, protectionism, and restrictive migration regimes, or transnational forms of social protection, global/dual citizenships, and sustainable economies? We hope for the latter.

References

Åkesson, L. (2011). Remittances and Relationships: Exchange in Cape Verdean Transnational Families. *Ethnos*, 76(*3*), 326–347. https://doi.org/10.1080/00141844.2011.577229

Amelina, A., Horvath, K., & Meeus, B. (2016). Migration and Social Transformation: Interdisciplinary Insights and European Perspectives. In A. Amelina, K. Horvath, & B. Meeus (Eds.), *An Anthology of Migration and Social Transformation: European Perspectives* (pp. 1–13). Springer.

Avanessian, A. & Malik, S. (2016). The Speculative Time Complex. In A. Avanessian & S. Malik (Eds)., Time Complex. Post Contemporary (pp. 7–56). Merve.

Bauböck, R. (Ed.). (2019). *Debating European Citizenship*. Springer International Publishing. https://doi.org/10.1007/978-3-319-89905-3

Bisong, A., Ahairwe, P. E., Njoroge, E. (2020). The Impact of COVID-19 on Remittances for Development in Africa. ECDPM, https://ecdpm.org/publications/impact-Covid-19-remittances-development-africa/

Bijak, Jakub (2016). Migration forecasting: Beyond the limits of uncertainty. Global Migration Data Analysis Centre Data Briefing Series, Issue 6, Berlin: IOM's Global Migration Data Analysis Centre GMDAC.

Bourbeau, P. (2013). *The Securitization of Migration: A Study of Movement and Order*. Routledge.

Bryant, R. & Knight, D. M. (2019). *The Anthropology of the Future*. Cambridge University Press.

Cabalquinto, E. C. & Wood-Bradley, G. (2020). Migrant Platformed Subjectivity: Rethinking the Mediation of Transnational Affective Economies via Digital Connectivity Services. *International Journal of Cultural Studies*, 23(5), 787–802.

Call to Action: Remittances in Crisis. How to Keep them Flowing. 2020. https://www.knomad.org/Covid-19-remittances-call-to-action/

Carling, J. (2014). Scripting Remittances: Making Sense of Money Transfers in Transnational Relationships. *International Migration Review*, *48*(4), 218–262. https://doi.org/10.1111/imre.12143

Castles, S. (2016). Understanding Global Migration: A Social Transformation Perspective. In A. Amelina, K. Horvath, & B. Meeus (Eds.), *An Anthology of Migration and Social Transformation: European Perspectives* (pp. 19–41). Springer.

Castles, S., Haas, H. de, & Miller, M. J. (2014). *The Age of Migration: International Population Movements in the Modern World* 5th ed.. Palgrave Macmillan.

Chakkalakal, S. & Ren, J (2021). Un/Doing Future. Unpublished Paper (under review).

Czaika, M. & Reinprecht, C. (2020). Drivers of migration. A synthesis of knowledge (Working Paper 163). Amsterdam: International Migration Institute.

Erdal, M. B. (2014). The Social Dynamics of Remittance-Receiving in Pakistan: Agency and Opportunity among Non-migrants in a Transnational Social Field. In M. M. Rahman, T. T. Yong, & A. K. M. A. Ullah (Eds.), *Migrant Remittances in South Asia* (pp. 115–134). Palgrave Macmillan UK.

Erdal, M. B. (2020). Theorizing Interactions of Migrant Transnationalism and Integration through a Multiscalar Approach. *Comparative Migration Studies*, 8(31), 1–16.

Fabian, J. (1983). *Time and the Other: How Anthropology Makes its Object*. Columbia University Press.

Faist, T. (2014). On the Transnational social question: How Social Inequalities are Reproduced in Europe. *Journal of European Social Policy*, 24(3), 207–222. https://doi.org/10.1177/0958928714525814

Faist, T. (2018). The Socio-Natural Question: How Climate change Adds to Social Inequalities. *Journal of Intercultural Studies, 39*(2), 195–206. https://doi.org/10.1080/07256868.2018.1446670

Faist, T. (2019). *The Transnationalized Social Question: Migration and the Politics of Social Inequalities in the Twenty-First Century*. Oxford University Press.

Foroutan, N. (2019): The post-migrant paradigm. In J.-J. Bock & S. Macdonald (Eds.), *Refugees Welcome? Difference and Diversity in a Changing Germany* (pp. 121–142). Berghahn Books.

Giriyan, S. (2020). Outlook 2020: Digital Trends that Will Shape the Remittance Industry. https://www.finextra.com/blogposting/18408/outlook-2020-digital-trends-that-will-shape-the-remittance-industry

Hill, M., & Yıldız, E. (Eds.). (2018). *Postmigrantische Visionen: Erfahrungen—Ideen—Reflexionen*. Transcript.

Isaacs, L. (2015). Blog: Predicting the Future? The Payments Market in 2025. https://www.developingmarkets.com/perspectives/blog-predicting-future-payments-market-2025

Kalantaryan, S. & Mcmahon, S. (2020). Covid-19 and Remittances in Africa, EUR 30262 EN, Publications Office of the European Union, Luxembourg. https://doi.org/10.2760/86710

Kloppenburg, S. & van der Ploeg, I. (2020). Securing Identities: Biometric Technologies and the Enactment of Human Bodily Differences. *Science as Culture*, 29(1), 57–76. https://doi.org/10.1080/09505431.2018.1519534

Levitt, P., Viterna, J., Mueller, A., & Lloyd, C. (2017). Transnational Social Protection: Setting the Agenda. *Oxford Development Studies, 45*(1), 2–19. https://doi.org/10.1080/13600818.2016.1239702

López-Calva, L. F. (2020, December 2). Stand by me: COVID-19 and the Resilience of Remittance Flows to LAC. UNDP in Latin America and the Caribbean. https://www.latinamerica.undp.org/content/rblac/en/home/

presscenter/director-s-graph-for-thought/stand-by-me%2D%2Dcovid-19-and-the-resilience-of-remittance-flows-to-.html
Lindley, A. (2010). *The early morning phonecall: Somali refugees' remittances.* Berghahn Books.
McKinsey & Co. (2018). A Vision for the Future of Cross-Border Payments. https://www.mckinsey.com/industries/financial-services/our-insights/a-vision-for-the-future-of-cross-border-payments
Metzger, M., Riedler, T. & Pédussel Wu, J. (2019). Migrant remittances: Alternative money transfer channels, Working Paper, No. 127/2019, Institute for International Political Economy (IPE), Berlin.
Mignolo, W. (2007). DELINKING. *Cultural Studies, 21*(2–3), 449–514. https://doi.org/10.1080/09502380601162647
Mignolo, W. (2011). *The Darker Side of Western Modernity: Global Futures, Decolonial Options.* Duke University Press.
Milanovic, B. (2012). Evolution of Global Inequality: From Class to Location, From Proletarians to Migrants, *Global Policy, 3*(2), 125–134.
Orozco, M. (2013). *Migrant Remittances and Development in the Global Economy: Diasporas in World Politics.* Lynne Rienner Publishers Inc.
Rahman, M. & Fee, L. K. (2012). Towards a Sociology of Migrant Remittances in Asia: Conceptual and Methodological Challenges. *Journal of Ethnic and Migration Studies*, 38(*4*), 689–706. https://doi.org/10.1080/1369183X.2012.659129
Ratha, D. & Sirkeci I. (2011). Remittances and the Global Financial Crisis. *Migration Letters 7*(2), 125–131.
Römhild, R. (2017). Beyond the bounds of the ethnic: For postmigrant cultural and social research. *Journal of Aesthetics & Culture*, 9(*2*), 69–75.
Schäfer, J. (2021). Transnationalität und soziale Ungleichheit. In D. Gerst, M. Klessmann, & H. Krämer (Eds.), *Grenzforschung* (pp. 206–220). Nomos.
Schatzki, T. R. (2002). *The Site of the Social: A Philosophical Account of the Constitution of Social Life and Change.* The Pennsylvania State University Press.
Singh, R. J. (2014). From Shock Absorber to Shock Transmitter: Determinants of Remittances in Sub-Saharan Africa. *Migration Letters, 7*(2), 231–240. https://doi.org/10.33182/ml.v7i2.196
Suri, T., & Jack, W. (2016). The Long-run Poverty and Gender Impacts of Mobile Money. *Science*, 354(6317), 1288–1292. https://doi.org/10.1126/science.aah5309
The White House (2021). Executive Order on Rebuilding and Enhancing Programs to Resettle Refugees and Planning for the Impact of Climate change. https://www.whitehouse.gov/briefing-room/presidential-actions/2021/02/04/executive-order-on-rebuilding-and-enhancing-programs-to-resettle-refugees-and-planning-for-the-impact-of-climate-change-on-migration/

Van Hear, N. (2014). Reconsidering Migration and Class. *International Migration Review*, *48*(1), 100–121. https://doi.org/10.1111/imre.12139

Waldinger, R. D. (2015). *The Cross-Border Connection: Immigrants, Emigrants, and their Homelands*. Harvard Univ. Press.

Welsh, Teresa (2021, January 11). Anticipated remittance dive bucked by Latin America and the Caribbean. *Devex*. https://www.devex.com/news/anticipated-remittance-dive-bucked-by-latin-america-and-the-caribbean-98880

World Bank (2020): Migration and Development Brief 32. COVID-19 Crisis through a Migration Lens. https://documents1.worldbank.org/curated/en/989721587512418006/pdf/COVID-19-Crisis-Through-a-Migration-Lens.pdfhttp://documents1.worldbank.org/curated/en/989721587512418006/pdf/COVID-19-Crisis-Through-a-Migration-Lens.pdf

World Bank. (2022). Remittances Brave Global Headwinds (=Migration and Development Brief 37). https://www.knomad.org/sites/default/files/publication-doc/migration_and_development_brief_37_nov_2022.pdf

Index[1]

[1] Note: Page numbers followed by 'n' refer to notes.

S. Meyer, C. Ströhle (eds.), *Remittances as Social Practices and Agents of Change*,
https://doi.org/10.1007/978-3-030-81504-2

D

N

S

T

U

The manufacturer's authorised representative in the EU is Springer Nature Customer Service Centre GmbH, Europaplatz 3, 69115 Heidelberg, Germany. If you have any concerns regarding our products, please contact ProductSafety@springernature.com

Printed and bound by CPI Group (UK) Ltd, Croydon, CR0 4YY
08/10/2026
02230271-0001